FIELD GUIDE TO THE

TREES AND SHRUBS OF BRITAIN

TREES AND SHRUBS OF BRITAIN
was edited and designed by
The Reader's Digest Association Limited, London

Editor: Michael W. Davison
Art Editor: Neal V. Martin

We are committed to both the quality of our products and the service we provide to our customers.
We value your comments, so please feel free to contact us on 08705 113366,
or via our Web site at www.readersdigest.co.uk
If you have any comments about the content of our books, you can contact
us at gbeditorial@readersdigest.co.uk

Reprinted 2001

Printed in Italy

ISBN 0 276 42507 3

READER'S DIGEST
NATURE LOVER'S LIBRARY

FIELD GUIDE TO THE TREES AND SHRUBS OF BRITAIN

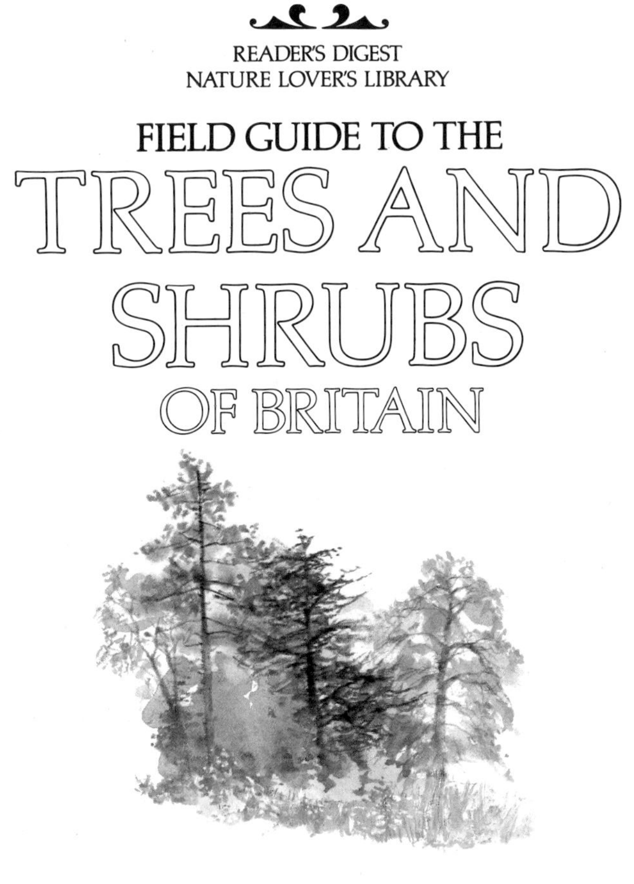

PUBLISHED BY THE READER'S DIGEST ASSOCIATION LIMITED

LONDON • MONTREAL • NEW YORK • SYDNEY

The publishers wish to express their gratitude to the following people for their major contributions to this Field Guide to the Trees and Shrubs of Britain

CONSULTANTS AND AUTHORS

Esmond Harris, B.Sc., Dip. For., F.I.For.,
Director, The Royal Forestry Society
of England, Wales and Northern Ireland

Jeanette Harris, B.Sc.

PHOTOGRAPHERS

For a full list of acknowledgments to the photographers whose work appears in this book, see page 304

ARTISTS

Dick Bonson
Brian Delf
Shirley Felts
Ian Garrard
Nick Hall
Delyth Jones
Charles Raymond
Derek Rodgers
Jim Russell
David Salariya
Ann Savage
Bruce Whatley

A full list of the plates contributed by each artist appears on page 304

The publishers would also like to thank The Royal Forestry Society of England, Wales and Northern Ireland for its valuable and expert assistance in the preparation of this book

Contents

Understanding trees and shrubs

For some 400 million years, ever since the first primitive land plants evolved tall stems and began to reach higher into the light than all other living things, trees have been the silent, stately guardians of everything below them. They have provided shade from the sun and shelter from the wind and rain; they have manufactured pure, life-giving oxygen with their leaves; they have enriched the soil and provided food, homes and shelter for a great variety of wildlife. Not only have they provided humans with one of their most valuable construction materials; but by their strength, beauty and stillness they have soothed the spirit and been a constant pleasure to the eye.

Trees and all other green plants manufacture food materials from minerals, carbon dioxide and water, deriving their energy from light; and, in the case of trees and shrubs, the unique material eventually produced is wood. Many plants, including trees and shrubs, have buds, leaves, flowers and fruit; but only trees and shrubs have wood. The difference between trees and shrubs is simple. Trees have a single woody stem, from which branches grow to form a crown. The branches of shrubs arise at ground level, forming a crown without a stem.

The power of trees and shrubs to make wood is contained in a tiny layer of cells, just below the bark, called the cambium layer. Every year the cambium produces new wood on its inner side, as well as a layer of tissue, called phloem, on the outside. At the same time, it reproduces itself, to surround the ever-growing bulk of the plant. As long as they live, trees and shrubs continue to grow all over. The trunk expands, the branches thicken, the shoots lengthen. Growth only ceases when the tree dies. Only then does the cambium finally stop making new wood.

In the growing season, life courses with ceaseless vigour through trees and shrubs; the impression of stillness on the outside belies the intense activity inside. Vast quantities of mineral-rich water flow upwards through the new wood, from the roots to the highest leaves. Sugar-rich sap descends through the phloem, from the leaves to all parts of the tree. All this energy is expressed in the tree's growth, in its flowers and fruit, in the seed which it produces in massive quantities. In effect, every tree or shrub is one of life's richest energy banks, storing food in its tissues, eventually returning everything to the earth when it dies and decomposes, immeasurably enriching the soil in which it stood rooted all its life.

The naming of trees

Many of the popular names of trees and shrubs describe some characteristic or use of the plant – for instance, crack willow owes its name to the brittleness of its twigs, and butchers once used the wood of dogwood to make 'dogs', or skewers. But popular names vary from country to country, and often between one part of the country and another. Dogwood has also been known as dogberry and dog-tree, and in parts of Wales, where its berries were used to make lamp oil, it was called the wax tree.

Sometimes the common names are misleading. The early settlers in America gave the trees which they found there the names of trees which they had heard of before; but often the species were not truly related. So they named many trees with fragrant wood cedars; but botanists now know that none of the American cedars truly belongs to the cedar family.

To eliminate this sort of confusion, scientists have applied the principle first proposed by the 18th-century Swedish naturalist Linnaeus, by which every tree and shrub has a double-barrelled scientific name. The first part is the generic name, which is common to all trees belonging to the same genus, or closely related group. The second part is the specific name, and refers to one particular species. All over the world, for instance, the Scots pine is called *Pinus sylvestris* – 'pine of the woods' – whatever popular names it may also have.

Within a species there are sometimes

small variations, of leaf or flower colour, for example. If these variations have occurred in the wild, the trees are called varieties, and a third scientific name is added. Thus *Pinus sylvestris* var. *scotica* is the Highland variety of Scots pine, with short, blue-green needles. If the variation has happened under cultivation, whether accidentally in a botanic garden or as a result of intentional breeding, the tree is called a cultivar. The cultivar's name is written after the scientific name and placed in single quotation marks – *Pinus sylvestris* 'Aurea' is a golden-leaved form of Scots pine which arose in a nursery.

Several species of tree have cross-fertilised with other species, and the resulting hybrid usually shows the characters of both. For example, European and Japanese larch growing near each other at Dunkeld in Scotland towards the end of the 19th century cross-fertilised to produce the hybrid or Dunkeld larch. Its scientific name is *Laris* x *eurolepis*, the x between the names indicates that both parents of the hybrid belonged to the same genus.

More rarely, a hybrid occurs between species of different genera. Leyland cypress, for example, is a hybrid between two American species – Monterey cypress (*Cupressus macrocarpa*) and Nootka cypress (*Chamaecyparis nootkatensis*), which in spite of its common name is not a true cypress at all. A symbol x is placed before the scientific name of such hybrids – so the Leyland cypress is called x *Cupressocyparis leylandii*.

The trees of Britain

Altogether more than 1,500 species of trees grow in Britain, and an even greater number of shrubs; trees in productive woodlands alone cover about 5 million acres of land. But of this great variety of species, many are rare and only grow in great gardens and botanic collections; and only a tiny number of the trees and shrubs which grow wild are truly native to this country.

Only 32 species of broad-leaved tree, three species of conifer and a few shrubs were established when the sea, swollen with melting ice, swept through the Strait of Dover some 7,500 years ago, cutting Britain off from the rest of Europe and from the trees and shrubs which grew there. The trees had been spreading northward since the end of the last Ice Age, some 10,000 years ago. They had survived the cold period in southern Europe, and had then spread at remarkable rates, often exceeding averages of 100 yds (300 m) a year. The broad-leaved trees included many of today's most common species, such as willow, oak, lime, ash and wych elm. The coniferous trees were yew, Scots pine and juniper. All the other trees now growing in Britain were introduced by humans, either for ornament, timber, or their fruit.

More than 200 species of tree and shrub are described and illustrated in this book, including all the native trees, all the common introduced trees, and a number of trees and shrubs grown mainly for ornamental purposes in gardens and tree collections.

How to use this book

The main purpose of this book is to enable anyone to identify without difficulty any of the trees and shrubs growing wild in Britain, or introduced for commercial timber production, and to serve as an introduction to the rarer, ornamental species growing in parks and gardens.

There are many ways to identify trees and shrubs – by their bark, buds or flowers, for example, or by their leaves or general character and appearance. On pages 8–23 the techniques of tree identification are explained in detail.

In the main part of this book, the trees and shrubs of Britain have been grouped according to the shape of their leaves or needles. To identify a particular tree or shrub, turn first to the keys to leaves and needles on pages 20–22, to find out to which broad group it belongs. Then turn to the indicated section of the book that deals with this group of trees. At the start of most sections will be found a detailed leaf or needle key for the group; this will lead directly to the page on which the particular tree or shrub that is sought is described and illustrated.

There are many other identification keys in the book – to help identify coniferous trees by their cones, for instance, or broad-leaved trees in winter by their twigs and buds. A complete guide to the identification keys is given on page 8.

How to identify trees

With experience it is often possible to identify a tree just by looking at its overall shape: the wide, rounded crown of a mature English oak and the spire-like profile of a Lombardy poplar are unmistakable even from a distance. But the shapes of trees vary according to their situation – oaks growing on mountains, for instance, tend to be stunted by the wind and shallow soil. So in most cases it is necessary to examine a tree in detail in order to name it correctly. The first thing to look at is the shape of its leaves, or – if the tree has shed its leaves – at the shape and colour of its twigs and buds. Other features which may help to identify it include the colour and pattern of its bark, and the size, shape and colour of its flowers or fruit. The recognition pages illustrate these features, many of which are also the subject of 'look-alike' charts on the pages indicated.

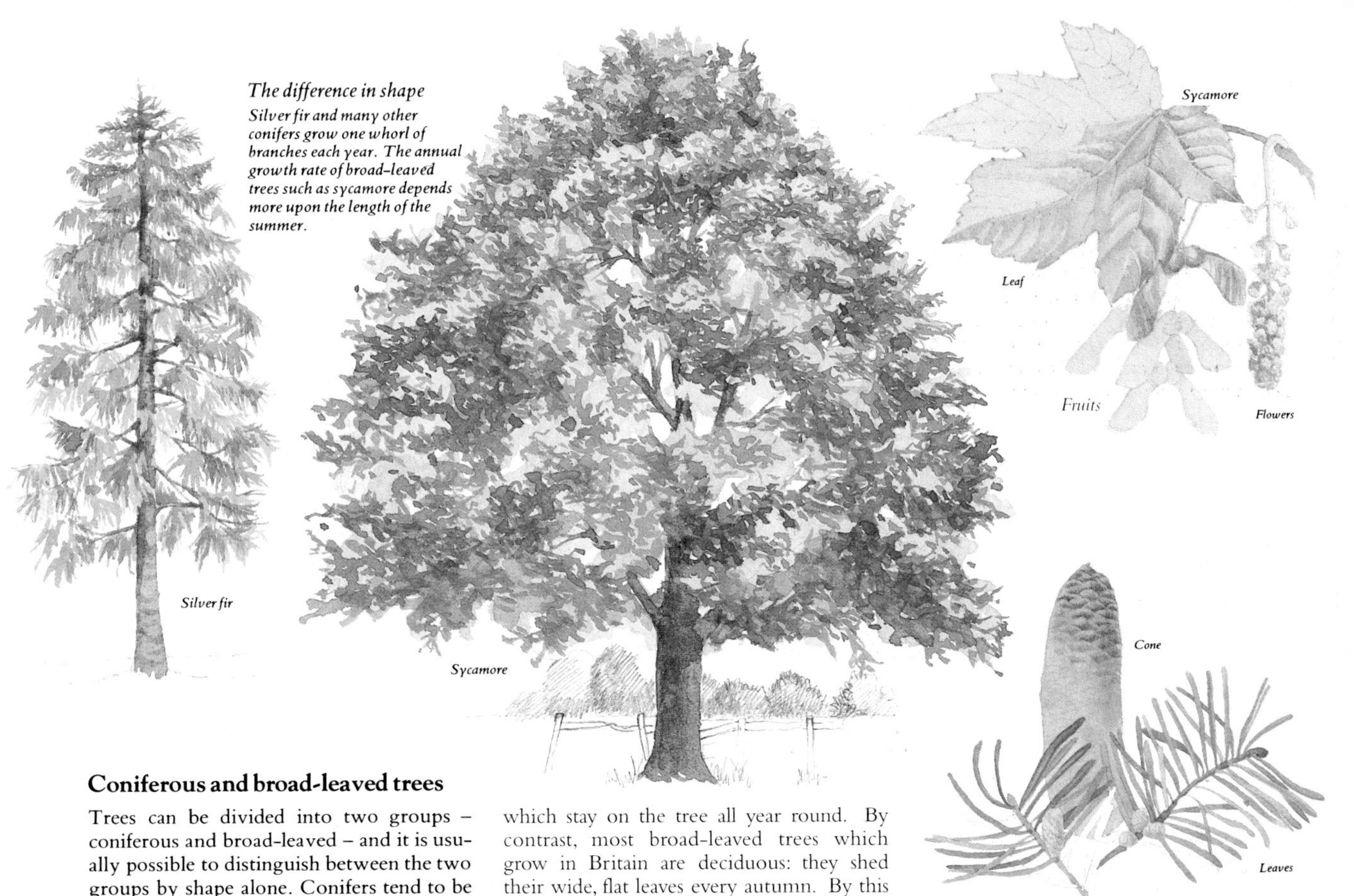

The evergreen leaves of most conifers are small and needle-like, with a layer of cuticle. Groups of fertilised female flowers grow into seed-bearing cones.

Coniferous and broad-leaved trees

Trees can be divided into two groups – coniferous and broad-leaved – and it is usually possible to distinguish between the two groups by shape alone. Conifers tend to be more regular in shape than broad-leaved trees, with their branches radiating in a symmetrical pattern from a straight central trunk. Conifers bear cones, and most have leaves like needles or small scales, many of which stay on the tree all year round. By contrast, most broad-leaved trees which grow in Britain are deciduous: they shed their wide, flat leaves every autumn. By this time it is becoming too cold to continue the process of food manufacture in the leaves (photosynthesis) and their broad surfaces would continue to lose water if they were retained.

Spreading the seeds

In autumn winged sycamore fruits spin away from the parent tree to the ground. The fruits contain the tree's seeds.

The first bud

When the sycamore shoot appears above ground, two fleshy seed leaves open to the light. Between them they enclose the tree's first bud.

From bud to leaf

The first true sycamore leaves grow from the bud between the seed leaves. By autumn, when the leaves fall, the shoot will have formed a new leading bud, containing next year's shoot.

Taking root

In spring the sycamore seed germinates, sending down its first root into the soil, to take up water and nutrients. A few days later the first shoot appears.

How trees grow

Each season of a tree's growth begins and ends with buds. In spring the buds open, new leaves and flowers dress the tree, new shoots grow. By autumn, next year's buds are already formed at the tip and sides of the twigs. Pines and some other conifers have one set of buds for a whole season's growth. The winter buds of other species, such as hemlocks, initiate only the first part of the year's growth, and other buds are formed during the growing season. Young broad-leaved trees follow a similar pattern, with the largest array of branches growing in the spring.

Every twig on a tree, with its leading bud extending its growth and its side buds forming new branchlets, is a miniature version of the tree itself. Small twigs grow from larger twigs, just as the larger twigs grow from the branches and the branches from the trunk.

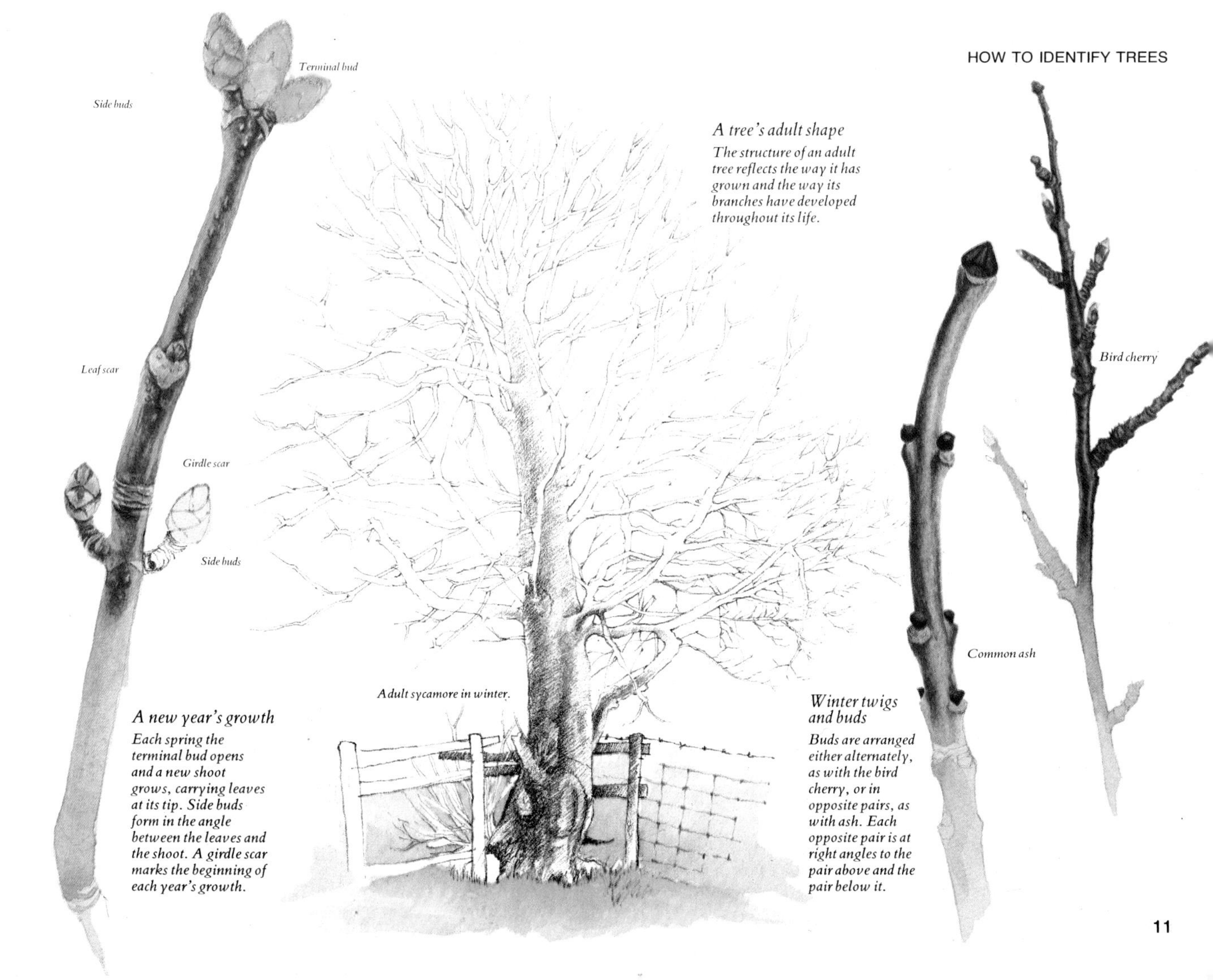

A tree's adult shape

The structure of an adult tree reflects the way it has grown and the way its branches have developed throughout its life.

A new year's growth

Each spring the terminal bud opens and a new shoot grows, carrying leaves at its tip. Side buds form in the angle between the leaves and the shoot. A girdle scar marks the beginning of each year's growth.

Winter twigs and buds

Buds are arranged either alternately, as with the bird cherry, or in opposite pairs, as with ash. Each opposite pair is at right angles to the pair above and the pair below it.

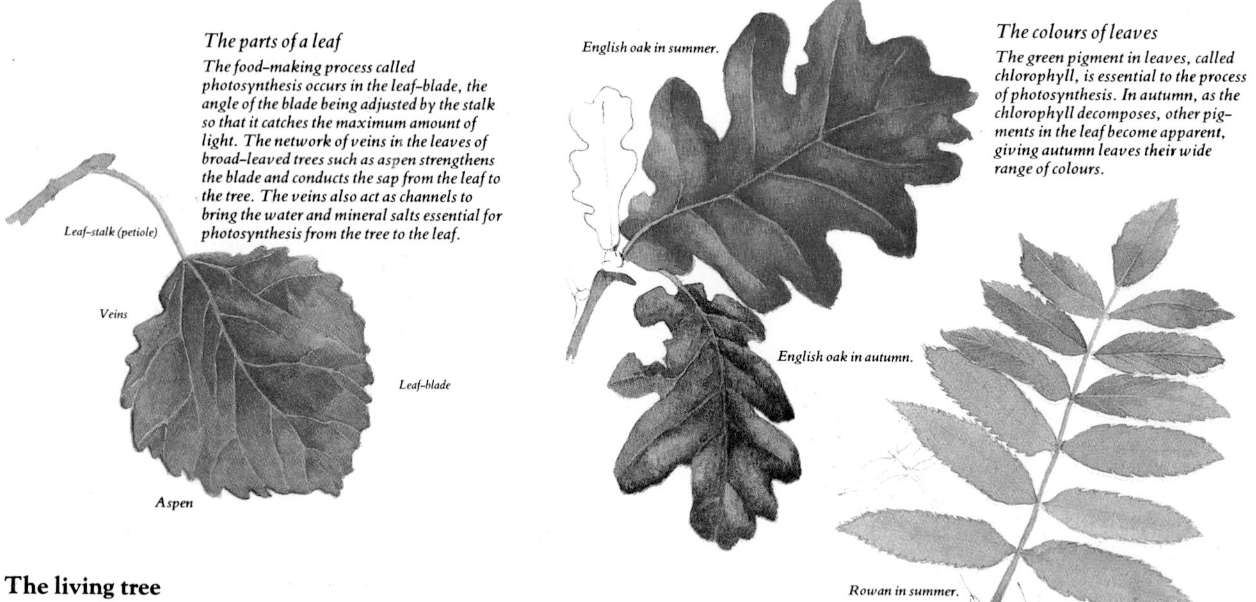

The parts of a leaf

The food-making process called photosynthesis occurs in the leaf-blade, the angle of the blade being adjusted by the stalk so that it catches the maximum amount of light. The network of veins in the leaves of broad-leaved trees such as aspen strengthens the blade and conducts the sap from the leaf to the tree. The veins also act as channels to bring the water and mineral salts essential for photosynthesis from the tree to the leaf.

English oak in summer.

English oak in autumn.

The colours of leaves

The green pigment in leaves, called chlorophyll, is essential to the process of photosynthesis. In autumn, as the chlorophyll decomposes, other pigments in the leaf become apparent, giving autumn leaves their wide range of colours.

Rowan in summer.

Rowan in autumn.

The living tree

A tree is nourished by its leaves. Every leaf is a complicated chemical workshop where carbon dioxide from the air, mixed with water taken in by the roots, is made into carbohydrates in the presence of light. These carbohydrates, which include sugar, are essential for the tree's growth and survival. The sugar-rich sap manufactured in the leaves is then carried down special channels from the leaves to all parts of the tree.

Leaves – especially the leaves of broad-leaved trees – are also efficient evaporating mechanisms. On a hot day they lose moisture to the air, keeping the tree cool, and they replace this moisture with water drawn up through the tree from its roots. The sugary sap from the leaves is borne downwards and outwards to the remainder of the tree in a tissue of cells called phloem. This downward flow takes place just below the bark, forming a casing of phloem which is easily damaged if the bark is stripped from the tree. Meanwhile, water with essential minerals from the soil flows upwards through a tissue of dead cells called the xylem, which forms the new wood of the stem and branches.

Horse chestnut

Alternate leaves

Common lime

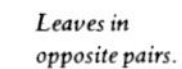

The arrangement of leaves

Leaves grow either in opposite pairs on the twig, or alternately first on one side of the twig and then the other. Each opposite pair grows at right-angles to the pair above and the pair below.

Evergreen leaves

The leaves of evergreen trees produce food all the year round when conditions are favourable. They last several years and then fall in spring and early summer, after new leaves have grown. In conifers, because the leaves are small and narrow, water evaporates slowly from them – an adaptation which helps them to survive cold northern winters.

Juvenile foliage

The early leaves or needles produced by young trees can be hard to identify. On trees such as the Chinese juniper, for instance, the young leaves are awl-shaped; sometimes these continue to grow on young shoots and mingle with the tree's adult foliage.

Chinese juniper

Norway spruce

Juvenile foliage

Adult foliage

The parts of a flower

The 'perfect' flower of a cherry has pollen-bearing stamens – the male parts of the flower – surrounding the female parts; these are a stigma, to which the pollen adheres, and a style connecting the stigma to an ovary. When the flower is pollinated the ovules inside the ovary grow into seeds, while the ovary forms the stony layer around the seed and the fleshy fruit around the stone.

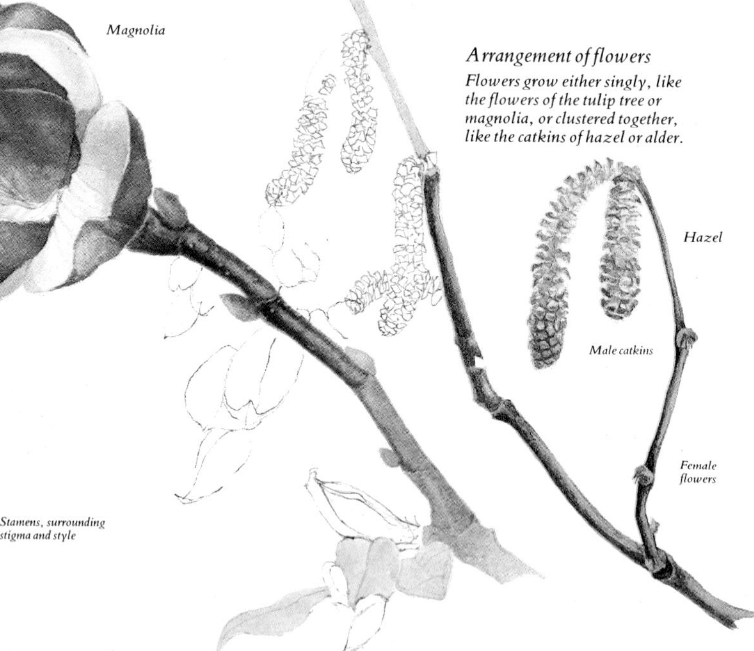

Arrangement of flowers

Flowers grow either singly, like the flowers of the tulip tree or magnolia, or clustered together, like the catkins of hazel or alder.

Petals

Stamens, surrounding stigma and style

Sepals

Sargent's cherry

From flower to seed

All trees have flowers, though conifer flowers are smaller and less conspicuous than those of broad-leaved trees. Flowers are a tree's reproductive organs; some are male, some are female, and some – the so-called 'perfect' flowers of cherries and maples, for instance – have both male and female parts. Conifers always have separate male and female flowers, sometimes on the same tree. Some broad-leaved trees bear separate male and female flowers on the same tree while others, such as willows, have them on separate trees. Pollen from the male flowers, carried by insects or by the wind, pollinates the female flowers, which then grow into fruit-bearing seeds or cones. Many fruits are eaten by animals which leave or excrete the seeds or stone. These can then germinate well away from the parent tree. Other fruits have wings and are dispersed by the wind.

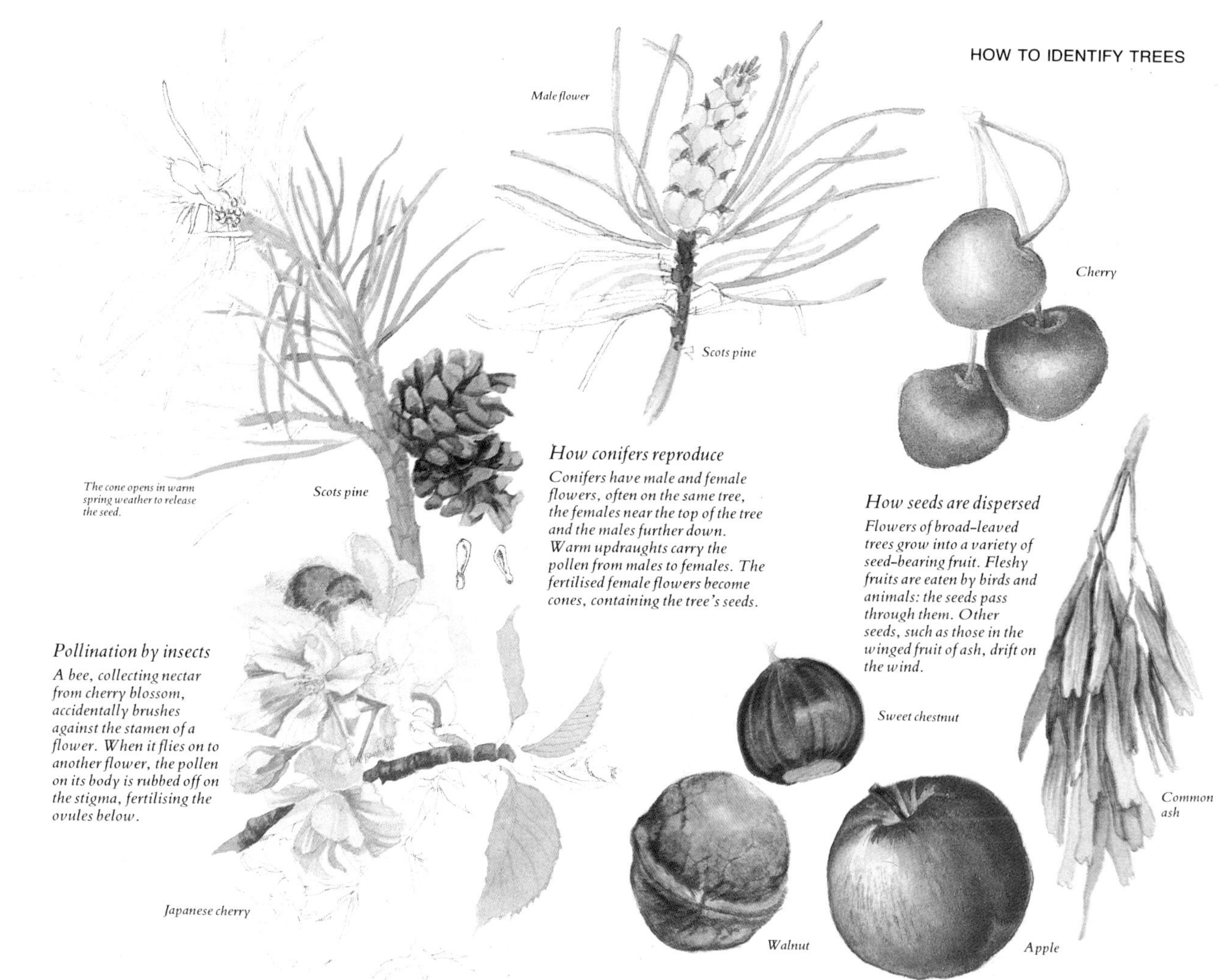

How conifers reproduce

Conifers have male and female flowers, often on the same tree, the females near the top of the tree and the males further down. Warm updraughts carry the pollen from males to females. The fertilised female flowers become cones, containing the tree's seeds.

How seeds are dispersed

Flowers of broad-leaved trees grow into a variety of seed-bearing fruit. Fleshy fruits are eaten by birds and animals: the seeds pass through them. Other seeds, such as those in the winged fruit of ash, drift on the wind.

Pollination by insects

A bee, collecting nectar from cherry blossom, accidentally brushes against the stamen of a flower. When it flies on to another flower, the pollen on its body is rubbed off on the stigma, fertilising the ovules below.

Lombardy poplar

Common alder

The shapes of trees

Every tree is an individual, whose adult shape reflects the conditions under which it lives. Trees growing close together in a forest are narrower in outline than trees of the same species standing alone in the middle of a park. Winds blowing off the sea make coastal trees grow lop-sided; harsh, mountainous conditions make trees stunted. Young trees put most of their energy into growing upwards, reaching for the light. Later they broaden to assume the typical adult shape of their species.

Pruning also drastically changes the natural shapes of trees. Coppicing and pollarding are well-tried methods for encouraging the growth of new shoots, for firewood, fencing or simply for ornament. In coppicing, the tree is cut off at ground level. In pollarding it is cut off higher up the trunk, out of reach of grazing animals. New shoots and branches grow quickly, because there is an existing root system.

Lozenge-shaped

An outline which is broad in the middle and pointed at the top distinguishes many pines, and some broad-leaved trees such as common alder.

Western red cedar

Triangular

Regular layers of branches growing horizontally from the trunk and decreasing in length give Wellingtonia, western red cedar and some spruces this shape.

Columnar

Many species have side branches which are all the same length, giving them a narrow, elegant shape. The branches of Lombardy poplar grow steeply upwards.

Rounded

A broad, widely domed crown radiating from the trunk characterises many familiar broad-leaved trees when mature, such as English oak, sycamore and ash.

English oak

Drooping

With some species, such as weeping willow, all the branches droop downwards. With others, such as morinda, only the branchlets droop.

Weeping willow

Atlas cedar

Upswept

Steeply ascending branches give many young trees such as Atlas cedars their shape.

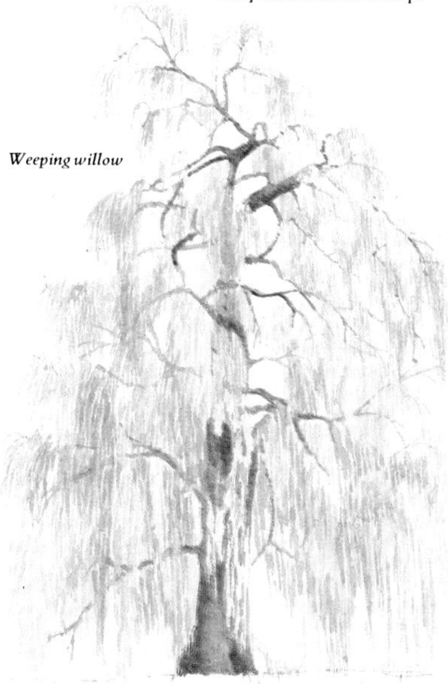

Scots pine

Flat-topped

Many pines, yews and cedars acquire this shape in old age as side-branches die and the crown flattens. The reddish colouring of the upper bark is characteristic of Scots pine.

Common ash
Green and smooth when young, becoming pale grey, uniformly networked with ridges.

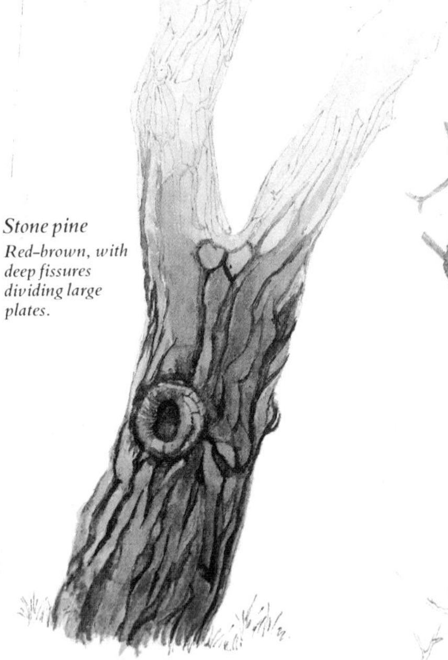

Stone pine
Red-brown, with deep fissures dividing large plates.

Wild cherry
Shiny red-brown, darkening with age, with horizontal rings of breathing pores.

Colours and patterns of bark

Every part of a tree is alive except its heartwood and outer bark, and from year to year all the parts keep growing, from the young shoots high on its crown to the base of its trunk and roots. The bark protects the life beneath it, by preventing the inside of the tree from drying out. It also protects the tree from insects, mammals, fire, fungus and extremes of heat and cold. Without bark a tree would die very quickly – as it does if a ring of bark is stripped off all round the stem. As the trunk of the tree expands, the outer skin of bark becomes tight. Soon it begins to split, cracking or flaking away to uncover new bark beneath.

The cracks and fissures form distinctive patterns that are characteristic of each species. In winter especially, the pattern and colour of a tree's bark are often the first and quickest clues to its identity. The trees illustrated here show some of the most striking contrasts in bark colour and pattern.

London plane

Dark grey or brown, with large flakes falling away and leaving pale yellow patches.

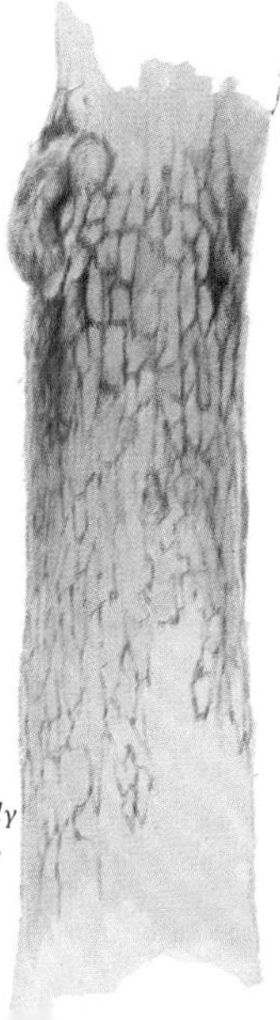

Crab apple

Dark brown, finely cracked into small, square plates.

Silver birch

White, peeling in strips around the trunk and leaving black diamond shapes.

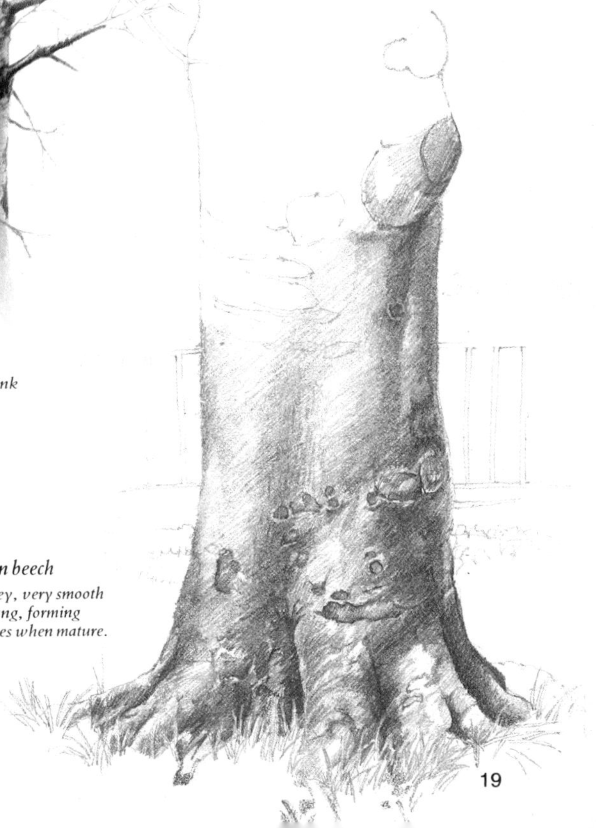

Common beech

Silver-grey, very smooth when young, forming small scales when mature.

KEY TO BROAD-LEAVED TREES

The trees and shrubs illustrated and described in the main part of this book have been grouped according to the shape of their leaves; for throughout most of the year this provides the single most obvious clue by which to identify them. When trying to put a name to a tree or shrub, first compare its leaves with those illustrated in this key; then, after deciding to which main group it belongs, turn to the detailed key for that group on the pages indicated. In winter, when the leaves have fallen from deciduous trees, their twigs and buds are the most obvious identification features: see charts on pages 184–93.

Common beech

Oval leaves Pages 50–91
Key, pages 48–49

Common lime

Heart-shaped leaves Pages 39–47
Key, page 38

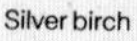

Triangular leaves
Pages 27–33
Key, page 26

Aspen

Round leaves Pages 34–37
Key, page 26

Wild cherry

Long leaves Pages 94–125
Key, pages 92–93

Maple-like leaves Pages 128–45
Key, pages 126–7

Sycamore

Hand-shaped leaves
Pages 158–61

Horse chestnut

Rowan

Feather-like leaves
Pages 164–79
Key, pages 162–3

Lobed leaves
Pages 147–57 Key, page 146

English oak

Gorse

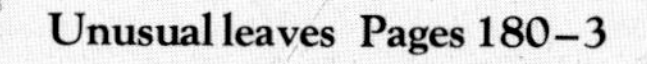

Unusual leaves Pages 180–3

Dwarf fan-palm

Tamarisk

KEY TO CONIFEROUS TREES

The leaves of coniferous trees can be divided into those which are needle-like and those which resemble scales. Trees with scale-like leaves sometimes also have awl-shaped juvenile leaves which persist on the adult tree. The needle-like leaves fall into four groups. Pines have long needles in groups of two, three or five. Spruce needles are sharp and arise on pegs. The needles of cedars and larches are in rosettes on the older twigs; those of larches are deciduous. Other trees have flat needles, including the silver firs whose needles leave a round leaf scar.

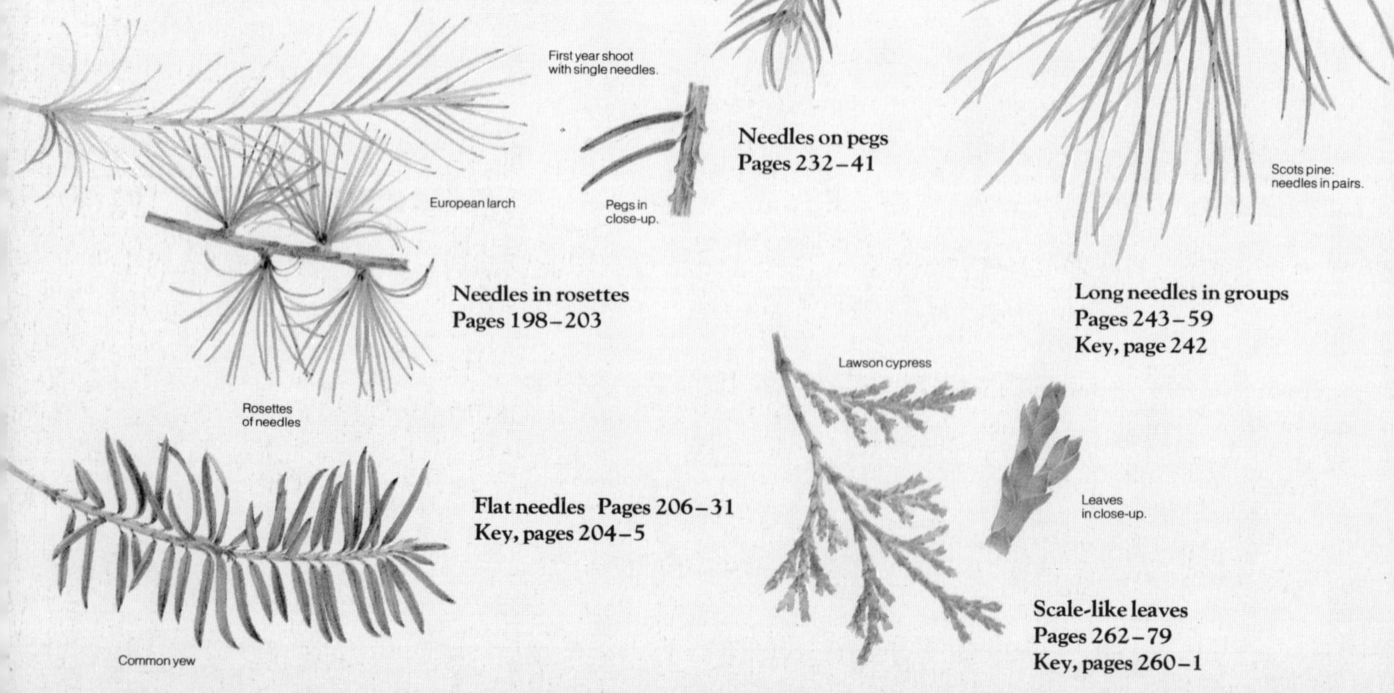

Needles on pegs
Pages 232–41

Long needles in groups
Pages 243–59
Key, page 242

Needles in rosettes
Pages 198–203

Flat needles Pages 206–31
Key, pages 204–5

Scale-like leaves
Pages 262–79
Key, pages 260–1

KEY TO CONES

Coniferous trees are grouped in this book according to the shape of their leaves. Their cones, however, offer a valuable alternative means of identification. Cones vary in size and shape from round and fat to long and narrow. Some remain upright on the tree, dropping their scales to release the ripe seed. Others turn to hang downwards as they ripen, so that the seed can be shaken out. The five main groups of cones are further sub-divided in the detailed cone chart on pages 280–3.

Long, hanging cones Page 281

The scales open to release the seeds, after which the cone falls to the ground where it can be found whole.

Scots pine

Norway spruce

Atlas cedar

Round, hanging cones Page 282

All these cones shake out their seeds while still on the tree. Some take more than a year to ripen. Spent cones may remain long on the tree.

Barrel-shaped, erect cones Page 280

These cones break up on the tree to release the seeds. The central axis always remains on the tree.

European larch

Round cones scattered on twig Page 283

Scales open to release seed. Spent cones often remain on the tree.

Cones with few scales Page 283

The scales open to release the seeds, and the spent cones usually remain on the tree.

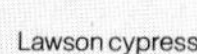

Lawson cypress

TREES AND SHRUBS OF BRITAIN

TRIANGULAR OR ROUND LEAVES

The woodland birch and the suburban lilac have one feature in common – a triangular leaf. Trees with round leaves include aspen and sometimes common alder. Leaves may have plain or toothed margins, and be alternate or in opposite pairs.

Triangular, large teeth, alternate

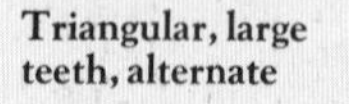

Silver birch

Silver birch
Betula pendula
Leaves $1-2\frac{3}{4}$ in. (2·5–7 cm) long, straight base, not hairy below. Page 28

Downy birch
Betula pubescens
Leaves $2-2\frac{1}{2}$ in. (5–6 cm) long, triangular base, hairy below. Page 29

Triangular, no teeth, opposite

Lilac

Lilac
Syringa vulgaris
Leaves $2\frac{1}{2}-2\frac{3}{4}$ in. (6–7 cm) long. Page 33

Triangular, small teeth, alternate

Lombardy poplar
Populus nigra 'Italica'
Leaves $1\frac{1}{2}-2$ in. (4–5 cm) long, flat stalk. Page 31

Black poplar
Populus nigra
Leaves 2–3 in. (5–7·5 cm) long, flat stalk. Page 30

Western balsam poplar
Populus trichocarpa
Leaves 4–12 in. (10–30 cm) long, metallic white below. Page 32

Lombardy poplar

Round, wavy margins, alternate

Aspen

Aspen
Populus tremula
Leaves $1\frac{1}{2}-2\frac{1}{2}$ in. (4–6 cm) long, very flat stalk. Page 35

Grey poplar
Populus canescens
Leaves $2\frac{3}{4}-3\frac{1}{2}$ in. (7–9 cm) long, felted white below. Page 34

Round, with fan-shaped veins

Judas tree
Cercis siliquastrum
Leaves alternate, $1\frac{1}{2}-4$ in. (4–10 cm) long, without teeth. Page 36

Katsura tree
Cercidiphyllum japonicum
Leaves opposite, 3 in. (7·5 cm) long, with small teeth. Page 37

Judas tree

Other round leaves

Cider gum

Cider gum, snow gum
Eucalyptus gunnii, E. niphophila
Juvenile leaves $\frac{3}{4}$ in. (2 cm) across, bluish. Adult leaves long and narrow. Pages 124–5

Common alder
Alnus glutinosa
Leaves though usually oval are sometimes round, 2 in. (5 cm) across. Leathery, sometimes with notched tip. Page 65

LIFE IN A BIRCH WOOD

Birch, together with willow, hazel and rowan, are 'pioneer' species that quickly colonise bare ground. Birch takes root readily in poor soils and its tight, winged fruits are blown far. Its thin leaves soon rot, enriching the soil and allowing more demanding species such as oak and beech to invade, whose seedlings grow into tall trees that deprive the protecting birch of light, eventually killing it. Birch provides food and shelter for a variety of wildlife and supports a rich variety of fungi.

Redpolls, tits and other birds feed on birch seeds. The caterpillars of the mottled umber moth eat the leaves.

Roe deer

Bracket

Heather and bilberry are among the plants that thrive on the acid soils colonised by birch. The light shade that birch cast encourages the growth of many other plants, too. Young birch trees and the grass beneath them provide food for hares and roe deer.

Razor strop

Hare

Razor strop and bracket fungus live on dead birch stems; fly agaric is associated with the still-living roots.

Heather

Fly agaric

Bilberry

Female catkins

Male catkins

Purple-brown male catkins and pale green female catkins open in April.

Yellow autumn leaf.

Leaves are alternate, thin and shiny, on slender, hairless stalks. Edges are ragged, with smaller teeth between large main teeth. The base of the leaf is straight.

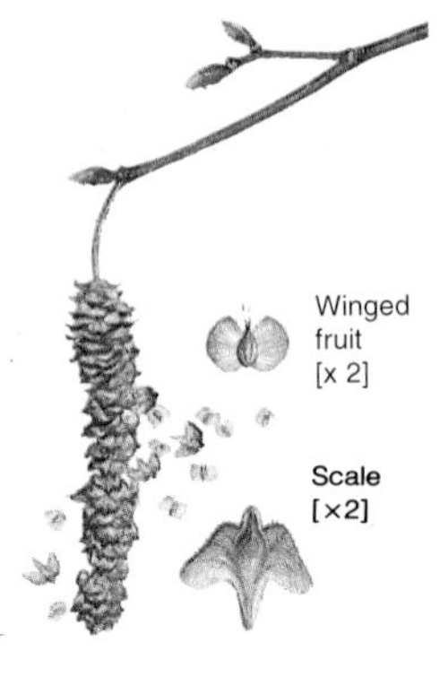

Fruiting catkins stay on the tree until winter, when they break up into scales and winged, wind-borne fruits.

Silver birch forms natural woodlands on light, dry soils throughout Britain, and is widely planted for its appearance.

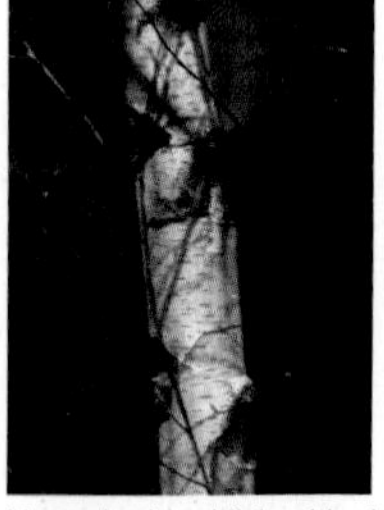

Young bark reddish; older is black-marked silver-white, raised in 'bosses'.

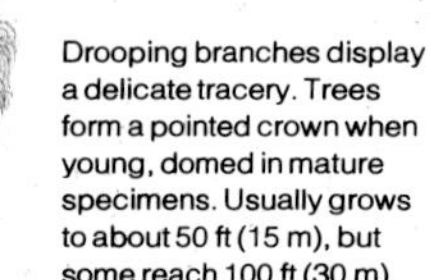

Drooping branches display a delicate tracery. Trees form a pointed crown when young, domed in mature specimens. Usually grows to about 50 ft (15 m), but some reach 100 ft (30 m).

Silver birch *Betula pendula*

Its straight silvery-white trunk and pendulous branches make the silver birch one of the most decorative and easily recognised of Britain's native trees. Despite its delicate appearance it is one of the world's hardiest trees, and in Britain, with rowan, will grow higher up mountains than any other deciduous tree. It grows particularly well on the sands and gravels of south-eastern England, and is often planted as an ornamental tree in gardens and streets, where its small size is an advantage.

The silver birch was a holy tree, revered by pagan Celtic and Germanic tribes: in Britain the Druids gave its name to a midwinter month. The birch was considered to have sacred powers of renewal and purification, so its twigs were used in the ritual of driving out the spirits of the old year. The belief persisted into historical times, when delinquents and the insane were birched to expel evil spirits.

The timber of silver birch shows no distinction between heartwood and sapwood. It is made into the backs of brushes and tool handles; it does not grow big enough in Britain for commercial use as timber. Birch twigs are cut in winter to make besom brooms for gardens and forest-fire beaters.

Winter reveals fewer and thicker branches than on silver birch. 80 ft (24 m).

The branches of this round-headed tree are twisting, and seldom hang down.

Bark usually red-brown, but can be silvery.

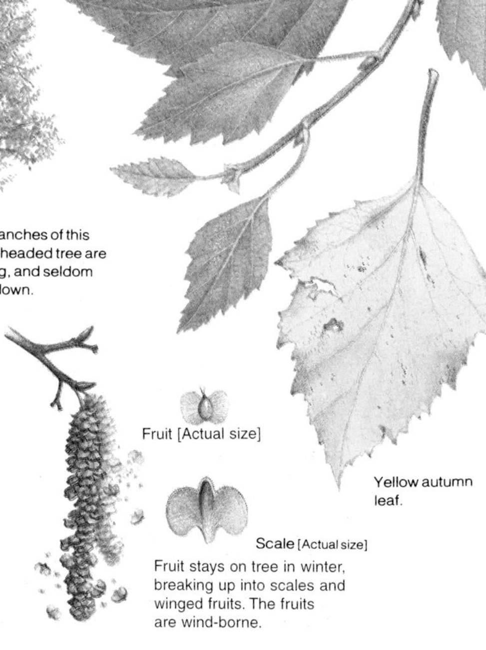

Fruit [Actual size]

Scale [Actual size]

Fruit stays on tree in winter, breaking up into scales and winged fruits. The fruits are wind-borne.

Yellow autumn leaf.

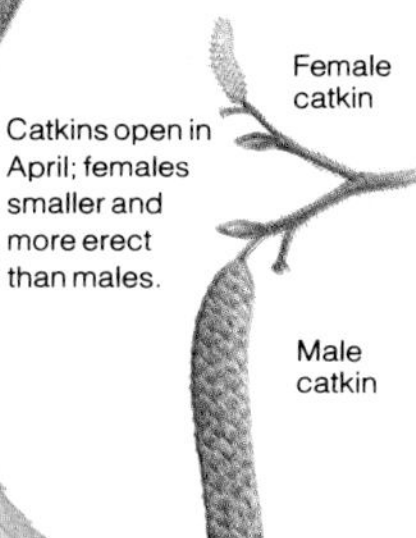

Catkins open in April; females smaller and more erect than males.

Veins on underside of leaf are hairy; teeth are more even in size than on silver birch leaves. Base is triangular, the stalk slender and hairy.

Downy birch thrives on wetter soils than silver birch and forms woodlands on damp uplands in the north and west.

Downy birch *Betula pubescens*

One of two birches native to the British Isles, the downy birch frequently crosses with the silver birch, the other native species, to produce hybrids that have the characteristics of both. All are closely related to a Canadian birch, the bark of which was used by the indigenous people to cover their canoes and dwellings. The bark of these birches is waterproof and resistant to fungus; often it can be seen as a shell, left intact around the collapsed and rotting wood of the tree.

In upland areas, downy birch woods provide useful shelter for sheep in winter, and they are a favourite habitat for roe-deer. Birches are short-lived (about 70 years), but play an important role as colonisers of poor soils. The wind-blown fruit is easily spread and quickly forms scrub woodland, while the fallen leaves improve the soil. Birch often colonises after heathland fires.

The sap of the birch is rich in sugar. Tapped in spring, it can be made into birch wine by adding honey, or it may be used as a shampoo. Birch oil is obtained from the bark and used as insect repellent. The wood is soft, and though it rots quickly out of doors, it can be used for furniture, tool handles and plywood. As firewood it burns with a particularly bright flame.

Female catkins

Alternate leaves are longer than they are broad, with translucent margins and small, regular teeth. The stalk is flattened.

Crimson male and green female catkins ripen on separate trees in March.

Male catkins

Female catkins release fluffy seeds in June.

Caterpillars of the wood leopard moth bore into poplar stems, sometimes causing them to break off.

Leaves turn banana yellow in autumn.

Fast-growing hybrid black poplars are often planted to make a screen and windbreak beside roads.

Bark is grey-brown, fissured, sometimes burred.

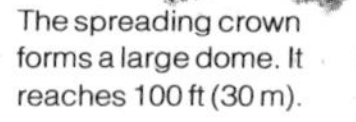

The spreading crown forms a large dome. It reaches 100 ft (30 m).

Black poplar *Populus nigra*

John Constable (1776–1837) immortalised the black poplar in many of his paintings of East Anglia, where it flourishes on fertile soil beside water. But this beautiful, spreading tree does not need pollution-free air to thrive, and since the 19th century it has been extensively planted in heavily industrialised areas, particularly in the north of England, where it is sometimes called the Manchester poplar. It makes an attractive screen for factories, railways and other industrial structures.

The black poplar is native to Britain but is scarce in the wild. It crosses easily with other poplars to produce vigorous hybrids valued for their fast growth and high-quality timber. The wood from black poplar and its hybrids is made into baskets for fruit and into matches and matchboxes.

The wood is particularly well suited for matches, because its open texture makes it easy to impregnate with paraffin wax, in which the matchsticks are soaked, and it is not liable to break or splinter when the match is struck. For all these commercial uses, poplar is cut into very thin veneers by rotating the logs against a blade, so that a continuous layer is peeled away. In Holland, however, the solid wood is used to make clogs.

Leaves are alternate, broader than they are long. The margin is translucent, with small, regular teeth. The stalk is long and flattened.

Most Lombardy poplars are male. Crimson catkins ripen in April.

Easily recognised by its tall, stately profile, the Lombardy poplar is a familiar sight along many avenues in Britain.

Grey-brown bark has low ridges; base often fluted.

Upright branches make the Lombardy poplar a lofty column of compact green in summer, growing to 100 ft (30 m).

Lombardy poplar *Populus nigra* 'Italica'

Planted along both sides of a country road, the Lombardy poplar is an unforgettable sight. It got its name when cuttings of a male tree were brought from Lombardy, in northern Italy, early in the 18th century for propagation in Britain. But the tree is now thought to be a native of Asia. In Europe it is hardly known in its female form. This has the advantage for garden and street planting that there are no woolly seeds to be swept up from lawns and pavements.

Because of its narrow shape, the Lombardy poplar lends tall grandeur to a scene without taking up too much ground space. However, like other poplars, it takes a lot of water from the soil during its rapid growth; and on shrinkable clays, such as that of London, this causes soil movement. In extreme cases, cracks can be caused in buildings near by. Sometimes poplar roots, in their search for water, can penetrate and block drains.

Lombardy poplar is not affected by soot and smoke, and as the dense, high crowns form an excellent screen it is commonly planted in a line to hide factories. The fluted stem and numerous branches mean that little timber for commercial use can be produced from the tree.

Large, thick leaves have a white, metallic-looking underside and small regular teeth. There is no translucent margin. The leaves, like the sticky buds, have a strong sweet smell.

Leaf in autumn.

Woolly female catkins break up into fluffy seeds in May.

Flowers appear as catkins in March. Female catkins are long and green; male catkins, on separate trees, are shorter and dull crimson.

Male catkin

Female catkin

Fast-growing western balsam poplars are often planted as shelter belts beside roads or individually in parks and fields.

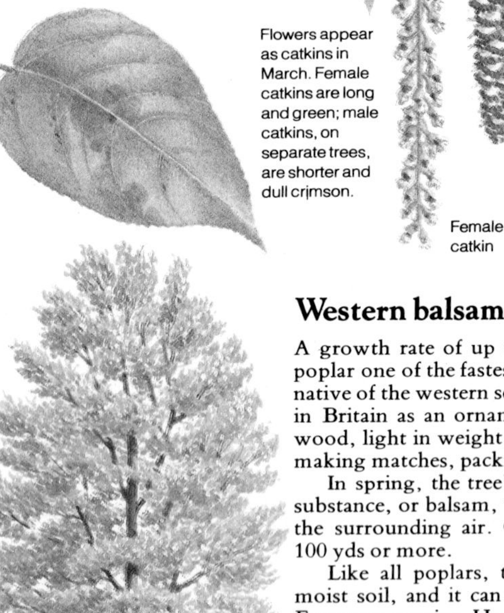

Regularly spaced branches give the tree a cone shape. It reaches 110 ft (33 m).

Smooth and greenish bark turns grey and ridged.

Western balsam poplar *Populus trichocarpa*

A growth rate of up to 6 ft a year makes the western balsam poplar one of the fastest-growing trees planted in Britain. It is a native of the western seaboard of North America, and is planted in Britain as an ornamental tree or to form a screen. Its soft wood, light in weight and colour, is used like other poplars for making matches, packing cases and baskets.

In spring, the tree's buds and young leaves exude a sticky substance, or balsam, with a heady, sweet odour that pervades the surrounding air. On hot, still days the smell carries for 100 yds or more.

Like all poplars, the western balsam requires low-lying, moist soil, and it can tolerate acid ground better than related European species. However, as a strong, fast grower, it needs freedom from competition from other trees, so it must be planted with plenty of space. Its roots die if the soil is stagnant and waterlogged. The main stem and branches are susceptible to ugly cankers, or growths, which detract from its decorative appeal, but it has been successfully crossed with other species to produce canker-resistant hybrids suitable for planting in parks or in corners of fields.

Leaves are opposite and undivided, with branching veins and a translucent margin. The sweet-scented flowers attract many butterflies.

Cultivated varieties offer a wide range of colours with single and double flowers.

The flower-head consists of many single flowers.

Each fruit contains two winged seeds.

Lilacs are widely planted in gardens for their showy flowers appearing in May, and many have spread to the wild.

The light brown, shaggy bark peels off in long strips.

The lilac, usually a shrub with many stems, may grow into a 25 ft (7·5 m) tree.

Lilac *Syringa vulgaris*

Britain owes the presence of this popular shrub to John Tradescant, the naturalist who became gardener to Charles I and his queen, Henrietta Maria. The lilac is native to eastern Europe and Asia Minor, and was brought to England by Tradescant in 1621 while he was in the service of the Duke of Buckingham. Since then the lilac has become sufficiently established to grow wild in many parts of Britain, as well as being cultivated in thousands of gardens for its glowing colours and sweet-smelling flowers.

Varieties of lilac have been produced in such profusion that it is difficult even for botanists to distinguish the many subtle shades of colour. Many of the most striking varieties were raised at Nancy, in France, by the 19th-century horticulturist Victor Lemoine and his son Emile. Some forms have single flowers, but others with double flowers have also been raised. The most highly scented varieties attract a host of butterflies in summer.

Lilacs are produced by pegging a branch into the ground to take root or, more often, by grafting on to the roots of common lilac or privet. If raised from seed, the flowers of different seedlings vary in colour. The wood of lilac is hard, with purple heartwood, and in Victorian times it was used for inlay work.

The grey poplar is distinguished by its open crown, and by the white of the upper bark and the undersides of the leaves. It grows to about 75 ft (23 m).

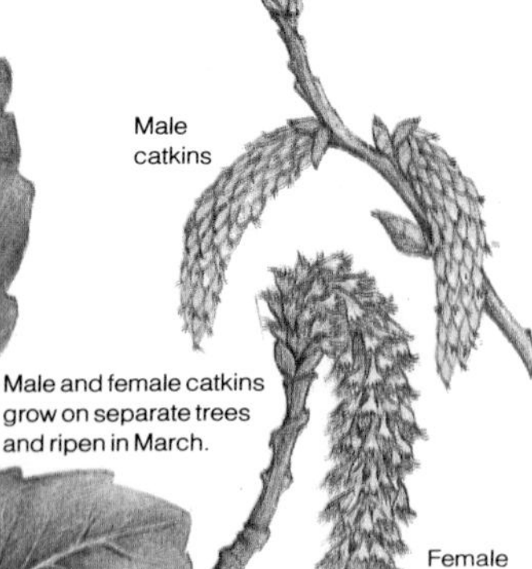

Male and female catkins grow on separate trees and ripen in March.

The grey poplar flourishes on ground that is constantly damp, particularly in water-meadows and river valleys.

Leaves are alternate and thick, and very variable in shape. Felted hairs on the underside of the leaf show pale when disturbed by wind. The leaf stalk is slightly flattened.

Lower trunk black; upper whitish with black lines.

Tree in winter.

Grey poplar *Populus canescens*

Experts cannot agree whether the grey poplar is a species in its own right or an ancient hybrid between the native aspen and the introduced white poplar. Certainly it has features in common with both species, but there are also noticeable differences. The leaf of the grey poplar is much rounder than that of the white poplar, and the down on the underside of the leaves, from which it gets its name, is grey rather than white. The leaves of the aspen, by contrast, are smooth on both sides.

The grey poplar is more tolerant of shade than other poplars and occurs in damp woods, where the young suckers it sends up from its roots often form dense thickets. It grows taller than the white poplar, producing a straight white upper trunk which, in maturity, is branchless for most of its height and pitted with lines of black diamonds. Like white poplar, the tree is resistant to salt-laden winds and is therefore often used to form shelter belts near the sea.

When dry, the wood of grey poplar is tough, and nails can be driven in without splitting it. It is used for packing cases and storage pallets. The sapwood is very white, contrasting with the dark brown heartwood.

Delicate open shape visible in winter.

Male and female catkins borne on separate trees. Male catkins brown in March, female catkins green. Pollination by the wind.

Female catkins shed white woolly fruits in May.

Leaves are 2 in. (5 cm) long, small and rounded with a wavy margin and flattened stalk.

This small poplar is easily recognised in summer by its trembling leaves. Up to 65 ft (20 m).

The leaves of the aspen turn a glorious amber-yellow in autumn. The tree is native and found throughout Britain.

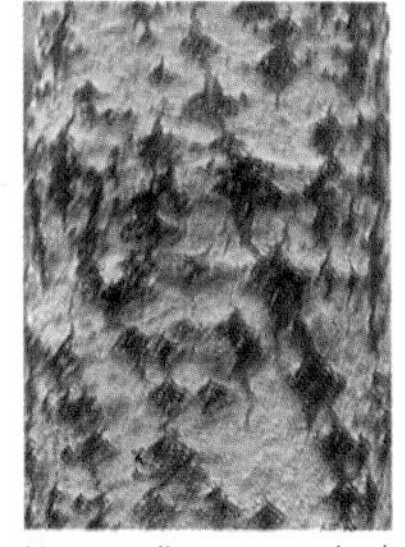

Young, silvery-green bark furrows with age.

Aspen *Populus tremula*

Country folk used to believe that the constant trembling of its leaves in the slightest breeze indicated some secret grief or guilt on the part of the aspen; some said the guilt was that of having provided the wood used for the cross on which Christ was crucified. Certainly 'to tremble like an aspen' became a common expression, though what makes the leaves quiver in the wind is now recognised to be the extreme flattening of the long stalks on which they are borne.

Constantly throwing up suckers to form new trees, the aspen pioneers the colonisation of new ground, particularly in the Scottish Highlands. In the Midlands and southern England the aspen occurs in mixed broad-leaved woodlands, but is nowhere abundant. Its quivering foliage and silver bark, strongly marked with black diamonds, make it an attractive garden tree.

Because its stem never grows very large, the aspen is not an important timber tree in Britain. The bigger American aspen (*Populus tremuloides*) is, however, grown commercially. Before the beaver became extinct in Scotland in medieval times the aspen must have provided the animal's staple food, as the American aspen still does for the beaver in Canada.

This spreading tree seldom grows to more than 33 ft (10 m), and has very light branches.

Tree in winter.

Flowers may sprout straight from the purplish trunk.

Pods ripen to purple in autumn, with long whiskers at base.

Leaves are alternate, with heart-shaped base, fan-like veins and a small spine at the rounded tip. The edge is wavy, with no teeth.

Pea-like rose-pink flowers appear singly or in bunches.

The narrow, dark red buds are distinctive in winter.

The fine display of decorative rose-pink flowers makes the Judas tree an attractive ornamental tree in southern England.

Judas tree *Cercis siliquastrum*

Legends abound to explain the name of the Judas tree, a native of the eastern Mediterranean and southern Europe, which was brought to Britain for the appearance of its rose-pink, pea-like flowers, some of which burst straight from the naked branches in late spring, before the leaves emerge. The tree is said to be the one on which Judas Iscariot hanged himself after betraying Christ, and its crooked stems are attributed to that event. Refinements of the same story hold that the blooms represent Christ's tears and that their colour is a blush of shame for Judas's perfidy.

The real explanation for the tree's name, however, is probably the more prosaic one that it is a corruption of 'Judaea tree', from the area of Israel in which it is particularly common. An alternative name for the Judas tree, and others of the same family, is 'redbud', which aptly describes the appearance of its twigs in winter.

The Judas tree is susceptible to the northern cold and grows best on dry, chalky soils in southern and eastern England or on the coast of western Scotland, warmed by the Gulf Stream. It can be grown elsewhere in Britain on south-facing walls.

Leaves are opposite, broader than they are long, blue-green above and glaucous below, edged with small, even teeth. Shiny green curved pods grow on female trees only.

Usually bushlike, with many stems, the katsura can grow to 45 ft (14 m).

This small oriental tree is grown in Britain's parks and gardens for the ever-changing colours of its foliage.

Tree in winter.

Bark is brown, ridged, and peels in strips.

Leaves, pink in spring, turn yellow and scarlet.

Male flowers

Female flowers

Male and female flowers grow on separate trees. Males have red stamens, females have red styles.

Katsura tree *Cercidiphyllum japonicum*

In its native forests of Japan and China the katsura tree is one of the largest deciduous trees, reaching heights of more than 100 ft (30 m) with numerous spiral, twisting trunks. In Britain, however, where the tree was introduced in 1865, it rarely grows to more than a bush; it starts to grow early in the spring, and the tender emerging shoots are often killed by spring frosts and cold winds.

In the Far East the katsura tree's yellow timber, light and fine-grained, is used for furniture and interior woodwork, but in Britain the tree is grown for ornamental purposes only. It thrives best on moist deep soils, in parks and gardens protected from frosts, and when established it rewards the care needed for its cultivation with a striking display of leaves, which turn from pink in spring to green in summer and then to a wide range of yellows, scarlets and crimsons in autumn.

The botanical name for the katsura tree, *Cercidiphyllum*, means 'leaf' (*phyllos*) 'like the Judas tree' (*Cercis*). The katsura tree's rounded leaves can easily be confused with those of the Judas tree, but the paired leaves of the katsura tree are opposite each other, whereas those of the Judas tree are alternate.

TREES WITH HEART-SHAPED LEAVES

Commonest of the trees with heart-shaped leaves are the tall, stately limes, of which there are four main species. Other, less common trees include two with alternate, toothed leaves and two with very large leaves, opposite and untoothed.

Medium-sized leaves, alternate, with drawn-out tip

Small-leaved lime

Small-leaved lime

Tilia cordata

Leaves 1½–3 in. (4–7·5 cm) long, with orange hairs in angles of veins. Page 43

Silver lime

Tilia tomentosa

Leaves up to 3½–4½ in. (9–12 cm) long, with dense silvery hairs on underside. Page 41

Common lime

Tilia × europaea

Leaves 2–4 in. (5–10 cm) long, with straight base. Page 40

Large-leaved lime

Tilia platyphyllos

Leaves 2½–6 in. (6–15 cm) long, hairy on underside. Page 42

Fairly large leaves, alternate, with regular triangular teeth

Black mulberry

Black mulberry

Morus nigra

Leaves 3–4½ in. (7·5–12 cm) long, rough on upper surface, with unpointed teeth. Page 47

Handkerchief tree

Handkerchief tree

Davidia involucrata

Leaves 5 in. (12·5 cm) long, with large triangular-pointed teeth. Page 46

Very large opposite leaves

Foxglove tree

Foxglove tree

Paulownia tomentosa

Leaves 5½–14 in. (14–36 cm) long, stalk with hairs. Page 45

Indian bean-tree

Indian bean-tree

Catalpa bignonioides

Leaves 5–10 in. (12·5–25 cm) long, stalk without hairs. Page 44

Various species of lime flower at different times, giving bees a continuous supply of nectar for much of the summer. The flowers of large-leaved lime open in June and July, hanging from long, pale green, leaf-like bracts.

The beauty of limes

As far back as Roman times, the tall, stately lime tree was planted for its shade and the sweet scent diffused by its flowers. Avenues of limes graced the formal gardens of Louis XIV in France and Charles II in England; afterwards, lime avenues took their place in the landscaped gardens of the great landowners. Many of these trees are now reaching the end of their lives, and need to be replaced by young trees. One lime, the silver lime, is particularly resistant to heat, drought and pollution, so does well as a street tree where there is space for it to grow.

Red nail galls caused by mites are often found on leaves.

Leaves are broad, 2–4 in. (5–10 cm) long, with almost straight bases. The undersides have white or buff hairs in the vein junctions. The shoots are often red-tinged.

Greenish-yellow flowers, sweet smelling in early July, produce abundant nectar sought by bees. Flowers hang from a long bract.

Decorative in shape, tall and long-living, the common lime is a familiar sight in British parks and gardens.

The rounded, hanging fruits are hairy and only faintly ribbed.

Young bark is smooth and grey, old is fissured.

A tall tree with long slender branches that start near the ground, the lower ones arched. It reaches 130 ft (40 m).

Common lime *Tilia x europaea*

The common lime is the tallest broad-leaved tree in Britain. Thought to be a hybrid between the large leaved and small-leaved limes, it grows vigorously and can live for 500 years. Some of the biggest British specimens date from the 18th century, when many limes were imported from the Netherlands to grace the gardens of stately homes.

Although limes become infested with aphids which feed on the leaves, causing sticky, partly digested leaf-sap to drip onto the pavements beneath, they are frequently planted alongside town streets. A mould fungus turns these droppings black, causing unsightly blotches. For streets, gardens and parks the silver pendent lime, *Tilia petiolaris*, is preferred nowadays as it is more resistant to aphid attack.

The stringy, inner bark of common lime, called bast or bass, was once used to make mats and ropes; in America the timber is known as basswood. The flowers provide a source of nectar for honey bees in July, after the nectar of the earlier-flowering large-leaved lime has been exhausted. Lime wood is light and fine-grained, used for wood carvings and for the making of musical instruments.

Leaves are alternate, green on top with dense silvery hairs on underside. The leaf margin has sharp teeth and the base is lopsided.

Yellow flowers appear in late July on light green leaf-like bracts. Their nectar is a narcotic to bees.

Fruit is five-sided and covered with fine down.

This shapely lime can be easily identified in summer by the silvery sheen of its leaves as the wind stirs them.

Silver pendent lime

Tilia petiolaris

The long leaf-stalk causes the foliage to droop. Sometimes called the weeping white lime, from its appearance and shape.

Smooth, grey-green bark cracks and darkens.

Ascending branches give a well-rounded, compact shape. The tree grows to 80 ft (24 m).

Silver lime *Tilia tomentosa*

A native of the Balkans and south-west Asia, the silver or white lime was introduced to Britain for its ornamental appeal in 1767. When disturbed by the wind the foliage has a striking dappled appearance, as the silver undersides of the leaves that give the tree its name contrast with the green upper surfaces. The silver lime is hardy and well able to withstand drought and frost. For that reason, it is used as a street tree in many parts of the United States, where the reflected heat from city pavements in summer can be desiccating.

A similar tree, the silver pendent lime, differs slightly in having drooping branches and leaves that hang downwards on long, slender stalks. Its origin is not known, but an early example was planted in the Cambridge Botanic Gardens in 1842.

As the pendent lime is so like the silver lime, there is doubt about whether it is genuinely a different species. It is more likely to be a 'sport', or natural variation, that has subsequently been propagated by gardeners, particularly as it is reproduced by grafting on to the rootstock of another lime. Both silver limes are best planted as a single specimen tree set in a lawn.

Leaves are alternate, and up to 6 in. (15 cm) long. They are dark green and hairy on top, paler and densely hairy on the underside. The stalk is also hairy.

The flowers are sweet smelling. [× 2]

Three globe-shaped fruits usually hang on each bract. They are five-ribbed and covered with short hairs.

The large-leaved lime is native in Britain, and is also often planted to lend dignity to avenues and parks.

Greenish-yellow flowers, appearing in late June, before other limes, are a valuable source of nectar for bees. Flowers hang in clusters of three or four from long bracts.

Bark is smooth and grey, becoming finely fissured.

This tall lime rises to 100 ft (30 m), with ascending branches and a narrow crown.

Large-leaved lime *Tilia platyphyllos*

Bees, moths, cattle and deer all make a feast of the lime tree, and the large-leaved lime, which flowers some weeks before other limes, draws bees to its nectar earlier than the rest. Lime seedlings are seldom seen in the wild, because they are very palatable to browsing animals. In parkland open to cattle or deer, older limes are often stripped of leaves to the height that the animals can reach. Lime leaves are popular, too, with the caterpillars of many moths, including the lime hawk moth, which lays its eggs on them early in May.

Nurserymen sometimes find it difficult to raise limes from seed, for unless it is gathered and sown as it ripens, it goes into dormancy and will not germinate easily. The seed of the large-leaved lime needs richer and damper soil than other limes if it is to flourish.

Once established, however, the lime is a hardy tree that graces many parks and public gardens. The large-leaved lime is long-lived and, unlike other limes, does not sprout at the base. Because it will stand hard pruning, it is a popular tree for planting in streets, especially in its red-twigged 'Rubra' form, which is more compact and erect.

Greenish-yellow flowers, sweet-smelling and attractive to bees, appear early in July in erect or spreading clusters of seven or eight on each bract.

Fruits are neither ribbed nor hairy like those of other limes.

The handsome small-leaved lime grows wild in Europe, and is a native tree of limestone soils in England and Wales.

Leaves are alternate and $1\frac{1}{2}$–3 in. (4–7·5 cm) long. They are dark green and shiny on top, with orange tufts of hair in vein junctions on the undersides. The stalk is not hairy.

Smooth, grey bark cracks into shallow plates later.

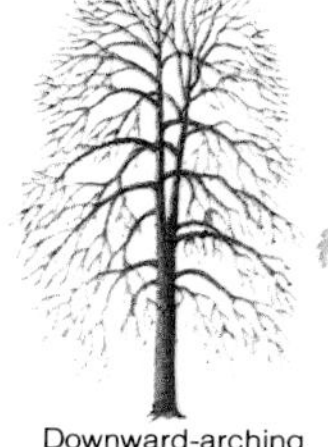

Downward-arching branches and a domed crown characterise this lime, which grows to 70 ft (22 m) high.

Small-leaved lime *Tilia cordata*

Its decorative appearance has long made the small-leaved lime popular for planting in stately avenues. For humbler folk, the lime was a holy tree, ranged along village streets to protect the peasants against evil. Limes have been planted to give shade, throughout history: records show that the ancient Greeks and Romans used the tree for this purpose.

Lime wood, being soft and even-grained, is ideal for carving and turning and has inspired generations of artists and craftsmen. The best-known woodcarver to use lime was Grinling Gibbons (1648-1721), whose work can still be seen in many of Britain's churches, cathedrals and great houses. The intricate and detailed portrayal of flowers and foliage for which Gibbons was celebrated would only have been possible with a fine-textured and easily worked wood such as lime.

Because it does not warp, lime wood is still used for the sounding boards and keys of pianos and organs. For the same reason it is a popular material for drawing boards. Fibres used to tie up plants are sometimes made of lime bark. Lime trees have nothing in common with citrus fruit. The name derives from *Linde*, the German word for lime tree.

Yellow catalpa
Catalpa ovata
The leaves of this catalpa have three pointed lobes and its flowers are yellow. It is smaller and darker-looking than the Indian bean-tree.

Numerous white flowers, flecked with yellow or purple, are carried on an upright head.

Pointed leaves, set opposite each other or in whorls of three, grow up to 10 in. (25 cm) long. They are smooth on top, hairy beneath.

Bean-like pods stay on the tree all winter.

The Indian bean-tree, from the southern United States, ornaments parks in the warmer parts of England.

Tree in winter.

Light brown bark scales into fine flakes.

The tree spreads to a wide, shallow crown, growing to 50 ft (15 m) only in areas where summers are warm.

Indian bean-tree *Catalpa bignonioides*

This summer-flowering tree is usually the last in the garden to produce leaves: they do not appear until June. It is a native of the southern United States, first cultivated in Britain in the 18th century, and its alternative name of catalpa is a corruption of Catawba, a Red Indian tribe in the area where botanists first recorded it.

In Britain, the fruit rarely ripens and the tree is reproduced from cuttings. Because it comes into leaf so late, some leaves are still emerging when the first frost arrives, and in a hard winter the last three or four bud clusters on each branch may be damaged by the cold. Nevertheless, the catalpa flourishes throughout southern Britain where it is planted in parks, gardens and streets. It is a fast-growing tree, putting on 3–4 ft (1 m) a year when young.

The golden Indian bean-tree, a cultivated variety called 'Aurea', has deep yellow leaves if planted in the open, though they remain green if the tree is planted in shade. *Catalpa ovata*, a hybrid between the Indian bean-tree and the Chinese or yellow catalpa, has leaves that are deep purple when young. Its yellow flowers bloom in July.

The fruit is green, oval in shape and beaked. It contains winged seeds.

The leaves are opposite and felted underneath, and grow to 14 in. (36 cm) long. The stalk is hairy.

The erect, purple flowers, shaped like those of the foxglove, open in May before the leaves appear.

One of the most striking of all ornamental trees, the foxglove tree is planted in parks and gardens in southern England.

The greyish bark is broken by orange blisters.

This tree has huge leaves and its flower buds are conspicuous all winter. It grows to 23 ft (7 m).

Foxglove tree *Paulownia tomentosa*

Purple foxglove-like flowers that cover the tree in May, before the leaves appear, give this tree its common name. Young plants have been pruned back hard to produce leaves more than 24 in. (60 cm) across, giving a remarkable display of foliage. The tree's botanical name derives from Anna Paulowna (or Pavlovna), daughter of Tsar Paul I of Russia and wife of the Dutch prince who became King William II. It was named in the 17th century by the German physician and botanist Englebrecht Kaemfer, who discovered the tree on an expedition to Japan for the Dutch East India Company.

The tree came originally from China, where for hundreds of years it had been attributed with almost magical powers to preserve beauty and health. An 11th-century Chinese manuscript was devoted entirely to the tree and described, for example, how a carefully prepared infusion from its leaves and fruit would prevent the skin from wrinkling and the hair from turning grey.

The foxglove tree grows well in southern England, but its buds are vulnerable to late spring frosts. Its wood is soft when first felled, but quickly turns hard and is very light in weight.

Green, buff-speckled fruit grows to more than $1\frac{1}{2}$ in. (4 cm) long, turning purple when ripe.

Davidia involucrata var. *vilmoriniana*
A narrower leaf, hairless and shiny on the underside, distinguishes this variety, which is commonly planted in parks and gardens.

Leaves are alternate and edged with large, sharp triangular teeth. They have dense white hair on the underside. Each white 'flower' comprises a pair of long bracts, hiding the purple blossom.

Displays of large white bracts give the handkerchief tree its name, and its alternative names of dove or ghost tree.

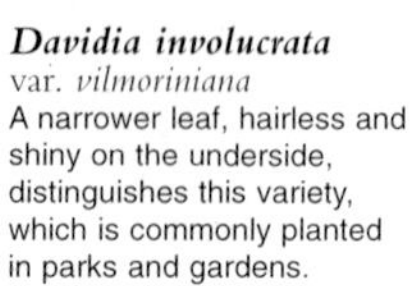

Radiating branches form a high-domed crown, sometimes topping 60 ft (18 m). The tree grows well in the south.

Fine cracks streak the grey-brown bark.

Handkerchief tree *Davidia involucrata*

This tree's spectacular white crown of flowers found its way into Britain's private gardens only after a series of adventures. It was first seen by the French Jesuit priest Père David, after whom it is named, when he travelled into remote China in 1868 at a time when few Europeans were allowed into the country. Specimens sent to Kew attracted the interest of the Victorian nurseryman Henry Veitch, who in 1899 commissioned a botanist named Ernest Wilson to bring seeds of the tree from China.

Wilson, who had never been abroad before, set off on a nightmare journey, full of danger and frustration. In China's remote Yunnan province he was imprisoned on suspicion of spying; he came unscathed through an epidemic of deadly fever; and he nearly drowned when his boat ran onto rocks.

When Wilson found a handkerchief tree it was a mere stump beside a house built from its timber. Bitterly disappointed, Wilson turned to collecting other plants, only to come across a clump of handkerchief trees by accident. But the trees were in full flower; with the Boxer Rebellion in progress around him, Wilson had to wait weeks for the seeds to ripen before he could at last send them back to England.

White mulberry

Morus alba

The food plant of the silk-worm is distinguished by its shiny, less downy leaf as well as by its white or pinkish fruit.

Leaves are alternate, toothed and pointed with a heart-shaped base, and hairy on both sides.

The fruit of the black mulberry is a deep wine red. It ripens in August or September.

In May and June, male and female flowers grow in separate catkins, sometimes on different branches.

Black mulberries have been grown in Britain since 1550. In the north they need protection from cold winds.

The short trunk soon divides into spreading branches to form a bushy, round-headed tree with coarse, dark leaves, reaching 20 ft (6 m) in height.

Bark is orange-brown, often scaled and rough.

Black mulberry *Morus nigra*

According to Classical fable, the fruit of the mulberry was once white, but was reddened by the blood of the tragic lovers Pyramus and Thisbe, whose story is parodied by Shakespeare in *A Midsummer Night's Dream.* They arranged to meet under a mulberry tree. Thisbe, who arrived first, was scared by a lion and fled, dropping her veil, which the lion smeared with blood. Pyramus, on finding it, believed Thisbe to be dead and killed himself. When Thisbe returned she committed suicide.

The fable is set in Babylon and the black, or common, mulberry may have originated in the Middle East, but it no longer grows in the wild anywhere. It was introduced to Europe by the Greeks and Romans for its fruit, which has a bitter-sweet taste and can be eaten raw or as a preserve. In the 17th century, James I encouraged the planting of black mulberry trees in an attempt to rear silk-worms for the home production of silk, but the silk-worms prefer the white mulberry, *Morus alba*, a native of China that does not grow well in Britain.

Mulberry was at one time planted in prison exercise yards. The rhyme 'Here we go round the mulberry bush' is said to have originated from daily exercise round the tree.

TREES WITH OVAL LEAVES

Oval-leaved trees range from forest giants like the elm and beech to crab apple and common pear. Clues to identification include the size of the leaf, its plain or toothed margins, its pointed or blunt ends and whether it is evergreen or not.

Small leaves

Box

Box
Buxus sempervirens

Leaves opposite, evergreen, ½–1 in. (1·3–2·5 cm) long, blunt or notched tip. Page 56

Shining honeysuckle
Lonicera nitida

Leaves opposite, evergreen, to ½ in. (1·3 cm), round base, tip blunt. Page 54

Californian lilac
Ceanothus thyrsiflorus

Leaves alternate, evergreen, to 2 in. (5 cm); three veins spread from leaf base. Page 50

Firethorn
Pyracantha coccinea

Leaves alternate, evergreen, to 1½ in. (4 cm); hairy stalks, thorny twigs. Page 51

Escallonia
Escallonia macrantha

Leaves alternate, evergreen, to ½ in. (1·3 cm); stalkless, glands beneath. Page 53

Barberry
Berberis vulgaris

Leaves to 1½ in. (4 cm); hairless, bristly margins; thorns in threes. Page 55

Blackthorn
Prunus spinosa

Leaves to 1½ in. (4 cm); small teeth, hairy undersides; twigs thorny. Page 57

Leaves with double toothing

Hazels
Corylus

Leaves alternate, 3–4 in. (7·5–10 cm) long, broad with even base. Pages 68–70

Grey alder
Alnus incana

Leaves alternate, 2½–4 in. (6–10 cm) long, with grey hairs on underside. Page 66

Elms
Ulmus

Leaves alternate, 4–7 in. (10–18 cm) long, broad, with unequal base. Pages 76–79

Common hazel

Leaves with triangular teeth

Keaki
Zelkova serrata

Leaves alternate, 2–4¾ in. (5–12 cm) long, with large pointed teeth. Page 81

Caucasian elm
Zelkova carpinifolia

Leaves alternate, ¾–3½ in. (2–9 cm) long; large teeth lack points. Page 80

Keaki

Leaves with rounded ends

Common alder

Common alder
Alnus glutinosa

Leaves alternate, 1½–4 in. (4–10 cm) long, dark green. Edges wavy and toothed; tip may be notched. Page 65

Snowberry
Symphoricarpos rivularis

Leaves opposite, ¾–2 in. (2–5 cm) long, with wavy edges. Page 90

Goat willow
Salix caprea

Leaves alternate, 2–4 in. (5–10 cm); woolly beneath, no teeth. Page 64

Leaves felted below

Whitebeam
Sorbus aria

Leaves alternate, 2–4 in. (5–10 cm) long, with felted white undersides and small teeth. Page 86

Wayfaring tree
Viburnum lantana

Leaves opposite, 2–4 in. (5–10 cm) long, with felted white undersides and small teeth. Page 87

Whitebeam

Alternate leaves with parallel lateral veins

Hornbeam

Hornbeam
Carpinus betulus
Leaves $1\frac{1}{2}$–4 in. (4–10 cm) long, margins double-toothed, 10–15 pairs of veins. Page 71

Roble beech
Nothofagus obliqua
Leaves to 3 in. (7·5 cm), base unequal, margins toothed, 5–8 veins. Page 74

Raoul
Nothofagus procera
Leaves to 3 in. (7·5 cm), margins wavy, toothed, 15–18 veins. Page 75

Persian ironwood
Parrotia persica
Leaves 3–$4\frac{1}{4}$ in. (7·5–11 cm) long, margins wavy, base tapered, 5–6 veins. Page 89

Common beech
Fagus sylvatica
Leaves 3–4 in. (7·5–10 cm) long, wavy margins, 6–11 veins. Page 72

Alder buckthorn
Frangula alnus
Leaves $\frac{3}{4}$–$2\frac{3}{4}$ in. (2–7 cm) long, margins slightly wavy, 7–9 veins. Page 61

Leaves with spiny teeth

Holly
Ilex aquifolium
Leaves alternate and evergreen, $2\frac{1}{4}$–3 in. (5·5–7·5 cm) long, very spiny. Page 58

Holm oak
Quercus ilex
Leaves alternate and evergreen, 2–4 in. (5–10 cm) long, lower leaves holly-like, upper leaves not spiny. Page 109

Leaves with side veins curving forwards

Dogwoods
Cornus
Leaves opposite, $1\frac{1}{2}$–3 in. (4–7·5 cm) long, with no teeth. Veins hold leaf together when it is broken in half. Pages 62–63

Purging buckthorn
Rhamnus catharticus
Leaves opposite or almost opposite, 1–$2\frac{3}{4}$ in. (2·5–7 cm) long, with teeth. Page 60

Dogwood

Leaves with pointed ends

Italian alder

Italian alder
Alnus cordata
Leaves alternate, to 3 in. (7·5 cm); glossy green on top; paler beneath. Page 67

Oval-leaved privet
Ligustrum ovalifolium
Leaves opposite and semi-evergreen, to 2 in. (5 cm); no teeth; base wedge-shaped. Page 52

Mock orange
Philadelphus coronarius
Leaves opposite, to 4 in. (10 cm); few widely spaced teeth on margins. Page 91

Strawberry tree
Arbutus unedo
Leaves alternate, evergreen, to 4 in. (10 cm); dark green on top, white main vein beneath. Page 59

Crab apple
Malus sylvestris
Leaves alternate, 3 in. (7·5 cm); small teeth. Page 82. Similar: common pear, cherry plum, damson, pp. 83–85; snowy mespil, p. 88.

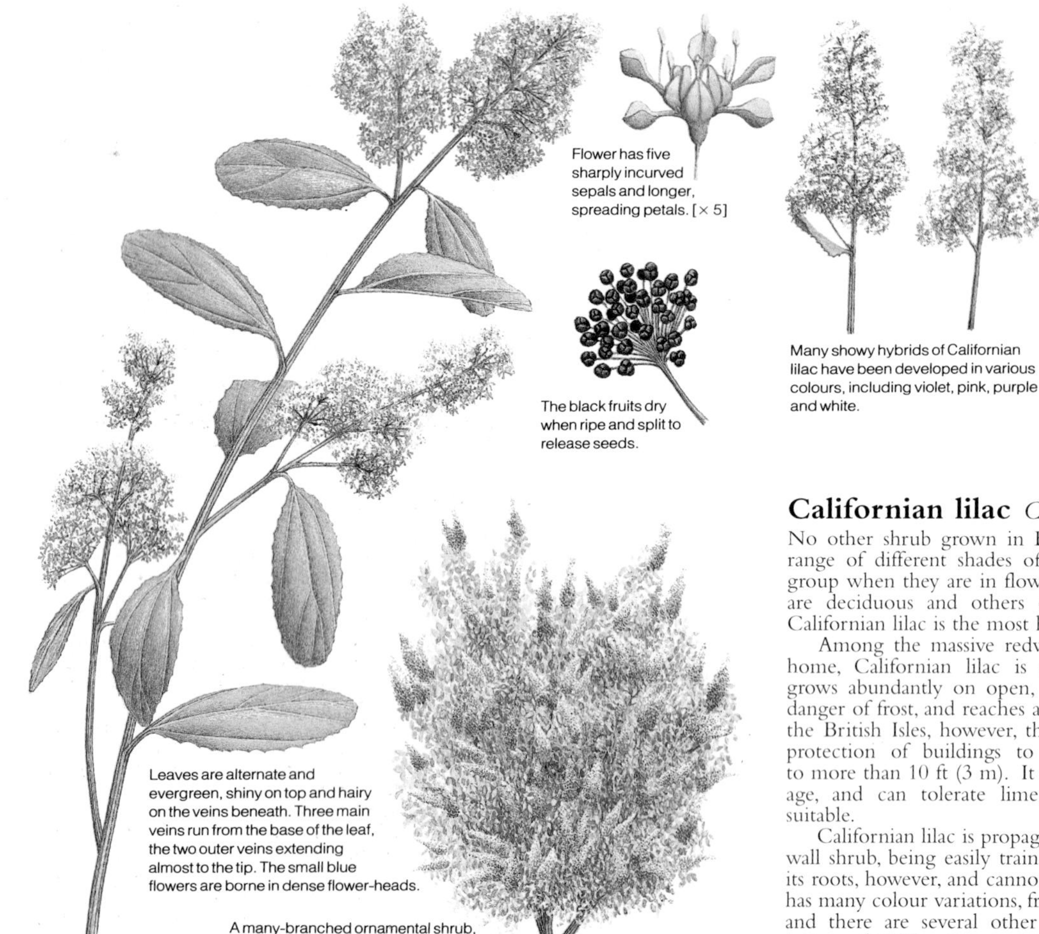

Flower has five sharply incurved sepals and longer, spreading petals. [× 5]

The black fruits dry when ripe and split to release seeds.

Many showy hybrids of Californian lilac have been developed in various colours, including violet, pink, purple and white.

Leaves are alternate and evergreen, shiny on top and hairy on the veins beneath. Three main veins run from the base of the leaf, the two outer veins extending almost to the tip. The small blue flowers are borne in dense flower-heads.

A many-branched ornamental shrub, growing to 7–10 ft (2–3 m).

In full bloom, covered with blue flowers, the Californian lilac is unmistakable. It needs a sunny, sheltered site.

Californian lilac *Ceanothus thyrsiflorus*

No other shrub grown in Britain can match the magnificent range of different shades of blue produced by the *Ceanothus* group when they are in flower in May and June. Some species are deciduous and others evergreen; of the evergreens, the Californian lilac is the most hardy.

Among the massive redwood trees of its North American home, Californian lilac is a big woodland shrub that also grows abundantly on open, sunny hillsides where there is no danger of frost, and reaches a height of 35 ft (11 m). Grown in the British Isles, however, the shrub needs warm sun and the protection of buildings to flower well, and seldom grows to more than 10 ft (3 m). It needs a light soil with good drainage, and can tolerate lime; seaside gardens are particularly suitable.

Californian lilac is propagated from cuttings and is a valuable wall shrub, being easily trained. It is sensitive to disturbance of its roots, however, and cannot be easily transplanted. The shrub has many colour variations, from purple and deep blue to white, and there are several other species, almost all of which are natives of California.

Thrushes feast on the firethorn's berries; blackbirds also find them good eating.

Leaves are alternate with small, regular teeth, dark green and glossy above; thorns bear leaves, and leaf-stalks are hairy. Berries are bright red.

Firethorn is a thorny, evergreen bush, growing in gardens to 5 ft (1·5 m).

Dense heads of white flowers appear in late May and June.

The 'Lalandei' cultivar is widely grown for its big, orange-red berries.

This hardy, flowering shrub is grown all over Britain for its bright and shiny berries that last all winter.

Firethorn *Pyracantha coccinea*

Despite its highly evocative common name, firethorn is a shrub that gardeners invariably call by its scientific name of *Pyracantha.* A native of southern Europe, where it occurs naturally in hedges and thickets, *Pyracantha coccinea* was introduced to Britain in the 17th century for the glow of bright red berries which it displays so conspicuously in the autumn. Nowadays the most popular form is the 'Lalandei' cultivar, with orange-red berries. Other species, mostly from China, have also been introduced, some with bright yellow or orange-yellow berries.

Firethorn is particularly suitable for the small garden. Grown as a free-standing bush, it requires no pruning and forms an effective screen; but more frequently it is trained along a wall, where it contrasts happily with red brick or white stone.

The shrub is reproduced by seeds or cuttings and will grow well in most kinds of soil, whether in sun or shade. It tolerates exposure to wind and the atmospheric pollution of cities. It does not, however, like to be moved once established, so it should be transplanted only when young; and although it will accept trimming, it will not bear so many berries for several seasons if it has been pruned to shape.

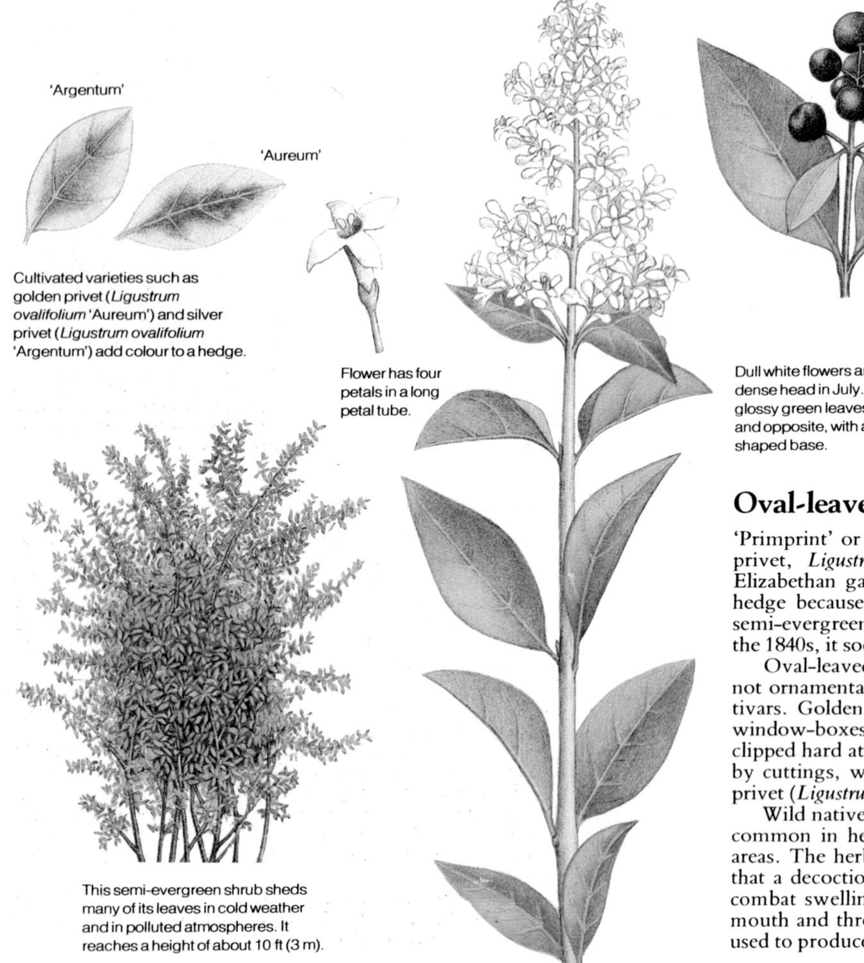

Cultivated varieties such as golden privet (*Ligustrum ovalifolium* 'Aureum') and silver privet (*Ligustrum ovalifolium* 'Argentum') add colour to a hedge.

Flower has four petals in a long petal tube.

Fruits are round, shiny black berries.

Dull white flowers are borne in a dense head in July. The smooth, glossy green leaves are toothless and opposite, with a wedge-shaped base.

This semi-evergreen shrub sheds many of its leaves in cold weather and in polluted atmospheres. It reaches a height of about 10 ft (3 m).

The oval-leaved privet is one of the commonest shrubs used for garden hedges, as it is easy to grow and maintain.

Oval-leaved privet *Ligustrum ovalifolium*

'Primprint' or 'prim' were Old English names for the native privet, *Ligustrum vulgare*, which was used for hedging in Elizabethan gardens. It was not particularly satisfactory as a hedge because it lost all its leaves in winter, and when the semi-evergreen oval-leaved privet was introduced from Japan in the 1840s, it soon took the place of the native variety.

Oval-leaved privet makes a dense and effective screen, but is not ornamental, except in its gold-leaved or silver-leaved cultivars. Golden privet, in particular, is a favourite choice for window-boxes in towns. It will tolerate poor soil, and can be clipped hard at any time of the year, and reproduces by seed or by cuttings, which will take root very easily. Chinese glossy privet (*Ligustrum lucidum*) forms a small, handsome tree.

Wild native privet, with its smaller, narrower leaves, is still common in hedgerows and woodlands, particularly in chalk areas. The herbalist John Gerard, writing in 1597, contended that a decoction of privet leaves could be used as a gargle to combat swellings, apostemations (abscesses) and ulcers of the mouth and throat. The blue-black berries of privet were once used to produce dyes.

The pinkish-red flower has glands on the calyx.

The fruit is shaped like a top, with the style protruding.

Many cultivated hybrids have been developed with larger, showier flowers and a variety of colours.

Leaves are alternate and in clusters, shiny above and dotted underneath with glands. The leaf edges have small and large teeth; the base is tapered, joining the twig without a stalk.

This evergreen shrub forms a rounded leafy bush, and is covered with numerous clusters of pinkish-red flowers in summer. 7–13 ft (2–4 m).

Escallonia is planted as a garden shrub. In western areas it forms hedges that are resistant to salt winds.

Escallonia *Escallonia macrantha*

Early Victorian plant collectors combed the world in search of new and rare species to brighten English gardens. Among them were two Cornish brothers, William and Thomas Lobb, who worked for a firm of nurserymen in Exeter. On a trip to South America in 1845 William Lobb visited Chiloe, an island off the coast of southern Chile, and collected specimens of the shrub later named escallonia. This was marketed in Britain with great success; the first hybrids were produced by John Seddan, a master among hybridisers who worked by trial and error at a time when the scientific study of genetics was unknown.

The island of Chiloe has a warmer climate than Britain's; consequently, though escallonia is today a popular garden shrub in Britain, it is only really hardy in south-west England and in Ireland, where the climate is softened by the warm waters of the Gulf Stream. In these areas the shrub grows well, forming thick attractive hedges and windbreaks that give protection to other plants.

Further north and east the shrub can only flourish if it has the protection of a wall. The Donard cultivars, with their varied forms and colours, are the most widely known.

One variety of shining honeysuckle, 'Baggesen's Gold', has yellow leaves. [× 2]

Leaves are opposite, blunt at the tip and round at the base; they are dark green on top and pale green beneath. The stem is purplish and hairy. Scented flowers form in pairs at the leaf bases in April. [× 2]

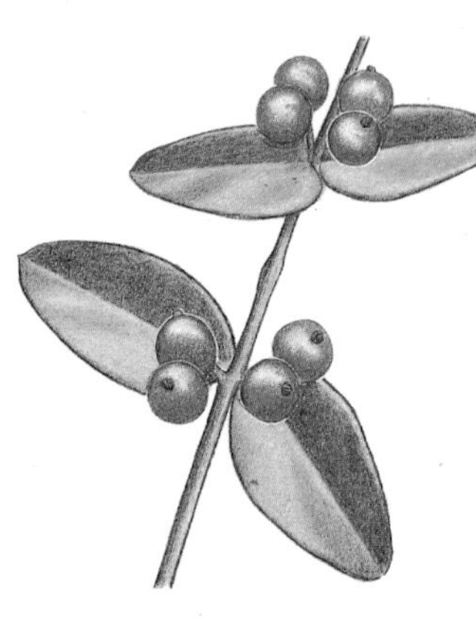

Fruits are small purple berries in pairs. [× 2]

A row of shining honeysuckle bushes is often planted in parks or gardens, and can be clipped to form a thick, low hedge.

This fast-growing shrub is quite dense and grows to about 6 ft (1·8 m) tall.

Shining honeysuckle *Lonicera nitida*

Though strikingly different in form, this sturdy shrub is in fact a close relative of the sweet-scented climbing honeysuckle. It is a native of western China, and was introduced to Britain in 1908 by the plant collector Ernest Wilson; the most popular modern cultivar of the shrub is called 'Ernest Wilson', but is commonly sold as Chinese honeysuckle. Evergreen and very leafy, the shrub bears unremarkable flowers, but is a vigorous grower.

In its native home, shining honeysuckle grows at altitudes of 4,500–7,000 ft (1,370–2,130 m). The shrub is hardy in Britain's climate. It has become popular for hedging because it withstands clipping well, and its rapid growth ensures that the hedge is established quickly. Indeed, constant trimming is needed to shape the shrub so that the top remains narrow, otherwise wind and snow tend to break it apart. When planted on its own, shining honeysuckle forms a dainty, spreading bush.

Propagation is simple, using cuttings taken in July or August. These need only to be planted in the desired position and they will root easily. There are, worldwide, about 200 species of *Lonicera*, embracing a wide variety of evergreen and deciduous flowering shrubs and woody climbers.

Leaves and clusters of yellow flowers grow on the short side-shoots, in the axils of the spines. The spines are grouped in threes. Leaves fall in winter.

In autumn the lozenge-shaped scarlet berries hang in bunches from the spiny twigs.

Hooker's barberry (*Berberis hookeri*) is an evergreen garden shrub with longer leaves; berries black.

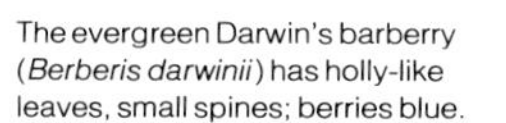

The evergreen Darwin's barberry (*Berberis darwinii*) has holly-like leaves, small spines; berries blue.

One of the most popular British garden shrubs, barberry is sometimes found in the wild in woods and hedges.

The purple-leaved cultivar 'Atropurpurea' is often grown in gardens for the sake of its colourful foliage.

Its thorny branches make the barberry a useful hedge. It grows to 10 ft (3 m) tall.

Barberry *Berberis vulgaris*

The sharp-thorned barberry has become rarer in the countryside in recent years, but it has won a new place as a decorative garden shrub. At one time barberry grew wild in hedgerows, and on commons and scrubland that was being re-invaded by woodland. The shrub was, however, discovered to be a host to rust, a fungus that attacks the leaves and stems of wheat and other cereals, and it has been uprooted from grain-growing areas.

In country districts the barberry was prized for a variety of household uses. Its showy red berries, edible but tart and avoided by birds, are rich in vitamin C and can be made into jelly, jam or sweets. Barberry jams and jellies were given to sufferers from liver and stomach disorders. The leaves, too, are edible and can be added to salads or as seasoning to meats. In the Middle Ages, the bark was a source of yellow dye. The small size of the stems and branches limits the use of the hard yellow wood to inlay work.

Some 170 species and varieties of barberry, including the common wild barberry and the related purple-leaved barberry, flourish in Britain's gardens, either as ornamental plants or as hedges. They are easy to grow in most soils and situations.

This small, rounded tree is often no more than a bush, but can reach 35 ft (11 m).

[× 2]

Seed capsules are blue-green, with three horns; they ripen and turn brown in September, releasing black seeds.

Slow-growing box has been widely used in topiary work – the art of clipping trees into ornamental shapes.

The evergreen leaves are opposite, and not toothed. They are shiny, dark green on top and paler beneath, with a notch at the tip.

Box *Buxus sempervirens*

Box is most familiar either as a dense evergreen hedge, or clipped into unusual shapes in ornamental gardens. Although a native tree, occurring naturally on chalky soils, it is seldom seen in the wild today except in a few areas such as Box Hill in Surrey. In the past the trees reached a considerable size, but most of the best have now been felled for their wood, leaving only the least vigorous specimens.

Box wood is yellow, hard and even-textured, and so heavy that it sinks in water when it is green. It is very stable and does not warp, and has long been used for high-class wood carving, for chessmen and mathematical instruments. It was particularly in demand in the 18th century for the blocks from which artists such as Thomas Bewick made their wood engravings.

Together with yew, box is much used in the layout of formal gardens. The dwarf form, known as 'edging box', was once popular for making borders around flower beds and graves. While its use for this purpose has gone out of fashion, the popularity of box for use in forming thick hedges is evident from the fact that more than 30 varieties are available from nurseries. They include 'Gold Tip', with yellow-tipped leaves.

Bark is light brown, turning grey with age.

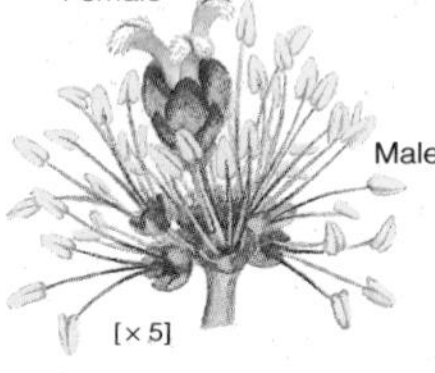

Greenish-yellow male and female flowers, growing together in the same cluster in the leaf-axils, flower in April and are pollinated by insects.

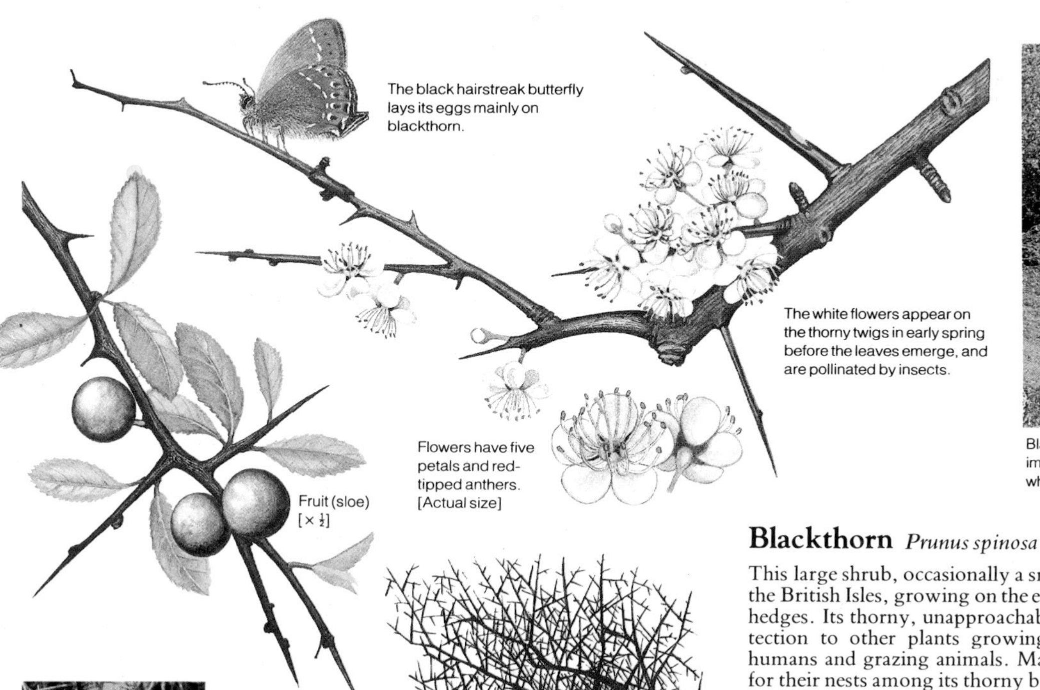

The black hairstreak butterfly lays its eggs mainly on blackthorn.

The white flowers appear on the thorny twigs in early spring before the leaves emerge, and are pollinated by insects.

Flowers have five petals and red-tipped anthers. [Actual size]

Fruit (sloe) [× ½]

Leaves are small and alternate, dull above and hairy beneath. Fruit is round and blue-black.

Blackthorn spreads by suckers to form impenetrable thickets, covered with white blossom in spring.

Bark when scraped shows orange beneath.

A thorny shrub, often producing dense hedges up to 13 ft (4 m) high in which birds can nest undisturbed.

Blackthorn *Prunus spinosa*

This large shrub, occasionally a small tree, is native throughout the British Isles, growing on the edge of scrub woodlands and in hedges. Its thorny, unapproachable thickets give valuable protection to other plants growing beneath it by warding off humans and grazing animals. Many birds also find protection for their nests among its thorny branches.

The blue-black fruits, known as sloes, are made into jam and wine and used to flavour gin. It is thought that blackthorn may be one of the parents of the damson and other domestic plums. The wood has a light yellow sapwood and brown heartwood. It is hard and tough, and takes a good polish. Since it is never available in large sizes, its main use is for the teeth of hay-rakes, for marquetry and for walking-sticks; it is also the traditional wood for the Irish shillelagh, or cudgel.

As the blossom of blackthorn often appears in March, during the period of cold east winds, a cold spring was traditionally known as 'a blackthorn winter'. Special varieties of blackthorn are cultivated for gardens, including 'Purpurea', with purple leaves, 'Rosea', with salmon-pink flowers, and a white double-flowered form called 'Plena'.

This narrow-crowned, conical tree has regular branching when young but becomes straggly with age. It can reach 65 ft (20 m).

Caterpillars of the holly blue butterfly feed on the leaves.

Leaves are alternate and evergreen, with sharp spines. They are glossy and waxy on top, matt and paler green beneath. Only female trees bear berries.

Male flower

Female flower

The small, scented male and female flowers appear in May on separate trees. [Actual sizes]

The holly is one of the most easily recognised of our native trees. Its bright red berries provide winter food for birds.

Holly *Ilex aquifolium*

Many a holly tree was spared the woodman's axe in days gone by because of a superstition that it was unlucky to cut down a holly tree. As a result, many hollies are today seen growing in the midst of hedgerows that have grown up around them. The superstition probably arose because of the tree's evergreen leaves and its long-lasting berries, leading people to associate the tree with eternity and the power to ward off evil and destruction. In addition, the holly has long been a symbol of Christmas.

Another tradition associated with the holly tree is that a good crop of berries is a warning of a hard winter on the way. This tradition probably arose out of the fondness shown by birds – especially thrushes – for the fruit as a source of food. In fact, a bumper crop of berries is not an augury of bad weather to come, but the result of a fine summer just past.

Holly is native to the British Isles, where it grows everywhere except on wet soils. Its presence in woodland often indicates past grazing, to which it is highly resistant. It forms a good hedge, and can be clipped and shaped. The wood of holly is white, sometimes with a greenish streak, and is dense, hard and heavy; like box it has been used for carving, inlay work and woodcuts.

Bark is green when young, smooth and grey later.

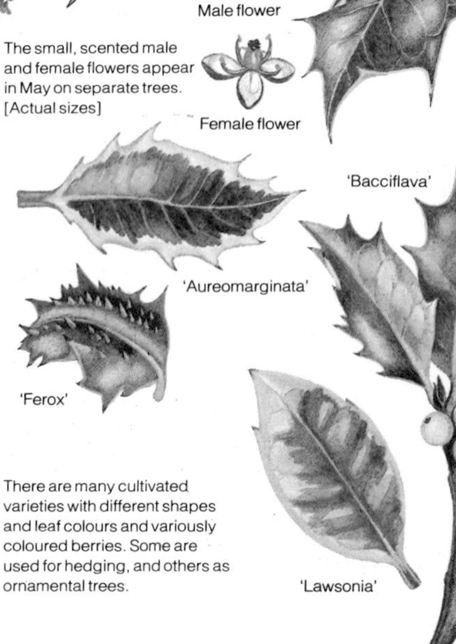

There are many cultivated varieties with different shapes and leaf colours and variously coloured berries. Some are used for hedging, and others as ornamental trees.

[× 2]

[× 2]

White, bell-like flowers appear in autumn, while the red strawberry-like fruits from the previous year's flowers are still ripening.

Rocky slopes in south-west Ireland are a natural setting for the strawberry tree; it is sometimes planted in parks.

Leaves are alternate and evergreen, with a toothed margin. The underside is paler than the upper side, the main vein white. The stalk is short and hairy. Fruits ripen in small clusters.

Hybrid strawberry tree

Arbutus × andrachnoides

The branches of this hybrid are red. The leaves are green on top and yellow-green beneath.

Bark is reddish-brown and peels into thin strips.

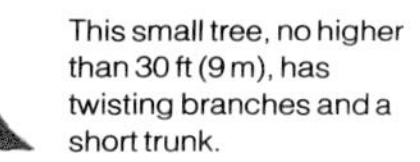

This small tree, no higher than 30 ft (9 m), has twisting branches and a short trunk.

Strawberry tree *Arbutus unedo*

The popular name of this tree is derived from its round, red fruits which ripen in autumn, but the fruits are not as palatable as the name suggests. In fact the species name of *unedo* comes from the two Latin words *un edo*, 'I eat one (only)'.

The distribution of the strawberry tree is oddly patchy. In the British Isles it grows wild only in western Ireland. It occurs again in western France and on the Mediterranean coast. Once it was believed that it might have survived the last glaciation in western Ireland, but it is more likely that it spread northwards rapidly after the glaciation and was then cut off by rising sea levels. Within historical times it certainly grew more widely than it does today, and its disappearance may be accounted for by the fact that it makes good charcoal and burns well. Its reddish-brown wood is hard and close-grained, though liable to splitting, and is used for inlay and marquetry.

With its cinnamon-red bark, the strawberry tree makes an attractive garden bush, but its seedlings need considerable protection until they are established. Though able to withstand the sea winds of the Irish coast, the tree quickly succumbs to cold northerly and easterly winds.

The caterpillar of the brimstone butterfly feeds on buckthorn.

Female flower [× 4]

Male flower [× 4]

Yellowish-green flowers appear on small shoots in May. Male and female flowers are on separate trees.

The purging buckthorn is a common shrub or small tree in hedgerows and woodland on chalk soils.

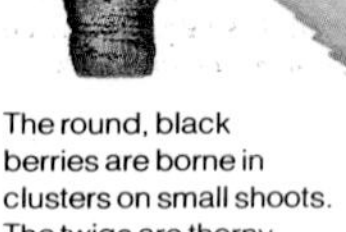

The round, black berries are borne in clusters on small shoots. The twigs are thorny.

This shrub or small hedgerow tree is many-branched and thorny. Thick foliage grows close to the ground. The bark is rough and scaly. Up to 16 ft (5 m).

Leaves are opposite, or nearly so, on the long shoots but grow bunched together on the short shoots. The edges are fine-toothed; veins point to the tip of the leaf.

Purging buckthorn *Rhamnus catharticus*

The common name of this shrub is derived in part from the use in former times of its bark and berries to concoct a violent purgative. This use for the shrub declined with the discovery of the milder cascara, made from a related North American shrub, *Rhamnus purshiana*.

Buckthorn shoots are of two kinds – long shoots, which extend growth, and short ones which bear bunches of leaves, flowers and fruit. The short shoots, resembling the antlers of a roebuck, may be the origin of the name buckthorn. Another name was crossthorn, as the short shoots occur opposite each other, forming a cross; this was thought to provide protection against witchcraft and evil.

It is only when the black, sharp-flavoured berries are borne on the female tree that the buckthorn becomes conspicuous, although it grows fairly widely on chalk and limestone soils in central and southern England. It can stand a certain amount of shade. The sapwood is yellow and the heartwood reddish-brown. Nowadays the wood has no uses, but in Iron Age Britain it was cut and used with other woods such as oak for making the charcoal then necessary for smelting.

The shiny leaves are alternate and untoothed, with 7–9 pairs of parallel veins. Greenish flowers appear in early summer at the junctions of leaves and twigs. Bark is smooth and black.

The branches ascend, the lowest from ground level, to form a bushy outline up to 15 ft (4·5 m) high.

The berries turn from green to red and purple. Turning yellow in autumn, the leaves hang downwards before falling.

Alder buckthorn grows in damp woods, in peaty soils and on the edges of raised bogs, where it often grows with alder.

Alder buckthorn *Frangula alnus*

From explosives to laxatives, from dyestuffs to butchery, this attractive, shrubby little tree has served man in a variety of roles. Charcoal from its wood was sought after as an ingredient of gunpowder and for making fuses, because of its even, slow-burning properties. It remained in use until after the Second World War. The berries and bark when fresh cause vomiting, but a drug extracted from the dried bark can be used safely as a purgative. Natural dyes in shades of yellow or brown come from the bark, while the fruit yields green or bluish-grey dyes. Butchers used to favour its hard, easily sharpened wood for skewers, and some trees are still cut for pea or bean sticks.

Alder buckthorn is not related to the alder, although they are often seen together and their leaves bear a superficial resemblance. Nor does it have thorns, although some other buckthorns have them. An alternative name is black dogwood, because the butcher's spikes and skewers made from it were once called 'dogs'. Its hanging yellow leaves and purple berries make it particularly attractive in autumn. While it is usually seen around marshes, alder buckthorn also occurs as a shrub layer in open, deciduous woodland such as the New Forest.

Caterpillars of the green hairstreak butterfly feed on the leaves.

The round, bitter, black berries grow in clusters, ripening in August or September.

Leaves are opposite, with short hairs on both sides and pointed, with veins curving towards the tip. Greenish-white flowers appear in June. Their unpleasant smell is attractive to insects.

This tall deciduous shrub sends out suckers freely to form dense thickets. It can grow to 13 ft (4 m).

The red shoots and leaves of dogwood make a blaze of colour in autumn. It grows chiefly on chalk soils.

Ridged bark gives off fetid smell when bruised.

The blood-red shoots and crimson colouring of the leaves in late autumn, give this species the Latin name *sanguinea*.

Dogwood *Cornus sanguinea*

From medieval times until early this century, butchers used 'dogs', or skewers, made from the hard, white wood of this native shrub to hold cuts of meat in shape. Dogwood was also used to make goads for beasts of burden, and to burn for making charcoal; a 17th-century account talks of the wood as a source of 'Mill-Cogs, Pestles, Bobins and Spokes for Wheels'.

The shrub is inconspicuous for most of the year but proclaims its presence in autumn with its red leaves and black fruit. It usually occurs in chalk and limestone soils, often invading abandoned pasture land. It spreads both by suckers from the parent plant and by seeds dropped by birds.

The bitter and inedible berries that grow on dogwood were once used as a source of lamp oil; their oily consistency led the Welsh country folk to call dogwood the 'wax tree'. It was also known as the 'dog-tree' or 'dogberry' because its fruit was not even fit for dogs. With the wide variety of uses to which its timber and berries were put, dogwood has played a prominent part in British country life. This was reflected by Shakespeare when he gave the name of Dogberry to the character of the comic constable in *Much Ado About Nothing*.

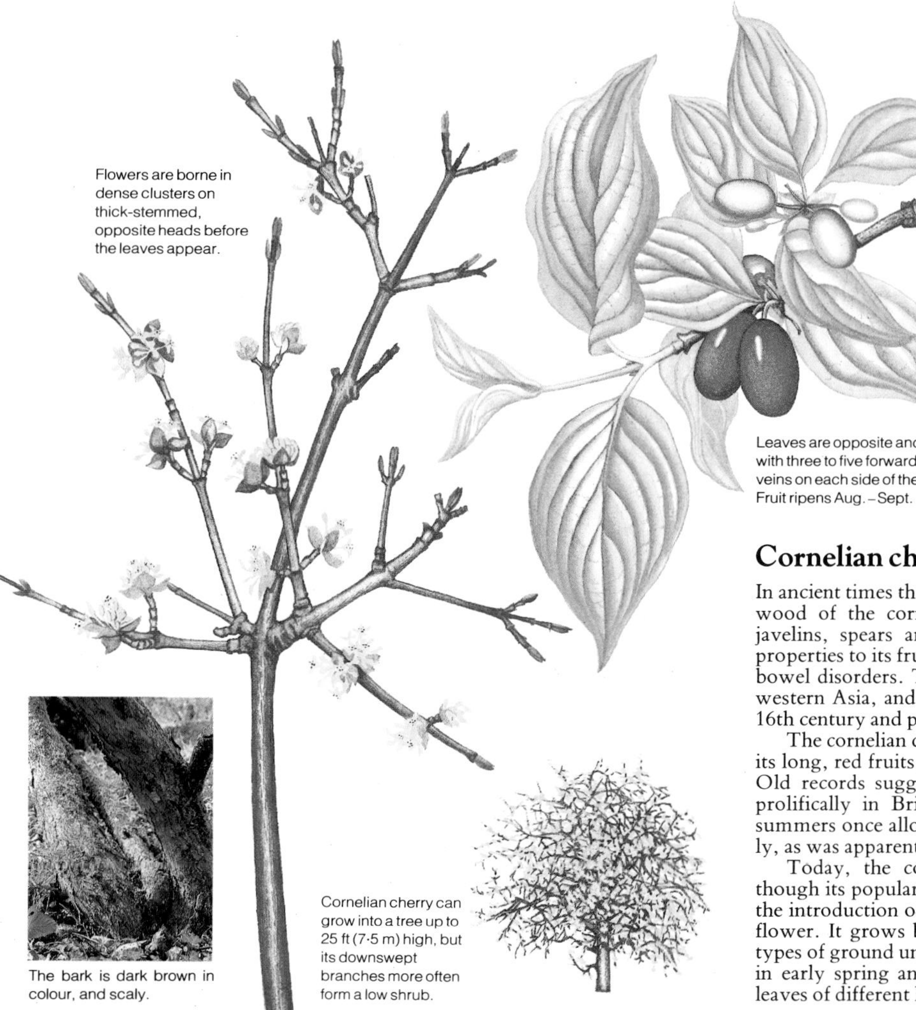

Flowers are borne in dense clusters on thick-stemmed, opposite heads before the leaves appear.

Leaves are opposite and pointed, with three to five forward-pointing veins on each side of the central rib. Fruit ripens Aug.–Sept.

The bark is dark brown in colour, and scaly.

Cornelian cherry can grow into a tree up to 25 ft (7·5 m) high, but its downswept branches more often form a low shrub.

Cornelian cherry is planted ornamentally for its bright yellow blossoms, which cover the tree in February and March.

Cornelian cherry *Cornus mas*

In ancient times the Persians, Greeks and Romans used the hard wood of the cornelian cherry, or cornel, for the shafts of javelins, spears and arrows. They also attributed medicinal properties to its fruit, which reputedly prevented dysentery and bowel disorders. The tree is a native of south-east Europe and western Asia, and has been planted in Britain at least since the 16th century and possibly much earlier.

The cornelian cherry was probably introduced to Britain for its long, red fruits, which were made into jellies and preserves. Old records suggest that the tree once produced fruit more prolifically in Britain than it does today. Possibly warmer summers once allowed the fruit to set and ripen more frequently, as was apparently also the case with grape vines.

Today, the cornelian cherry is planted for decoration, though its popularity waned at the end of the last century, after the introduction of the wych hazel, which it resembles when in flower. It grows best in chalky soil, but will flourish in most types of ground unless they are acid. Its yellow blossoms appear in early spring and there are several cultivated varieties with leaves of different hues.

Male catkins

Female catkin

Male and female catkins grow on separate trees. Male catkins are grey at first, turning yellow when ripe with pollen; females are greenish-white. [Actual sizes]

Leaves are alternate and short pointed, edged with small teeth, dark grey-green on top and woolly beneath.

Bark is smooth and grey; old trees fissure at base.

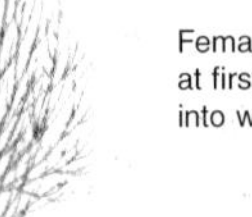

Tree in winter.

Female catkins are green at first, then break up into woolly fruits.

A small, many-stemmed shrubby tree, which grows to 50 ft (15 m) high.

Goat willow – the familiar 'pussy willow' – grows widely throughout Britain, and will quickly colonise unoccupied land.

Goat willow *Salix caprea*

Goat willow or great sallow comes into the public eye once a year when its golden, male catkins are used to decorate churches on Palm Sunday. The female catkins are less spectacular, but their smooth, silky surface has gained the tree its popular name of 'pussy willow'. Often the branches gathered for indoor decoration are not true goat willow, but come either from the closely related sallow or from one of the numerous natural crosses between goat willow and other species.

Goat willow flowers early and provides the bees with both pollen and nectar when few flowers are out. The tree is also pollinated by wind. It reproduces easily from seed and colonises waste ground, particularly in damp places, where it flourishes in woodland, scrub and hedges.

The bark contains tannin and, like that of other willows, the drug salicin which is used in medicines. The wood is very soft, the sapwood yellowish-white and the heartwood brown. Although little used now, the light wood was once made into clothes pegs, rake teeth and hatchet handles. A pendulous variety of goat willow found on the banks of the river Ayr in 1840 is cultivated in gardens as the Kilmarnock willow.

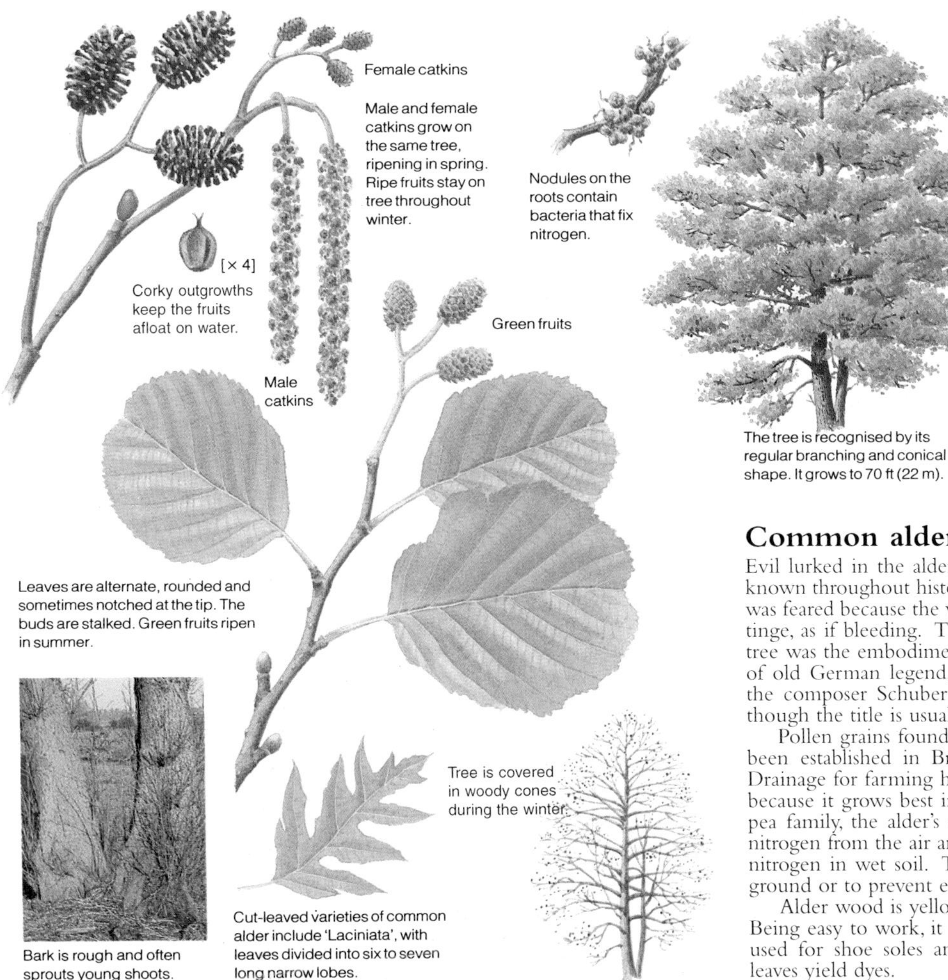

Bark is rough and often sprouts young shoots.

Cut-leaved varieties of common alder include 'Laciniata', with leaves divided into six to seven long narrow lobes.

The tree is recognised by its regular branching and conical shape. It grows to 70 ft (22 m).

The common alder thrives in wet ground and is often seen lining the banks of rivers and streams in all parts of Britain.

Common alder *Alnus glutinosa*

Evil lurked in the alder, according to ancient belief. The tree, known throughout history from Western Europe to the Far East, was feared because the wood, when cut, takes on a blood-orange tinge, as if bleeding. This gave rise to the superstition that the tree was the embodiment of a malign spirit, such as the *Erlkönig* of old German legend, made famous by the poet Goethe and the composer Schubert. *Erlkönig* meant originally 'alder king', though the title is usually translated as 'elf king'.

Pollen grains found in peat deposits show that the alder has been established in Britain for at least eight thousand years. Drainage for farming has made it less abundant in recent times, because it grows best in wet ground. Like the members of the pea family, the alder's roots contain bacteria which can utilise nitrogen from the air and 'fix' it, making up for the usual lack of nitrogen in wet soil. The alder can be planted to enrich poor ground or to prevent erosion of river banks.

Alder wood is yellow when seasoned, and durable in winter. Being easy to work, it was favoured for clog making, and is still used for shoe soles and broom handles. The bark, fruit and leaves yield dyes.

Male catkins

Male and female catkins, borne on the same tree, ripen in early spring. Males are long, females smaller and egg shaped.

Female catkins

Cones mature in autumn and hang on tree all winter.

Female catkins develop into green cones.

Grey alder is a broad, rather cone-shaped tree reaching about 80 ft (24 m) in height.

Grey alder is often planted as a shelter belt, as it grows rapidly on poor sites. Long catkins cover the tree in spring.

Smooth grey-green bark has distinct pores.

Tree in winter.

Leaves are alternate and pointed, and edged with small teeth on bigger teeth. They are light, dull green on top, grey and hairy beneath.

Grey alder *Alnus incana*

An ugly slag heap can be transformed into a hilly copse within a few years by the planting of grey alder. One of the few trees that will flourish on so loose and infertile a site, it suckers freely and binds the heap together. It has another outstanding virtue: its ability to fix nitrogen from the air increases the fertility of poor soil. Because of this, it has been planted in British woodlands as a 'nurse', helping more demanding trees to grow.

The grey alder is not a native of Britain, but was introduced in 1780 from the Continent, where it grows widely in mountainous areas from Scandinavia to the Alps, and as far east as the Caucasus. It grows naturally by streams, and its numerous suckers bind the gravel beds and protect them from being washed away by flood water.

In Britain too, the grey alder flourishes in cold and wet places, where it is often planted as an ornamental tree. It is also planted on motorway verges, and in the wake of bulldozers on earth-shifting projects. Easily propagated by seeds or cuttings, it unfortunately produces poor quality wood of little commercial value. Several distinct varieties of the tree have been developed, including 'Aurea', which has reddish catkins.

Leaves are alternate, with point and heart-shaped base. They are glossy green on top; the underside has tufts of orange hairs at vein junctions. Stalks are long and thin, cones the largest of any alder.

Hanging male catkins and tiny, red females develop on the same twig in spring.

Ripe cone after seed is shed.

Italian alders are often planted to line motorways. More densely leaved than most alders, they quickly form a screen.

Italian alder *Alnus cordata*

The piles on which the buildings of Venice stand are of alder wood; since the Italian alder attains a more useful size than other European alders, and grows well in southern Italy, it could well be this species on which the city dubbed 'Queen of the Adriatic' was literally founded. Alder wood is durable – particularly under water, where it is almost indestructible owing to the preservative chemicals, such as tannin, that it contains.

To the untrained eye, the Italian alder is a deceptive tree. The fruits are contained in cone-like structures, but not the true cones of conifers. On the other hand, its shape and its dense, shiny, bright green leaves make it resemble a pear tree rather than an alder. This lovely and shapely tree is, however, distinguished from other species of alder by its leaves, which are pointed and oval.

The Italian alder usually occurs in dense thickets on damp soils, but grows well in dry soil, too, and is very vigorous, growing rapidly to form a tall, compact tree. These features make the Italian alder suitable for lining roads and streets. It does not take up too much space, yet is attractive to look at, and will tolerate a dust-laden atmosphere.

Bark is smooth and grey, later developing cracks.

This dense, conical alder, shaped like a pear tree, grows up to 80 ft (24 m).

Hazel nuts are a favourite food of squirrels and mice. Pigeons, jays and pheasants also eat them.

Leaves are alternate, with sawtooth edges, a drawn-out tip and hairy surfaces. They grow to 4 in. (10 cm) long and broad, with a variable outline. Nuts grow in clusters of up to four, each partly enclosed in leafy, overlapping bracts.

Light brown, scaly bark has yellow breathing pores.

Many stems rise from the 'stool' of a coppiced hazel, which if uncut can reach 30 ft (9 m) across.

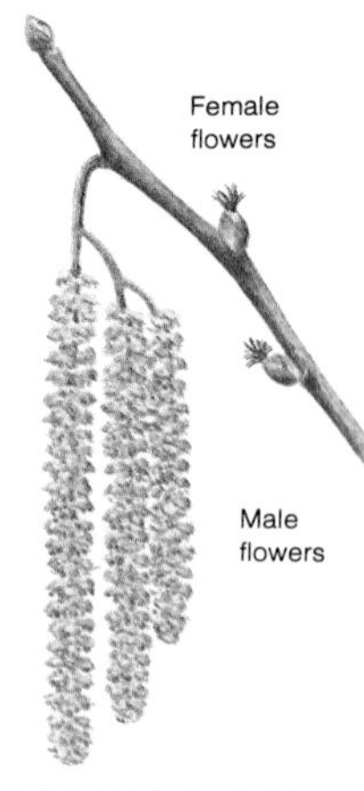

Male flowers hang in 'lambstail' catkins; female flowers appear as tiny buds with protruding red tassels.

Common hazel grows throughout Britain, and is striking in February, when it is covered with catkins.

Common hazel *Corylus avellana*

Since prehistoric times, pliant hazel rods have been woven into a variety of useful products. The primitive coracle, used by Welsh fishermen for 3,000 years, has a basket-like frame of hazel covered by a skin of stretched animal hides or, today, of canvas. Panels of interwoven hazel rods were used in the building technique known as 'wattle and daub': the hazel panels, or wattles, were placed between the wooden posts forming the frame of the house and then daubed with a mixture of mud and straw. Similar woven panels, undaubed, are still used as hurdles to pen sheep, and hazel rods are used in basketwork.

To ensure a steady supply of hazel rods, hazel bushes were 'coppiced' – that is, cut back to ground level at regular intervals, usually of seven years. Where the rods were required for house-building, the hazels were sometimes grown together with tall, scattered oaks that would provide the timber for the main frames.

Both hazel rods and the living bushes are used for hedging in country districts. The rods are woven between thorns, which have their main stems partly broken and 'laid' or bent over, giving added strength to the hedge. Alternatively, hazel bushes may be planted and used to form a dense living barrier.

The bracts holding the nuts have long, pointed lobes.

Female flowers

The flowers ripen in early spring. Female flowers are small and red; male flowers are long yellow catkins.

Male flowers

Unlike other hazels which are naturally bushy in shape, Turkish hazel grows into a true tree when it is not cut back.

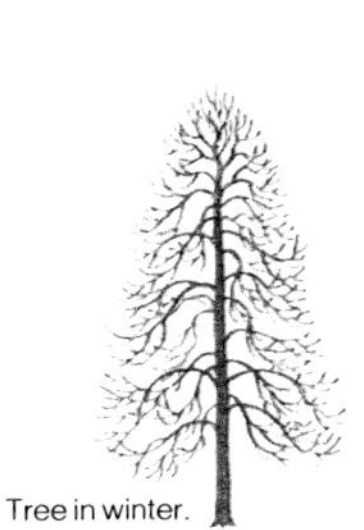

Tree in winter.

The dark green, alternate leaves are very regular in shape and grow to 4½ in. (12 cm) long, with large and small teeth. The leaf-stalk is stout and hairy and reddish in colour.

Bark has coarser fissures than common hazel.

The tree has a regular pyramidal shape, with fairly level branches. It seldom grows to more than 20 ft (6 m) in Britain.

Turkish hazel *Corylus colurna*

When Turkish hazel was introduced to Britain in the 17th century it was probably for its nuts. For an alternative name for the tree is Constantinople nut. Although it produces prolific crops in its native lands of south-east Europe and western Asia, where the summers are hot and the winters are cold, it does not fruit well in Britain. As a result, the tree has not been widely planted. Most of the home-grown hazel nuts eaten in Britain are from the cob, an improved form of common hazel (*Corylus avellana*), the filbert (*Corylus maxima*), and various hybrids raised in orchards in Kent and elsewhere in the south-east.

Where the Turkish hazel does occur in parks and gardens, it is planted chiefly for its ornamental value. It tends to produce suckers around the base, but when those and the lower branches are removed it can become a stately tree, taller than the other hazels and with an attractive pyramid shape. In south-east Europe, the tree can reach a height of 80 ft (24 m), though it is generally much smaller in Britain.

In its native lands, the Turkish hazel is greatly valued for its timber, used in furniture making. It does not warp and has an attractive grain, resembling that of the bird's eye maple.

The yellow flowers, with red stamens, are sweetly scented and appear soon after Christmas.

'Ruby Glow'

'Brevipetala'

Numerous varieties have been developed for gardens. 'Ruby Glow' is a hybrid of *Hamamelis mollis* and *Hamamelis japonica*.

Leaves are alternate, with small teeth, an unequal base and a long-pointed tip. The undersides are downy.

Wych hazel in its various forms is widely planted in shrubberies and gardens for its display of flowers in mid-winter.

Wych hazel is a relatively small shrub, seldom more than 8–10 ft (2·5–3 m) tall. It has upward-pointing branches and flowers Dec.–Mar.

Wych hazel *Hamamelis mollis*

This shrub, introduced from China in 1879, brings much-needed colour to a winter garden. Its twigs bear clusters of bright yellow, sweet-scented flowers. For this reason it has become a very popular garden shrub, and many cultivars and hybrids have been developed by crossings with other species.

Wych hazel was given its name by early settlers in North America. They thought that the leaves of the American species looked very like those of the common hazel of Britain, and therefore judged that their twigs would be equally suitable for water-divining, which had been practised for a long time in Europe using forks of common hazel. The word *wych* is Old English for 'pliant'; this quality had long been exploited by water-diviners, or 'dowsers', who grip one fork of a hazel twig in each hand and pull them apart until they are under great pressure. As the twig is passed over underground water it will sometimes twist violently in the hands of the 'dowser'. There is as yet no scientific explanation for this phenomenon.

The bark, leaves and twigs of wych hazel, when distilled with alcohol, yield an extract which is used in medicine to prevent inflammation and control bleeding.

Female flowers

Male flowers form in drooping catkins up to 2 in. (5 cm) long. The female flowers, with crimson styles in green bracts, are grouped in shorter catkins.

The pointed leaves are alternate, with reddish stalks and double-toothed edges. There are 10–15 pairs of parallel veins. Triangular, ribbed nutlets grow in clusters of about eight pairs, each in a leafy, three-lobed bract.

Male flowers

Pollarded hornbeams in Epping Forest were a source of fuel and beansticks for London until the early 20th century.

The compact cultivated variety 'Fastigiata' is widely planted in parks.

Boles are deeply fluted but silver-grey bark is smooth.

Steeply rising branches form a rounded crown, up to 80 ft (24 m) high.

Hornbeam *Carpinus betulus*

The hedges forming the maze at Hampton Court are said to have been originally of hornbeam, though they were replaced later by yew and holly. Hornbeam is suitable for hedges, as it is easily clipped, becomes very dense and retains some of its dead leaves in winter. It occurs in oak and beech woods, surviving among beeches because it will tolerate deep shade. Only in the south-east is hornbeam a native tree; elsewhere it has been planted.

Hornbeam seldom grows to its full stature of 80 ft (24 m) or more, and until the end of the 19th century hornbeams were frequently coppiced or pollarded. Trees that were coppiced were cut almost to the ground to make fresh shoots grow from side-buds just above ground level; the shoots were used to provide faggots, charcoal and beansticks. Pollarded trees were cut at head height, above the reach of grazing animals which would otherwise have eaten the young shoots.

The name of hornbeam refers to the tree's tough wood, 'horn' meaning hard and 'beam' a tree in Old English. As it resists heavy blows, the wood is used for making butchers' chopping blocks, mallets, balls and skittles. Before the days of cheap steel it was fashioned into spokes and cogwheels.

Ornamental forms of common beech include the narrow, upright-branched 'Dawyck' beech, and the copper beech, or 'Purpurea', with its reddish-purple leaves.

Autumn leaves turn yellow at first, then orange or red-brown.

Female flower

Male flowers

Leaves are alternate, shiny green on both surfaces, with a wavy margin and six to seven pairs of parallel veins.

In a four-valved husk are two triangular nutlets.

Young leaves appear with yellow, long-stalked male flowers and greenish-white female flowers.

The mature beech creates a thick canopy overhead, casting dense shade which prevents the growth of plants beneath it.

Older trees have a massive, many-branched dome; young trees are slimmer and more conical in outline. They grow to about 120 ft (36 m).

Smooth grey bark may break into small squares.

Common beech *Fagus sylvatica*

In the village of Meikleour, near Perth, can be seen a magnificent beech hedge more than two centuries old; it is almost 110 ft (33 m) high, and 600 yds (550 m) long. The story goes that while it was being planted in 1745, the men downed tools on hearing that Bonnie Prince Charlie had landed, and did not return for a year. Afterwards it was left to grow, and it has flourished to become a famous landmark. Less ambitious but still impressive beech hedges are quite common: the tree can be clipped closely and remains dense because it tolerates shade. It thrives in a wide variety of soils, and many ornamental varieties are grown.

Beech wood bends beautifully and can be turned easily, making it an ideal material for furniture, particularly chairs. It is fine-grained and knot-free, the branches falling off early to leave a clean bole. Furthermore its light red-brown colour with darker flecks polishes to a superb natural finish.

Beech chairs have been made in the Chilterns for centuries, and until recently the woodlands there were managed to supply this still-thriving industry. The chairmakers – or 'bodgers' – once worked within the woods, setting up primitive lathes to turn the legs. Nowadays local factories use imported beechwood.

LIFE IN A BEECH WOOD

In spring, bluebells and anemones splash beech woods with colour, but in full summer the woods are dark and relatively colourless places, for the opened beech leaves let little sunlight through to encourage growth below. The leaves are so arranged that all get some light, but very little filters between them.

In the same way, the leaves intercept most of the rain that falls. This lies on the leaves, to be evaporated again after a shower, and does not reach the soil beneath. But the woodland floor, though dry, does provide food for fungi; and for small birds and mammals.

Jays are among the birds that frequent beech woods to seek fallen beech nuts.

Jay

Beech roots thrive in shallow but fertile soil, spreading laterally just below the surface.

Grey squirrel

Death cap [poisonous]

Bluebell

Bluebells and wood anemones come up before the beech leaves have fully opened, while enough light is still available for growth. They will continue to grow in heavy shade, while bird's-nest orchid, which feeds on dead organic matter such as beech leaves, needs no light at all. Fungi feed in the same way.

Wood anemone

Wood mice and grey squirrels prize the beech nuts on the woodland floor. Squirrels damage beech trees by gnawing at the sapwood below the bark.

Bird's-nest orchid

Cep [edible]

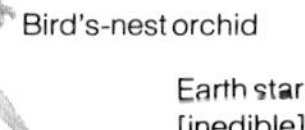

Earth star [inedible]

Wood mouse

Beech nuts

Female flower

Male flowers

Leaves are alternate, dark green on top and paler beneath, with 7–11 pairs of parallel veins; they have an unequal base. Male flowers are single and consist of many stamens; female flowers are small and nut-shaped, at base of leaf.

Fruit opens into four valves, releasing its nutlets in September. At about the same time the leaves turn yellow or red.

This attractive, South American relative of the common beech has become popular in large gardens in the south of Britain.

The smooth grey bark becomes rough and flaky.

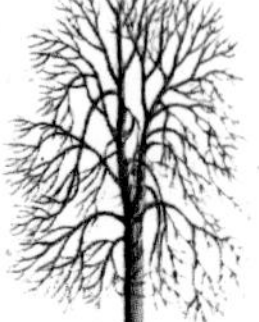

The tall roble beech has an open crown and arching branches. It grows to 75 ft (23 m).

Roble beech *Nothofagus obliqua*

When Spanish explorers reached the areas of South America where this tree grows, its shape reminded them of the oaks they had left behind in Spain, so they called it *roble*, which means oak in Spanish. In fact roble beech is one of several species of *Nothofagus*, or 'false beech', which occur in the Southern Hemisphere. They are also known as southern beeches; some are evergreen and others, like the roble, are deciduous.

Like the other southern beeches, roble once formed extensive forests in South America and especially in Chile, from which country the tree was introduced into Britain in 1903. It is a vigorous, fast-growing tree, frequently growing at the rate of 5–6 ft (1·5–1·8 m) a year. It does not like lime-rich soils, and requires space in which to grow.

The timber of the roble beech, dull reddish-brown in colour, is like that of common beech and is used for similar purposes. It appears to be one of the few hardwoods whose bark is not stripped by the grey squirrel, a menace which makes the growing of hardwood for timber almost impossible in some parts of southern Britain. If this immunity continues, the tree will have increasing value as a source of timber.

Male flowers

Female flower

Leaves are alternate and prominently ridged between the veins, of which there are 15–18 pairs. The leaf margin is finely toothed, and the stalk is green. Female flowers are small, green and nut-shaped, at base of leaf; male flowers consist of many stamens.

The fruit, dark green then turning brown, resembles a small beech nut. The leaves turn red, gold or pink.

This fast-growing beech from Chile is planted as an ornamental tree in parks, especially in western Britain.

Smooth, grey bark cracks vertically with age.

The tree is conical in profile, with dense foliage. In young trees the branches reach steeply upwards. The raoul grows to 45 ft (14 m).

Raoul *Nothofagus procera*

Under the name *rauli*, the timber of the raoul – like the roble, a form of southern beech – is commercially the most important hardwood in Chile, and natural forests containing the tree have been plundered throughout South America. Generally, the forests have not been replanted; the cleared ground has been used for food crops which give a quicker cash return.

The timber is cherry-coloured, like a redder version of the wood of the common beech, and is fairly dense. It is easy to season, and gives a smooth finish when worked in any direction. It is used to make furniture, floors, doors and stairs.

Both the raoul and the roble beech are being studied by forestry experts in Britain with a view to planting in this country. The raoul grows well here although, since it likes a moist soil, it is best suited to rainier western districts. Once established, it grows quickly, but the buds open early and are susceptible to frost damage in cold springs. Some small stands of raoul are already established as timber trees in British forests, but the species has so far been planted mainly as an ornamental tree in gardens and parks. Its foliage turns from green to rich shades of gold, crimson and pink in autumn.

Crimson flowers tinge the boughs in spring before the leaves appear.

Winged fruits turn brown when ripe, and fall in July.

Leaves are alternate, about 3 in. (7·5 cm) long, and rough on upper surface. Edge is double-toothed and tip rounded. Base is unequal and does not overlap the stem. Stalk and midrib are hairy.

The single seed is set nearer to the notched tip of fruit than that of the wych elm. [Actual size]

The English elm was typical of the lowland English landscape, before Dutch elm disease reduced its numbers.

Dutch elm disease is borne by the scolytid beetle, which burrows under the bark and spreads a fungus that blocks the tree's sap.

The bark is dark and divided by long fissures.

This tall, narrow-crowned tree, with billowing foliage, grows to 120 ft (36 m).

English elm *Ulmus procera*

Long regarded as one of the traditional sights of hedgerows in the Midlands and southern England, the English elm is a prime example of the way in which humans have influenced the landscape. For elms, though native trees, were comparatively rare until the 17th and 18th centuries, when great landowners planted them at intervals along the hedges used to enclose farm land, and landscape gardeners introduced them as ornamental trees to beautify their parklands.

Ironically, in establishing the elm as one of our most familiar trees, we were also responsible for its susceptibility to disease. To meet the demand for a stately looking tree that retained its leaves until well into the autumn, nurseries propagated a few such strains by taking the suckers that sparang up around the roots of selected trees. All Britain's elms are therefore genetically similar, and any disease to which they have little resistance can spread unchecked.

Dutch elm disease, so called because it was first identified in Holland, entered the country in 1964, and has destroyed one in five of the timber trees of our hedgerows, about 25 million English elms being the principal victims.

Leaves turn a distinctive yellow in autumn.

Purplish flowers appear before leaves.

Leaves are alternate, about 6 in. (15 cm) long, hairy on top and below. Edge is double-toothed and tip long and pointed. Base is unequal and sometimes covers short, stout stalk. Winged fruits fall in July.

Seed is larger than that of English elm, and set in centre of fruit. [Actual size]

Wych elm occurs mainly in the north and west of Britain, often in hilly country. It is often found beside water.

Wych elm *Ulmus glabra*

Hardiest of the many species of elm, the wych elm grows further north than other elms and can flourish even on hillsides and near the sea, and in polluted atmospheres. It is unlike most elms also in reproducing itself by seed, and not by suckers from the roots of the parent tree; this means of propagation has given wych elm a greater resistance to Dutch elm disease. The name 'wych' comes from an Anglo-Saxon word meaning pliable, and refers to the tree's twigs. It used to be thought good luck for a horseman to carry a riding-switch cut from an elm tree.

The heartwood of wych elm is an attractive reddish-brown, with an occasional green streak, and the sapwood broad and yellow. Elm wood is extremely tough, and has many uses. Because it is durable, even in perpetually wet conditions, elm was much used in the past for underground water pipes, which were made by hollowing out entire tree trunks with an auger.

Today, elm is used for the keels of boats, for groynes and for harbour works. Being almost impossible to split, elm is also the ideal wood for the seats of chairs and the hubs of wooden wheels, into which legs and spokes have to be firmly driven. Elm also provides the traditional wood used for coffins.

The bark is grey, with a few long fissures.

Wych elm is broader than English elm but grows to only 100 ft (30 m) high.

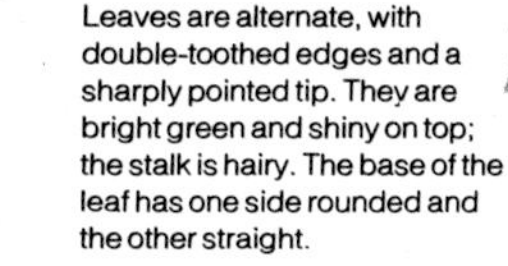

Leaves are alternate, with double-toothed edges and a sharply pointed tip. They are bright green and shiny on top; the stalk is hairy. The base of the leaf has one side rounded and the other straight.

Flowers mature into winged fruits.

Seed is near notch in tip of wing, as in English elm. [Actual size]

The flat fields of the east Midlands and East Anglia are the setting for most of England's smooth-leaved elms.

Wheatley elm

Ulmus minor var. *sarniensis*

The leaves of this variety are darker and rounder. Its compact crown and vertical branches make it especially suitable for avenues and street planting.

Smooth-leaved elm *Ulmus minor*

Preferring warmer climates than other elms, the smooth-leaved elm occurs in Britain only in southern and eastern counties. On the Continent, however, it used to be as familiar a sight as the English elm was in England, before the ravages of Dutch elm disease greatly reduced the numbers of both species. Like the English elm, the smooth-leaved elm produces suckers from around the base of the trunk. Unlike the English elm, however, the smooth-leaved elm does not rely entirely on these suckers as a means of propagation, for it also produces fertile seeds.

In East Anglia the smooth-leaved elm is pollarded, or cut off at about head-height, to produce a crop of shoots which are used as peasticks. More commonly seen than the smooth-leaved elm itself are two tall, narrow varieties of it that are often planted as ornamental trees. These are the Cornish elm and the Wheatley, or Jersey, elm. Developed in coastal regions, both varieties are tolerant of salty winds, and so are useful for forming windbreaks near the sea.

A rarer form is the lock elm, which occurs in the Midlands and East Anglia; the name refers to its timber, which is so hard to saw or plane that the tools become 'locked' into the wood.

The bark has deep cracks and appears corky.

This narrow tree has branches ascending from the trunk, then turning down at the ends. It grows to a height of about 90 ft (27 m).

The leaves of Huntingdon elm (*Ulmus* x *vegeta*) are about 4 in. (10 cm) long, with a double-toothed edge and lop-sided base. They are smooth and shiny on top with hairy tufts in the axils beneath.

Huntingdon elm is one of the most popular of several hybrids in the Dutch elm group. It is often planted in parks.

Commelin elm

Ulmus × *hollandica* 'Commelin'

The leaves of this variety are smaller than those of Huntingdon elm.

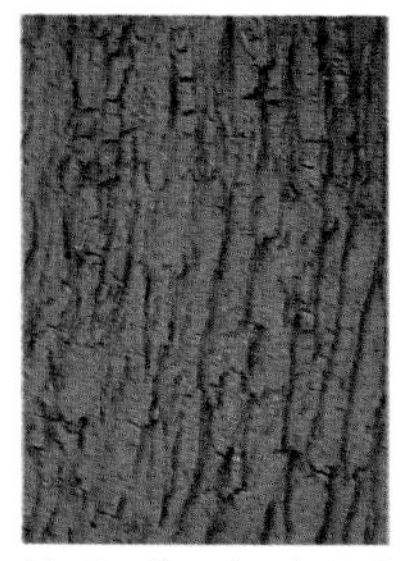

Huntingdon elm bark is brown and ridged.

All Dutch elms have ascending branches and fairly narrow crowns, growing to 100 ft (30 m).

Dutch elm *Ulmus* x *hollandica*

Dutch elms are natural hybrids between the smooth-leaved elm and the wych elm, both of which occur together on the European continent. Most of these hybrids are vigorous and have characters intermediate between those of the parents.

The varieties of Dutch elm most commonly planted as street trees are Huntingdon elm, called after the nursery in Huntingdon where they were first raised in this country, and a Commelin elm, bred in Holland in an attempt to produce a strain resistant to Dutch elm disease. Unfortunately this was not wholly successful, and no elm with complete immunity has yet been grown.

All elms have a reputation for shedding their branches without warning, and boughs occasionally crash to the ground, particularly when there has been a long season of drought. This characteristic gave rise long ago to the saying: 'Ellum hateth man and waiteth'. Campers are often warned not to pitch their tents under elms.

The wood of Dutch elm is like that of wych elm, and has similar uses. It is particularly suitable for interior work, as it warps less than other elm wood.

Female flower
[Actual size]

Male flower
[Actual size]

Female flowers

Male flowers

Male and female flowers grow on the same twig and appear with the emerging leaves in spring.

This elm graces parklands with its symmetrical profile and has escaped the worst ravages of Dutch elm disease.

Leaves are alternate, with saw-like margins. The leaf tip is not long-pointed as in other elms, and the base of the leaf is even, not lop-sided. The leaves are hairy beneath; the largest are at the tips of the twigs.

Tree in winter.

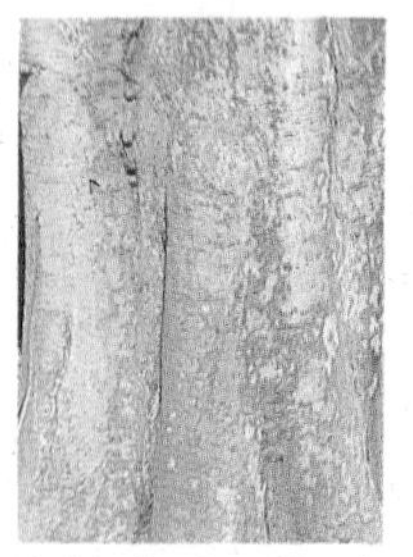

Bark is like that of beech, and flakes in patches.

The short bole, oval shape and uprising branches with dense foliage are characteristic of this elm, which rises to 85 ft (26 m).

Caucasian elm *Zelkova carpinifolia*

Although it is a relative of the European elms, the Caucasian elm cannot be mistaken for any other tree. Its short trunk breaks into numerous upright branches, to give a unique fan-shaped crown. It is a handsome tree, despite its habit of producing unsightly suckers from its base, and it is particularly attractive in the autumn when its leaves turn golden-yellow. The tree was introduced from the Caucasus for its attractive shape in 1760; its generic name, *Zelkova*, is the name of a town in that area.

Caucasian elm grows very slowly when young, and is long-lived. Some British trees are more than 200 years old, and many alive today have not yet reached their full size. In its native home, Caucasian elm grows together with oak on moist, loamy soils, and it thrives best in similar situations in Britain. Although the timber is tough and durable, the trunk of the tree is so short that wood cannot be obtained from it in useful lengths.

The elm bark beetle that has destroyed so many of Britain's elms by spreading Dutch elm disease, has been defeated by the smooth, resistant bark of younger Caucasian elms. Older specimens, however, are more vulnerable, for the beetle finds crevices through which it can burrow.

In autumn, the leaves turn rich shades of yellow and orange.

Male flowers

Female flowers

Male and female flowers grow on the same twig and emerge before leaves.

Alternate leaves have a long, sharp tip and large saw-like teeth with small points. There are no hairs on the underside. Foliage has a drooping, scattered appearance.

This tree from Japan grows well in Britain and, though an elm, has not been seriously affected by Dutch elm disease.

Keaki *Zelkova serrata*

A temple garden in Japan was the setting of this highly ornamental tree when it was found in the 19th century by a German collector, Karl von Siebold. It was introduced to Britain in 1861, but is still not commonly planted. It is a graceful and at times spectacular tree, as can be seen from the infrequent specimens in country house gardens and city parks, notably in London.

The keaki is not hard to grow from seeds or cuttings, and once the young tree is established, it is quite hardy, tolerating a certain amount of shade and preferring a moist soil. In such situations it develops a neat, rounded shape with attractive foliage which displays striking colours in the autumn. Like the related Caucasian elm, it has fairly smooth bark when young.

Its timber resembles that of other members of the elm family, with reddish-brown heartwood and yellow-brown sapwood. It is very tough and durable, lasting for a long time without special treatment. Although it branches low down and lacks a tall trunk, keaki has been used in Japan in the building of temples – especially for the roofs and pillars. Burrs – big growths on the trunk – are common on keakis, and finely grained veneers are cut from them for decorating furniture.

Older bark becomes flaky, exposing orange patches.

The spreading branches and straight, slender shoots form a neat, regularly shaped crown up to 65 ft (20 m) tall.

Cultivated apple has pinker flower.

Leaves are alternate, with pointed tips. Undersides are smooth, not hairy as on cultivated apple.

In autumn, the fruit becomes flushed with red.

The crab apple is still seen in copses, thickets and hedgerows. It grows from pips dropped by people or by birds.

Bramley's Seedling

Cox's Orange Pippin

Numerous cultivated apples have been developed from the crab apple.

Crab apple *Malus sylvestris*

Small, bitter, hard and generally insignificant though its fruit may be, the humble wild crab apple is the ancestor of all the cultivated apples of today – Beauty of Bath, Laxton's Fortune and many other familiar varieties. Centuries of selection and improvement by growers have created a major food and drink industry from the cultivated apple; but the wild crab apple still has a part to play, for it continues to furnish the root stock on to which grafts are made to produce new varieties.

A wide range of ornamental flowering crab apples has been bred for street planting. In spite of its bitterness the fruit is made into jelly, jam and wine, while birds seek it out eagerly. In former times fermented crab-apple juice – called verjuice – was regarded as a remedy for scalds and sprains. The wood of crab apple, like that of cultivated apple, is excellent both for carving and for burning.

The crab apple recolonised Britain after the Ice Age and is therefore regarded as a native British tree. It is found scattered throughout the countryside, often in oak woods. The wild crab apple has thorns, which may have been intentionally bred out by growers of the cultivated apple.

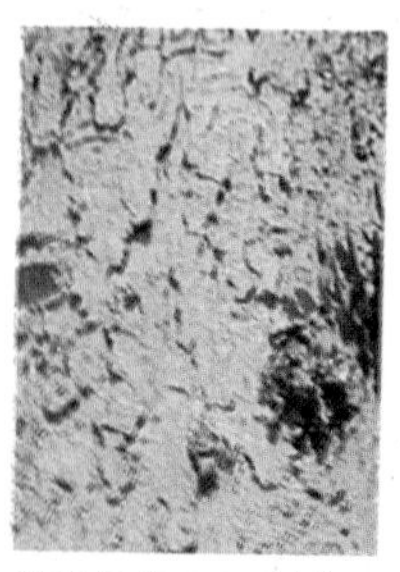

Bark is brown; old trees flake in patches.

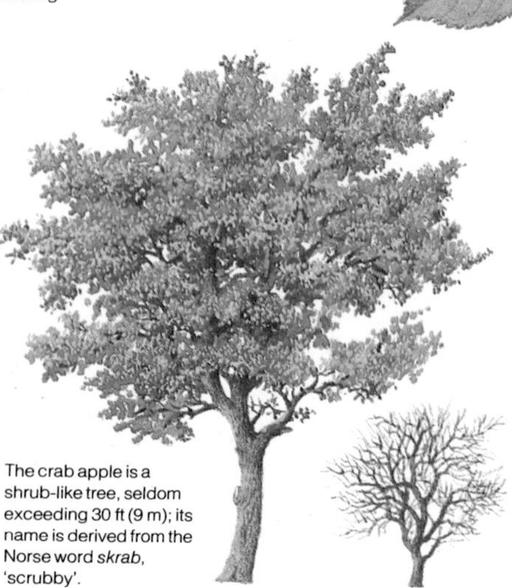

The crab apple is a shrub-like tree, seldom exceeding 30 ft (9 m); its name is derived from the Norse word *skrab*, 'scrubby'.

White flowers distinguish pears from apple trees.

Leaves are dark, glossy green, with smaller teeth than apple and a longer leaf-stalk. Fruits ripen from yellow-green to brown.

Pear is narrow, with sparse branches, and often leans; it grows to 50 ft (15 m). Suckers may form a thicket round the parent.

Dark grey or brown bark cracks into small plates.

All cultivated pears are derived from the common pear, which itself is probably of hybrid origin.

'Williams' Bon Chrétien'

'Conference'

The common pear can still be found growing wild in hedgerows and along the edges of country roads.

Common pear *Pyrus communis*

Unlike the crab apple, the common or wild pear is not thought to be native to Britain; it is more likely to have escaped from orchards, to which it had been brought from Continental Europe. Originally, the common pear came from western Asia, but its fruit has been eaten in Europe for thousands of years. It was cultivated by the ancient Greeks, and is mentioned by Homer in the *Odyssey*.

In its wild state, the common pear is a thorny tree with bitter and gritty fruit. It sends out suckers freely from its roots, multiplying to form thickets distinguished by the snowfall of white blossom which covers them in April. The wood is a pale pink-brown in colour, easily stained and polished and used for musical instruments, carving, turning and veneers.

The wild pear is used as a root stock on which are grafted the many cultivated orchard varieties of the tree, which provide dessert pears, fruit for stewing, and perry, a cider-like drink probably introduced by the Normans. Like apples, pear trees often have mistletoe growing on them. Birds leave the sticky seeds on the bark, where the mistletoe develops as a parasite, drawing its sustenance partly from the host tree.

The numerous, solitary white flowers appear Feb.–Mar., before the leaves come out.

Leaves are alternate, glossy green on top and hairless. The leaf margin has small, regular, round-ended teeth. Fruits, pale green in summer, turn the colour of ripe tomatoes.

The purple-leaved cherry plum, *atropurpurea* or 'Pissardii', is grown in suburban gardens.

The cherry plum, smothered with small white flowers in early spring, grows wild in thickets in southern England.

Cherry plum *Prunus cerasifera*

The pure white flowers of the cherry plum splash hedgerow and garden by the beginning of March, heralding the spring before winter is properly over. Because it spreads freely by suckering, the tree is useful for forming dense hedges, and its thorny twigs make it an effective barrier. Its common name describes its cherry-like fruits; the alternative name of myrobalan plum is thought to come from Greek words meaning a fruit producing a sweet-scented ointment.

Like other members of the *Prunus* genus, the cherry plum was cultivated for its fruits before being replaced by more rewarding fruit trees. It is one of the parents from which cultivated plums and gages have arisen, and such trees are often grafted onto its rootstock.

The cherry plum is probably best known in the form of the purple-leaved 'Pissardii'. This was named after Pissard, French-born gardener to the Shah of Persia in the late 19th century. It arose by chance in the Imperial gardens and Pissard cultivated it, and sent specimens to France. It is now grown extensively in suburban gardens for its decorative foliage, and for the pinkish flowers it produces in the early spring.

The smooth, dark bark becomes crinkled with age.

This spreading, open-crowned tree resembles blackthorn, but it blooms earlier, and its foliage is not so thick. It grows to 25 ft (7·5 m).

Leaves are alternate, and hairy on both sides. They are smaller than plum leaves. The small, round, purple fruit has a waxy bloom.

The white flowers, which open Apr.–May, are pollinated by insects.

The damson has long been cultivated for its small, plum-like fruits which ripen during September and October.

Plum and greengage are larger-fruited than the damson, but all are varieties of *Prunus domestica*.

The smooth brown bark becomes rough with age.

The damson is a small tree not reaching more than 20–25 ft (6–7·5 m) in height.

Damson *Prunus domestica*

The damson gets its name from the city of Damascus in Syria where, according to tradition, it was first cultivated. Many major food plants were developed in the Middle East, some of the more important, such as wheat, evolving into superior forms by the crossing of species and doubling of the chromosomes. When this happens, the resulting plant is very vigorous and much larger than its parents. Such doubling has occurred with plums.

Like the greengage and the plum, the damson has been developed from crosses between the blackthorn and the cherry plum. In Britain it is seldom cultivated in orchards, occurring more frequently as a single tree near a house or farm. It spreads easily, either by suckering or by germinating from the stones dropped by people and birds after eating the fruit.

Unlike most fruit trees, the damson does not need pruning to produce a good crop every year. Its fruit can be stewed, bottled, jellied or made into jam. The wood of all plum trees has a reddish heartwood and pale brown sapwood; it is hard and dense, taking polish well. Because of the attractive colour contrast between heartwood and sapwood, damson is used for turning and cabinet-making.

Creamy-white flowers appear in May and are sweet-scented.

Leaves are alternate, with a white felt of thick hairs on the underside. Each leaf has 9–12 pairs of parallel veins and is irregularly toothed.

The berries, green at first, ripen to bright scarlet and provide food for birds.

Silvery-white leaves, emerging in spring, make the tree appear to be covered in blossom, before its flowers emerge.

Smooth, light grey bark becomes ridged with scales.

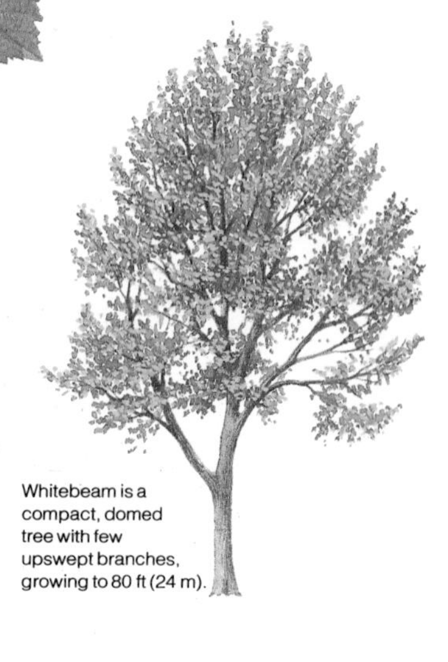

Whitebeam is a compact, domed tree with few upswept branches, growing to 80 ft (24 m).

Whitebeam *Sorbus aria*

The hard, tough wood of the whitebeam was used for making cogs in early machinery, before it was replaced by iron. Over-ripe whitebeam berries were made into jelly for eating with venison. Although both of these uses are largely things of the past, the whitebeam has found an important new function as a decorative street tree. The whitebeam's compact shape and relatively modest size allow it to be planted in restricted spaces; and the hairy undersides of its leaves resist pollution and sea winds and help the tree to conserve moisture on dry sites. In addition, for most of the year the whitebeam is strikingly handsome. From spring onwards, the white down beneath the leaves decks the tree in silver, until red berries and golden leaves bring a new array of colours in autumn.

The Anglo-Saxons, who gave the tree its name ('beam' meant tree, like *Baum* in modern German), used it as a boundary marker because of its distinctive appearance. In its natural state it grows on dry limestone and chalk, as well as on more acidic soils, a number of different forms growing in various parts of the country. It also hybridises with other members of its family and has been developed into numerous varieties by human intervention.

Flowers are all alike and fertile. [× 2]

The oval berries, borne in a flat head, are red at first, then ripen to a shiny black.

The colourful berries of the wayfaring tree often brighten the edge of woods or hedgerows in southern Britain.

Leaves are opposite, with dense, white hairs on the underside. The edges have regular, pointed teeth; the stalks are hairy. Unlike those of the related guelder rose, all flowers making up the flower-head are the same size.

This small, spreading shrub seldom rises to more than 20 ft (6 m).

Wayfaring tree *Viburnum lantana*

The 16th-century botanist John Gerard found this shrub so widespread along lanes and byways in southern England that he called it the 'wayfarer's tree'. The shrub usually grows on the edges of woods and in hedgerows on chalk and limestone soils, and does not occur naturally further north than Yorkshire.

Wayfaring tree is a corruption of wayfarer's tree, but the shrub has a still older name – hoarwithy. 'Hoar', meaning white, refers to the white, silky hairs on the underside of the leaves, which reduce water loss on dry soils; and 'withy' means a pliant stem. The young twigs are so flexible that they were used to bind faggots in the days before string. They were also cut to make switches for driving livestock. In the past the black berries were used to make ink, and the very hard wood from the tree stem was fashioned into mouthpieces for tobacco-pipes.

The wayfaring tree provides a bright splash of white when it flowers in May and June. Its red berries, turning black with maturity, are also attractive in appearance. To human taste they are so astringent as to be inedible. Birds like them, however, and spread the seeds on to nearby pastures, which are readily invaded by seedlings or suckers when fields are abandoned.

Leaves are alternate, toothed and with a short point at the tip. They are pink when unfolding in April.

The snowy mespil may grow to 40 ft (12 m). It usually has several stems, but is sometimes pruned back to one.

The bark is dark grey and smooth.

Snowy mespil produces profuse quantities of white flowers with strap-shaped petals.

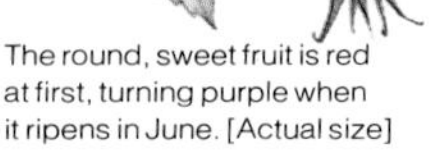

The round, sweet fruit is red at first, turning purple when it ripens in June. [Actual size]

White flowers in May and rich red autumn leaves make the snowy mespil a decorative tree for much of the year.

Snowy mespil *Amelanchier lamarckii*

Mespil is derived from the Latin word for medlar, a once-popular apple-like fruit that is edible only when it is partly rotten. Mespil fruits resemble small medlars, but are sweeter-tasting. The Red Indians of North America gathered and dried them for winter eating, and they can be used in puddings and pies or made into jam. The word 'snowy' refers to the brilliant white flowers which appear in May and whose nectar is particularly attractive to bees and wasps. Snowy mespil is sometimes confused with the related shrub *Amelanchier canadensis*; this has young leaves that are woolly on both sides, whereas those of snowy mespil are smooth. Both have rich autumn colours.

Mespils grow well in Britain on light, acid soils and are hardy so long as they are planted where they receive plenty of sunlight. Their rootstock is often used for the grafting of pears and quinces. The wood is heavy, strong and close-grained, the heartwood is dark brown tinged with red, and the sapwood is lighter. The wood is used to make tool handles and fishing rods.

In their native North America the trees are sometimes called June berries, shad berries or shad blow, because they flower and fruit when shad – a migrating fish – are present in the rivers.

In autumn, leaves turn brilliant hues of yellow, orange and red before they fall.

Crimson stamens forming the flowers appear on the naked branches during March. Bracts are brown.

Leaves are alternate with wavy edges, and undersides have red parallel veins. The stalks are hairy.

Its spectacular autumn colours have made Persian ironwood popular for large gardens since it was introduced in 1841.

Smooth bark peels off in flakes, leaving patches.

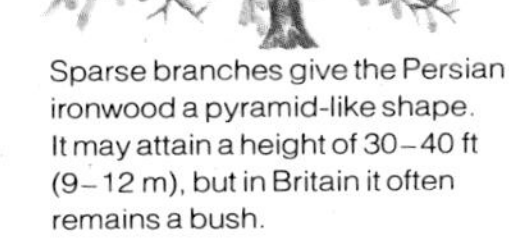

Sparse branches give the Persian ironwood a pyramid-like shape. It may attain a height of 30–40 ft (9–12 m), but in Britain it often remains a bush.

Persian ironwood *Parrotia persica*

Its hard, virtually indestructible timber gives the Persian ironwood its name; but the wood has no commercial use, even in its native homeland of Iran and the Caucasus. The botanical name *Parrotia* was given to this tree in honour of the Russian naturalist F. W. Parrot. Among other achievements, Parrot in 1829 made the first recorded ascent of Mount Ararat, the mountain on the borders of Iran, Turkey and Armenia on which Noah's ark reputedly came to rest.

In its homelands, the Persian ironwood grows on wet hillsides and forms a substantial tree. In Britain, it remains a shrub unless the lower branches are pruned. It does best if planted in a sunny position on moist, well-drained soil where there is plenty of room for it to spread; unlike the closely related wych hazel it can tolerate lime.

It is grown in Britain purely for its ornamental value. In late winter and early spring it produces crimson flowers which appear before the leaves unfold, and in autumn its foliage turns striking shades of yellow, orange and red. The bark on older trees peels and flakes in patches like that of the London plane, making an attractive feature throughout the year.

Snowberry suckers freely and forms dense, tangled thickets unless it is regularly pruned. It grows to 3–6 ft (1–1·8 m).

The pink, bell-shaped flowers appear from June to September, attracting bees. [× 3]

Caterpillars of the death's head hawk moth, *Acherontia atropos*, which commonly feed on potato leaves, also eat those of the snowberry.

The smooth oval leaves are set opposite each other in pairs. Their edges are wavy.

Pheasants and other birds may feed on the berries in a hard winter when food is scarce.

Its long-lasting, round white berries, have made the quick-spreading snowberry a popular garden shrub.

Snowberry *Symphoricarpos rivularis*

Snowberry is the name given to several related North American shrubs introduced to Britain in the 19th century for the attractive appearance of their fruit. They have been crossed to give garden forms grown for ornamental hedging. Snowberry has also been widely planted in woods where pheasants are reared. The most common species readily forms thickets, grows on any soil, and tolerates deep shade, so it makes ideal ground cover in which game can hide; on the other hand, so long as the shrub is cut back periodically to prevent it becoming too thick, pheasants can easily be flushed from it.

The large white berries gave the shrub its name because they frequently adorn it throughout the snows of winter. Eating them can have ill effects, they are not palatable to humans, and they are not much liked by birds. Pheasants sometimes eat them if no other food is available, but generally the berries survive unplundered. They have a spongy texture and are full of air, so they explode with a popping sound when stamped on or squeezed hard – a feature which delights children.

In some districts, the snowberry has naturalised itself in hedges, by streams and on banks, spreading mainly by suckers.

A straggly, rather untidy shrub, mock orange is redeemed for ornamental use by its profuse flowers. It grows to 12 ft (3·6 m).

Leaves are borne in opposite pairs, and have a few, widely spaced teeth. The stalks are short and hairy.

Cup-shaped white flowers appear in early June on shoots that grew in the previous year.

Mock orange is a gardener's favourite, thriving even when left to take care of itself, and doing well on poor soils.

'Virginal'

'Variegatus'

'Belle Etoile'

Cultivated forms of mock orange include varieties with large or double flowers, and one with a creamy-white margin to the leaf.

Mock orange *Philadelphus coronarius*

In early summer, the showy flowers of mock orange give off a heady fragrance reminiscent of orange blossom that is overpowering if the blooms are brought indoors. Flowers and scent have made the mock orange a popular garden shrub since the 16th century. Sir John Danvers, who helped to introduce the Italian style of garden design to England, planted clumps of it in the grounds of his Chelsea house.

Even when neglected by a gardener, mock orange survives, and it flourishes on dry, chalky soils as well as on loam. The shrub flowers on the shoots formed in the previous year, so after it has flowered gardeners remove the old wood, to ensure good flowering in the following year.

Mock orange is often called 'syringa' – an error, because that is the botanical name for lilacs. The confusion may have arisen at the beginning of this century, when the Lemoines, a family of French nurserymen who developed many cultivated varieties of lilac, also created various mock orange cultivars. In its native south-east Europe and Asia Minor, mock orange is, by tradition, a symbol of deceit, even though its generic name of *Philadelphus* means 'brotherly (or sisterly) love'.

LONG-LEAVED TREES AND SHRUBS

Familiar species that have leaves longer than they are broad include most shrubs, many willows, some oaks and the sweet chestnut. Long-leaved trees and shrubs can be divided into five distinct groups according to their texture, colour and shape.

Very long narrow leaves, alternate

Willows
Salicaceae

Leaves 3–4½ in. (7·5–12 cm), with teeth, pale below. Pages 116–18

Osier
Salix viminalis

Leaves 4–10 in. (10–25 cm), with leaf margin rolled in. Page 119

Sea buckthorn
Hippophaë rhamnoides

Leaves ¾–3 in. (2–7·5 cm), grey above and silvery below; no teeth. Page 121

Thick, shiny evergreen leaves

Cherry laurel

Cherry laurel
Prunus laurocerasus

Leaves alternate, 2–6 in. (5–15 cm), almond-smelling. Page 96

Portugal laurel
Prunus lusitanica

Leaves alternate, 3–4½ in. (7·5–12 cm), many teeth, red stalks. Page 97

Spurge laurel
Daphne laureola

Leaves alternate, 2–4½ in. (5–12 cm), dark, no teeth. Page 123

Phillyrea
Phillyrea latifolia

Leaves opposite, 1–2 in. (2·5–5 cm), small teeth, dark above. Page 120

Rhododendron
Rhododendron ponticum

Leaves alternate, 2½–5 in. (6–12·5 cm), no teeth; base tapered. Page 95

Sweet bay
Laurus nobilis

Leaves alternate, 2–4 in. (5–10 cm), wavy margin, red stalks. Page 98

Spotted laurel
Aucuba japonica

Leaves alternate, 2½–5 in. (6–12·5 cm), spotted yellow. Page 99

Blue-green leaves

Snow gum

Snow gum
Eucalyptus niphophila

Leaves alternate, 5½ in. (14 cm), leaf stalk red. Page 125

Cider gum
Eucalyptus gunnii

Leaves alternate, 3–4 in. (7·5–10 cm), narrow; stalk yellow. Page 124

Toothed leaves

Bird cherry

Cherries
Prunus

Leaves alternate, 4–6 in. (10–15 cm), with lumpy glands at leaf base. Pages 100–5

Cotoneaster
Cotoneaster frigidus

Leaves alternate, 2½–5 in. (6–12·5 cm), silvery white below, with blunt tip. Page 111

Almond
Prunus dulcis

Leaves alternate, 2¾–4½ in. (7–12 cm), folded at base. Page 106

Snowbell tree
Styrax japonica

Leaves alternate, 2½–3 in. (6–7·5 cm), small glandular, teeth on margin. Page 112

Snowbell Tree

Dwarf quince
Chaenomeles japonica

Leaves alternate, 2–2¾ in. (5–7 cm), long point, small teeth, stipules at base. Page 115

Spindle
Euonymus europaeus

Leaves opposite, 1½–2¾ in. (4–7 cm), long point, small teeth. Page 113

Forsythia
Forsythia × intermedia

Leaves opposite, 3–4 in. (7·5–10 cm), large teeth. Page 122

Sweet chestnut
Castanea sativa

Leaves alternate, 6–8 in. (15–20 cm), saw teeth, parallel veins. Page 110

Sweet chestnut

Leaves woolly below

Medlar

Medlar
Mespilus germanica

Leaves alternate, 3–6 in. (7·5–15 cm), thick, and toothed near tip. Page 107

Holm oak
Quercus ilex

Leaves alternate, 2–4 in. (5–10 cm), dull, with fawn hairs on underside and without teeth. Page 109

Buddleia
Buddleia davidii

Leaves opposite, ¾–4 in. (2–10 cm), grey-green above. Page 114

Magnolia
Magnolia × soulangiana

Leaves alternate, 4½–6 in. (12–15 cm), leathery and without teeth. Page 94

Cork oak
Quercus suber

Leaves alternate, 1½–2¾ in. (4–7 cm), sharp teeth, white hairs below. Page 108

Cork oak

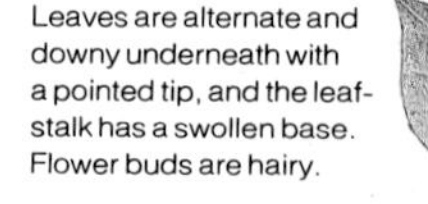

Leaves are alternate and downy underneath with a pointed tip, and the leaf-stalk has a swollen base. Flower buds are hairy.

Large, pink or purple-tinged white flowers appear in April, before the leaves emerge, and continue to open until May.

The striking pink or purple-white flowers of the popular hybrid magnolia brighten parks and gardens in early spring.

Fruits are arranged spirally in cone-like structures and appear in early autumn.

Magnolia liliiflora

Yulan (*Magnolia denudata*)

The widely planted magnolia is a fertile hybrid of two Chinese species, *Magnolia liliiflora*, and the Yulan.

Greyish bark has horizontal pores and vertical fissures.

An oval and straggly bush of up to 25 ft (7·5 m), the magnolia is also pruned and trained against walls.

Magnolia *Magnolia × soulangiana*

Although the magnolia is a familiar feature of British gardens, it has longer associations with other countries – it is a cross between two Chinese species, and was originally cultivated near Paris in the 19th century. The buds of one of its parents, the yulan, were used by the Chinese as a medicine and for flavouring rice dishes. The French connection is continued in the use of the tree's botanical name; it commemorates Professor Pierre Magnol, Director of the Botanical Garden at Montpellier in the 17th century.

When it is in flower, the magnolia is unrivalled among ornamental shrubs. It tolerates pollution and the clay soils of southern Britain, but this deciduous shrub demands shelter from the wind and protection from spring frost if its flowers are to show their full beauty and last as long as possible. It has been planted against garden walls since Victorian times.

Of all the species of magnolia in cultivation, *Magnolia × soulangiana* is the most easily grown, and is quickly recognised by its pinkish or purplish-white flowers. The wood has a hard, close grain which has proved suitable for making angles in mouldings and on decorative woodwork.

The leaves are alternate, unlobed and untoothed with tapered base and short-pointed tip; they are dark on top and paler below, often dusted with red.

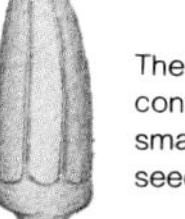

The long capsule contains many small, flattened seeds. [Actual size]

The purple flowers appear in May and June in clusters of 10–15. They are 2 in. (5 cm) across.

A native of Asia Minor, the rhododendron now grows wild in many parts of Britain, often shading out other plants.

Rhododendron *Rhododendron ponticum*

When the rhododendron was introduced to the British Isles from Asia Minor more than 200 years ago, it was extensively planted for game cover in woods. It was chosen for this purpose because it adapts to all kinds of soils and situations, and can survive under the heavy shade of beech trees. In some areas it now forms a dense and almost impenetrable shrub layer beneath the trees. It spreads freely by seed and is very difficult to eradicate, either by cutting or with the use of weed-killers.

Along with the cherry laurel, rhododendron is the most common evergreen to have been introduced to Britain. Some of the earlier ornamental rhododendrons were obtained by crossing *Rhododendron ponticum* with other hardy species from the Himalayas and China. It is still used as rootstock on which to graft the hundreds of cultivars and hybrids now in existence. These provide a wide range of colour, flowering from early spring until well into summer.

Although the shrub enjoys the sun, rapid warming-up damages the beautiful flowers, as they need time to thaw out slowly on frosty mornings. Ideally therefore, the shrub should be planted in sheltered places.

Among hundreds of cultivated species of rhododendrons and azaleas is *Rhododendron luteum*, a deciduous form with smaller, yellow flowers.

This evergreen shrub, with dark green, glossy foliage, grows to 20 ft (6 m) high. It spreads rapidly and smothers all other growth in its vicinity.

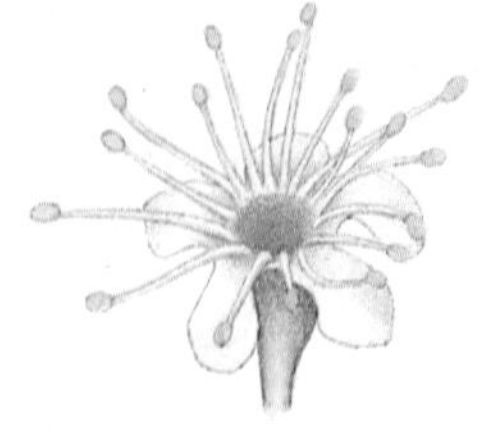

Erect heads of dull, white flowers are borne in the leaf axils in April. [× 3]

The alternate, bright green glossy leaves are leathery and pointed. They have small, wavy teeth and thick stalks. When crushed, the leaves smell of almonds.

This evergreen grows to 20 ft (6 m) and spreads to form hedges.

The round berries are red at first, ripening to shiny black. [Actual size]

Cherry laurel is tolerant of shade, and when growing wild forms dense cover for game and many forms of wildlife.

Cherry laurel *Prunus laurocerasus*

When the cherry laurel, a native of south-east Europe, was introduced into this country in 1576 it immediately found favour as an ornamental evergreen hedge. The laurel hedge which is such a familiar feature of suburban gardens is in fact cherry laurel and not a true laurel. It is hardy, and grows on most soils except those which contain chalk.

This shrub is, apart from the rhododendron, the most common introduced evergreen in Britain. It is planted as game cover in woods because it can tolerate shade and the moisture dripping from the trees above, and its large evergreen leaves keep the ground warm in winter for game birds. In such shady situations it does not flower or fruit well, but as a hedge it freely produces flowers and cherry-like fruit, which when ripe are eaten by birds.

In the days when amateur naturalists made collections of butterflies, the leaves of cherry laurel formed part of their simple equipment. The leaves smell of bitter almonds when crushed and contain prussic acid or cyanide; butterflies dropped into a 'killing jar' containing the crushed leaves quickly died, but remained relaxed enough to be pinned out.

The flower is creamy-white, waxy and fragrant with a hawthorn-like scent. There are about 20 five-petalled flowers on each stalk; only a few develop into berries. [×5]

This laurel has dense foliage; it usually develops a rounded shrubby profile, but can reach 20 ft (6 m) in height.

The alternate leaves are on red stalks; they are dark glossy green on top and yellow-green below, with many teeth and long, pointed tips. Long, drooping flower spikes appear in June.

The hanging berries are at first red, turning later to purplish-black.

This native of Spain and Portugal is widely grown in Britain for its ornamental flowers and evergreen foliage.

Portugal laurel *Prunus lusitanica*

The main distinguishing feature of the Portugal laurel is the dark crimson colour of its twigs and leaf-stalks. It is a native of Spain and Portugal, and was introduced to Britain as an ornamental plant in 1648. Together with cherry laurel and holly, it was then one of the few evergreens available for planting.

Portugal laurel is much hardier than cherry laurel, and unlike cherry laurel it can grow in chalky areas. However, it is not so frequently planted. Where it is planted it is usually grown as a hedge, but if it is given plenty of room and allowed to grow naturally it forms a beautiful ornamental tree. Portugal laurel can also be grown in tubs for decoration, and is kept within bounds by clipping. Unlike the other laurels it has not become naturalised in Britain.

Because it is easily controlled, the plant is often grown in game coverts, where it acts as a windbreak between other trees and keeps the wood warm in winter. It also suppresses the growth of ground plants beneath it, which allows the pheasants to move about freely without becoming trapped. As it often grows into a small tree, pheasants can roost in its branches away from foxes and other predators.

The big, green, oval berries turn black when ripe in October.

Leaves are evergreen, alternate and thick, tapering at both ends, with wavy margins. Oil glands give off rich smell when leaf is crushed. Twigs and leaf-stalks are red.

Male flower [× 4]

Female flower [× 4]

Yellowish-green flowers appear in leaf axils in spring; male and female flowers are borne on separate trees.

Sweet bay can withstand training and heavy clipping, and is often grown in a tub to decorate terraces or drives.

A densely branched shrub of pyramidal shape, often grown where space is limited. When not clipped back, it reaches 10 ft (3 m).

Sweet bay *Laurus nobilis*

In ancient Greece the bay tree, or true laurel, was sacred to the god Apollo. The highest honour a Greek poet or warrior could receive was to be crowned with a garland of fruiting laurel leaves. The Romans adopted the laurel wreath as a symbol of high achievement, especially in war. In modern Britain, the title of the office of Poet Laureate maintains the age-old significance of the laurel as a mark of supreme distinction in poetry.

But it is in the kitchen that the bay leaf is best known today, whether used on its own to flavour meat or, combined with thyme, parsley and other herbs, in a *bouquet garni*. In the past, the bay leaf had many other uses apart from cookery. The 16th-century doctor-monk Andrew Boorde recommended burning bay leaves 'to expel corrupt and contagious air in the buttery, the cellar, the kitchen, the larder-house'. It was believed that the sweet, pungent odour of the leaves disinfected the air. Bay leaves were also prescribed for persistent coughs and as a laxative.

Originally from northern Asia, the laurel is now distributed widely throughout Europe and the Mediterranean, flourishing especially in cities, as it stands up well to pollution.

The small, white, male and female flowers are borne on separate plants in March and April.

This native of Japan tolerates dense shade, and grows in corners of gardens where little else will thrive.

A rounded, bushy shrub, growing to 12 ft (3·6 m) high. It is hardy and evergreen.

Shiny, dark green, leathery leaves are opposite and often have yellow spots. They have a pointed tip, few teeth, a prominent midrib and a long stalk.

The round berries are green at first, ripening to scarlet in the following spring. Each has a single seed. The berries are not usually eaten by birds.

Many male trees, such as those of the cultivated variety 'Concolor', lack spots on the leaves.

Spotted laurel *Aucuba japonica*

When the botanist John Groefer introduced this native of Japan to Britain in 1783, it was not realised that all the plants he had brought, with their decorative spotted leaves, were female. It was not until the early 1840s that male plants, with pure green leaves, were brought to Britain. They then fertilised the female plants, which produced the handsome scarlet berries favoured by Victorian gardeners.

The berries remain on the shrub throughout the autumn, winter and spring, adding to the ornamental effect of its foliage. At one time spotted laurel was a popular house-plant, while out of doors it became a favourite for planting in banks with other ornamental shrubs and trees alongside garden paths.

The spotted laurel is still popular today, and many different forms of male and female bushes, with variously coloured leaves, have been developed. Since it does not demand much light, it is a very suitable plant for filling in the dark corners of shrubberies or planting under dense trees; it will make a thick hedge to obscure unsightly buildings. It tolerates the polluted air of industrial Britain, and will thrive on almost any soil, however poor. In some areas it now grows wild.

Birds feed on the bright red cherries in July.

[Actual size]

Leaf turns crimson in autumn.

The white flowers of wild cherry appear before the leaves in April.

The white blossom of the wild cherry is conspicuous in beech woods in spring, especially on clay soils over chalk.

Wild cherry *Prunus avium*

The cherry, like other fruit trees, has been crossed and selected to produce better fruiting varieties. Many of these derive from the wild cherry, or gean, which is still used as the rootstock on which its more productive relatives are grown. The wild cherry can be found in woods – especially beech and oak woods – where its blossoms stand out in snow-white patches in spring.

Wild cherry grows rapidly to timber size, and its wood is used to make fine furniture, veneers and sweet-smoking cherry pipes. The wood is of good quality, although sometimes larger trees suffer from heart rot.

The 'cherry ripe' of the old London street cry came from the cultivated varieties of the tree grown in Kent, where farmers grazed their sheep beneath the trees, making double use of the land. Harvesting the fruit was once a social occasion: on cherry-picking Sunday in Cambridgeshire, over a century ago, a small payment enabled people to eat as many cherries as they could manage in a day. The fruit is now eaten fresh or prepared in a variety of ways, and is also used in syrups and cough mixtures. Liqueurs are distilled from the fermented pulp, with which the stones are also crushed.

Shiny, chestnut-brown bark peels in horizontal strips.

Leaves are alternate, with long points and regular, forward-pointing teeth. There are glands at the base, and the stalk is red and grooved.

The tree is pyramidal in shape, reaching 30–40 ft (9–12 m).

This native British tree is found more in the north than the wild cherry, and is common by streams in limestone areas.

The black cherries, called 'hags' in Scotland, are taken by birds, though they have a bitter taste. They contain a hard, oval stone.

The bird cherry is usually smaller than the wild cherry, reaching about 20–30 ft (6–9 m).

Bark peels and has scattered pores.

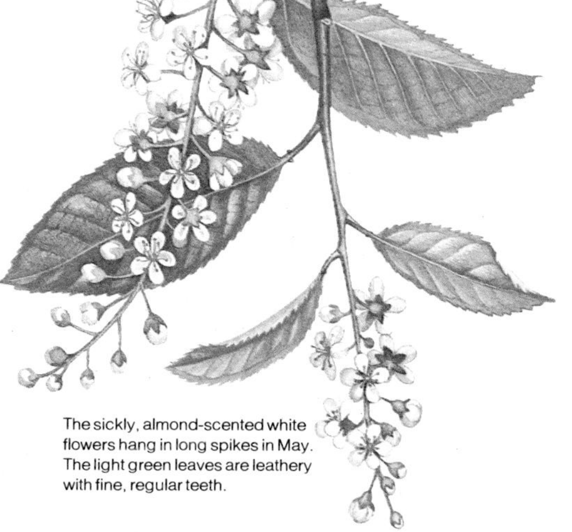

The sickly, almond-scented white flowers hang in long spikes in May. The light green leaves are leathery with fine, regular teeth.

Bird cherry *Prunus padus*

Few trees can match the outstanding beauty of the bird cherry's display in May, when long, hanging bunches of blossom fill the air with an almond fragrance. As the tree's name implies, however, its bitter fruit is edible only to birds. Its bark, though, was once used by humans: in the Middle Ages it was the source of an infusion used as a tonic and as a sedative for upset stomachs, while pieces of the bark were hung outside doors and put in drinking water as a guard against plague.

The tart taste of the cherry is due to its richness in tannin, and the fruit itself has its uses – to flavour brandies and wines. A very similar species, the black or rum cherry, is used for flavouring rum. Timber from the tree has a reddish-brown heartwood and white sapwood, and gives off a somewhat disagreeable smell.

Bird cherry is often planted as an ornamental tree: a number of cultivars have bigger and more varied flowers – white, pink and double. One of them, 'Watereri', has spectacular hanging blossoms. Bird cherries are found much farther north than the wild cherry, and have a variety of local names, among them 'hag cherry', 'hawkberry' or 'hagberry' in Scotland and Northumberland, from the tree's old Norse name *heggr*.

The leaves are alternate and broad, with abrupt, drawn-out points and sharp teeth.

The autumn leaves, crimson or orange, fall early.

Smooth, red-brown bark has pores in raised lines.

Clusters of shell-pink flowers appear in late March at the same time as the leaves.

This cherry has a rounded crown, and reaches 60 ft (18 m) in the wild.

A native of Japan and Korea, this ornamental cherry is often planted for its beautiful spring blossom.

Sargent's cherry *Prunus sargentii*

This lovely cherry is cultivated in Britain primarily for its display of pink spring blossom, but it has other ornamental features too. Its young leaves are purplish, and its autumn leaves change colour earlier than those of most trees, turning orange or crimson in September. Sargent's cherry has been widely planted in streets, gardens and parks, but unlike some other flowering cherries it has particular soil requirements, thriving best on a moist loam. However, it adapts well to the British climate, and its flower buds are not ravaged by bullfinches before they can blossom as those of other cherries are.

Charles Sprague Sargent, the American botanist after whom the cherry is named, found it in 1890, growing on mountainsides in the shadow of Mt Fujiyama in Japan, and subsequently introduced it to the West. In Japan the even, close-grained wood is used extensively to make blocks for colour printing. It is so sought after that mature trees are now rare in their native land.

When sold by nurserymen the stem of Sargent's cherry is usually grafted on to the rootstock of its relative, the wild cherry or gean, *Prunus avium*; this produces a vigorous and attractive garden tree.

In autumn the leaf turns golden pink. Some cultivars turn red.

The large leaves have many bristly teeth and a wedge-shaped base. They have a smooth and polished appearance.

Brown bark is ringed with breathing pores.

White or rose-tinged flowers appear in April or May.

The bullfinch strips cherries of their flower-buds.

This small tree with wide-spreading branches, often grafted, reaches 10–15 ft (3–4·5 m).

The tree often develops a flat top. It was the first flowering cherry from the East to be planted in European gardens.

Japanese cherry *Prunus serrulata*

Pink and white flowers wreathing the branches of Japanese cherry trees splash many a suburban street with colour in spring. They vary widely in the precise shade of their flowers, their fragrance and the autumn and spring colours of their foliage, but they are nearly all varieties of one tree, *Prunus serrulata*.

The tree is thought to have originated in China, and then been extensively cultivated in innumerable forms in Japan. The first specimen was introduced to England via China in 1822. Most will not grow true from seed but have to be reproduced by grafting or budding, usually onto a seedling of wild cherry.

One of the most attractive Japanese cherries is 'Tai Haku', a superb, robust tree with dazzling white single flowers. For decades this tree was lost to its native land, and known to the Japanese only through paintings. It was rediscovered by Captain Collingwood Ingram, an authority on cherry trees, who in 1923 spotted a specimen growing in a garden in Sussex. Ingram realised that the tree was a rare one, and on a subsequent visit to Japan he identified it as the 'Great White Cherry' regarded by the Japanese as a long-lost species. Ingram later re-introduced the tree to its country of origin.

'Tai Haku'
Prunus serrulata

Flowers are single, pure white and the largest of any flowering cherry.

'Longipes'
Prunus serrulata

The large, double, pure white flowers appear later than those of most Japanese cherries.

[Actual size]

'Watereri'
Prunus padus

In spring, this form of bird cherry bears spectacularly long hanging spikes of white flowers.

Flowering cherries

For over a thousand years flowering cherries have been cultivated in Japan, but it is only in the last two centuries that they have been introduced into Britain. Now they are probably our most widely planted ornamental trees, for they are very adaptable. Cherries come in many different shapes and sizes, and in a wide range of colours: pure white, pink, deep rose or even, occasionally, sulphur-yellow. In autumn many cherries burst into colour for a second time, as their leaves turn to gold and crimson; in winter the bark is a deep shiny red. The trees flower early in the year, so the leaves, which are only just emerging, do not hide the blossom but, in some cases, grace it with a striking bronze background.

'Kanzan'

Prunus serrulata

This cultivar is the most commonly planted of all the flowering cherries. The large, semi-double, deep pink flowers are bunched.

'Plena'

Prunus avium

This variety of wild cherry, or gean, produces masses of double white flowers on long stalks. They grow in spreading branches.

'Cheal's Weeping'

Prunus serrulata

This grafted tree has drooping branches reaching nearly to the ground. Its big, bright pink flowers bloom early.

'Amanogawa'

Prunus serrulata

This cultivar is a narrow, column-shaped tree with nearly perpendicular branches. Its shape makes it suitable for small gardens.

'Amanogawa'

Prunus serrulata

The semi-double flowers are $1\frac{1}{2}$–2 in. (4–5 cm) wide, and pale pink in colour. The flower-stalks are long. This cultivar produces a profusion of fragrant blooms.

Leaves are alternate, long-pointed and finely toothed. They are folded about the midrib, to make a V-shaped 'valley'.

In southern Britain in a hot summer, the green fruits sometimes ripen to release an oval, pitted nut containing an edible kernel.

'Roseoplena'

Pink flowers appear in March or April, before the leaves emerge. Some cultivated varieties, such as 'Roseoplena', have showy double blooms.

In Britain, almonds are grown for decoration rather than for their fruit. Their blossom is an early herald of spring.

Almond *Prunus dulcis*

More than 1,000 years before the birth of Christ, the Phrygians of Asia Minor regarded the almond as the sacred tree of life. It has since become rich in legend, perhaps because its flowers are among the earliest to appear after the winter. The Greeks believed that Phyllys, wife of Demophon, King of Athens, was turned into an almond tree by the gods after killing herself because she feared her husband had deserted her. They looked upon the tree as a symbol of fruitfulness. Another legend says that the almond provided Aaron's rod in the Bible story.

Almonds probably originated in western Asia or the Balkans, but they have been planted in Mediterranean lands since ancient times and have naturalised themselves in many areas. They are valued for their fruits, the kernels of which are added to cakes or ground to make marzipan. The kernel of the bitter almond is the source of highly poisonous prussic acid. Once that has been removed, the oil is used as a food flavouring.

In Britain, where almonds have been grown since the 16th century, the fruit rarely ripens fully because the summers are too cold. The hard, usually reddish, wood is used for tool handles, ornamental carvings and decorative veneers.

Yellow, horizontal bands of pores ring the trunk.

The almond is an open-branched, decorative tree, with hanging leaves. It grows to 30 ft (9 m).

The fruit, which ripens Oct.–Nov., is round and yellow-brown. A deep hollow at the end is surrounded by large, withered sepals. The fruit does not fall from the tree after ripening.

Leaves are alternate, finely toothed near the tip, hairy on the upper surface and downy beneath. A single showy flower appears at the end of each short, leafy twig in early summer, and is pollinated by bees.

Popular in Shakespeare's day for its fruit, the medlar is now more often planted for its flowers and russet autumn leaves.

Medlar *Mespilus germanica*

For centuries the fruit of the medlar, sometimes called 'medle' or 'merle', was a delicacy. It was eaten by the Greeks and the Romans, who dedicated it to the god Saturn, and was believed by herbalists to cure a variety of ailments, including excessive bleeding, kidney stones and digestive disorders.

Medlar fruit cannot be eaten raw until it is 'bletted' – that is, allowed to become over-ripe to the point at which the flesh softens and starts to rot, but before the outer skin shows signs of decay. If the fruit is left on the tree, frost will start the bletting process. Alternatively, the medlars can be picked in the autumn and laid out under cover for two weeks or so to soften. The need to let medlars blet was well known to Shakespeare, who punned on the fruit's name in *As You Like It.* Rosalind tells the interfering clown Touchstone: 'You'll be rotten ere you be half-ripe, and that's the right virtue of the medlar.'

Medlar fruit can also be made into jelly, but the tree is now more commonly grown for ornament. An infertile form called Smith's medlar, which flowers profusely, is a cross between the medlar and the hawthorn. Medlars originally came from the Caucasus, and some now grow wild in south-east England.

Grey-brown bark has deep vertical fissures.

This low-growing, gnarled and rather sprawling tree grows to 20 ft (6 m).

Leaves are alternate, similar to those of holm oak, but they have spine-tipped lobes. They are dark green on top, white underneath. Acorns are in a loose, shallow cup.

Male flowers appear on the young, grey-green shoots in May or June.

In Portugal and Spain trees are stripped for their cork, revealing the red inner bark. In Britain the trees are only ornamental.

Cork oak *Quercus suber*

Every ten years or so, the cork oaks of Portugal, Spain and Algeria have their outer bark stripped from their trunks to furnish the world with bottle stoppers, insulating materials, flooring tiles and other cork products. In Britain cork oaks are not exploited commercially, but grown simply for their ornamental value as attractive evergreens.

Cork is light, buoyant and impervious to liquids, and it does not conduct heat. These qualities have been known for 2,000 years: the Romans used cork to make sandals and floats to buoy up fishing nets. But it was not until glass bottles were first manufactured on a large scale in the 15th and 16th centuries that the foundations of the modern cork industry were laid.

In Mediterranean lands, the cork is cut from trees in rings of up to 3 in. (7.5 cm) thick, using an axe. The tree then survives to grow another layer; some 500-year-old Portuguese oaks have been stripped 40 or 50 times. Care has to be taken not to damage the living tissue immediately below the bark, for this layer transports the food manufactured in the leaves to all parts of the tree. The very thick bark of the cork oak protects it from fire in its native habitat.

Thick, grey, gnarled bark has long cracks.

The evergreen cork oak, native to the Mediterranean, has low gnarled branches. It grows to 65 ft (20 m).

Leaves are alternate. The younger, lower leaves are broad and spiny; the older, upper leaves are narrower and do not have teeth. Both are dark green on top, with felted white undersides.

Male flowers are long yellow catkins, appearing in June.

Salt-laden sea winds do not harm the rugged holm oak, which flourishes even in exposed sites on coasts and estuaries.

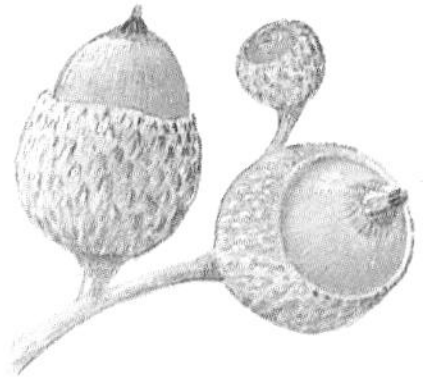

Light green acorns are up to two-thirds enclosed in their scaly cups. [Actual size]

Bark is ash-grey and cracked into small squares.

The evergreen holm oak grows into a round-headed tree up to 90 ft (27 m) high.

Holm oak *Quercus ilex*

Most kinds of oak familiar in Britain lose their leaves in winter, but holm oak is one of the evergreen species. Its leaves are spiky when young and give the tree its names in English and Latin: holm and *ilex*, both mean holly. In some parts of England the tree is called the holly oak or the live oak, as it remains 'alive', or green, through the winter.

Holm oak is native to the Mediterranean lands and was brought to Britain more than 400 years ago. It is very hardy and grows well on most poor soils, although it does not like heavy clay. Its leaves are adapted to withstand drying out in hot dry summers, so it flourishes in exposed locations, particularly by the sea, where it is useful for shade or, if clipped back hard, for hedging.

In southern Europe the hard, dense wood is used in furniture making and for the handles of tools, and also as a source of charcoal. As with other oaks, the freshly cut timber produces a blue stain around nails driven into it, as the tannin in the wood reacts with the iron. The presence of tannin made the holm oak a source of material for treating leather and skins in Greek and Roman times.

Female flowers

Leaves are alternate, with saw-like teeth and parallel veins. Catkins may have male flowers only, like long yellow tassels, or male flowers towards the tip, and smaller green female flowers nearer the base.

Male flowers

British-grown nuts seldom ripen to full size.

The fruit is a green spiny husk which splits in autumn to release one to three edible nuts.

Sweet or Spanish chestnut was probably introduced by the Romans, and is now planted largely for its decorative value.

Bark soon develops long spiral fissures.

Sweet chestnuts are tall and narrow with many low branches, but spread wider when older. They reach 100 ft (30 m).

Sweet chestnut *Castanea sativa*

Sweet chestnuts roasted beside an open fire have been a winter delicacy in Britain for generations, and chestnut stuffing has become a traditional part of the Christmas turkey dinner. Few chestnuts sold in shops in this country, however, are home grown. Britain's summers are too cool for the chestnut to ripen to full size, and most of those used in the kitchen are imported from the south of France and from Italy.

The sweet chestnut is a native of the Mediterranean lands and was probably introduced to Britain by the Romans. From the fruits they made a form of porridge, called *pollenta* in Latin, which is still sometimes eaten in the poorer regions of southern Europe. The chestnuts were slowly dried over an open fire, then ground and mixed with milk.

Because chestnuts do not germinate freely in Britain, few sweet-chestnut trees are genuinely wild. Most have been planted for decorative purposes in gardens or in public parks. Chestnut wood is very similar to oak wood, although it lacks the silver grain of oak. It is used, like oak, for panelling and beams; because it resists the weather well, it is used for the palings of rough fences, the poles being produced by coppicing.

Fruits ripen to red in the autumn and remain on the tree throughout the winter, attracting birds.

[× 3]

Leaves are alternate, tapered at the base and silver-white underneath. Sweet-scented white flowers are borne in flat heads and appear in June.

Hardy cotoneasters will grow in all types of soil and conditions. They make an attractive garden shrub.

Cotoneaster *Cotoneaster frigidus*

Birds love the brilliant red berries of the cotoneaster, and strip the branches early in winter. Among the rarer birds that are attracted by the berries are waxwings, which periodically invade this country from Scandinavia in winter. The berries are also one of the favourite foods of the pheasant, and cotoneasters are often planted in woods to attract them.

Many species of cotoneaster are grown in gardens, from dwarf, creeping evergreens that are attractive in rockeries to small deciduous trees. *Cotoneaster frigidus*, a native of the Himalayas, brought to Britain in the 19th century, is one of the hardiest and tallest, and is sometimes called the Himalayan tree-cotoneaster. It can become a shapely tree if it is pruned back to one stem when young.

Some of the most popular cotoneasters are hybrids between *Cotoneaster frigidus* and other species. They grow on most types of soil, can withstand urban pollution and do not mind being placed in the shade of larger trees. *Cotoneaster simonsii*, a vigorous grower with many stems, is particularly suitable for hedges as it retains some of its leaves during the winter and so remains decorative throughout the year.

Tree in winter.

Bark is grey-brown, with horizontal pores.

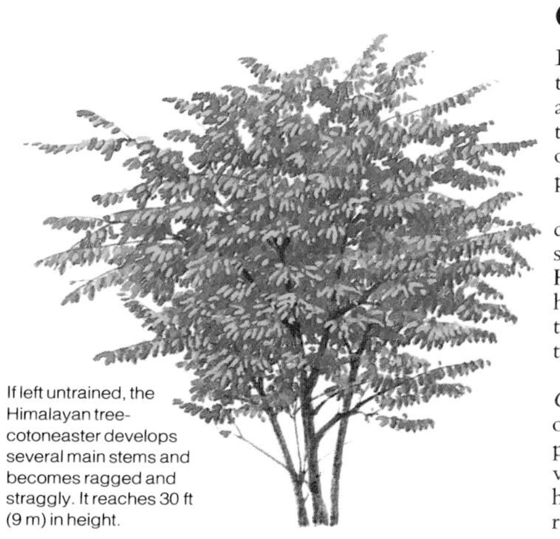

If left untrained, the Himalayan tree-cotoneaster develops several main stems and becomes ragged and straggly. It reaches 30 ft (9 m) in height.

Greenish egg-shaped fruits hang down on long stalks, splitting in autumn to show brown seeds.

Leaves are alternate and taper at both ends, with a few very small teeth on the edges. The snowdrop-like flowers, with yellow stamens, bloom in mid-June.

A dainty native of the Far East, the snowbell tree needs little room to grow and is suitable for planting in small gardens.

Tree in winter.

Snowbell tree *Styrax japonica*

Masses of snowy-white, delicate flowers which hang under the fan-like branches in early summer give the snowbell tree its common English name. It was brought from Japan at the end of the last century purely as an ornamental tree, but in the Far East its light, yellowish, soft and close-grained timber is used for household utensils and decorative carving.

The snowbell flowers can be best appreciated if they are seen from below, so the tree should be planted on rising ground or a grassy knoll. The snowbell thrives in sunny places on rich, lime-free soils and is quite hardy, though it may be damaged if the tissues of its twigs and buds thaw out too quickly after frost in early spring.

Other types of snowbell tree are also grown in British gardens, including one from the Mediterranean which is the source of a balsam or aromatic gum called storax. This is obtained by making incisions in the bark and then collecting the liquid that exudes from it. Balsam was formerly used in medicine to treat asthma and bronchitis, and is still burned as incense. In some European countries, hardened drops of balsam are made into rosary beads.

Mature bark is dull grey, often with orange cracks.

The snowbell tree is broader than it is tall. It can grow to 30 ft (9 m).

[Actual size]

The fruits are four-lobed capsules which turn a deep pinkish-red when ripe. They are matt, not glossy, and contain four orange-coloured seeds.

[× 2]

The light green leaves are opposite, thin and pointed, with small teeth. The small, greenish-yellow flowers have narrow petals.

The spindle, a decorative tree, grows throughout England and Wales, but is rarer in Scotland and Ireland.

Spindle *Euonymus europaeus*

The white, hard and dense wood of this small tree was used from ancient times for making spindles. The 'spinsters', usually unmarried girls, held the raw wool in one hand and rotated it on to the spindle with the other; the rotation kept the wool fibres tight and helped draw the loose wool into a thread. A round, flattish stone with a hole in the middle – a spindle whorl – was threaded over the end of the spindle to act as a primitive fly-wheel and keep the spindle turning – a device improved upon by the spinning wheel. The wood of the spindle was also known as skewerwood and pegwood, indicating its other uses; and today it makes high-quality charcoal for artists.

For most of the year the spindle is an inconspicuous shrub, but in the autumn it declares its identity with a display of dark red leaves and pinkish-red, four-lobed fruits. Because of its autumn show, the spindle is cultivated in gardens and parks as a decorative tree, and some attractive varieties have been developed.

The tree has an unpleasant smell if bruised and the fruit is an emetic. In former times the powdered leaves and seeds were dusted on the skin of children and animals to drive away lice.

Young, smooth, greenish bark later turns grey.

Spindle is a small tree or big bush reaching 20 ft (6 m) in woods and hedgerows. Cultivated forms occur in parks. The tree does particularly well on chalk soils.

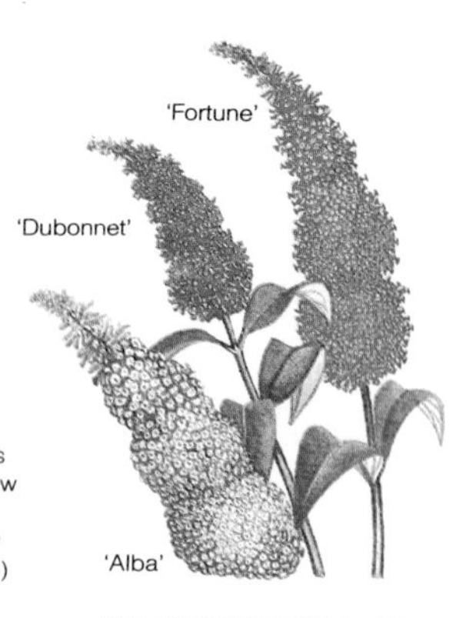

Since the first buddleias were introduced in the 19th century, many colourful varieties have been bred to enhance gardens.

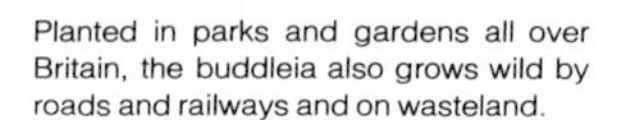

Planted in parks and gardens all over Britain, the buddleia also grows wild by roads and railways and on wasteland.

Buddleia *Buddleia davidii*

Butterfly bushes, as buddleias are sometimes called because of the attraction their flowers have for butterflies, were introduced to Britain from China by way of Russia at the end of the 19th century. Since then, the buddleia has established itself so successfully that it has become naturalised in many parts of the country, as far north as central Scotland. Its wind-borne seeds quickly sprout on any sunny patch of waste ground, provided that the soil is not heavy.

The buddleia most often seen in the wild has lavender or purple-coloured flowers, but cultivated varieties and hybrids may be white, mauve, pink or orange-yellow. All can be grown in sunny gardens and all have the same allure for butterflies. To get the best flowers, the shrub should be well pruned in March.

The name buddleia commemorates the botanist Adam Buddle, a Lincolnshire-born clergyman who specialised in the study of mosses and grasses and who wrote a completely new English *Flora* in 1708. Buddle's master-work, describing thousands of native wild plants, never found a publisher, but it was heavily drawn upon by later botanists, few of whom bothered to give credit to the author.

Round, speckled yellow fruit ripens in October. It tastes tart, but makes good preserves.

Leaves are alternate, long-pointed and finely toothed.

Dwarf quinces have a low-lying, straggling shape and grow best against a wall or fence. 36–60 in. (90–152 cm).

The dwarf quince, which is also known as 'Japonica', is widely cultivated for its bright flowers and edible fruit.

Variety *alpina* has orange flowers.

Spiny branches of the dwarf quince bear clusters of pink or brick-red flowers in April and May.

Dwarf quince *Chaenomeles japonica*

Quinces have been cultivated for many thousands of years for their fruit. Hard and bitter when eaten raw, they can be made into delicious jelly or marmalade, used sparingly to add flavour to an apple pie, or crushed and fermented into a potent wine.

The ancient Greeks regarded the quince as sacred to the goddess Aphrodite, and a symbol of love, happiness and fruitfulness. Some scholars believe that the fruit, which turns yellow in the autumn, was the 'golden apple' of Greek mythology, placed in the keeping of a dragon in the Garden of the Hesperides by Hera, wife of Zeus. Hercules was required to obtain one of the golden apples as the 11th of his 12 labours. Another legend says that the quince was the forbidden fruit of the Tree of Knowledge in the biblical story of Adam and Eve.

The quince probably originated in central Asia and came to Britain by way of the Mediterranean lands. The dwarf, or Japanese, quince and the early flowering species *Chaenomeles speciosa*, a native of China, are grown in Britain as ornamental shrubs or hedges. They have been crossed to produce various hybrids with double or single flowers of white, orange, pink, brick-red and crimson. Quince flourishes in most types of soil.

'Britzensis', or scarlet willow.

Various forms of white willow include the scarlet willow, with red twigs; the cricket-bat willow, with purple twigs and blue-grey leaves; and 'Vitellina', the yellow-twigged parent of the golden weeping willow.

Male catkins

Leaves are alternate on short stalks, finely toothed and pointed. They bear silver hairs which are denser on the underside.

'Coerulea', or cricket-bat willow.

The white willow is a shapely tree, with a stout trunk and spreading branches, that grows to 60 ft (18 m).

Dark grey bark forms network of thick ridges.

'Vitellina', or golden willow.

Yellow male catkins and green female catkins form on separate trees in spring.

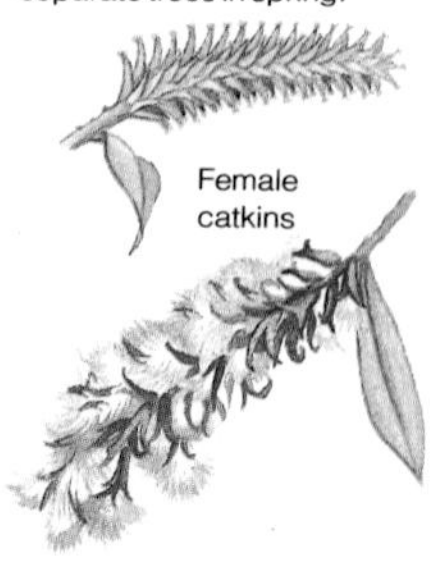

Female catkins

Female catkins ripen to produce fluffy fruits that are distributed by the wind.

White willows are native to Britain and flourish beside water in low-lying districts. Silvery leaves distinguish them.

White willow *Salix alba*

Pollarded willows used to be a frequent sight in the low-lying regions of England. The practice of pollarding involved cutting off the tops of the trees at head height, out of reach of grazing animals, to give a regular crop of small poles suitable for fencing, basketry or firewood. In modern times, however, pollarding has declined, and the willows themselves have become scarcer as they are uprooted to make the cleaning of rivers and ditches by machinery easier.

The decline of the willow may well prove to be to the eventual detriment of the countryside, for the roots of waterside trees bind the soil of the banks together and reduce erosion. One area in which white willows are still commonly seen is East Anglia, where a cultivated variety is widely grown as a source of wood for cricket bats.

Cricket-bat willows are planted in rich riverside soil, where they grow exceptionally fast. They are felled at 12–15 years old, by which time they may be 60 ft (18 m) tall. The trunk is cut into 'rounds' about 30 in. (76 cm) long, and then divided lengthwise into triangular segments with a wedge and mallet. Each triangular 'cleft' is then shaped into a bat.

Salix babylonica

The leaves of this species are not hairy like those of the golden weeping willow. The twigs are brown. The tree grows to 50 ft (15 m) in Britain.

Golden weeping willow in winter.

Branches and twigs of the golden weeping willow are a striking yellow; the leaves are hairy.

The greyish-brown bark is criss-crossed by ridges.

From its early days, the golden weeping willow produces a round cascade of yellow twigs and green leaves, reaching almost to the ground. It grows to 65 ft (20 m).

The golden weeping willow is a hybrid very popular in gardens and parks. It is often found growing beside water.

Golden weeping willow *Salix* x *chrysocoma* (or 'Tristis')

Small creeping willows were among the earliest trees to recolonise Britain after the last Ice Age. Since then, so many species have arrived here that it is very difficult to tell them apart. Most willows hybridise freely with one another. Of the weeping willows planted in the past, many were selections and crosses propagated by nurseries, and have been given different names according to different opinions about their origins.

The most commonly planted ornamental weeping willow today is golden weeping willow, thought to be a cross between *Salix babylonica* and a form of *Salix alba*. Golden weeping willow is a fast-growing tree that can be propagated by pushing a long twig into the ground; it will soon root itself and grow into a graceful sapling.

Weeping willows have traditionally been regarded as symbols of mourning. The botanical name *Salix babylonica* recalls the sadness of the Psalm: 'By the rivers of Babylon, there we sat down, yea, we wept . . . Upon the willows in the midst thereof we hanged up our harps.' In fact, the riverside trees of Babylon were poplars, not willows; the species of willow known as *Salix babylonica* is now known to have originated in China.

The hairless leaves, often twisted, are shiny green on top and grey-green below.

Green female catkins appear in May.

In summer, female catkins mature into white woolly fruits.

The familiar pollarded willows that grow along river banks are usually crack willows. They are native to Britain.

Yellow male catkins are borne on separate trees from the female catkins. The twigs break off easily.

Crack willow *Salix fragilis*

The twigs of this willow are very brittle (*fragilis* in Latin) and can be snapped off easily; from this characteristic are derived both its common and botanical names. This brittleness has proved of great value to the crack willow, as it has allowed it to develop a peculiar method of spreading far afield. Usually the tree grows by the side of a river, so many of its broken twigs fall into the water, to be carried off and lodged in the mud downstream, where they take root and grow into new trees. This willow does not, therefore, rely entirely on its seed to reproduce itself. The seeds stay fertile for only a short time, and require moist soil on which to germinate soon after they are shed.

Paradoxically, charcoal obtained from willow twigs is less brittle than other kinds, except perhaps for that made from spindle, and is therefore preferred by artists for drawing. In some places the roots of crack willow were once boiled to produce a purple dye, used at Easter to decorate hens' eggs.

Crack willows play an important role on river banks in preventing erosion by holding the soil together with their long, penetrating roots. They tolerate a polluted atmosphere, and can also grow well in salty air near the coast.

The grey bark is deeply ridged and cracked.

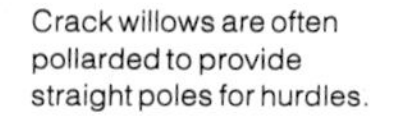

If allowed to grow to its full height, the crack willow will reach 80 ft (24 m), producing a rounded, green crown.

Crack willows are often pollarded to provide straight poles for hurdles.

Leaves are very long and narrow, green on top, with dense, silvery hairs beneath. They are sharp-pointed and without teeth; edges are rolled inwards on the underside.

Straight, flexible shoots are felted when young; male and female catkins grow on separate twigs before the leaves.

Leaf margins rolled inwards.

Female flower [× 5]

Male catkin (actual size)

Female catkin (actual size)

Male flower [× 5]

The common osier is a shrub that has been coppiced to produce many quickly grown shoots; it reaches 33 ft (10 m).

The osier is commonly grown by water, sometimes commercially to provide 'withies' for the basket-making industry.

Osier *Salix viminalis*

As this willow is a shrub rather than a tree, it is not pollarded like other willows to produce straight poles. Instead it is coppiced – that is, cut down to ground level once a year, so that the osier grows a mass of long, pliant stems, or 'withies'. These are ideal for basket-work, and in the past there was heavy demand for them in the manufacture of fish-traps, lobster-pots, chairs and countless other objects, including the shopping basket. Even today, commercial withy-growing is still practised in Britain, especially in Somerset, and the willow is still used for remedial therapy and basket-making by blind people.

When the one-year-old shoots are harvested, they are known as green willows. Brown willow is obtained by steaming the osier shoots and then drying them, the bark being left on. To make buff willow the shoots are boiled and the bark is stripped off; it is tannin from the bark that turns the rods their buff shade. White willow can be prepared only in spring, when the sap starts to rise in lengths that have been stored on end in standing water over winter. The bark is then stripped off. A traditional dance known as 'strip the willow' owes its name to the 'peeling-off' sequence of the dancers' movements.

Phillyrea is tolerant of sea winds and grows well along the south coast of Britain, but it is not commonly planted.

The dark evergreen leaves are glossy on top, with shallow teeth. Flower clusters grow where upper leaves join stems.

Small, greenish-white flowers appear in May–June. [× 4]

The small, round fruits turn purple and eventually black; each contains a single seed.

Greyish bark is smooth, or lightly ridged.

A native of the Mediterranean, phillyrea is a densely leaved, rounded tree with tiny leaf-buds. It is similar in appearance to holm oak, and can grow to 30 ft (9 m).

Phillyrea *Phillyrea latifolia*

According to Greek legend, the gods created this tree from a sea nymph. The nymph's name was Philyra, and her beauty was so great that Kronos, the youngest son of Heaven and Earth and father of Zeus, fell in love with her. To escape the watchful eye of his wife Rhea, so the legend runs, Kronos turned Philyra and himself into horses. The offspring of their love-making was the centaur Chiron, part man and part horse. Philyra was so appalled by the monstrous appearance of her son that she begged the gods to turn her into a tree; her prayer was granted.

The tree was introduced to England from the Mediterranean in 1597 by John Gerard, the herbalist, who in the same year published his celebrated *Herball.* Phillyrea was first planted in gardens belonging to the Earl of Essex.

In the formal gardens of the 17th century, phillyrea was clipped and trimmed by topiarists into ornamental shapes. Today, however, it is usually planted as a single tree and allowed to grow freely. Most types of soil suit it, and the tree is not harmed by polluted atmospheres. The alternative name of jasmine box is a reference to the tree's sweet-scented spring flowers and its use as an alternative to box in topiary.

The willow-like leaves, about 3 in. (7·5 cm) long, are very short-stalked and droop from spiny twigs. They are alternate and untoothed, dark green on top and silver-haired beneath. The acid-tasting orange berries stay on the tree all winter.

The sea buckthorn has been widely planted as an ornamental shrub for its attractive berries and foliage.

This spiny shrub sometimes sprawls along the ground in windswept sites. It usually grows only to 5–8 ft (1·5–2·5 m), but can become a small sturdy tree in more sheltered places.

Female flower [× 4]

Male flower [× 4]

Male and female flowers grow on separate bushes in clusters within angles of twigs. They are small and green, appearing Mar.–Apr.

Sea buckthorn *Hippophae rhamnoides*

Pollen grains of sea buckthorn have been found in lake deposits dating back more than 10,000 years. These show that it was one of the pioneer trees that brought vegetation back to Britain in the bleak and desolate centuries following the last Ice Age. No doubt it colonised the beds of shingle left by glaciers and rivers, in much the same way as it does in central Europe today. Sea buckthorn is able to sucker – to spread by growing new bushes from outlying roots – and in this way soon stabilises the ground, binding the soil together with its roots and forming thickets.

Like other pioneer trees, sea buckthorn needs plenty of light and space in which to grow; and its associated root bacteria take nitrogen from the air and 'fix' it in the ground in a form that is available to plants. But these characteristics have been the tree's undoing, for no sooner has it created a stable, fertile soil than bigger trees encroach and steal the light and space it needs. As a result, the plant now grows naturally only by the sea in Britain.

The generic name *Hippophae* is derived from the Greek words meaning 'to brighten the horse', suggesting that the juice of the berries may have been used in the past to give the coats of horses a healthy shine.

Leaves are opposite and pointed, with toothed margins. They appear after the flowers.

Stem is hollow with pith at junctions. Bark is pitted with breathing pores.

Four-petalled yellow flowers are borne in clusters on stems from previous year. The shrub flowers Mar.–Apr.

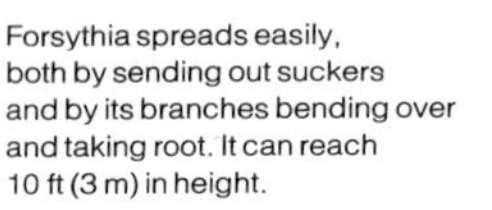

Forsythia spreads easily, both by sending out suckers and by its branches bending over and taking root. It can reach 10 ft (3 m) in height.

Thriving in almost any garden soil, forsythias brighten the spring in parks and gardens throughout Britain.

Forsythia *Forsythia × intermedia*

Thanks to a venturesome Scot named Robert Fortune, Britain has brighter springs. Fortune roamed the scarcely known Orient in the mid-1800s, collecting botanical specimens. To Britain he brought the kumquat fruit – called *fortunella* after him – and a range of decorative plants including several species of forsythia. The hardy hybrid *intermedia*, a cross between two Chinese species, has become Britain's most widely grown spring-flowering shrub.

A profusion of March and April blossoms earns forsythia the alternative name of golden bell. It is hardy, at home on almost any soil, and resists pests, disease and air pollution. It spreads rapidly and can make an attractive and unusual hedge. Because its spring blooms bud on the previous summer's growth of branches, these old branches need to be cut back after flowering to stimulate young growth.

Other hybrids can be produced among the seven Asian and east European species of forsythia. In some cases cross-breeding results in plants with extra chromosomes and oversized flowers – variations which scientists have started to imitate artificially, by temperature control and chemical treatment.

The long tubed flower contains the male stamens with the female ovary below. [× 4]

Spurge laurel, an uncommon though native shrub, thrives on chalky soil and can tolerate deep woodland shade.

The black berries are poisonous to humans, but birds can eat them without harm. [x 2]

Small green flowers appear Feb.–Apr. in clusters among upper leaves. They are pollinated by insects.

Leaves are evergreen, up to 4½ in. (12 cm) long and thick, dark and glossy. They taper to the base and are usually clustered near the top of the plant.

Small upright branches, usually bare except at the top, may rise to more than 40 in. (100 cm) in height.

Spurge laurel *Daphne laureola*

Dwarfed by oaks, beeches and other woodland companions, this fragile-looking shrub must make the most of its meagre share of sunshine. Evergreen leaves – thick and tough enough to withstand the repeated dripping of rainwater – help it to absorb much of the light it needs for growth at times when deciduous trees are bare. It starts to blossom in winter, before a new canopy of foliage above plunges it into summer-long gloom.

Spurge laurel is neither a spurge nor a laurel, although the flowers recall those of some members of the spurge family and the leaves bear a strong resemblance to laurel leaves. That similarity is borne out in the botanical name, *Daphne*. In Greek mythology, Daphne was a river nymph who appealed to the gods to help her to resist the advances of Apollo. They turned her into a laurel bush, whereupon he donned the head-wreath of laurel leaves which the Romans later adopted as a symbol of heroism and victory.

Britain has only one other native daphne, the deciduous *Daphne mezerium*, which has pink or red flowers. However, many species from other parts of the world are cultivated in Britain for their fragrance and decorative appearance.

[× 2] [× 2]
The bisexual yellow flowers are arranged in clusters of three. Each cluster grows on a single stem emerging from a leaf axil.

The adult, willow-like leaves are alternate and 3–4 in. (7·5–10 cm) long. They are evergreen, with a blue-grey bloom.

A tall, graceful and very open tree that grows up to 100 ft (30 m).

This fast-growing eucalyptus, sometimes known as Tasmanian cider gum, is now popular as an ornamental garden tree.

Small, urn-shaped fruits, in clusters of three, contain minute seeds. [× 2]

The thin, smooth, reddish bark flakes off in patches.

Leaves of trees up to about four years old are rounded and stalkless and almost encircle the stem, growing opposite each other in pairs.

Cider gum *Eucalyptus gunnii*

Several species of gum tree, or eucalyptus, have been introduced into Britain from Australasia for their ornamental qualities. The cider gum, which comes from the cool mountain regions of southern Australia and Tasmania, is the most widespread in gardens and parks. Its round juvenile leaves, which it puts forth until it is about four years old, are widely used in flower arrangements. Cider gums thrive on most soils, apart from chalk, as far north as Scotland. In common with other gums, they do not form winter buds but continue growing; as a result their younger leaves are susceptible to frost. If a frost-damaged gum is cut down to ground level it will reshoot from the base.

Compared with some forest giants in the gum family the cider gum is small, reaching a maximum height of 100 ft (30 m). The giant *Eucalyptus regnans*, for instance, grows to more than three times that height.

Gum trees take their name from the resinous substance that they exude from their bark. The leaves of many species give off the distinctive smell of eucalyptus oil when crushed, but those of the cider gum are practically odourless. The flowers have a hinged lid that opens to allow insects to pollinate them.

Fruits are small and cup-shaped, and grow in clusters, close to the branch. [× 2]

Green juvenile leaves are replaced in the first years by long, sickle-shaped alternate leaves, grey-green in colour, with red margins and red stalks.

Yellowish-white flowers appear in August in clusters of up to ten.

Open flower [× 2]

Grey-green bark peels to leave long, pale patches.

This rugged evergreen grows to 25–30 ft (7·5–9 m). In Australia it is often no more than a bush.

The snow gum, hardiest of eucalyptuses, is well adapted to the cold. In Britain the trunk is usually single.

Snow gum *Eucalyptus niphophila*

In its native Australia, the snow gum flourishes at altitudes of 6,000 ft (1,830 m) on the tree-line – the limit beyond which trees do not grow. At that height the snow gum has to endure snow and frost, and so it is hardy enough to withstand also the rigours of the British climate. Like the cider gum, it has become a popular ornamental tree, valued for the attractive colours of its buds and bark.

By comparison with the blue gum, *Eucalyptus globulus*, which in Australia and in the right conditions can leap upwards by 15 ft (4·5 m) in a single year, the snow gum grows slowly, rarely adding more than 40 in. (100 cm) in 12 months. When mature, it is one of the smallest of the eucalyptuses, making it suitable even for small gardens.

Most gums grow in dry places where the sunlight is intense and their leaves are specially adapted to reduce water loss. They are protected by a waxy covering and contain oil-secreting glands – the source of eucalyptus oil used in medicines. In strong light, the adult leaves turn their edges to the sun, to present the smallest surface area to direct sunlight; as a result, gum trees cast little shade on the ground below them.

TREES WITH MAPLE-LIKE LEAVES

Many trees outside the maple family have leaves closely similar in shape. They include the familiar hawthorn and London plane, as well as the less common guelder rose and wild service tree. The shape and number of the lobes assist identification.

Leaves silver beneath

Silver maple

Silver maple
Acer saccharinum

Leaves opposite, 3–6 in. (7·5–15 cm) long, five-lobed and deeply divided. Page 133

Red maple
Acer rubrum

Leaves opposite, 3–4 in. (7·5–10 cm) long, with three to five shallow lobes. Page 132

Rounded lobes

Field maple

Field maple
Acer campestre

Leaves opposite, 3 in. (7·5 cm) long, deeply divided, with few blunt teeth. Page 130

White poplar
Populus alba

Leaves alternate, $3\frac{1}{2}$ in. (9 cm) long and felted white beneath. Page 139

Fig
Ficus carica

Leaves 12 in. (30 cm) long, with wavy margins. Page 140

Hawthorn
Crataegus monogyna

Leaves alternate, $1\frac{1}{2}$–3 in. (4–7.5 cm) long, toothed and deeply divided. Page 144. Midland hawthorn, *Crataegus laevigata*, is similar. Page 145

Middle lobe absent

Tulip tree

Tulip tree
Liriodendron tulipifera

Leaves alternate 4–6 in. (10–15 cm) long, with four lobes. Page 141

Pointed lobes

Three lobes

Snake-bark maple
Acer rufinerve
Leaves opposite, $3\frac{1}{2}$ in. (9 cm) long; margins have small teeth. Page 134

Guelder rose
Viburnum opulus
Leaves opposite, 2 in. (5 cm) long; margins have coarse teeth. Page 143

Five to seven lobes

Smooth Japanese maple

Smooth Japanese maple
Acer palmatum
Leaves opposite, $2\frac{3}{4}$ in. (7 cm) long, with five to seven long pointed lobes, small teeth. Page 135. Downy Japanese maple, *Acer japonicum*, has 7–11 lobes. Page 135

Sweet gum
Liquidambar styraciflua
Leaves alternate, 6 in. (15 cm) long, with five long pointed lobes with small teeth. Page 137

Cappadocian maple
Acer cappadocicum
Leaves opposite, 3 in. (7·5 cm), five long pointed lobes, no teeth. Page 131

Cappadocian maple

Sycamore
Acer pseudoplatanus
Leaves opposite, 7 in. (18 cm) long, with five lobes with large regular teeth. Page 128

Norway maple
Acer platanoides
Leaves opposite, $4\frac{1}{2}$ in. (12 cm) long, with five lobes with a few large teeth; lobes and teeth have long points. Page 129

London plane
Platanus × hispanica
Leaves alternate, 8 in. (20 cm) long, with five lobes with few spiky teeth. Page 138

Wild service tree
Sorbus torminalis
Leaves alternate, 4 in. (10 cm) long, with five toothed lobes; lower pair are at right-angles to leaf-stalk. Page 142

The variety *atropurpureum* has purple seeds and leaf undersides and green upper leaf surfaces.

Angle between wings is narrower than in Norway maple.

Tar spot

Galls

A common leaf fungus called 'tar spot' disfigures but does not harm the tree. *Phytoptus* galls also appear on leaves.

Sycamores grow vigorously in all parts of Britain, and often shelter farmhouses in such areas as the Yorkshire dales.

Leaves are opposite and five-lobed; the lowest lobes are not fully separated. Upper sides are dark green. The greeny-yellow flowers appear with the leaves.

The grey, fissured bark ages to pinkish-brown.

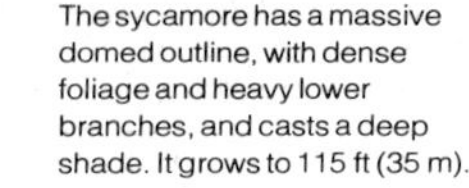

The sycamore has a massive domed outline, with dense foliage and heavy lower branches, and casts a deep shade. It grows to 115 ft (35 m).

Sycamore *Acer pseudoplatanus*

The sycamore is Europe's largest maple, growing to 115 ft (35 m), and is sometimes known as the great plane or great maple. It is unique among hardwood trees in its ability to withstand salty winds, so can be grown near the coast. On bleak uplands, especially in Scotland, it forms useful windbreaks and shelter round farmhouses; it was often planted around farms to provide shade and to keep the dairy cool.

Maturing quickly, the sycamore can be felled to provide valuable timber by the age of 60 years, though it can live for 200 years. Sycamore wood is creamy white, easy to work and does not warp; these qualities make it popular for furniture, and decoratively grained pieces are used for veneers and for musical instruments. In former days sycamore wood was used for many household utensils, and for the worktops of kitchens and dairies.

It was under a sycamore tree at Tolpuddle in Dorset that six farm labourers met in 1834 to form a society to fight starvation wages. For this deed, the so-called Tolpuddle Martyrs were sentenced to seven years' transportation to Australia. They were pardoned two years later and offered a passage home. The tree became known as the Martyrs' Tree, and still stands.

In autumn the leaves turn yellow or scarlet-brown.

The yellow flowers appear before the leaves.

The thin, light green leaves are opposite and have long points. The leaf-stalk is also long.

The angle between each wing of the seed is wider than in the sycamore.

The Norway maple, introduced in the 17th century, bears clusters of pale yellow flowers in early spring.

Bark is grey, with many small fissures.

The Norway maple is a shorter and more slender tree than the sycamore, reaching 90 ft (27 m).

Norway maple *Acer platanoides*

Harsh climatic conditions in the mountains of northern continental Europe which are its native home make the Norway maple very hardy and resistant to frost. It seeds freely, and has reproduced itself and become naturalised in Britain. In Scotland it is planted for both shelter and ornament, and in southern Britain it brightens many city streets and parks. It is suited for growing in towns because it tolerates smoke and grime. It thrives on most soils and the leaves, unlike those of some ornamental maples, do not lose their green colour on soils which contain lime.

Yellow clusters of flowers appear in early spring before the leaves. They provide a useful source of food for bees at a time of year when little other food is available. There are many ornamental forms of the Norway maple, some with variegated or purple leaves.

The young tree grows quickly but is prone to attack by grey squirrels, which strip off and eat the bark and also the sweet sap beneath. The wood is of good quality and indistinguishable from that of the sycamore, but is less useful because, coming from a smaller tree, it is not available in the larger sizes.

In autumn, leaf turns amber-yellow.

Leaves are opposite and small, with three main, round-tipped lobes and two smaller basal lobes. In summer they are dull green above, downy below.

Each pair of seed wings lies in an almost straight line. Wings are often tinged with pink.

The small yellow-green flowers form erect clusters. Emerging leaves have a pinkish tinge.

This native maple brings a red-gold glow to parks and hedges in the southern half of England early in autumn.

Bark is grey or light brown, with fine shallow fissures.

The field maple is a round-headed tree with a sinuous trunk; the ends of its branches droop, then turn up. It grows up to 85 ft (26 m).

Field maple *Acer campestre*

The decorative 'bird's-eye maple', used for furniture veneers and wall panelling, comes from the field maple. The distinctive figured pattern is obtained by cutting across the small knots which form on the trunk. At one time the wood was also used for making domestic utensils, such as drinking bowls.

All the maples produce useful wood, but field maples of timber-producing size have disappeared and not been replaced, as the wood of other maples has become more freely available. Maple wood is used for violin-making and forms the back, sides and neck of the instrument. The rippled grain used for the backs is known as 'fiddle back'. The supreme violin-maker, Antonio Stradivarius (1644–1737), was the first to use a bridge of maple to support the strings. The quality of his instruments owed much to the way in which the wood was seasoned, and to the composition of the finishing varnish.

Usually the field maple is seen only in hedgerows growing in the chalky soils of the southern half of England, and it is often cut back to form a trim hedge. In the past it was used for topiary work. If it is allowed to grow unclipped or is planted as a single tree, it can reach a considerable height.

The paired seeds are in clusters of 'keys'. Each pair has widely spread wings about $1\frac{1}{2}$ in. (4 cm) long.

Leaves are opposite with five to seven untoothed, long-pointed, triangular lobes. They are smooth except for tufts of hair in vein axils on the underside.

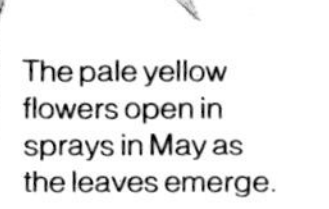

The pale yellow flowers open in sprays in May as the leaves emerge.

This tree from the Caucasus is planted in large gardens in Britain for the sake of its butter-yellow autumn foliage.

The bark is greyish-brown and smooth.

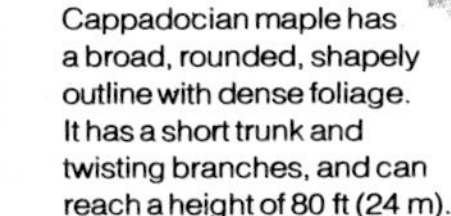

Cappadocian maple has a broad, rounded, shapely outline with dense foliage. It has a short trunk and twisting branches, and can reach a height of 80 ft (24 m).

Cappadocian maple *Acer cappadocicum*

Most maples become a delight to the eye in their autumn colours, but two park and garden cultivars of the Cappodocian maple provide a splash of colour in spring as well. The leaves of the cultivar 'Aureum' are pale yellow as they unfold in spring, turning green in summer and a rich butter-yellow in autumn.

The leaves of the other cultivar, 'Rubrum', are red when they first come out, then turn a golden yellow. Later in the summer these leaves fade to green, but in some trees there is further growth, which is yellow. The paler parts of these leaves lack chlorophyll, the chemical that normally gives leaves their green colour and absorbs energy from sunlight to power the food-manufacturing processes of trees and plants.

The Cappadocian maple is a native of the Caucasus, the Himalayas and China. It derives its name from an ancient region of Asia Minor, which is the mountainous central area of present-day Turkey. The tree was introduced to Britain about 100 years ago. It is hardy and fast-growing and does well in most soils. It never attains a great height, and is therefore being increasingly planted for ornament in large gardens.

Clusters of red flowers appear in spring before the leaves emerge.

Leaves are opposite, in pairs. Each has three to five toothed lobes. Emerging leaves have a reddish tinge, becoming yellow-green and then dark green on top; the underside is whitish, and leaf stalks are red.

The paired, reddish seeds are winged. They begin to form in May and are shed in late summer.

The red maple, a native of North America, is planted in Britain for its red spring flowers and wine-red autumn foliage.

Red maple *Acer rubrum*

Bright colour is provided by this ornamental tree throughout most of the year. It has red flowers that emerge before the leaves; its twigs and buds are red; and early in autumn its leaves turn brilliant hues of red and yellow.

When tree leaves die in autumn, the chlorophyll that gives them their green colour breaks down so that other colours in the leaf are revealed; these are produced by chemical changes brought about when abundant sunshine raises the tree's sugar content. Maples are particularly rich in sugar, so in sunny autumns bright red and purple colourings result. The young leaves are often red too, because sugar in the tree has been mobilised for spring growth.

For many years the national emblem of Canada was a stylised version of the leaf of the red maple, but the modern emblem is more like the leaf of the sugar maple. It is in eastern Canada and the United States that the red maple grows best, along the borders of streams and in swamps. Because it requires a lot of moisture for good growth, care is needed when siting an ornamental tree, for its roots will clog nearby drains in their search for moisture.

Smooth grey bark darkens and cracks with age.

Fast-growing red maple is lightly branched and has a tall slender crown. In autumn the tree turns a brilliant red. It grows to 70 ft (22 m).

Greenish-red or dark red flowers appear on the shoots in March, before the leaves.

The handsome silver maple, from eastern North America, is often planted in parks and beside main roads in Britain.

Slender branches of the silver maple thrust strongly upward, spreading near the top, to give the tree a tall, open appearance. It grows to about 100 ft (30 m).

Leaves are opposite, in pairs, and have five deeply divided lobes with large, irregular teeth. Undersides are silvery.

Paired seeds are set close together and have twisted wings.

Grey-brown bark may be flaky on older trees.

Tree in winter.

In autumn, leaves turn a delicate yellow, and sometimes a brilliant red.

Silver maple *Acer saccharinum*

Like most members of the maple family, the silver maple has sap so rich in sugar that in its North American homeland it is exploited commercially to produce both syrup and refined sugar. The tree can be tapped every year so long as it is healthy and growing in favourable conditions, such as the deep, wet soils of swamps and by riversides.

Incisions are made in the bark in February and collecting tubes are inserted. The sap is taken out daily for about six weeks. After that, the concentration of sugar in it falls, and collecting it becomes uneconomical. The collected sap is concentrated by boiling it into maple syrup; it is then sold in this form or refined into sugar. As it contains certain aromatic substances, the syrup and sugar have a distinctive flavour. The silver maple was the chief source of sugar for the early settlers of North America.

In Britain the tree yields little sugar, but it flourishes as an ornamental tree when planted on suitable sites. It is hardy and only casts a light shade. One disadvantage is that the twigs are rather brittle and easily snapped by the wind. But in light winds the tree is seen to advantage, as the undersides of the leaves reveal their silvery colour.

Leaves are opposite. Each has three shallow lobes, sharply and unevenly serrated. The small, paired seeds are very widely angled.

The tree flowers in mid-April as the leaves unfold. Both the flowers and the young leaves are an attractive yellow-green colour.

This often short-lived tree is frequently found in gardens throughout Britain. It flowers abundantly from an early age.

Snake-bark maple *Acer rufinerve*

Many gardens in Britain and Japan owe some of their beauty to this grey-budded maple, which is grown mainly for its attractively striped bark. In autumn, the leaves add their splash of orange and rust-red colour to the scene. The leaves are similar to those of the red snake-bark maple, *Acer capillipes*, with which this tree is often confused; but the bark of the red snake-bark maple is always green with white or buff stripes, whereas that of the snake-bark may be either green and white or grey and pink.

Decorative, snakeskin-like patterns on the bark of older trees are caused by the splitting of the bark's outer layer of cork. The bark of all trees is waterproof and contains cork which prevents the delicate underlying tissues from drying out, and also saves them from damage by animals and insects. As the tree grows, the cork-producing cells expand, causing the dead outer layer of cork to split.

Snake-bark maple was brought to Britain from the Far East in 1879. Although it is hardy and can be grown in most soils, its upper leaves are inclined to colour early. It is mainly grown in large gardens, both in Britain and in Japan; but in fact it is also suited to smaller gardens, as it does not reach a great height.

Bark is green and white or grey and pink.

A very open tree, which can spread from a short trunk to a full bush. The upper branches are likely to colour early. It grows to about 42 ft (13 m).

'Atropurpureum'

'Dissectum Atropurpureum'

Two common cultivars are the purple-leaved 'Atropurpureum', and 'Dissectum Atropurpureum', which has deeply divided leaves.

The smooth Japanese maple is one of the smallest of maples. It is particularly popular in Britain as a garden tree.

The leaves have five to seven long, pointed lobes, with a hairless leaf-stalk. The winged seeds, which are set in wide-angled pairs, are about ⅜ in. (1 cm) long.

Downy Japanese maple

Acer japonicum

The autumn leaves, golden and red-fringed, have 7–11 short lobes and a hairy leaf-stalk. The deep red flowers emerge with the young greenish leaves.

The bark is rich brown, turning grey when old.

Tree in winter.

This bushy tree, with its sinuously ascending stem and branches, may grow to 50 ft (15 m).

Smooth Japanese maple *Acer palmatum*

Almost every Japanese garden boasts a maple, either in the form of a full-sized tree or bush, or as a *bonsai*– a miniature tree grown in a pot. Maples have been crossed and selected in Japan for more than 300 years. Regular expeditions were made into the countryside to view maples growing wild and to look for new forms to cultivate; *Acer palmatum*, which is naturally a very variable species, was particularly suited to this purpose.

A bewildering number of cultivars of smooth Japanese maple have been produced, varying in leaf form and colour. Some have broad leaves; some have leaves narrow and deeply incised. Colours range through green, purple and yellow to variegated forms with areas of pink or white. Many of these cultivars have delightful Japanese names which mean 'beautiful little red girl', 'coral tower', 'dancing peacock' and so on.

Maples vary in their requirements. Some coloured forms are affected by hot, direct afternoon sun, even in Britain. Too much fertiliser can alter growth and leaf form, and too much shade can cause variegated forms to revert to green. Downy Japanese maple, introduced to Britain in 1864, thrives best in situations that are sheltered and well-drained.

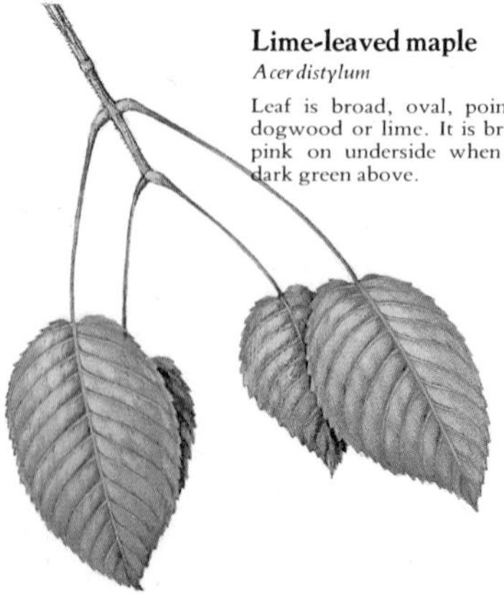

Lime-leaved maple

Acer distylum

Leaf is broad, oval, pointed like dogwood or lime. It is brownish-pink on underside when young, dark green above.

Japanese maple

Acer palmatum dissectum 'Red filigree lace'

Finely divided leaves give lacy appearance and are always red.

Hornbeam maple

Acer carpinifolium

Leaf lance-shaped like hornbeam, sharp-toothed. Green leaves turn pale yellow and brown in autumn.

Japanese maple

Acer palmatum 'Aureum'

Leaf has five lobes. Variegated colours turn yellow in autumn; margins are always pink.

Norway maple

Acer platanoides

Leaf has five pointed lobes with large teeth. Green when young, yellow or occasionally crimson in autumn. Cultivar 'Crimson King' always crimson.

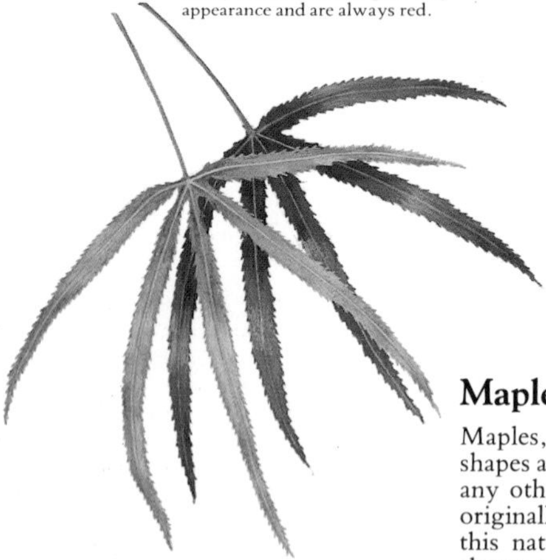

Japanese maple

Acer palmatum 'Koto ito komachi'

Leaves are stranded, usually forming five very long, narrow lobes. Green when young, they turn red in autumn.

Maples in many forms and colours

Maples, particularly Japanese maples, have a wider range of leaf shapes and a greater variety of summer and autumn colours than any other trees. Some are natural variations, and gardeners – originally in Japan and more recently in Europe – have exploited this natural variability to produce numerous cultivars. Leaf shapes range from the five lobes typical of most maples, to very deeply divided leaves, some of which are no more than strands. Other maple leaves resemble the leaves of quite different trees. The cultivars of Japanese maple fall into five leaf shape groups – ordinary hand-shaped leaves, dissected leaves, deeply divided leaves, strand-like leaves and variegated leaves. A few of the many leaf shapes and colours of maples are shown on this page.

Female flower

Male flowers

The five-lobed leaves are alternate, unlike those of maples. The round spiky fruit hangs from a long stalk and turns from green to brown when ripe.

Male flowers are round and yellow and grow in a cluster; female flowers are small and borne in a dense round head.

Brilliant autumn colours make the sweet gum a popular ornamental tree in parks in central and southern England.

Oriental sweet gum

Liquidambar orientalis

The leaf of this related species from Turkey is much smaller and more deeply divided, with a very long middle lobe.

The brown, deeply fissured bark becomes corky.

A conical crown that grows wider and more rounded with age characterises the sweet gum, which can reach a height of 80–85 ft (25 m).

Sweet gum *Liquidambar styraciflua*

In the 16th century, Philip II of Spain sent a naturalist named Hernandez to Mexico – which had been conquered by the Spaniards under Cortés in 1519 – to report on the natural products of the country. One of the trees he described was the sweet gum, which he called 'liquid amber', from the colour and texture of the gum it produces. About a century later, in 1681, the tree was introduced to England as an ornamental tree.

Although it does not like chalky soils or dry situations, it is hardy in Britain and grows on most other soils where there is adequate moisture. As its branches are not wide-spreading, it could be more frequently planted as a street tree. Like the red maple, which it much resembles, the sweet gum produces brilliant autumnal colours, ranging from bright scarlet to deep red, lemon and purple.

The sweet gum has no commercial value in Britain, but in the southern and eastern states of America it is still grown for its gum – which is used in adhesives, salves, perfumes and incense. The timber is of good quality, and in the United States is used to make 'satin wood' furniture. The oriental sweet gum was introduced in 1750 and is occasionally seen in Britain.

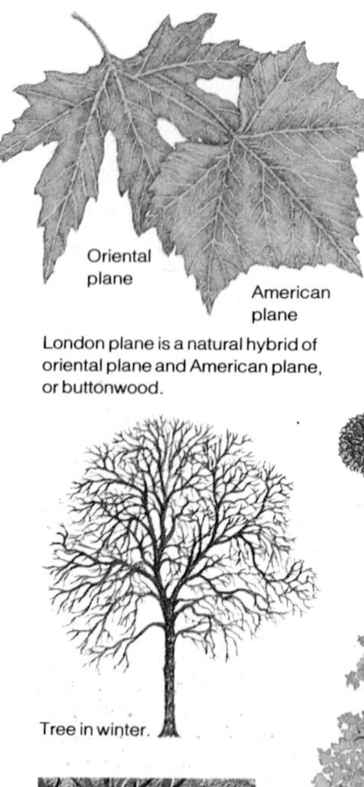

London plane is a natural hybrid of oriental plane and American plane, or buttonwood.

Tree in winter.

Leaves are alternate, with five lobes, and measure about 6 in. (15 cm) across. Bobble-like fruits do not drop, but remain on the tree during the winter – an advantage when planes are planted in cities, as pavements remain clear.

Reddish female flowers grow at the shoot tips; the yellow male flowers are further back.

Hardy and stately London planes have a domed crown, and thick, twisting branches. They grow to 100 ft (30 m).

Large bark plates flake off to leave creamy patches.

This tree is a useful avenue tree; it thrives on most soils and withstands heavy pruning and pollution.

London plane *Platanus × hispanica*

Many London planes planted 200 years ago are still growing vigorously in the squares of London. The plane survived as one of the few trees that could thrive in the soot-laden atmosphere of cities before the passing of the Clean Air Act. Its shiny leaves are easily washed clean by the rain and it sheds its bark regularly in large patches, preventing the tree from becoming stifled under a layer of sooty, sulphurous grime.

The fast-growing London plane is a hybrid between the western, or American, plane, and the eastern or oriental plane. It was first described in 1670 from a specimen growing in the Oxford Botanic Gardens, to which it may have been sent by John Tradescant the younger (1608–62), gardener to Charles I. Tradescant's father had established a 'nursery garden' for the study of plants at Lambeth in south London, and it passed on his death to his son. The records of the Tradescant garden show that both parent planes were growing there, so the conditions for producing a cross existed.

The wood from the London plane is hard and fine-grained, resembling that of beech. It is sold under the name of 'lace wood' because of the delicate tracery of its grain pattern.

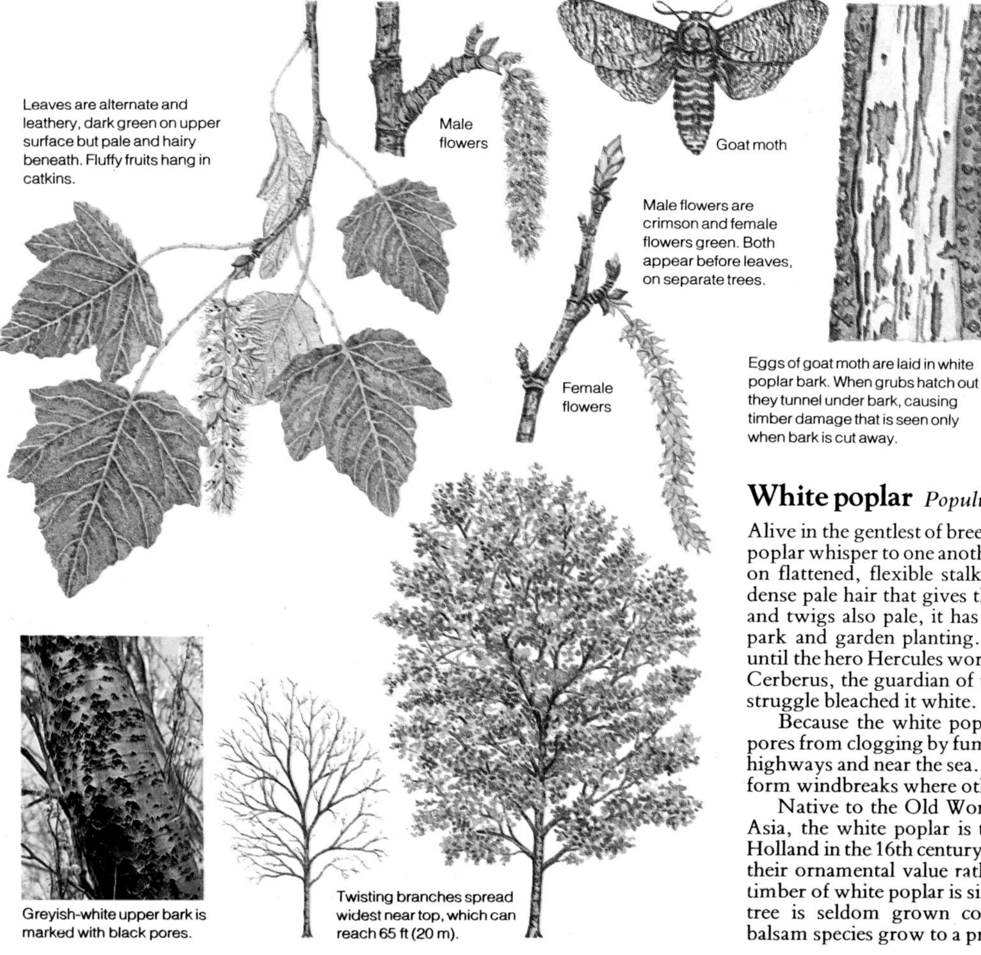

Leaves are alternate and leathery, dark green on upper surface but pale and hairy beneath. Fluffy fruits hang in catkins.

Male flowers are crimson and female flowers green. Both appear before leaves, on separate trees.

Eggs of goat moth are laid in white poplar bark. When grubs hatch out they tunnel under bark, causing timber damage that is seen only when bark is cut away.

White poplars, although smaller than most other poplars, are hardy trees, often grown as shelter belts.

Greyish-white upper bark is marked with black pores.

Twisting branches spread widest near top, which can reach 65 ft (20 m).

White poplar *Populus alba*

Alive in the gentlest of breezes, the trembling leaves of the white poplar whisper to one another with a sound like rain. The leaves, on flattened, flexible stalks, are covered underneath with the dense pale hair that gives the tree its name. With its upper bark and twigs also pale, it has a unique beauty which is prized for park and garden planting. In Greek legend the tree was black until the hero Hercules wore a garland of it during his battle with Cerberus, the guardian of the underworld. His sweat from the struggle bleached it white.

Because the white poplar's leaf hairs protect its breathing pores from clogging by fume particles or salt, it flourishes beside highways and near the sea. It suckers freely and can be grown to form windbreaks where other trees will not survive.

Native to the Old World from Western Europe to Central Asia, the white poplar is thought to have been brought from Holland in the 16th century, when trees were first recognised for their ornamental value rather than for their practical uses. The timber of white poplar is similar to that of other poplars, but the tree is seldom grown commercially because the black and balsam species grow to a profitable size much more quickly.

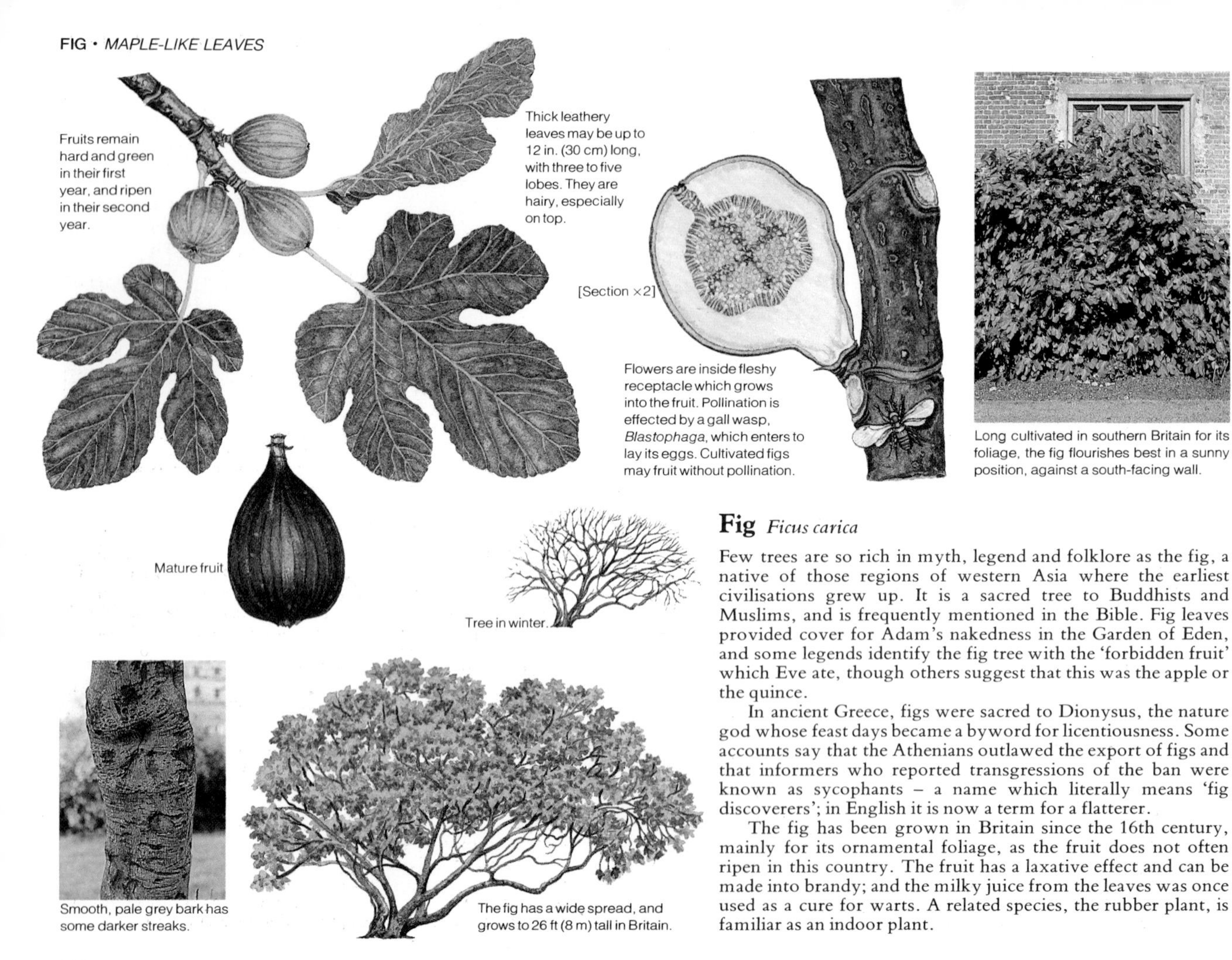

Long cultivated in southern Britain for its foliage, the fig flourishes best in a sunny position, against a south-facing wall.

Smooth, pale grey bark has some darker streaks.

The fig has a wide spread, and grows to 26 ft (8 m) tall in Britain.

Fig *Ficus carica*

Few trees are so rich in myth, legend and folklore as the fig, a native of those regions of western Asia where the earliest civilisations grew up. It is a sacred tree to Buddhists and Muslims, and is frequently mentioned in the Bible. Fig leaves provided cover for Adam's nakedness in the Garden of Eden, and some legends identify the fig tree with the 'forbidden fruit' which Eve ate, though others suggest that this was the apple or the quince.

In ancient Greece, figs were sacred to Dionysus, the nature god whose feast days became a byword for licentiousness. Some accounts say that the Athenians outlawed the export of figs and that informers who reported transgressions of the ban were known as sycophants – a name which literally means 'fig discoverers'; in English it is now a term for a flatterer.

The fig has been grown in Britain since the 16th century, mainly for its ornamental foliage, as the fruit does not often ripen in this country. The fruit has a laxative effect and can be made into brandy; and the milky juice from the leaves was once used as a cure for warts. A related species, the rubber plant, is familiar as an indoor plant.

Showy, tulip-like flowers are resplendent in a good summer.

Leaves have four lobes and a flattened top, and are borne on long stalks.

Planted as an ornamental tree, the tulip tree with its trembling leaves resembles the poplar in general appearance.

The brown, bud-like collection of fruits is unique in shape; it breaks up into long-winged individual fruits.

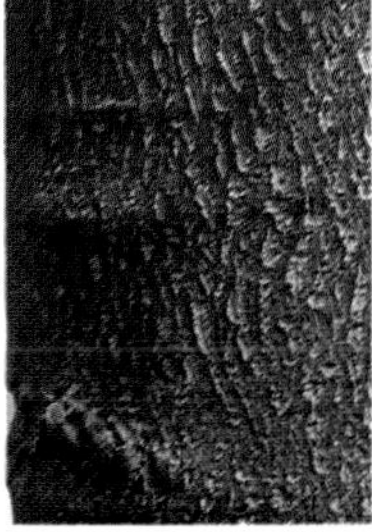

Smooth young bark later develops rough ridges.

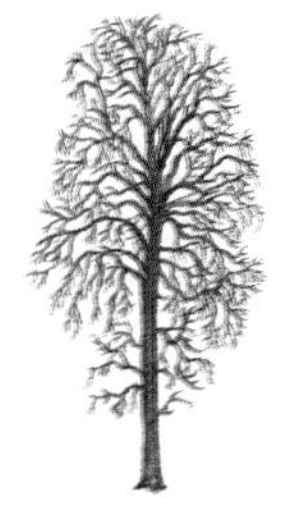

The rich yellow or russet leaves remain on the tree until late November. It grows to 115 ft (35 m).

Tulip tree *Liriodendron tulipifera*

North American Indians used to call the tulip tree 'canoe wood', since canoes to carry up to 20 people could be hollowed out of a single log. In its native habitat the trunk often reaches a height of 50 ft (15 m) before it branches. In addition to the North American species, there is also a Chinese tulip tree that has more deeply divided leaves.

The tree was introduced to Britain by the Tradescants, father and son, gardeners to Charles I. They described it in 1656 as 'Tradescant's white Virginia poplar', because the leaves flutter on their long, slender stems like those of poplars. This movement of the leaves increases the flow of air around them, so speeding up the rate of transpiration and the passage of water through the tree. The tree's modern name is derived from the tulip-like flowers of older trees.

Like the poplar, the tulip tree grows best on deep, moist soils. The timber is of good quality, especially from trees that are encouraged to grow rapidly. The sapwood, known as canary whitewood or yellow poplar, is soft and easily worked, and is commonly used to make 'white wood' kitchen furniture. The bark, which is bitter to taste, has quinine-like properties.

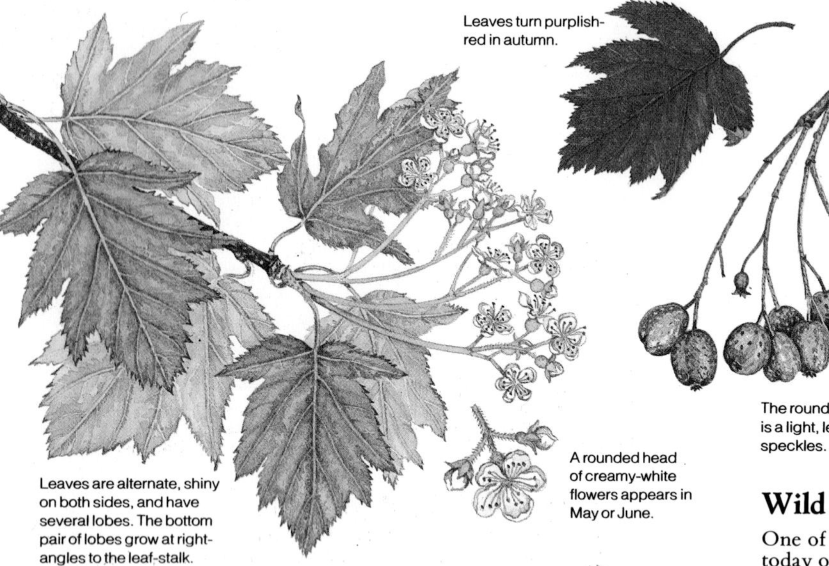

Leaves turn purplish-red in autumn.

The seeds in fruit are brown. [Actual size]

Leaves are alternate, shiny on both sides, and have several lobes. The bottom pair of lobes grow at right-angles to the leaf-stalk.

A rounded head of creamy-white flowers appears in May or June.

The rounded fruit, borne in clusters, is a light, leathery brown with speckles. It ripens in September.

Although a native of Europe, this tree is uncommon in Britain, growing mainly in Kent, occasionally in gardens.

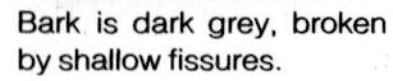

Bark is dark grey, broken by shallow fissures.

Ascending branches form a conical shape when tree is young, but broaden into a spreading, domed head with maturity; up to 65 ft (20 m).

Wild service tree *Sorbus torminalis*

One of the rarest of Britain's native trees, the wild service tree today occurs only singly in patches of old woodland of oak and ash. In the past, however, the tree was much more widespread – it has even been identified in the charcoal found on the sites of pre-Roman settlements. The tree's disappearance from its old habitat is probably due to the depredations of the charcoal burners in bygone days, coupled with the fact that it grows only slowly and does not germinate freely.

Superficially the wild service tree resembles a maple in leaf shape and autumn colouring, but its leaves are alternate. Its unusual name is apparently a corruption of the Latin genus name of *Sorbus*. A local name for the tree in Kent and Sussex, the chequer tree, may be derived from the way the bark peels off in rectangular strips, producing a chequered effect; this name has been adopted by many public houses called The Chequers.

The gritty fruit of the wild service tree used to be sold in south-east England as the 'chequers berry' and eaten as a cure for colic and dysentery, as the acid-tasting berries have a binding effect. Because of this medicinal use, the tree was known locally as the 'griping service tree'.

Small, fertile flowers are surrounded by bigger, showy, infertile flowers. [Actual size]

Leaves are opposite, with three to five lobes, smooth on top and hairy below; the base is flat and the edge has large teeth. Flower-heads are dense and white.

The leaves turn a dull, loganberry red in autumn.

This spreading shrub has few branches and grows to 13 ft (4 m). It bears fragrant flowers in May–June and red berries in autumn.

The drooping berries often stay hanging after the leaves have fallen.

This shrub grows wild on damp ground and in oak woods, and brightens garden shrubberies in several cultivated forms.

Guelder rose *Viburnum opulus*

Guelder rose was better named in former times when it was called water or swamp elder; these old names point to the elder-like berries of this native shrub and its preference for growing in damp situations. It is one of the shrubs found in wet areas of land grown over with low bushes. In such sites it flourishes alongside other shrubs, such as alder buckthorn and sallow, and trees such as birch and alder.

The name 'guelder' rose correctly refers only to an unusual form of the wild tree, which arose in the Dutch province of Guelderland about 400 years ago. This form produces big but sterile white flowers, which bunch together in a tight head and earn it the alternative name of snowball tree. As it is sterile, the snowball tree can only be propagated by bending its branches to the ground and letting them layer themselves there.

In the original wild form of the shrub, two types of flower are produced in the same head. The showy, outer flowers, which are sterile, attract insects to the smaller, fertile flowers farther in. In the snowball tree, the fertile flowers have disappeared and the showy ones have taken over the whole head. The leaves, bark and berries of the guelder rose are all poisonous.

Hawthorn berries are winter food for many birds, including redwings and fieldfares. They can be made into a jelly rich in vitamin C.

Leaves are alternate, with deeply divided lobes and paired stipules at the base of each leaf. The showy white flower heads have a sickly sweet scent.

Quick-sprouting hawthorns can grow almost anywhere and have been used for centuries as field boundaries.

Each fruit contains a single seed.

Fleshy fruits, called haws, turn dark wine-red in the autumn.

Bark is greyish-brown, with many small scales.

Hawthorns are often trimmed, but left untended they can reach 45 ft (14 m) in height.

Hawthorn *Crataegus monogyna*

Fast-growing, sturdy hawthorn makes an almost impenetrable barrier when it is cut back and laid. During the land enclosures, between the 16th and 19th centuries, hawthorns were planted in their thousands in the hedges with which landowners surrounded their estates. In recent years, the hedges have been destroyed to make mechanised farming easier and the hawthorn's sharp spines have been replaced by electric fences or barbed wire.

Hawthorns, sometimes called 'may' or 'quickthorn', were associated by early Christians with Joseph of Arimathea, owner of the tomb in which Jesus was placed after his crucifixion. Joseph was said to have planted his hawthorn staff in the ground during a visit to Glastonbury in Somerset, and it sprouted to produce a 'Holy Thorn' that blooms at Christmas. The thorn 'Biflora' is still found in the Glastonbury area.

Another legend links the hawthorn with licentious pagan and medieval rites to greet the advent of summer. This legend probably arose because hawthorn blossoms in mid-May – around May Day in the unreformed Christian calendar. In country areas, destruction of a hawthorn is believed to invite peril, and to bring the blossom indoors is to court disaster.

'Paul's Scarlet'

There are many ornamental forms. These may have double or single flowers, which may be white, pink or red.

Leaves are alternate. Lobes are more rounded and shallower than on common hawthorn, with stipules at the base of most leaves. The flowers are white.

Fruits are rounder and redder than those of common hawthorn.

Each fruit contains two seeds. [Actual size]

Much less frequent than common hawthorn, this tree occurs in southern England on heavy soils and in woodlands.

'Rosea Pleno-flore'

The Midland hawthorn is a thorny, densely branched tree with a fluted bole. 25–30 ft (7·5–9 m).

Midland hawthorn *Crataegus oxyacanthoides*

Unlike the more abundant common hawthorn, Midland hawthorn is usually found as a tree rather than as a hedge plant. It differs, too, in being more tolerant of shade, so that it is often found in woodland and it prefers heavy clay soils.

The tree, which has a characteristic fluted bole, is probably best known for its garden cultivars, many of them hybrids between this species and the common hawthorn with which it crosses freely. One of the most spectacular of these is 'Paul's Scarlet', which has bright red flowers. There are many other highly decorative hybrids, frequently found in parks and gardens. The flowers may be single or double, and pink, white or scarlet in colour. All make excellent ornamental trees.

Hawthorn rapidly colonises any open space: the fruits, or haws, are eaten greedily by birds and the seeds are spread in their droppings. When Britain's rabbit population was devastated by the myxomatosis epidemic of the 1950s, hawthorn and other trees and shrubs quickly invaded areas which had previously been kept open by grazing rabbits. Downlands, where sheep grazing had also declined, were especially vulnerable and soon covered with dense scrub.

TREES WITH LOBED LEAVES

The indenting of the margin of each leaf to create a series of lobes is a characteristic feature of many species of oaks, and of some other trees. The lobes can be rounded or sharp-pointed. The leaves of all these trees are arranged alternately.

Long pointed lobes

Red oak

Red oak
Quercus rubra
Leaves 5–9 in. (12.5–23 cm) long; matt on both sides. Page 153

Scarlet oak
Quercus coccinea
Leaves 5–6 in. (12·5–15 cm) long; shiny on both sides. Page 152

Pin oak
Quercus palustris
Leaves 3–6 in. (7·5–15 cm) long; sharp, deep lobes. Page 154

Many lobes

Turkey oak
Quercus cerris
Leaves $3\frac{1}{2}$–5 in. (9–12·5 cm) long; deep irregular lobes, stipules at leaf base. Page 157

Hungarian oak

Hungarian oak
Quercus frainetto
Leaves 6–10 in. (15–25 cm) long; regular lobes, largest near tip. Page 155

Shallow pointed lobes

Lucombe oak
Quercus × hispanica
Leaves $1\frac{1}{2}$–$4\frac{1}{2}$ in. (4–12 cm) long; dark shiny green above, grey-green and hairy below. Page 156

Lucombe oak

Shallow rounded lobes

English oak
Quercus robur
Leaves $3\frac{1}{2}$–5 in. (9–12·5 cm) long; small ear-like extensions at base of leaf. Page 148

Sessile oak
Quercus petraea
Leaves 3–5 in. (7·5–12·5 cm) long; with wedge-shaped leaf base. Page 149

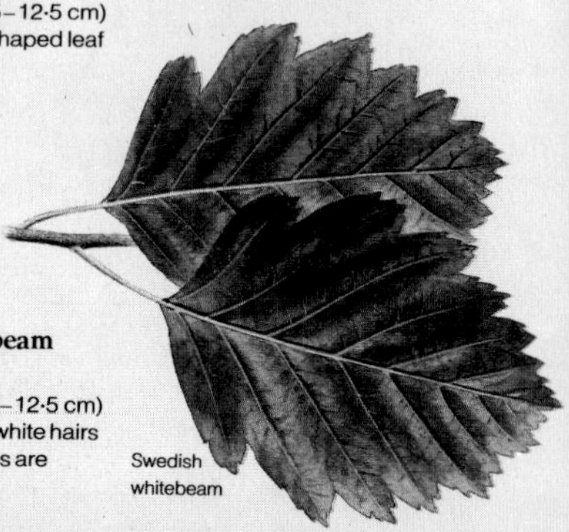

Sessile oak

Swedish whitebeam
Sorbus intermedia
Leaves 3–5 in. (7·5–12·5 cm) long; covered with white hairs on underside. Lobes are toothed. Page 147

Swedish whitebeam

The flowers, borne in dense clusters, are whitish, with pale pink anthers.

Underside

The broad, shallow-toothed leaves are alternate, with lobes that are more pronounced near the base of leaf than at the tip. They are green on top, yellowish grey-green and hairy below. The bunched, oblong-ovoid fruits are scarlet.

The soft, grey-green foliage of Swedish whitebeam is a feature of streets and parks throughout Britain.

Tree in winter.

The bark has horizontal rings of breathing pores.

A small, compact tree with a dense, broad-domed crown on a short bole. It grows to 50 ft (15 m).

Swedish whitebeam *Sorbus intermedia*

Town dwellers need not travel far to find the Swedish whitebeam, for its chief use is as a street tree. It was introduced to Britain from Scandinavia many years ago, and in some places has become naturalised by bird-sown seeds from its berries. The Swedish whitebeam is attractive at all times of the year. In spring, white flowers with pink stamens appear. The leaves are dark green, with a white underside, and turn to an attractive yellow in the autumn, when bright red berries crown the tree.

There are many reasons why the tree is suitable for urban planting. Apart from its decorative appeal, its round-headed shape and relatively short life mean that the tree does not get large and so require constant lopping. The leaf fall is slight, and the berries are so quickly taken by birds that they do not drop and litter the pavements.

The texture and colour of the underside of the leaves solve two problems in town sites. Firstly, the hairy surface reduces the amount of water given off, thereby compensating for the restricted water supply. Secondly, the white colouring protects the leaves from being damaged by reflected light from pavements and the walls of buildings.

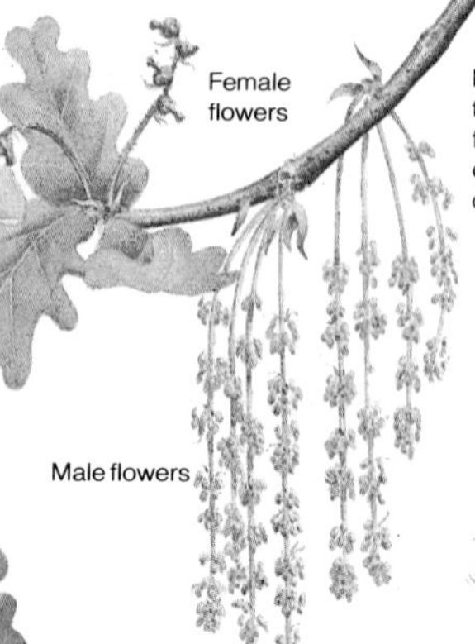

Flowers and leaves appear together in May. Male flowers hang in slim catkins; female flowers occur at tips of shoots.

Even in winter the oak supports many forms of life. Insect larvae hibernate in its bark.

Oaks in such areas as the New Forest are among Britain's oldest trees, their branches resembling stags' heads.

Leaves are alternate and almost stalkless, with 'ears' at the base and four or five lobes on each side. Acorns often in pairs on long stalks.

Young bark, smooth and shiny, becoming fissured.

Large branches rise from a short trunk to form a massive crown, rising to 115 ft (35 m).

English oak *Quercus robur*

Druids in Celtic Britain held the oak tree sacred and gathered mistletoe from its boughs for their secret rites. Ever since those days the English oak has been the 'king' of British trees. Not for nothing did the botanists name it *robur*, 'sturdy'. Its timber became the foremost construction material, for it was strong and durable and could be grown into the curved shapes suitable for the cruck frames of houses and the knees, or frame supports, of ships.

By the time of Elizabeth I, felling of oak trees had become so extensive that laws had to be passed to protect the tree. Later, the demands of the navy led to the extensive planting of oaks in royal forests; many of the trees planted for this purpose survive today, to give pleasure to the countrygoer.

Tall, lightly branched trees are still in demand for oak panelling and for furniture, in which the silvery grain can be displayed to advantage. The acorns were once an animal foodstuff of prime importance, feeding the pigs that were turned loose in the forest in the autumn – a right of 'pannage' that is still jealously guarded by commoners living in the New Forest. The oak supports more insect species than any other British tree.

Female flowers

Male flowers

Male flowers resemble those of English oak, but bud-shaped female flowers are stalkless.

Leaf bases are wedge-shaped, without the 'ears' of English oak and with distinct stalks. The acorns are stubbier, without stalks.

Sessile oak is the dominant native oak of the less-fertile, wetter northern and western upland regions of Britain.

Sessile oak *Quercus petraea*

After humans discovered how to separate iron from its ore by roasting it, timber that would produce steadily burning charcoal to heat furnaces became a valued crop. Oak made excellent charcoal, and in the north and north-west of Britain the iron smelters' furnaces were fed by charcoal from the sessile oak, which tolerates the lighter, more acid, less fertile soils of the region. Although much woodland was cleared to supply this demand, the use of coppicing provided a renewable energy resource.

The sessile oak and the English oak are Britain's two native species of oak. The word 'sessile' means unstalked and refers to the acorns which are stalkless, unlike those of the English oak. The leaf stalks of the sessile oak, however, are longer than those of the English oak.

Oak bark used to be a source of tannin, a substance widely used for making leather from hides until man-made chemicals replaced it. After the hides had been softened in a lime pit, and all the hairs and flesh removed, they were passed through tanning baths containing pounded-up oak bark and water. The resultant leather was then rinsed and dried.

Bark is finely cracked and ridged, as on English oak.

Branches rise at different levels from a long trunk, forming a fan-shaped crown. The tallest trees reach 130 ft (40 m).

LIFE IN AN OAK WOOD

Oak woodland, mixed with elm, became established in Britain around 9,000 years ago. Few kinds of woodland are so rich in life as an oak wood. This is partly due to the fact that it is 'climax vegetation' – the culmination of a succession of plant communities growing and competing on the same piece of ground. The soft leaves of oak rot quickly when they fall, forming a rich, mild leaf mould. These conditions support an abundance of other tree and shrub species, particularly ash, hazel and holly, and encourage a wide variety of plants to grow. These in turn provide food and cover for mammals and insects. For instance, many insects feed on oak trees, and the caterpillars of moths can strip oaks of their leaves in some years.

Buzzards

Acorns provide food for wood-pigeons, rooks, grey squirrels and mice. Smaller animals and birds fall to buzzards, sparrowhawks and owls, while badgers root in the leaf mould for earthworms and caterpillars.

Wood-pigeons

Green woodpeckers hunt insects and beetle larvae in the bark of oak trees, among which the rare purple emperor butterfly flits. The galls or growths called oak apples and the greenish-red spangle galls on oak leaves are caused by the grubs of gall-wasps.

Spangle galls

Oak apple

Purple emperor

Bramble

Plants such as primroses, violets, ferns and bramble thrive due to the rich soil and plentiful light.

Primroses

Violets

Leaf is 3–6 in. (7·5–15 cm) long and turns rich scarlet in early autumn.

Leaves are alternate, with bristle-tipped lobes and deep, semi-circular indentations. They are shiny on both sides and have long, slender stalks.

This oak provides some of Britain's richest autumn colour. It is often planted on roadsides, mainly in southern England.

Acorns are squat and fat, and grow in shallow cups. They ripen in the autumn of their second year.

The greyish bark fissures and darkens with age.

A tall-domed tree with a slender trunk and many fine upswept branches in the crown. It reaches 85 ft (26 m).

Scarlet oak *Quercus coccinea*

Henry Compton, Bishop of London in 1675, was an avid collector of exotic plants and trees with which he filled the gardens of Fulham Palace. His collection of North American trees owed much to the zeal of the Reverend John Banister, whom he had sent to North America as a missionary. In addition to his clerical duties, Banister collected specimens for the Bishop; among them was the scarlet oak, which Banister found in Virginia and sent to England in 1691.

A fast-growing tree which thrives on most soils except those that contain lime, the scarlet oak is today planted as an ornamental tree in parks and along city streets. In a dry autumn the tree turns bright scarlet, the colour spreading like a blush from branch to branch instead of appearing suddenly throughout the crown as in most other trees. Scarlet oak in its native home cannot tolerate shade, and is not found in dense woodland; it is usually scattered wherever there is adequate light.

The wood of the scarlet oak is heavy, hard and strong. But unlike that of the white oaks that are native to Britain, the timber of the scarlet oak is not resistant to decay. It is, however, imported for making whisky barrels in Scotland.

The leaf turns a dark red in autumn.

First-year acorns.

Leaves are alternate, broader than those of scarlet oak, with shorter, stouter stalks. Both sides are matt green.

The red oak is fast-growing, and is common in parks and gardens. It is often used to screen conifer plantations.

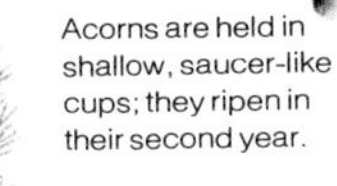

Acorns are held in shallow, saucer-like cups; they ripen in their second year.

Tree in winter.

Bark is shiny grey, turning dark brown and fissuring.

This North American oak has a large dome with straight branches. It reaches 115 ft (35 m).

Red oak *Quercus rubra*

In its choice of habitat the red oak falls between scarlet oak and pin oak, growing best on deep, well-drained soil, where it grows rapidly into a big tree. The red oak does not tolerate a lot of shade, so it prefers open situations where it can spread itself without competition. Like the other red oaks, *Quercus rubra* (the red oak proper) is planted for its autumn colour, which in this species colours the entire crown at the same time.

Red oaks in America are susceptible to a disease known as oak wilt, caused by a fungus of the same type that attacks elm trees and carried in a similar way by bark beetles. The onset of oak wilt is signalled by a browning of the leaves. Stringent precautions are being taken to prevent the disease from entering Britain; when red oak timber is imported, the beetles are killed before shipment by de-barking and fumigation.

The Forestry Commission has planted red oaks on the edge of woodland rides to add diversity and colour to commercial plantations. The tree has not, however, proved a success as a city tree: the crowns are too broad for avenues and the fallen leaves make pavements slippery in the autumn. In its native America, the tannin-rich bark was used for tanning leather.

Leaves are alternate; the acorns are green when immature, and take two years to ripen.

Acorns are very small, squat and fat, in a thin-shelled, shallow cup.

The leaves have long points and deep, narrow indentations; they are shiny on both sides. The leaf is narrower, smaller and more deeply lobed than that of the red oak *Quercus rubra*.

The pin oak is one of the less common ornamental red oaks, so called because their leaves turn red in the autumn.

Pin oak *Quercus palustris*

In the winter the short, slender twigs that stand out from the branches of this tree have a pin-like appearance at a distance, giving it one of its names. It is also known as water oak and swamp oak, both of which names describe situations in which it grows in its native North America. In Britain the tree is grown as an ornamental species, on a wide variety of soils. Although it does not grow as large as the red oak, it probably does best on soils containing a good deal of moisture.

The pin oak has brilliant red autumn colouring that starts at the tips of the shoots before spreading to the rest of the leaves on the branches. Like the other red oaks, it grows fast but suffers from yellowing of the leaves on chalky soils, which inhibit the formation of the green pigment chlorophyll.

The heavy timber of the pin oak, with its red-brown heartwood, is similar to that of other red oaks, and of poorer quality than that of the white oaks, being less resistant to decay. In its native home it has been used for making charcoal, and its bark for tanning leather. The acorn is bitter with tannin, not sweet like those of the white oaks, and is not so attractive to foraging animals. The tree is planted mainly in southern England.

Lichen often coats the smooth, grey-brown bark.

Pin oak can be recognised by its narrow, dome-shaped profile and dense crown. It can grow to 85 ft (26 m).

The acorn cup has large, loose-fitting scales.

Leaves are alternate, about 8 in. (20 cm) long with many deep lobes. They taper towards the stalk and are dark green above, grey and hairy below.

With its rapid growth and large, rich green leaves, the Hungarian oak makes a magnificent park tree in Britain.

Tree in winter.

Bark is greyish with a network of fissures.

Branches fan out to a large domed crown. The tree reaches 90 ft (27 m).

Hungarian oak *Quercus frainetto*

This stately, ornamental oak has not been widely planted in Britain, and most of the specimens found in parks and large gardens have been grafted onto the roots of other oaks. The part to which the desired tree is grafted is known as the 'stock', and it must be closely related or else the graft will not take. The piece to be added to the stock is called the 'scion'.

The essential factor in grafting is the matching of the stock and the scion while they are growing rapidly – preferably in the spring. They are bound in place and covered to prevent their drying up or becoming diseased. By grafting, vigorously growing trees can be produced much more quickly than from seed.

Like most oaks, the Hungarian oak needs plenty of space in which to grow and it thrives on all but very wet soils. Sometimes fallen oak trees have been covered by encroaching bogs and impregnated with chemicals, which act as a preservative. They are then found as 'bog oak', and their dark, almost black timber is extremely hard and heavy. Acorns from most oak trees are sweet and form a valuable food for various animals. The acorns of the Hungarian oak have the additional quality of being suitable for grinding into a form of coffee.

The acorns are half-enclosed in a mossy 'cup'. They ripen at the end of their second year.

The underside of the leaf has felted, greyish-white hairs.

First-year acorns

The small leaves are alternate, with triangular, sharp-pointed lobes. They are shiny green on top. Acorns grow singly or in pairs, on a short stalk.

This natural hybrid has been widely planted in parks and gardens in England, particularly in the West Country.

Lucombe oak *Quercus × hispanica*

The original Lucombe oak was felled by the man after whom it was named, to provide wood for his own coffin; and for many years before his death at the age of 102 he kept the boards beneath his bed. In the 1760s, Mr Lucombe – an Exeter nurseryman – discovered that the oak, a cross between Turkey and cork oaks, occurred naturally when the two parent trees grew together. He raised a number of seedlings from the acorns of Turkey oak in his nursery, and noticed one that retained its leaves in the winter like the cork oaks; this he called 'evergreen Turkey oak'. He propagated thousands of trees from it by making grafts onto ordinary Turkey oaks.

In 1792, seedlings were raised from the acorns of the Lucombe oak itself, but being a hybrid they were variable in form. Some of these were also selected and propagated by grafts. They vary in bark thickness and the extent to which they retain their leaves.

The Lucombe oak – also known as the Spanish oak – retains the timber qualities of cork oak, being of dense texture with a good close grain. But it is not a commercial timber, and trees are only grown individually, for ornamental purposes.

The corky bark is usually a light, creamy brown.

This evergreen oak has an open crown. It grows to 90 ft (27 m).

Female flowers

Male flowers

The male flowers hang in dense bunches. The female flowers are small and inconspicuous.

Acorns are borne in very 'mossy' cups, and mature in the second season.

Leaves are alternate, with deeply cut lobes. They are rough, dark green and shiny on top. Stipules occur around the leaf base.

This introduced tree grows more vigorously than native British oaks. Ascending branches are typical.

The tall broad profile of this oak makes it a handsome parkland tree. It grows to 125 ft (38 m).

Bark is more fissured and rougher than native oaks.

Turkey oak *Quercus cerris*

An earlier name for Turkey oak was wainscot oak, its timber being considered suitable only for making wall panelling. The tree was introduced from Turkey in the second half of the 19th century, when its timber was recommended for all kinds of uses. But it did not live up to expectations. Although the tree grows quickly and has a straight trunk, the timber is of poor quality. It warps easily, distorts, and is liable to split during seasoning. It cannot be used out-of-doors, as it quickly decays, so it was relegated to the role of lining and decorating living rooms.

The tree was also once known as iron oak because of the weight of its timber when green; or mossy-cupped oak, from the distinctive acorn cups which hold the bitter acorns until they ripen in the second year. The acorns are freely produced and the tree has become naturalised in many parts of southern Britain.

Turkey oak makes a distinctive ornamental tree and, unlike other oaks, it grows well on chalky soil. It is often used as the stock onto which other ornamental oaks are grafted. The tree is very late in losing its leaves in autumn, and in younger trees they persist throughout the winter in a withered state. Being shallow rooted, the tree is easily blown over.

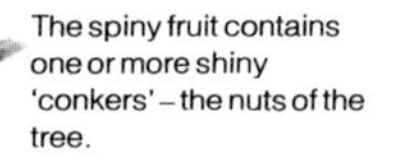

The spiny fruit contains one or more shiny 'conkers' – the nuts of the tree.

The leaf has five to seven large, thick, stalkless leaflets with pronounced veins and a long, tapering base. The flowers are a showy white spike.

White-flowered horse chestnut and red horse chestnut make attractive avenue trees, popular in parks and gardens.

Red horse chestnut

Aesculus × carnea

A common decorative hybrid between horse chestnut and the red buck-eye from North America. Leaves are darker, often smaller; flowers pink or dull red.

Bark is red-brown or dark grey-brown and scaly.

Tree in winter.

The horse chestnut, which can attain 115 ft (35 m), has arching branches that are usually turned up at their ends.

Horse chestnut *Aesculus hippocastanum*

Each autumn, schoolboys avidly gather horse chestnuts with which to play conkers. The tree was introduced to Britain from the Balkans in the late 16th century; but it was not until some 200 years later that chestnuts were used for the game. Before that, conkers – the name derives from 'conqueror' – were played with cobnuts or snail shells.

The glossy conkers give the tree its American name of 'buck-eye', as the chestnuts are said to resemble the eye of a deer. Conkers are eaten by deer and cattle, and were sometimes ground up as meal to fatten sheep. There is a tradition that the Turks once fed them to horses to cure broken wind (a respiratory disorder).

Horse chestnuts are often grown as ornamental avenue trees for their 'candles' of flowers, and were frequently planted for this purpose as early as the 17th century. The wood is pale cream or brown; it is very light and weak and of limited economic value. It is used for toys and, being absorbent, for making trays in which to store fruit. Until recently, artificial limbs were made from it, as it is light and easily shaped. The tree grows rapidly on most soils, but requires plenty of space.

The leaflets are stalked, and narrower than those of the common horse chestnut. The pyramid-shaped spikes of flowers are white, touched with pink, red or yellow.

The husks of the fruits are thin, and have no spines. The fruits contain wrinkled, glossy, dark brown nuts.

This ornamental tree is becoming popular in parks and large gardens, and on roadside verges.

Bark is grey-green or pinkish-grey and smooth.

Tree in winter.

A tall, rounded outline and steeply angled branches help to identify this tree, which can reach a height of 60–65 ft (18–20 m).

Indian horse chestnut *Aesculus indica*

The flowers of the Indian horse chetnut bloom towards the end of June – about six weeks after those of the common horse chestnut. For this reason, the tree is being increasingly planted in parks and on roadsides, to extend the flowering season after the 'candles' of common horse chestnuts have flowered in May. The later flowering of the species is valuable to bees, too, for the insect-pollinated flowers come out during an otherwise rather barren period between the spring and summer flowering of other trees and shrubs.

The tree's leaves and flowers are more delicate in appearance than those of other horse chestnuts, and the whole tree is less massive. The seeds are smaller, and of little use to 'conker' players. Many flowers and trees have developed devices to avoid self-fertilisation: in the horse chestnut, the stigma, or female part of the flower, ripens before the stamen, or male part.

The Indian horse chestnut is a native of the Himalayas, and was introduced to Britain in 1851. It requires soil with rather more moisture than other horse chestnuts. 'Sidney Pearce', a form bearing more and larger flowers than the original, was developed from the Indian horse chestnuts in Kew Gardens.

Each leaf consists of three leaflets, the middle one being on a stalk. The leaflets are bluntly lobed and have white, hairy undersides.

The paired, winged fruits are large, growing to $1\frac{1}{2}$–$1\frac{3}{4}$ in. (4–4.5 cm), and ripen when the leaves turn crimson in the autumn.

The yellow flowers open in late May, hanging in groups on the twigs. They appear with the young bronze or pink leaves.

Its decorative leaves and bark make this native of China one of Britain's most popular ornamental trees.

Tree in winter.

Paper-bark maple *Acer griseum*

Its bark makes this small, attractive maple easy to identify at any time of year. The old, dead layers of bark form thin, papery strips which peel off the trunk and branches to expose the coppery-red younger bark below, which is protecting the vulnerable growing tissues. A native of China, this maple was brought to Britain by the collector E.H. Wilson in 1901, when on an expedition to gather seeds of the elusive handkerchief tree.

In spring and summer the paper-bark maple is identifiable by its leaves, which are divided into three leaflets – only one or two rare maples have leaves of a similar shape. The leaves change colour throughout the year, being various shades of pinkish-brown in the spring before becoming green, and then turning to brilliant shades of crimson and red in the autumn. As with other maples, the fruits are wind-borne, but they are not carried any great distance from the tree, as the shape of the fruits' 'wings' is not aerodynamically efficient.

Like those of the beech and other maples, the paper-bark maple's leaves are arranged to catch as much light as possible. The lower leaves on a branch are often larger and have longer stalks than the upper leaves, so that they are not shaded by them.

The copper-coloured bark peels off like paper.

Paper-bark maple has an open, domed crown and upward-reaching branches. It is a small tree, reaching about 40 ft (12 m) in height.

Each alternate leaf consists of three leaflets, from 1–3 in. (2·5–7·5 cm) long. The leaflets are grey-green on top and have silky white hairs below. The sweet-scented but poisonous flowers hang in long chains in May and June.

Brown pods hang on the tree in winter and contain poisonous black seeds.

The yellow-garlanded laburnum is a familiar sight in many suburban gardens. It is common in streets and parks.

Scotch laburnum

Laburnum alpinum

This hardier species is distinguished by its larger, hairless leaves and brown seeds. It flowers in June, two or three weeks later than common laburnum.

Smooth, brownish bark has buff breathing pores.

A tree with ascending and arching branches, laburnum can reach a height of 23 ft (7 m).

Laburnum *Laburnum anagyroides*

One of the most poisonous trees that can be grown easily in British gardens is also one of the most popular. Thousands of small gardens have a specimen of this striking ornamental tree which produces long chains of golden-yellow flowers in the spring; these have earned the tree the name of 'golden rain'. It is a native of southern Europe and was first introduced into Britain in 1560.

Many of the trees now planted are a cross between the common and Scotch laburnum; the selected cultivars produce numerous flowers. The cross also produces fewer seeds, which makes it more suitable for planting in places where children play. The pea-like pods, which gave the tree its old name of 'peascod', attract children, especially when ripening in July and August, and at this time of year many young children are taken to hospital after eating the seeds.

The sapwood of laburnum is butter-yellow, while the heartwood is dark chocolate-brown and very hard. Before cabinet makers perfected the art of staining wood, the heartwood of laburnum was much in demand as a substitute for ebony.

TREES WITH FEATHER-LIKE LEAVES

The feather-like appearance of these leaves arises from the division of each leaf into numerous leaflets on the same stalk. The number of these leaflets varies. Leaves may be opposite or alternate; leaflets may be stalked or toothed-edged.

Opposite leaves, five to seven leaflets

Elder
Sambucus nigra

Leaves 1–3½ in. (2·5–9 cm) long; leaflets rounded, stalked, with small teeth. Page 176

Box elder
Acer negundo

Leaves 6 in. (15 cm) long; top pair of leaflets stalkless. Page 177

Alternate leaves, 13–36 unstalked leaflets

Caucasian wing-nut
Pterocarya fraxinifolia

Leaves to 24 in. (60 cm); leaflets rounded, toothed; terminal leaflet stalked. Page 169

Stag's horn sumac
Rhus typhina

Leaves 6–8½ in. (15–22 cm) long; large, saw-like teeth. Page 178

True service tree
Sorbus domestica

Leaves 6–8½ in. (15–22 cm); leaflets rounded, stalkless, large teeth. Page 171

Honey-locust
Gleditsia triacanthos

Leaves 4–6 in. (10–15 cm) long; leaflets small and numerous, no terminal leaflet. Page 175

Caucasian wing-nut

Alternate leaves, 13–28 stalked leaflets

Tree of heaven

Tree of heaven
Ailanthus altissima

Leaves 12–24 in. (30–60 cm) long; leaflets long, with few teeth, often no terminal leaflet. Page 170

Locust tree
Robinia pseudoacacia

Leaves 6–8 in. (15–20 cm); leaflets round, no teeth. Page 174

Varnish tree
Rhus verniciflua

Leaves 20–32 in. (50–80 cm) long; leaflets long, without teeth. Page 179

Black walnut
Juglans nigra

Leaves 18 in. (45 cm); leaflets long, toothed, no terminal leaflet. Page 167

9–15 leaflets

Rowan

Rowan
Sorbus aucuparia

Leaves 8½ in. (22 cm); alternate; leaflets rounded, stalkless, toothed. Page 172. Hupeh rowan, page 173, is similar.

Common ash
Fraxinus excelsior

Leaves 8–12 in. (20–30 cm) long, opposite; leaflets stalked, toothed. Page 164

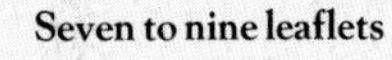

Seven to nine leaflets

Bitternut

Bitternut
Carya cordiformis

Leaves to 8 in. (20 cm) long, alternate; terminal leaflet unstalked, toothed. Page 168

Walnut
Juglans regia

Leaves to 18 in. (45 cm); alternate; toothless; terminal leaflet stalked. Page 166

Manna ash
Fraxinus ornus

Leaves to 12 in. (30 cm); opposite; leaflets rounded, small teeth, stalked. Page 165

Male and female flowers often occur on the same tree on separate twigs, giving the tree a purple colour before the leaves come out.

Leaves are opposite and toothed, and have 9–13 stalked leaflets, with long tips. The single fruits have a long wing.

This widespread tree flourishes on a lime-rich soil, such as that of the limestone 'pavement' of the Peak District.

Common ash in winter.

Weeping ash
F. excelsior 'Pendula'

The grafted weeping ash has a round head and long, drooping branches. It is very common in gardens.

The greenish-grey bark fissures with age.

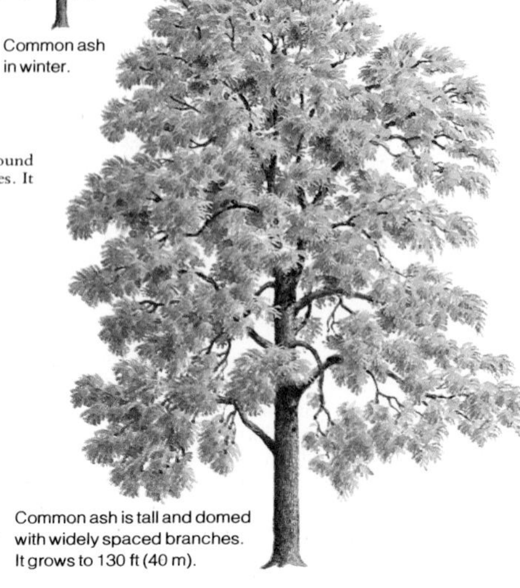

Common ash is tall and domed with widely spaced branches. It grows to 130 ft (40 m).

Common ash *Fraxinus excelsior*

Before the coming of Christianity, the people of Scandinavia worshipped the ash as a sacred tree, symbol of the life-force. In Norse mythology Odin, greatest of the gods, carved the first man out of a piece of ash wood. Yggdrasil, the Tree Of The World, was a giant ash whose roots reached down into the deepest pits of hell, but whose crown touched the highest points of heaven and whose massive trunk united the two.

The ash was supposed to have medicinal as well as mystical properties. It was believed that if a sick child was passed through the cleft of an ash tree it would be cured. Burning ash logs were said to drive out evil spirits from a room.

If such beliefs are now dismissed as superstition, the wood of the ash still has a justifiably high reputation for strength and pliability. Almost pure white, coarse-grained and exceptionally tough, it is in steady demand for a wide variety of products including oars and spars, handles for tools such as axes and hammers, hockey sticks, tennis rackets and skis. Though grown mainly for its timber, the ash in different forms – such as the weeping ash – is also a versatile and popular ornamental tree. The winged fruits, often called 'keys', grow in bunches.

Flowers of manna ash are creamy-white, unlike those of common ash, and are borne in dense heads in May and June.

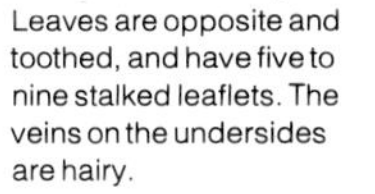

Leaves are opposite and toothed, and have five to nine stalked leaflets. The veins on the undersides are hairy.

The single fruits have a slender wing and hang in dense bunches, turning brown in autumn.

This decorative tree from the south of Europe is often planted in city parks for its early summer flowers.

Manna ash is more regular and rounded in outline than the common ash, and the foliage is denser. Branches are sinuous. The tree is often grafted onto common ash, and grows to 80 ft (24 m).

Bark smooth and grey, rougher below graft.

Manna ash *Fraxinus ornus*

The Bible tells how the Children of Israel, escaping from Egypt across the Sinai Desert, were kept alive by a miraculous food called manna that fell from the sky (Exodus 16). It was once thought that the biblical manna might have been the viscous, sugary gum obtained from the manna ash, which accounts for its name. But as ash trees do not grow in desert regions, the manna is more likely to have been a sweet exudation from tamarisk bushes resulting from the feeding activities of small insects.

But it was probably the exudation of the manna to which Keats was referring in his poem *La Belle Dame Sans Merci*:

'She found me roots of relish sweet,
And honey wild and manna-dew.'

The manna ash is still cultivated in southern Italy and Sicily for its gum. Shallow cuts are made in the branches and from these oozes pale yellow gum, which hardens on contact with the air. The gum is made into a syrup that is used as a mild laxative.

In Britain, where it was introduced in 1700, the manna ash is usually grafted onto rootstock of common ash whose growth rate is much faster; differences in the bark show up the union.

The green, rounded fruit contains the familiar crinkled nut with its edible kernel.

Each leaf usually has seven leaflets, larger towards the tip. The leaves are set alternately on the twig.

Young leaves are bronze-coloured. Male flowers are borne in catkins; female flowers stand upright, in twos or threes.

The walnut has often been planted near farmhouses for its edible nuts, though the crop is frequently spoiled by frosts.

The walnut is a handsome, spreading tree with a broad crown and thick bole, reaching 100 ft (30 m).

The smooth, grey bark has occasional deep fissures.

Walnut *Juglans regia*

As the legions of Imperial Rome marched north to conquer the barbarian lands of Gaul and Britain they carried with them the seeds of the walnut tree. The 'royal nut of Jove' was their name for the fruit of the tree, which they prized as a food and as a source of cooking oil.

The walnut, a native of Asia Minor, was imported to Rome from Greece by about 100 BC. The Greeks called it the 'royal nut' or 'Persian nut', names that reflect its importance and its origin, and many of the superstitions and myths about the walnut can be traced back to ancient Greece. The resemblance of the peeled nut to the human brain led to the medieval belief that it could cure mental disorders; this belief arose from the so-called 'doctrine of signatures', according to which preparations made from plants that looked like parts of the human body could be used to treat ailments affecting those parts.

The walnut had many more practical uses. Apart from the value of its timber in furniture making, the oil from the nut was used in the 19th century for soap manufacture, and one horticultural guide of the time, John Loudon's *Suburban Gardener*, recommends a decoction of walnut leaves for killing slugs.

Female flowers

Male flowers in catkins and female flowers, open on the same tree in late May or early June.

Male flowers

Leaves are alternate. Each leaf has 11–23 leaflets, the largest in the middle and toothed. The terminal leaflet is often missing.

The green, rounded fruit contains a round, corrugated nut.

The black walnut is found occasionally in gardens in the south and east of England, rarely in the north and Ireland.

Black walnut *Juglans nigra*

In 1709 a particularly severe winter devastated the walnut trees of continental Europe; the result was a prohibition on exports of the valuable timber to Britain where, since the late 17th century, it had been increasingly used for making furniture. British cabinet makers were forced to turn to the New World where the black walnut grew in abundance, especially in Virginia.

The dark brown, richly grained wood of the black walnut proved immediately popular with cabinet makers and their customers – especially for veneers – and remained so until the mid-18th century, when it was to some extent eclipsed by mahogany. One of the prime uses of black walnut was in the manufacture of gun stocks; the wood has a particular capacity to absorb the shock of recoil, it does not splinter and is smooth to handle. In the 18th and 19th centuries the expression 'to shoulder walnut' meant to enlist as a soldier.

In 1633 the gardener John Tradescant was recorded as having a black walnut in his garden at South Lambeth, but the tree has not been planted in Britain in any quantity. The main reason for its rarity is that its tap root is easily damaged, making it difficult to transplant. Container-growing may increase its numbers.

The chambered pith in the twigs is typical of walnuts.

Dark brown bark is fissured into broad ridges.

A fast-growing tree reaching 100 ft (30 m), with fuller foliage than common walnut.

Autumn leaf

Leaves are alternate and consist of seven to nine almost stalkless leaflets, smaller near the base. Leaflets have fine hairs on underside, and are dark yellowish-green, turning bright gold in autumn. Fruit are in pairs or threes.

Although the bitternut is not commonly grown in Britain, it is found in some parks, botanical gardens and tree collections.

Husk

Nut

Ripe husk splits, allowing reddish, bitter-tasting nut to emerge. The nut is ridged.

Thick bark of older trees becomes ridged.

The tree has long, straight ascending branches, its crown is conical, and pointed until old. The tree grows to 80 ft (24 m).

Bitternut *Carya cordiformis*

Of the many species of North American hickory grown in Britain, the bitternut, introduced in 1766, is by far the hardiest and most successful, though it is not often seen. As the name implies, the nuts are inedible, even though the tree is a close relative of the walnut.

An attractive tree with foliage which turns a lovely yellow in autumn, the bitternut is distinguished in winter by its sulphur-yellow buds. It is tolerant of shade; once established it grows quickly, but needs to be planted when small to avoid damage to the tap-root which is especially vulnerable during transplanting. Its preferred habitat is wet land near streams: in America it is often called swamp hickory.

The wood is white, tinged with pink, resembling ash in appearance. It is tough, hard and elastic, can be bent easily and will absorb shock without splintering. Like ash, hickory is used in the manufacture of sports goods such as skis, and also for tool handles. In the days of sail the mast hoops – wooden rings attaching fore-and-aft sails to the mast – were of hickory wood. Hickory is still burned to cure and smoke meats, to which it imparts a distinctive flavour.

Winged fruit

Leaves are alternate, with 7–21 leaflets that are stalkless and toothed. Leaflets are almost opposite; they are shiny, bright green on top and paler below.

The long, fruiting female catkins carry many winged seeds.

Grey bark is broken into a network of shallow cracks.

Female catkin

Male catkins

The flowers open in April and the thick, green, male catkins are 3–5 in. (7·5–12·5 cm) long. Female catkins are slightly longer.

The centre of the twig is hollow, and divided into sections by plates of pith.

A domed tree with many stout branches. Smaller branches are level, longer ones rise strongly. The tree grows to a height of 83 ft (25 m).

This fast-growing but uncommon tree flourishes in parks and gardens near water. It grows best in southern Britain.

Caucasian wing-nut *Pterocarya fraxinifolia*

A regular spreading shape and handsome ash-like foliage make this tree an unusual ornamental species in large gardens and parks. It is a native of the Caucasus that was introduced to Britain in 1782, and is easily identified by the round green 'wings' that surround the nuts, a feature from which it derives both its common and scientific names. *Pterocarya* comes from the Greek words *pteron*, meaning 'a wing', and *karyon*, 'nut'.

In autumn and winter the tree has distinctive buds which have no scales, leaving the undeveloped leaves and flowers exposed. On other trees, bud scales provide protection against drying-out of the young leaves, and against damage caused when the twigs rub together in a wind. Another feature of the wing-nut is that the pith of the twigs is divided into chambers.

In Britain the wing-nut thrives in damp areas near streams, but it will also grow well in other places. It needs to be grown in sheltered spots, where it will benefit from maximum protection from late frosts. A vigorous hybrid – *Pterocarya* × *rehderana*, a cross between this species and Chinese wing-nut – was developed in the United States in 1879, and was introduced to Britain in 1902.

The winged fruits are borne in dense bunches.

Each leaf has 13–25 stalked, opposite leaflets with long points. They are deep green on top and pale and hairless beneath. There is often no terminal leaflet.

Its resistance to atmospheric pollution makes the tree of heaven a suitable tree for planting in city streets.

Male flower

Female flower

Male and female flowers, which open in May, usually grow on separate trees.

Pale grey bark, smooth or scaly, has pale stripes.

Tree in winter.

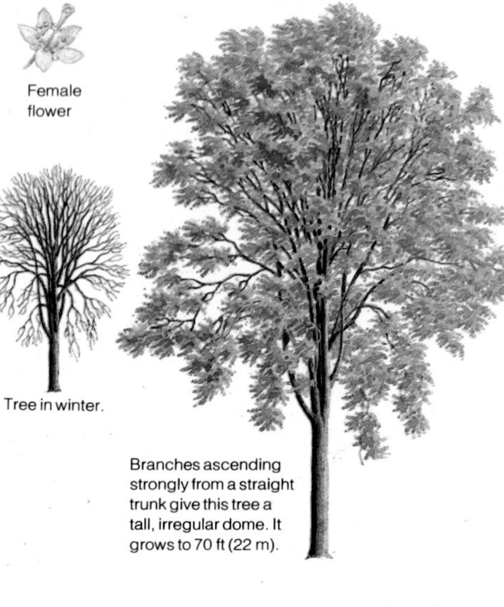

Branches ascending strongly from a straight trunk give this tree a tall, irregular dome. It grows to 70 ft (22 m).

Tree of heaven *Ailanthus altissima*

This tree from China lives under a false name. The name 'tree of heaven' rightfully belongs only to the species *Ailanthus moluccana*, whose branches – according to the people of its native East Indies – reach towards Paradise. The name was, however, transferred to the species *Ailanthus altissima* when this tree was introduced to England in the 1750s. It has frequently been planted to provide ornament for squares in London and other cities. At first the species was thought to be a member of the varnish tree family. Its large, feather-like leaves resemble those of the varnish tree, but they have longer stalks and larger rounded teeth at the base of the leaflets.

In warm climates the tree of heaven spreads rapidly on dumps and waste ground. This is due to its abundant production of suckers, some of them sprouting at a considerable distance from the parent tree. In Britain, the tree grows best in the warmer south. It does not require much moisture, and is commonly found in parks on lighter soils.

In the autumn, the leaves of the tree of heaven sometimes turn an attractive reddish-gold, as do the twisted, wind-scattered seeds. The wood is white, and resembles ash.

Flower-heads are less dense than those of the rowan, and domed rather than flat.

Leaves are alternate, each consisting of 11–21 leaflets with rounded bases and numerous sharp teeth. Sticky, hairless buds and small pear-like fruits distinguish the true service tree from the rowan.

Although the true service tree is a native of Europe, it is very uncommon in Britain, even in parks and gardens.

Tree in winter.

The orange-brown bark is scaly and rough.

A tree with ascending, spreading branches. It grows to 50 ft (15 m).

True service tree *Sorbus domestica*

In ancient times, the fruit of the true service tree was used to make an alcoholic drink. The fruit was fermented with grain, producing a cider-like beverage that is still made in continental Europe to this day. The Romans called this drink *cerevisia*, from which the name 'service' is derived. The fruit occurs in two forms, apple-shaped and pear-shaped; it is only edible raw when over-ripe, or when frost has sweetened it by turning the starch into sugar. Medicinal uses for the fruit were also found, and it was said, among other things, to be a cure for colic.

At one time this slow-growing tree – which in fact is native to North Africa, western Asia and southern Europe – was held to be a native of Britain. This was because of a famous, centuries-old tree which grew in the Forest of Wyre, before being destroyed in 1862.

The wood has a compact grain which, if well seasoned, takes a high polish. It is not readily obtainable in Britain, but is used on the Continent, where the tree is more commonly grown. The hard timber is used in joinery and to make wheels; in France, until the coming of modern materials, it was thought to be the best wood for making the screws of wine presses.

The ripe berries attract birds in autumn. Each leaf has numerous pairs of stalkless leaflets with sharp, forward-pointing teeth.

Creamy-white clusters of flowers form in May.

The rowan's finest display is in the autumn, with clusters of bright red berries. It flourishes by mountain streams.

Bastard service tree
Sorbus × thuringiaca

On this tree, the leaf is only partially divided. It is a hybrid of rowan and whitebeam, decorative in streets.

Bark is smooth, shiny and grey, with pores.

The rowan is a graceful, open tree up to 65 ft (20 m) in height.

Rowan *Sorbus aucuparia*

Connected with witchcraft from ancient times, the rowan tree's name is believed to be derived from the Norse word *runa*, meaning 'a charm'. The tree was often planted outside houses and in churchyards to ward off witches. On May Day, a spray of rowan leaves was hung over doors to repel evil, and wells were dressed with rowan to keep witches away.

The tree's alternative name of mountain ash reflects the fact that it grows higher up the mountain-sides than most other native trees, sometimes clinging to a rock-face after sprouting in a crevice from seed dropped by a bird. It is widely planted to decorate streets and gardens, not only for its beauty but also because its narrow shape does not take up much room and its sparse foliage allows grass to grow on the ground beneath.

The red berries of rowan is made into a jelly that is eaten with game, and being rich in vitamin C they were once made into a drink to prevent scurvy. Bird-catchers once used the berries as bait for traps to snare thrushes, redwings and fieldfares. The rowan's strong, flexible, yellow-grey wood was once widely used for making tool handles and small carved objects, and was sometimes used instead of yew for making long-bows.

The Hupeh rowan, introduced from western China in 1910, is a vigorously growing tree that thrives in urban surroundings.

White or purplish berries distinguish this tree from other rowans in autumn and winter. Earlier the berries are pale green.

Leaflets are greyish-green, and have teeth only on their upper halves. The leaf-stalk is red. White flowers appear in spreading heads in May.

The bark is smooth and purplish-brown.

The Hupeh rowan is a small tree up to 40 ft (12 m) tall, common in parks.

Hupeh rowan *Sorbus hupehensis*

A colourful tree growing in the mountainous areas of China's Hupeh province caught the eye of a British plant collector, E.H. Wilson, in the early 1900s, and was introduced to this country as the Hupeh rowan. It makes an attractive display for most of the year. The leaves are a striking red in autumn, and the silver-grey summer foliage singles out the tree from other rowans.

In autumn, in contrast with the red leaves, the rather pendulous berries turn from pale green to white, or purplish-white, and acquire a distinctive porcelain-like appearance. The berries do not seem to be as attractive to birds as those of red-berried rowans, as they are not stripped so rapidly from the tree.

The Hupeh rowan is very suitable for lining urban streets. It is modest in size, and has fairly sparse foliage that does not accumulate in masses on the ground when it falls. The tree retains a pleasing shape at all seasons, without the need for pruning. It withstands drought and heat well, and therefore tolerates town surroundings where paving reduces the amount of water available and heat is reflected from buildings and roads. The Hupeh rowan also tolerates pollution, thriving in a contaminated atmosphere.

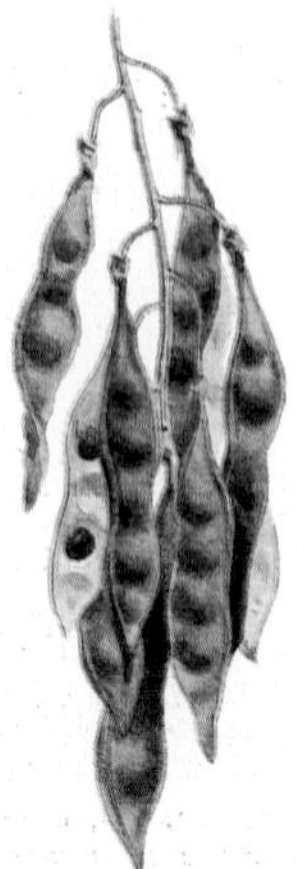

In autumn, smooth brown pods split to release black seeds, shaped like kidneys. The pods remain hanging on the tree in bunches into the winter.

Leaves are alternate. Each has 11–15 stalked leaflets, oval and hairless with small spines at their tips; they are bluish-green beneath.

Pea-like flowers hang in sweet-scented clusters.

This tree from North America has long been grown in England on light soils, chiefly in southern parts of the country.

The brown or grey bark is furrowed and twisted.

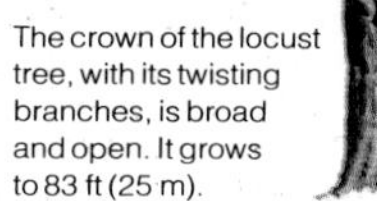

The crown of the locust tree, with its twisting branches, is broad and open. It grows to 83 ft (25 m).

Locust tree *Robinia pseudoacacia*

Double confusion surrounds the locust tree, or false acacia. In the first place, the 'locusts' upon which John the Baptist is said to have fed in the wilderness were probably the fruits of the carob, or locust bean – not of this locust tree, which belongs to a different genus. The two trees acquired similar popular names because their pods are alike. Furthermore, neither tree has anything to do with locusts – in the eastern Mediterranean the same Greek word came to be used for the insect and for the carob pod simply because they looked somewhat alike.

Nowadays, the locust tree is less common in England than it was in the first half of the 19th century. At that time the radical journalist William Cobbett, author of *The English Gardener*, advocated the use of its hard wood for the pegs once used to fasten together the timbers of ships. Cobbett made a handsome profit by buying the trees from nurserymen and selling them to planters and speculators; but by the time they were ready for exploitation, iron was superseding timber in shipbuilding.

The tree's generic name honours the 17th-century gardener Jean Robin, who obtained seeds of the tree from America and grew trees from them in the Jardin des Plantes in Paris.

Leaves are alternate, with numerous leaflets that taper towards the tip and are yellowish-green below. Some leaflets have smaller leaflets of their own.

Pods contain flat seeds and are often twisted.

Bark has shallow fissures and branched thorns.

Older honey-locusts have a spreading, flattened top. Clusters of long, thorny spines on the branches and trunk make this tree unique. It grows to 60 ft (18 m).

Male flowers

Female flowers

Male and female flowers grow in separate clusters on the same tree. Male clusters contain numerous flowers, female clusters fewer.

'Sunburst' is a cultivar with yellow young leaves.

The honey-locust, which turns gold in autumn, is largely restricted to parks and gardens in the east and south.

Honey-locust *Gleditsia triacanthos*

When British missionaries in North America came across the honey-locust and locust tree in the 17th century, they saw similarities between them and the carob or locust bean of the eastern Mediterranean, and named their discoveries accordingly. The tree was introduced to Britain by Henry Compton, Bishop of London in 1675.

Another name for the honey-locust is three-thorned acacia – a reference to the vicious spines that the tree has developed, which prevent its seed-pods and foliage being eaten by browsing animals. These spines make the tree suitable for stock-proof hedges. Thornless cultivars have been developed for planting in streets and gardens.

The honey-locust will thrive on most soils, but prefers moist, deep loams similar to those on which it occurs naturally. It is short-lived but fast-growing. It can tolerate a certain amount of shade and pollution, and is not damaged by frost. In autumn, the foliage turns a rich, attractive gold. One weakness of the tree is that its branches are brittle and easily broken by the wind, so it is best planted in sheltered places. The seeds have a hard coat, and acid is used to dissolve this for quick germination.

Flower [Actual size]

Autumn berries hang in bunches.

The pith inside an elder stalk resembles white, spongy cork.

The elder does well in rich, neglected ground such as deserted cottage gardens. Its flowers are used to make tea.

The elder usually remains a bushy shrub, with many stems arising at ground level.

The stalked, toothed leaves are opposite and consist of five to seven leaflets, which smell offensively. The numerous creamy-white flowers form a flat-topped head with a heavy, sweet scent.

Elder *Sambucus nigra*

Elder flourishes wherever the nitrogen content of the soil is high: near abandoned dwellings, in churchyards and around rabbit warrens and badger setts. In these places the soil has been enriched by the breakdown of organic matter such as dung and refuse. The seeds are spread in the droppings of birds which eat the berries. The plant colonises an area quickly and it soon becomes established, for it grows very vigorously.

Nowadays some cultivars are grown in gardens for their ornamental value, but the tree has been cultivated by humans for centuries. The fruit and flowers make excellent wines and jams and are rich in vitamin C. Coughs were treated with a tea made from the flowers, and an extract of the bark was used as a purgative. Dyes were obtained from different parts of the tree: black from the bark, green from the leaves, and blue or lilac from the flowers.

The pith from the stem is easily cut, and was once used for holding botanical specimens while they were sectioned. The wood, which is hard and yellowish-white, makes small items such as toys, combs and wooden spoons. Generations of children have hollowed out the stems to make whistles and pea-shooters.

The light brown bark is thick, ridged and corky.

If it is given light and space, the elder may grow from a shrub into a small tree up to 30 ft (9 m) tall.

Male flowers

Female flowers

Red male flowers and green female flowers are borne on separate trees.

Each leaf is made up of five to seven thin, opposite leaflets with a few small lobes. The lower leaflets are stalked. The paired fruits, arranged in a V-shape, have long seeds and curved wings.

Fruits

'Variegatum'

'Auratum'

Cultivars of box elder are grown for ornament. The leaves of 'Auratum' are rich yellow, turning bright gold; those of 'Variegatum' have a pale margin.

This fast-growing native of North America is a common ornamental tree of parks, town gardens and streets.

Greyish-brown bark cracks into fissures with age.

An irregularly shaped crown and sprouting from the bole characterise box elder. It is short-lived, and never grows to more than 45 ft (14 m).

Box elder *Acer negundo*

This fast-growing, bushy-headed tree – also called ash-leaved maple – was introduced to Britain from North America in 1688 by Bishop Henry Compton, an avid collector of exotic trees. In its ordinary form it has green leaves which turn yellow in autumn, but it is probably better known for its various cultivars. The most popular of these is a variegated form 'Variegatum', the leaves of which have a pale margin. This cultivar originally occurred in France as a 'sport', or aberrant form arising naturally. It must be propagated by grafting and maintained by regular pruning; otherwise the stock sends up shoots and replaces the graft with the ordinary green form.

Other cultivars of box elder include 'Violaceum', which has purple or violet shoots covered with a white bloom, and 'Auratum', which has bright, golden-yellow leaves. Box elder is resistant to drought and frost, and because it grows so fast it is often used in public parks to screen unsightly features.

As with most maples, sugar can be obtained from the sap in spring. The wood, which is light, soft and creamy-white in colour, has little commercial value because the tree does not become large; its timber is therefore available only in small sizes.

Male flowers

Male and female flowers are borne on separate trees. The male flowers are a greenish-yellow; female flowers a rusty red.

Female flowers

Autumn leaves are brilliant oranges and reds. The fruiting heads remain on the tree in winter.

This ornamental tree adds autumn colour to gardens throughout Britain. It suckers freely, producing dense thickets.

Leaves are alternate and consist of 11–29 leaflets. The leaflets are pointed and stalkless, with saw-like teeth; the largest are in the centre.

Stag's horn sumac *Rhus typhina*

In winter when the leaves have fallen, the bare branches and thick twigs of this tree resemble the antlers of a stag. It is a native of North America, and was introduced to Britain in 1629 by John Parkinson, who had been apothecary to James I and who kept medicinal gardens in London's Long Acre. An extract of the roots of sumac was used to treat fevers.

Easily grown in any fertile soil, sumac tolerates pollution but requires plenty of light if it is to flourish. It responds well to severe pruning, and can therefore be maintained at a manageable size in small gardens. Very large specimens can also be obtained. The tendency of sumac to throw out suckers provides a useful means of propagation. The cultivar 'Lacinata' has particularly beautiful, fern-like leaves.

It is uncertain where the name 'Sumac' came from – perhaps from the North American Indians, who hollowed out the stems and used them as tobacco pipes and tubes. This practice spread to the white settlers in North America, who employed such tubes for tapping sugar maples. Nowadays the tree is grown in Britain for its decorative qualities; in Canada its light, soft, orange-coloured wood is used for making toys.

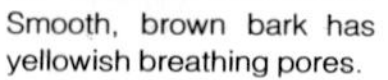

Smooth, brown bark has yellowish breathing pores.

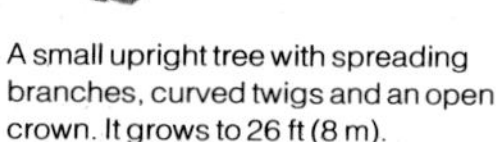

A small upright tree with spreading branches, curved twigs and an open crown. It grows to 26 ft (8 m).

The small, yellowish-white flowers are borne in branching spikes.

The green, poisonous fruits ripen to a pale, creamy brown in September.

The varnish tree, though uncommon, is planted for its decorative foliage in some parks and large gardens.

The large leaves are alternate, each leaf consisting of numerous thick leaflets; these are stalked and in pairs which are often not quite opposite.

Bark cracks into long, vertical fissures.

An upright tree with a straight stem and upward-curving branches. The crown is domed and open. The tree grows to 45 ft (14 m).

Varnish tree *Rhus verniciflua*

Before the development of synthetic varnish derived from chemicals, the varnish tree was important in Japan as a natural source of varnish for lacquer work. Incisions were made in the trunk, and the syrupy fluid that the tree exuded was collected in containers. This fluid is yellowish at first, but on exposure to air becomes thicker and darker. When a thin layer is painted onto ornamental boxes and furniture, it hardens and shows up the grain underneath. Gold leaf was sometimes mixed with the varnish when decorating woodwork.

Some people are allergic to the sap, which may cause a rash. Other members of the varnish tree's family, such as the American poison ivy, contain even more toxic substances. An oil produced by crushing the seeds of the varnish tree is still used as a lamp oil in the Far East.

The tree was introduced to Britain about a century ago. It is not common, growing chiefly in parks in the southern part of the country, though some occur further north. It forms a medium-sized tree with the distinctive feature of large, aromatic leaves that turn red in the autumn. On female trees poisonous, yellowish-green or brown berries are sometimes found.

In exposed positions, the tamarisk may be bent into shape by the prevailing wind. Often planted as a shrub, it can grow to tree size. As a shrub, it reaches 10 ft (3 m).

[×3]

The tiny pink or white flowers have five petals and five stamens. The twigs are reddish, and papery triangular bracts cover the base of each shoot.

Because the alternate leaves are so numerous and tiny, they give a feathery appearance to the foliage.

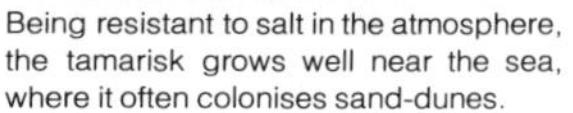

Being resistant to salt in the atmosphere, the tamarisk grows well near the sea, where it often colonises sand-dunes.

Tamarisk *Tamarix anglica*

This shrub was exploited in the Middle East from ancient times for its medicinal properties. It was for this reason that tamarisk was introduced to Britain in 1582 by Dr Edmund Grindal, Bishop of London in the reign of Elizabeth I. First grown in Dr Grindal's 'physic garden', or herb garden, the plant was used to treat rheumatism and bruises, and also as a tonic.

Tamarisk now grows wild on Britain's south and east coasts; being tolerant of salt and sea winds, it thrives near the ocean. To minimise the water loss caused by the drying effect of salt, the leaves are reduced to small scales. As an ornamental shrub, tamarisk is cultivated for its feathery foliage and haze of pink flowers in midsummer. In mild areas, it can be found flowering up to Christmas.

Tamarix anglica and *Tamarix gallica*, originally classified as separate species, are now regarded as being of the same species. One form produces a honey-like substance when the stem is cut. This is edible, and provided food for desert Bedouins. The name tamarisk is thought to be derived from the Hebrew *tamaris*, 'broom': if tied together, the shrub's flexible, twiggy branches are well adapted for sweeping.

Female flowers

Male flowers

Male and female flowers grow on separate trees. Males appear as small green catkins, females are small, stalked, round and knob-like.

The tumbling foliage of this relic of primeval forests can still grace parks and gardens in the south and south-west.

Leaves are two-lobed and fan-shaped, with radiating veins reflecting the leaf shape. The fruits resemble small green plums on long stalks.

In autumn, foliage turns amber coloured before falling.

Light brown bark roughens into corky fissures.

A tall, slender trunk and drooping foliage consisting of distinctively fan-shaped leaves identify this tree, which can reach a height of 100 ft (30 m).

Maidenhair tree *Ginkgo biloba*

Fossils of the maidenhair tree have been found in coal seams formed 250 million years ago, yet this ancient, primitive tree lives on today, the sole survivor of its family. It is unique in other ways too. Fertilisation is by free-swimming male sperm which reach the ovules through a film of water – a method found in ferns, but in no other tree living today. The unusual, fan-shaped leaves – partly divided in the middle and with parallel veins – resemble the maidenhair fern and give the tree its common name.

The tree survived through the centuries by cultivation in temple and palace gardens in China; its generic name *Ginkgo* is said to be derived from the Chinese *yin kuo*, meaning the 'silver fruit' that the tree sometimes bears. It was introduced to Europe early in the 18th century, and has also been extensively planted in America as a street tree.

In a dry autumn, the leaves turn a brilliant amber before falling to expose the short, blunt twigs which, in winter, give the maidenhair the appearance of a pear tree. The pale yellow wood is light, lacking in strength and without commercial use. In Japan the hard fruits are roasted and eaten as a hangover cure.

Chusan palm leaf.

Round brown fruits occur in large bunches on female trees.

The dwarf fan-palm's coarsely segmented leaves are distinctive; in the wild it is usually low growing, but in cultivation in Britain it can grow to a height of several metres.

The mild climate of south-western England and western Scotland favours exotic trees such as the dwarf fan-palm.

Chusan palm
Trachycarpus fortunei

Each of this palm's finely divided leaves has about 50 segments. The tree can be grown in mild areas of Britain, and reaches a height of about 35 ft (11 m).

Trunk shows the ragged bases of fallen leaves.

The leaves are stiff and fan-shaped, with 12–15 segments. Flowers grow in drooping heads.

Dwarf fan-palm *Chamaerops humilis*

With their strange trunks – straight, unbranched and barkless, topped by a cluster of fronds – the palms present an outlandish appearance to eyes accustomed to the more gently spreading outlines of most trees seen in Britain. Large evergreen leaves form a succession of rosettes which persist for a few years before falling off, leaving behind the whiskery leaf-bases. Botanists class palms as monocotyledons – plants that have only one seed-leaf within the seed. Most temperate trees belong to the second main division of flowering plants, the dicotyledons, which have two seed-leaves.

Fan palms are, as the name indicates, a group of palms with large, rounded, fan-like leaves. These leaves are very susceptible to wind damage, and the trees have therefore to be grown in sheltered sites. The dwarf fan-palm grows wild on mountain-sides along the coast of the Mediterranean. The only palm native to Europe, it was introduced to Britain in 1731. It grows in gardens in south-western England and the west coast of Scotland, warmed by the Gulf Stream.

The Chusan palm, introduced from China in 1836, is a hardier tree which will survive moderately severe frosts.

The shoots are rigid, furrowed spines, with smaller side shoots, often in threes, on the larger spines. The bright yellow flowers are pollinated by bees and other insects.

The blackish pods burst to release their seed on hot summer days.

The rare Dartford warbler uses gorse as one of its favourite nest sites.

Gorse flourishes on light soil, and its colourful flowers brighten heathland throughout the British Isles.

Broom
Cytisus scoparius

Similar to gorse but without spines, broom grows to 7 ft (2 m) on heaths and sandy places over most of Britain. Its golden flowers open in May and June.

This dense, prickly, evergreen shrub first blooms in spring and summer, but may be in flower throughout the year. It grows to 7 ft (2 m) or more.

Gorse *Ulex europaeus*

'When the gorse is out of bloom, kissing is out of season,' says one old country saying, and according to another 'while the gorse is in flower Britain will never be conquered'. But neither lovers nor patriots need be alarmed, for gorse of one or other species is in bloom almost all the year round.

The warm, coconut smell of gorse and the sharp reports of ripe pods bursting epitomise high summer, especially in those parts of the country where the plant is the predominant feature of the landscape. Gorse, also known as furze or whin, grows naturally on acid, sandy heaths, often in exposed, windy situations. It is a very resilient plant, with thick stems which reduce the rate at which water is lost, and although liable to frost damage, it recovers quickly and sends up new shoots. It also survives fire.

Gorse is an excellent fuel and in warm, dry weather burns fiercely, causing heath fires to spread rapidly. It is often planted as a hedge or a windbreak for livestock, and in the past was grown near dwellings so that washing could be laid out to dry on the thorny branches without fear of it blowing away. The sharp foliage affords protection to the nests of birds such as linnets, whinchats, stonechats and the rare Dartford warbler.

WINTER TWIGS AND BUDS

Although leaves provide the easiest means of putting a name to a tree, it is still possible to tell one species of deciduous tree from another in winter, when the leaves have fallen. At this time of the year, clues to a tree's identity are provided by the colour of the leafless twigs and the buds they bear ready to produce next year's leaves and flowers.

The most suitable twigs to examine for identification purposes are those at the ends of the branches. On some trees – particularly cherries and other fruit trees – the presence of short shoots is a further aid to identification. These grow more slowly and have close rings round them.

The first feature to be looked for on the selected twig is the arrangement of the buds. They may be in opposite pairs, each pair at right-angles to the next, or they may arise alternately from one side of the shoot and then the other all the way along the twig; on deciduous conifers they are arranged in spirals.

The next step towards identification is to look more closely at an individual leaf bud. How many scales, if any, are protecting the young leaves inside? Are the scales fringed with hairs and, if so, what colour are they? Is the bud itself hairy or sticky? The shape and size of each bud must also be considered. The size, however, to some extent depends upon how vigorously the parent tree is growing.

Flower buds and leaf scars as clues

Flower buds, which contain the blossoms for the following spring or summer, are usually much fatter than leaf buds. Buds on short shoots tend to be smaller than those on vigorous, long shoots. The way the buds grow on the twig is also important. For example, the close-set buds of willows, growing flat against the twig, are distinctive; beech can be distinguished from the similar hornbeam by the way the buds of beech stand away from the twig, while those of the hornbeam lie close to it.

Frequently, the most important marks on a twig are the scars left by a fallen leaf. These vary considerably in shape and size; those of the horse chestnut, for instance, are most conspicuous. The colours of the twigs should be noted – especially those of the younger shoots from the previous summer. Another significant 'identity-tag' is the abundance and arrangement of the breathing pores, which can vary from tree to tree. It is also worth examining the shape of a twig in cross-section. Many of these are round, but in the small spindle tree it is four-sided.

Thorny twigs

Some trees and shrubs have developed thorns that protect them from grazing animals, and many for this reason make good hedges. Some cultivated trees that were spiny in their wild form have been developed in thornless forms to make the picking of their fruit easier. Because thorns are a disadvantage in streets, thorn-bearing trees that are otherwise suitable for street use, such as the locust tree or false acacia, have been bred without thorns.

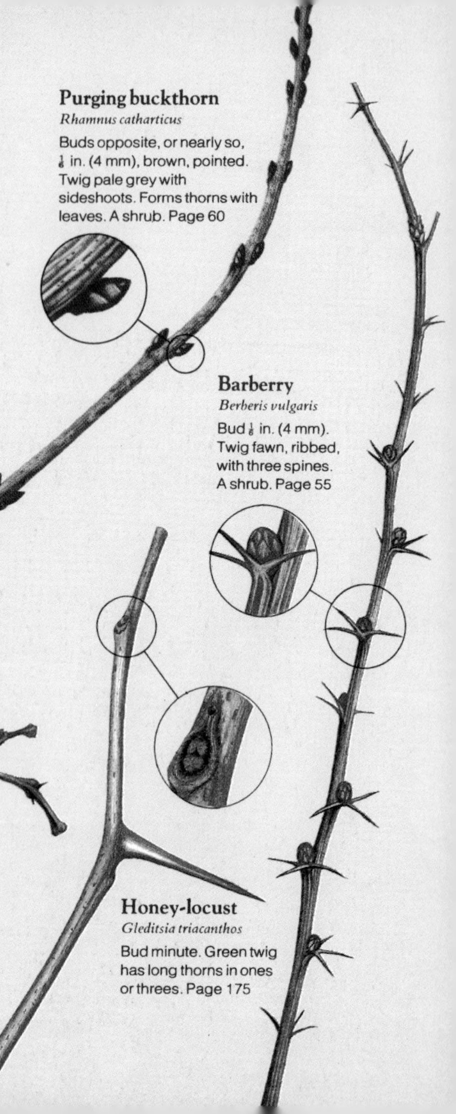

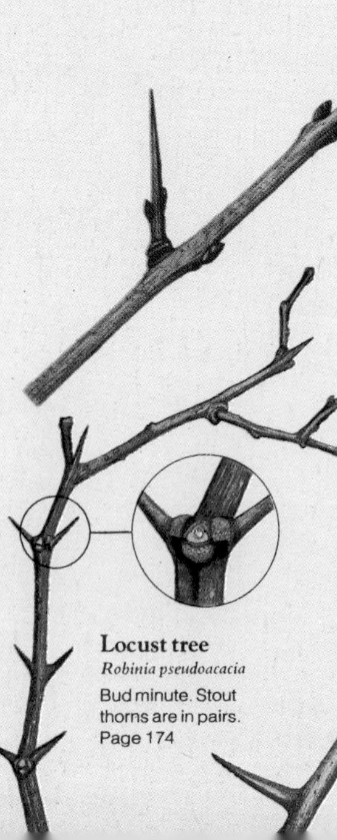

Purging buckthorn
Rhamnus catharticus
Buds opposite, or nearly so, ⅙ in. (4 mm), brown, pointed. Twig pale grey with sideshoots. Forms thorns with leaves. A shrub. Page 60

Barberry
Berberis vulgaris
Bud ⅙ in. (4 mm). Twig fawn, ribbed, with three spines. A shrub. Page 55

Honey-locust
Gleditsia triacanthos
Bud minute. Green twig has long thorns in ones or threes. Page 175

Locust tree
Robinia pseudoacacia
Bud minute. Stout thorns are in pairs. Page 174

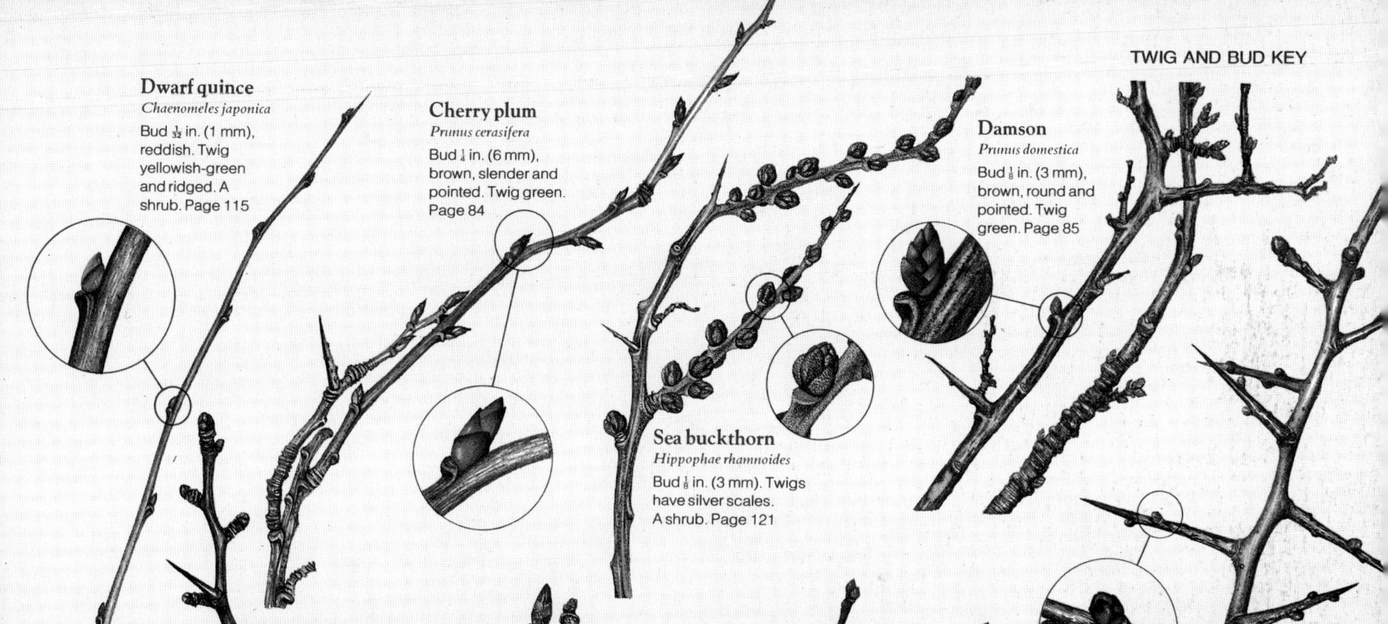

Dwarf quince
Chaenomeles japonica
Bud $\frac{1}{32}$ in. (1 mm), reddish. Twig yellowish-green and ridged. A shrub. Page 115

Cherry plum
Prunus cerasifera
Bud $\frac{1}{4}$ in. (6 mm), brown, slender and pointed. Twig green. Page 84

Damson
Prunus domestica
Bud $\frac{1}{8}$ in. (3 mm), brown, round and pointed. Twig green. Page 85

Sea buckthorn
Hippophae rhamnoides
Bud $\frac{1}{8}$ in. (3 mm). Twigs have silver scales. A shrub. Page 121

Blackthorn
Prunus spinosa
Bud $\frac{1}{16}$ in. (2 mm). Twigs grey or black. Short, dark brown shoots become thorns bearing rounded buds. Page 57

Crab apple
Malus sylvestris
Bud $\frac{1}{6}$ in. (4 mm), dark red, rounded and usually hairy. Twig grey-brown. Page 82

Common pear
Pyrus communis
Bud $\frac{1}{5}$ in. (5 mm), yellow-brown, hairless and rounded. Twig grey. Page 83

Common hawthorn
Crataegus monogyna
Bud $\frac{1}{16}$ in. (2 mm), single. Brown twigs bear thorns. Page 144. Midland hawthorn is similar. Page 145

Clustered buds

Characteristically, cherries and related trees have their buds clustered on short side-shoots, many of which contain the flowers. By contrast, the buds and therefore the leaves of oaks are clustered at the tips of their shoots, around the large terminal bud. The buds also have many scales.

AT TIPS OF SIDE-SHOOTS

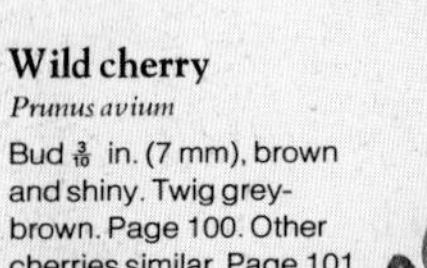

Wild cherry
Prunus avium
Bud $\frac{3}{10}$ in. (7 mm), brown and shiny. Twig grey-brown. Page 100. Other cherries similar. Page 101

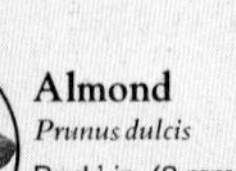

Almond
Prunus dulcis
Bud $\frac{1}{8}$ in. (3 mm), brown. Twigs green. Page 106

AT TIP OF TERMINAL SHOOT

English oak
Quercus robur
Bud $\frac{1}{5}$ in. (5 mm), round, brown, hairless. Twig grey-brown. Page 148. Sessile oak bud hairy, larger. Page 149

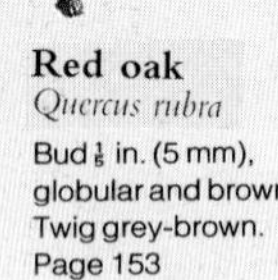

Red oak
Quercus rubra
Bud $\frac{1}{5}$ in. (5 mm), globular and brown. Twig grey-brown. Page 153

Turkey oak
Quercus cerris
Bud $\frac{1}{16}$ in. (2 mm), whiskered. Twig brown. Page 157. Lucombe oak: terminal buds whiskered. Page 156

Hungarian oak
Quercus frainetto
Bud $\frac{2}{5}$ in. (1 cm), globular and hairy. Twig brown. Page 155

Scarlet oak
Quercus coccinea
Bud $\frac{1}{8}$ in. (3 mm), reddish, pointed. Twig yellowish. Page 152. Pin oak bud smaller, twig brown. Page 154

Large leaf scars

Twigs of deciduous trees all bear leaf scars that have formed where the leaf stalk was attached when the leaf was alive. On some species these scars are very conspicuous, often showing characteristic shapes and patterns such as those on the horse chestnut. The buds of such trees may be in opposite pairs, or arranged alternately along the twigs.

BUDS OPPOSITE

Sycamore
Acer pseudoplatanus
Bud $\frac{2}{5}$ in. (1 cm), round, green scales with brown edges. Twig brown with paler breathing pores. Page 128

Common ash
Fraxinus excelsior
Bud $\frac{2}{5}$ in. (1 cm), squat and black. Twigs greyish. Page 164

Manna ash
Fraxinus ornus
Bud $\frac{1}{2}$ in. (1·3 cm), hairy and pale brown. Twig greyish. Page 165

BUDS ALTERNATE

Indian bean-tree
Catalpa bignonioides

Bud minute and round. Twig grey-brown, ridged, with raised, paler breathing pores. Page 44

Norway maple
Acer platanoides

Bud $\frac{3}{8}$ in. (1 cm), round, chestnut-brown and shiny. Twig chestnut-brown with paler breathing pores. Page 129

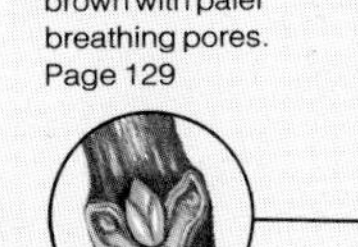

Horse chestnut
Aesculus hippocastanum

Bud $\frac{5}{8}$ in. (1·5 cm), dark, sticky. Twig fawn. Page 158. Red horse chestnut scales dull green, purple margins. Page 158. Indian horse chestnut bud slender, sticky. Page 159

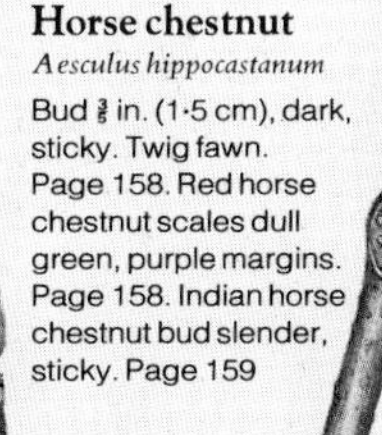

Foxglove tree
Paulownia tomentosa

Bud minute and round. Twig fawn, smooth with larger, paler breathing spores. Page 45

Stag's horn sumac
Rhus typhina

Bud minute. Twig very hairy and red-brown. A shrub. Page 178

Varnish tree
Rhus verniciflua

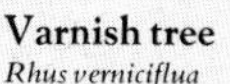

Bud $\frac{1}{8}$–$\frac{1}{6}$ in. (3–4 mm), chestnut-brown. Twig downy and greenish-yellow, with orange breathing pores. Page 179

Handkerchief tree
Davidia involucrata

Bud $\frac{1}{3}$ in. (9 mm), dark brown and pointed. Twig brown, ridged with breathing pores. Page 46

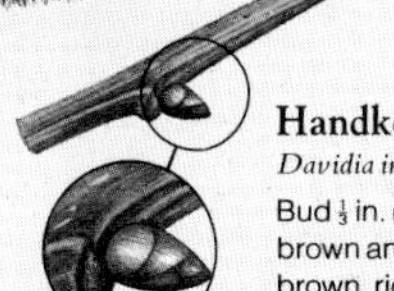

Fig
Ficus carica

Terminal bud $\frac{3}{8}$ in. (1 cm). Green with long, thin point. Twig green or brown, sometimes with maturing fruit. Page 140

Walnut
Juglans regia

Bud $\frac{1}{5}$ in. (5 mm), rounded and black-purple. Twig grey and knobbly. Page 166. Black walnut bud light brown, twig blackish. Page 167

Tree of heaven
Ailanthus altissima

Bud $\frac{1}{16}$ in. (2 mm). Shoot hairless, whitish, round pores. Page 170

Hairy buds, alternate

All trees and shrubs in this group are distinguished by having buds covered in dense, silky hairs, although they may also show features, such as leaf scars, that occur in other groups. All the plants in the group also have alternate buds.

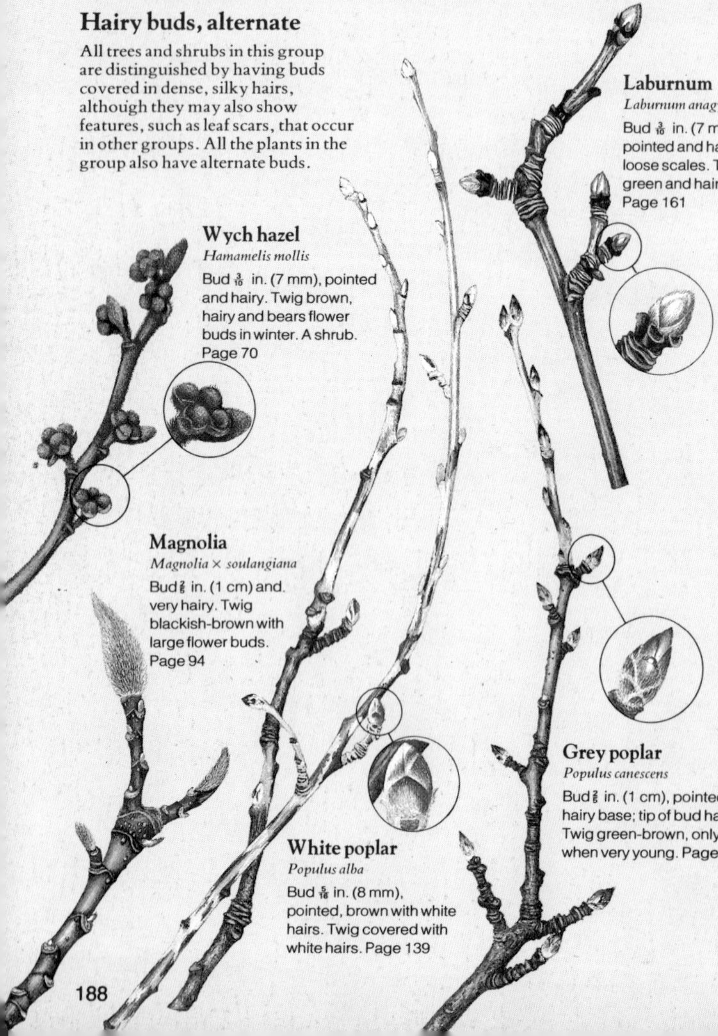

Wych hazel

Hamamelis mollis

Bud $\frac{3}{10}$ in. (7 mm), pointed and hairy. Twig brown, hairy and bears flower buds in winter. A shrub. Page 70

Magnolia

Magnolia × soulangiana

Bud $\frac{3}{8}$ in. (1 cm) and very hairy. Twig blackish-brown with large flower buds. Page 94

White poplar

Populus alba

Bud $\frac{5}{16}$ in. (8 mm), pointed, brown with white hairs. Twig covered with white hairs. Page 139

Laburnum

Laburnum anagyroides

Bud $\frac{3}{10}$ in. (7 mm), pointed and hairy with loose scales. Twig green and hairy. Page 161

Grey poplar

Populus canescens

Bud $\frac{3}{8}$ in. (1 cm), pointed with hairy base; tip of bud hairless. Twig green-brown, only hairy when very young. Page 34

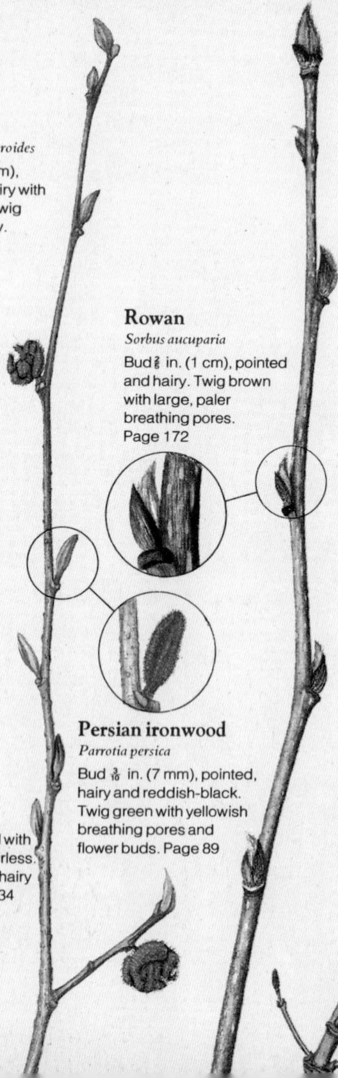

Rowan

Sorbus aucuparia

Bud $\frac{3}{8}$ in. (1 cm), pointed and hairy. Twig brown with large, paler breathing pores. Page 172

Persian ironwood

Parrotia persica

Bud $\frac{3}{10}$ in. (7 mm), pointed, hairy and reddish-black. Twig green with yellowish breathing pores and flower buds. Page 89

Buds without scales (young leaves exposed)

The buds of most deciduous trees and shrubs are protected from damage and drying out during the winter by tough scales. But a small number of trees have their buds exposed; they may be set in opposite pairs, or arranged alternately. Having been tightly folded against the cold during the winter, the leaves grow with the coming of warmer weather in early spring.

OPPOSITE

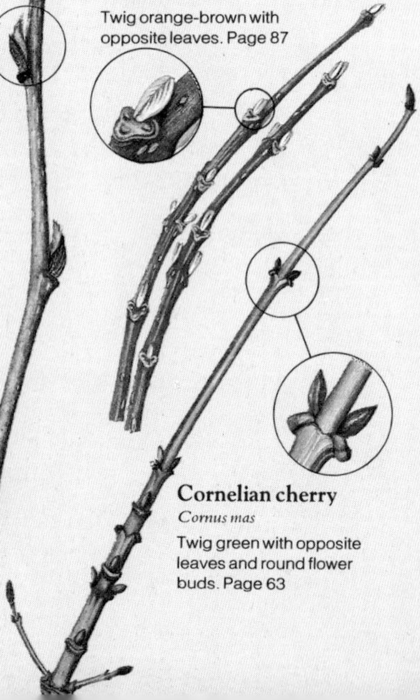

Wayfaring tree

Viburnum lantana

Twig orange-brown with opposite leaves. Page 87

Cornelian cherry

Cornus mas

Twig green with opposite leaves and round flower buds. Page 63

Buddleia
Buddleia davidii

Twig fawn. Short shoots opposite with leaves in bunches. Fruits remain in winter. A shrub. Page 114

Elder
Sambucus nigra

Twig fawn, brittle, with raised breathing pores. Young leaves opposite and purplish. Page 176

Dogwood
Cornus sanguinea

Twig red with opposite leaves. A shrub. Page 62

ALTERNATE

Cotoneaster
Cotoneaster frigidus

Twig green with ridges. A shrub. Page 111

Alder buckthorn
Frangula alnus

Twig brown with ridges and long, paler breathing pores. Page 61

Caucasian wing-nut
Pterocarya fraxinifolia

Twig shiny green or brown with scattered breathing pores. Page 169

Alternate buds on stalks

Alders are distinguished from other trees by their stalked leaf buds. The tulip tree is one of the few other trees that has stalked buds; it also has conspicuous leaf scars to identify it.

Tulip tree
Liriodendron tulipifera

Bud $\frac{3}{8}$ in. (1 cm), green tinged with purple. Twig shiny chestnut-brown with leaf scars. Page 141

Common alder
Alnus glutinosa

Bud $\frac{1}{5}$ in. (5 mm), dark purple with 'pinched' tip. Twig shiny brown with raised pores. In winter, bears catkins and fruit. Page 65. Italian alder bud is round and pointed. Green tinged with red. Page 67. Grey alder bud very hairy and twig grey. Page 66

Buds with two scales of different sizes

This group contains only lime trees, some with and some without hairy buds. The larger of the two scales almost covers the bud.

Common lime
Tilia × europaea

Bud $\frac{3}{8}$ in. (1 cm), green or tinged with red. Twig hairless and green. Page 40. Large-leaved lime bud is larger and twig hairy, reddish or green. Page 42. Small-leaved lime twig is hairless, red above, brown below. Page 43. Silver lime bud is round, green, hairy; twig is grey-brown, hairy. Page 41

Pointed, alternate buds

Buds in this group may be set at an angle to the twig, or pressed close to it. Some buds have many scales, but the angled bud of the plane tree is protected by a single large, prominent scale. Among the trees with buds pressed close to the twig, the willows have a single large scale. Balsam poplar is distinguished by its very sticky buds.

BUDS AT ANGLE TO TWIG

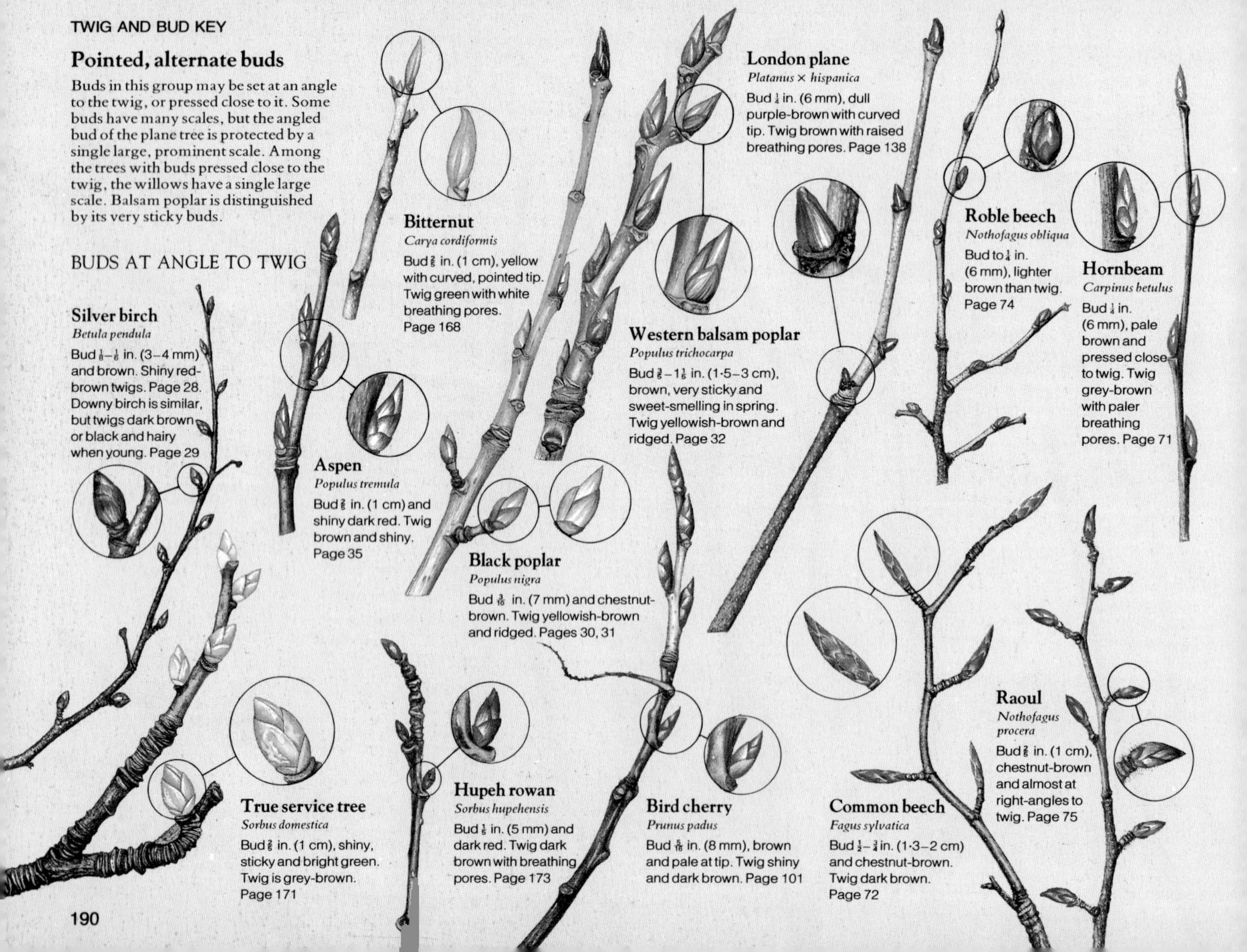

Silver birch
Betula pendula
Bud $\frac{1}{8}$–$\frac{1}{6}$ in. (3–4 mm) and brown. Shiny red-brown twigs. Page 28. Downy birch is similar, but twigs dark brown or black and hairy when young. Page 29

Aspen
Populus tremula
Bud $\frac{3}{8}$ in. (1 cm) and shiny dark red. Twig brown and shiny. Page 35

Bitternut
Carya cordiformis
Bud $\frac{3}{8}$ in. (1 cm), yellow with curved, pointed tip. Twig green with white breathing pores. Page 168

Black poplar
Populus nigra
Bud $\frac{3}{10}$ in. (7 mm) and chestnut-brown. Twig yellowish-brown and ridged. Pages 30, 31

Western balsam poplar
Populus trichocarpa
Bud $\frac{3}{5}$ – $1\frac{1}{5}$ in. (1·5–3 cm), brown, very sticky and sweet-smelling in spring. Twig yellowish-brown and ridged. Page 32

London plane
Platanus × hispanica
Bud $\frac{1}{4}$ in. (6 mm), dull purple-brown with curved tip. Twig brown with raised breathing pores. Page 138

Roble beech
Nothofagus obliqua
Bud to $\frac{1}{4}$ in. (6 mm), lighter brown than twig. Page 74

Hornbeam
Carpinus betulus
Bud $\frac{1}{4}$ in. (6 mm), pale brown and pressed close to twig. Twig grey-brown with paler breathing pores. Page 71

True service tree
Sorbus domestica
Bud $\frac{3}{8}$ in. (1 cm), shiny, sticky and bright green. Twig is grey-brown. Page 171

Hupeh rowan
Sorbus hupehensis
Bud $\frac{1}{5}$ in. (5 mm) and dark red. Twig dark brown with breathing pores. Page 173

Bird cherry
Prunus padus
Bud $\frac{5}{16}$ in. (8 mm), brown and pale at tip. Twig shiny and dark brown. Page 101

Common beech
Fagus sylvatica
Bud $\frac{1}{2}$–$\frac{3}{4}$ in. (1·3–2 cm) and chestnut-brown. Twig dark brown. Page 72

Raoul
Nothofagus procera
Bud $\frac{3}{8}$ in. (1 cm), chestnut-brown and almost at right-angles to twig. Page 75

BUDS CLOSE TO TWIG

Goat willow
Salix caprea

Bud $\frac{1}{6}$ in. (4 mm), red-brown. Twig red-brown and shiny. Page 64

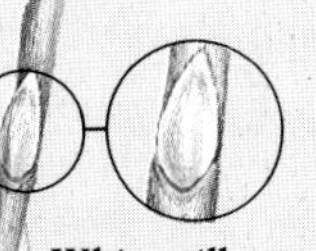

White willow
Salix alba

Bud $\frac{1}{8}$–$\frac{1}{6}$ in. (3–4 mm), and covered with greyish-white hairs. Twig slender with greyish-white hairs. Page 116

Osier
Salix viminalis

Buds $\frac{2}{5}$ in. (1 cm), green with some hairs. Twig dark brown and hairy. Page 119

Crack willow
Salix fragilis

Bud $\frac{1}{5}$ in. (5 mm), and twig yellow to brown. Page 118

Weeping willow
Salix babylonica

Bud $\frac{1}{4}$ in. (6 mm), green to brown, hairless. Twig brown. Page 117

Golden weeping willow
Salix × chrysocoma

Bud $\frac{1}{4}$ in. (6 mm), yellow-ish-green and not very hairy. Twig bright yellow. Page 117

Large buds

All buds in this group are more than $\frac{1}{5}$ in. (5 mm) in length. Lilac is distinguished by its opposite buds, and the maidenhair tree by its buds being carried on short, woody shoots.

Common hazel
Corylus avellana

Buds alternate, $\frac{5}{16}$ in. (8 mm), round, green, hairy. Twig hairy. Page 68. Turkish hazel is similar. Page 69

Maidenhair tree
Ginkgo biloba

Buds alternate, $\frac{1}{4}$ in. (6 mm), short shoots with leaf scars. Young twig green, turning brown. Page 181

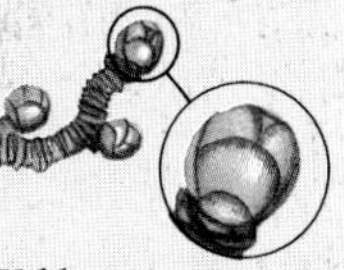

Wild service tree
Sorbus torminalis

Buds alternate, $\frac{2}{5}$ in. (1 cm), round, shiny. Twig brown. Page 142

Sweet chestnut
Castanea sativa

Buds alternate, $\frac{2}{5}$ in. (1 cm), pointed and red-brown. Twig purple-brown, ridged, with hairs and breathing pores. Page 110

Lilac
Syringa vulgaris

Buds opposite, $\frac{2}{5}$ in. (1 cm), green with brown scale edges. Twig brown, ridged with paler breathing pores. A shrub. Page 33

Whitebeam
Sorbus aria

Buds alternate, $\frac{3}{10}$ in. (7 mm), green, pointed with red-edged scales. Tip with long, white hairs. Twig red-brown. Page 86. Swedish whitebeam bud has grey hairs. Page 147

Black mulberry
Morus nigra

Buds alternate, $\frac{1}{4}$ in. (6 mm), red-brown, shiny and pointed. Twig pale fawn and hairy. Page 47

Small buds

The only point of similarity between the buds in this group is that all are $\frac{1}{5}$ in. (5 mm) in length or less. They are divided into trees with opposite buds, those with buds arranged spirally (the larches), and those with alternately arranged buds.

OPPOSITE

Box elder
Acer negundo

Buds $\frac{1}{8}$ in. (3 mm), green and globular. Twig green. Page 177

Field maple
Acer campestre

Bud $\frac{1}{8}$ in. (3 mm), lower scales brown, upper scales green with hairs. Twig dark brown. Page 130

Red maple
Acer rubrum

Bud $\frac{1}{32}$ – $\frac{1}{16}$ in. (1–2 mm) and red. Twigs reddish-brown or green. Page 132. Silver maple, page 133, and smooth Japanese maple, page 135, are similar

Paper-bark maple
Acer griseum

Bud $\frac{1}{8}$ in. (3 mm), dark-brown and pointed. Twig red or grey-brown. Page 160. Cappadocian maple is similar. Page 131

Forsythia
Forsythia × intermedia

Bud $\frac{1}{32}$ – $\frac{1}{16}$ in. (1–2 mm), yellow-brown. Twig yellow-brown with prominent breathing pores. Terminal flower buds chestnut-brown and clustered at shoot tip. Page 122

Mock orange
Philadelphus coronarius

Bud minute. Twig brown. Page 91

Dawn redwood
Metasequoia glyptostroboides

Bud $\frac{1}{32}$ – $\frac{1}{16}$ in. (1–2 mm), yellow-brown, under red-brown twig. Page 224

Spindle
Euonymus europaeus

Bud $\frac{1}{16}$ in. (2 mm), green scales with brown edges, pointed. Twig bright green. Page 113

Guelder rose
Viburnum opulus

Bud $\frac{1}{5}$ in. (5 mm), green with purple edges. Twig greyish-brown. Page 143

Snowberry
Symphoricarpos rivularis

Bud $\frac{1}{32}$ in. (1 mm), brown. Twig very slender. Page 90

Katsura tree
Cercidiphyllum japonicum

Bud $\frac{1}{5}$ in. (5 mm) and red. Twig olive-brown. Page 37

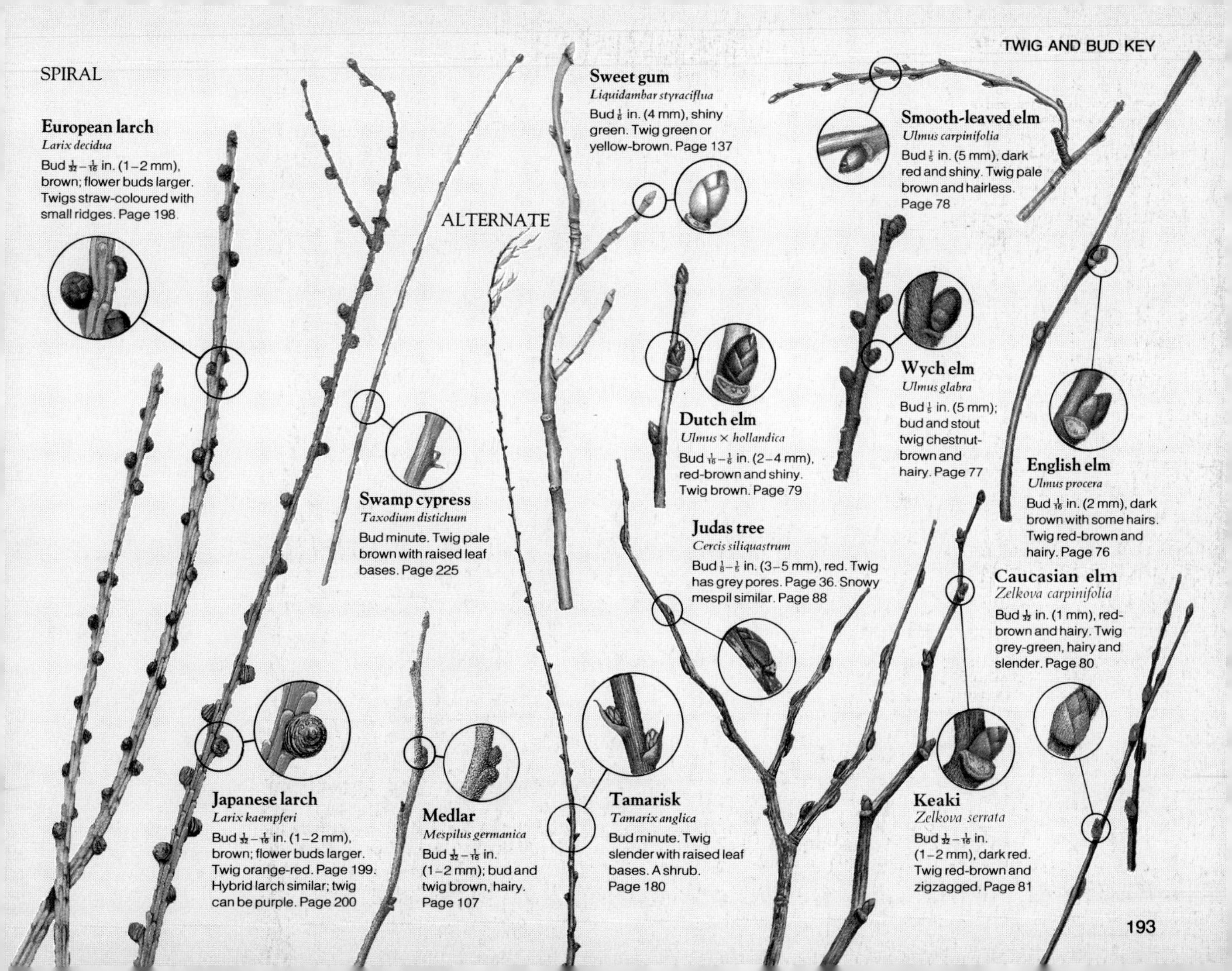
SPIRAL
European larch
Larix decidua
Bud 1/32–1/16 in. (1–2 mm), brown; flower buds larger. Twigs straw-coloured with small ridges. Page 198
ALTERNATE
Swamp cypress
Taxodium distichum
Bud minute. Twig pale brown with raised leaf bases. Page 225
Sweet gum
Liquidambar styraciflua
Bud 1/6 in. (4 mm), shiny green. Twig green or yellow-brown. Page 137
Smooth-leaved elm
Ulmus carpinifolia
Bud 1/5 in. (5 mm), dark red and shiny. Twig pale brown and hairless. Page 78
Dutch elm
Ulmus × hollandica
Bud 1/16–1/6 in. (2–4 mm), red-brown and shiny. Twig brown. Page 79
Wych elm
Ulmus glabra
Bud 1/5 in. (5 mm); bud and stout twig chestnut-brown and hairy. Page 77
English elm
Ulmus procera
Bud 1/16 in. (2 mm), dark brown with some hairs. Twig red-brown and hairy. Page 76
Judas tree
Cercis siliquastrum
Bud 1/8–1/5 in. (3–5 mm), red. Twig has grey pores. Page 36. Snowy mespil similar. Page 88
Caucasian elm
Zelkova carpinifolia
Bud 1/32 in. (1 mm), red-brown and hairy. Twig grey-green, hairy and slender. Page 80
Japanese larch
Larix kaempferi
Bud 1/32–1/16 in. (1–2 mm), brown; flower buds larger. Twig orange-red. Page 199. Hybrid larch similar; twig can be purple. Page 200
Medlar
Mespilus germanica
Bud 1/32–1/16 in. (1–2 mm); bud and twig brown, hairy. Page 107
Tamarisk
Tamarix anglica
Bud minute. Twig slender with raised leaf bases. A shrub. Page 180
Keaki
Zelkova serrata
Bud 1/32–1/16 in. (1–2 mm), dark red. Twig red-brown and zigzagged. Page 81

IDENTIFYING BERRIES

The main evolutionary objective of both plants and animals is to develop efficient means of reproducing themselves. One way by which trees and shrubs achieve this is by producing fruit which contains a seed or seeds for dissemination by the wind or other means. The fruit of many trees takes the form of berries which turn red or black when ripe, drawing the attention of animals and birds to them.

The same conspicuous colouring of berries that attracts wildlife also provides a ready means of identifying various trees and shrubs in autumn and winter. For though red and black are the predominant colours, the exact shade varies from tree to tree; so, too, do the size, shape and arrangement of the berries.

Most berries, being succulent, and rich in sugars, starch and other foods, are eagerly sought by wildlife. Some berries, such as those of rowan and yew, are eaten whole; the seeds within them have hard coats that resist digestive juices, and therefore pass intact through the bird or animal. Others, such as cherries, are not swallowed whole – birds eat only the fleshy covering and discard the stone containing the seed. The seeds of the mistletoe stick to birds' beaks and are wiped off onto the branches of trees where they then grow. The seed is usually dropped well away from the parent tree, and so has space in which to grow.

How fruits take shape

Fruits are formed from the female part of the flower, or ovary, after the ovules have been fertilised, and they contain the seed or seeds. The wall of the ovary becomes fleshy, and the resulting fruit contains one or more seeds. Berries containing one seed include gean, damson and blackthorn, while holly, some of the buckthorns and elder have few seeds. Whitebeam and rowan may contain many seeds, and the strawberry tree's fruit always does so. The mulberry is a fused collection of small fruits.

As berries are rich in sugar and starch, they are valuable to man as well as to wildlife. The berries of most British trees and shrubs have long had a place in kitchen, medicine cupboard and work-place. Many such as elderberry are used to make wine, while blackthorn and juniper are used to flavour gin. Jellies and jams are made from damson, rowan and hawthorn. Many old remedies used berries such as buckthorn and spindle as purgatives, and rowan was believed to be beneficial to the kidneys. A number of natural dyes can be obtained from berries: for example green from buckthorn, and blue, lilac and violet from elder.

Red berries

Hawthorns
Crataegus
Fruits ripen to deep red; withered remains of flower persist. ⅓ in. (9 mm). Pages 144–5

Snowy mespil
Amelanchier lamarckii
Withered remains of flower persist on fruits. ¼–5/16 in. (6–8 mm). Four to six seeds. Page 88

Spotted laurel
Aucuba japonica
Round scarlet berries on female tree only; 5/16–½ in. (8 mm–1·3 cm). Popular tub plant. One seed. Page 99

Holly
Ilex aquifolium
Round, bright red, clustered berries on female trees only. ¼–½ in. (6 mm–1·3 cm). Four poisonous seeds. Page 58

Black mulberry
Morus nigra

Fleshy fruit, edible when ripe, consisting of many single-seeded berries; resembles raspberry. $\frac{3}{4}$–1 in. (2–2·5 cm). Page 47

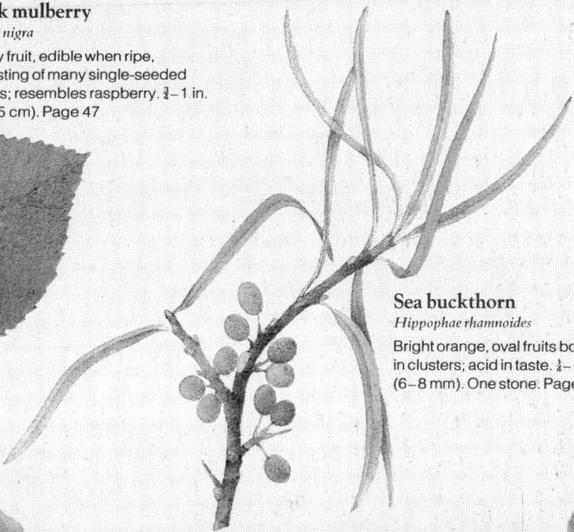

Sea buckthorn
Hippophae rhamnoides

Bright orange, oval fruits borne in clusters; acid in taste. $\frac{1}{4}$–$\frac{5}{16}$ in. (6–8 mm). One stone. Page 121

Common yew
Taxus baccata

Bright red, fleshy seed-covering; $\frac{1}{4}$–$\frac{1}{3}$ in. (6–9 mm). One poisonous seed. Page 230

Wild cherry
Prunus avium

Round fruits hanging in pairs, often bitter; $\frac{1}{2}$ in. (1·3 cm). One stone. Page 100

Cornelian cherry
Cornus mas

Long, egg-shaped, glossy cherries; acid, but can be made into jam. $\frac{5}{8}$ in. (1·5 cm). One stone. Page 63

Barberry
Berberis vulgaris

Long, red edible fruits hang in clusters; $\frac{5}{16}$–$\frac{1}{2}$ in. (8 mm–1·3 cm). One or several seeds. Page 55

Red berries turning black

Rowan
Sorbus aucuparia

Round scarlet berries in heads, sharp-tasting; made into wine or jelly. $\frac{1}{4}$–$\frac{5}{16}$ in. (6–8 mm). Two to eight seeds. Page 172

Whitebeam
Sorbus aria

Long bright scarlet fruits, made into jelly for venison. $\frac{1}{2}$ in. (1·3 cm). Two to eight seeds. Page 86

Portugal laurel
Prunus lusitanica

Numerous round fruits hang in clusters; $\frac{5}{16}$ in. (8 mm). One stone. Page 97

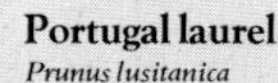

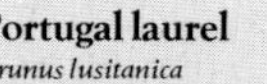

Cherry laurel
Prunus laurocerasus

Round, glossy fruits; bird cherry very similar; $\frac{1}{4}$–$\frac{5}{16}$ in. (6–8 mm). One stone. Page 96

Cotoneaster
Cotoneaster frigidus

Round, bright red fruits borne in heads, much favoured by birds. $\frac{1}{5}$ in. (5 mm). Two seeds. Page 111

Wayfaring tree
Viburnum lantana

Numerous, flattened oval berries borne in dense heads; green at first, then red, then black. $\frac{5}{16}$ in. (8 mm). One flattened stone. Page 87

Guelder rose
Viburnum opulus

Shiny round berries hang loosely in open heads, may remain on branches after leaves have fallen. $\frac{5}{16}$ in. (8 mm). One flattened stone. Page 143

Strawberry tree
Arbutus unedo

Warty fruits take a year to ripen; yellow turning orange-red; acid, edible when ripe. $\frac{3}{5}$–$\frac{3}{4}$ in. (1·5–2 cm). Many seeds. Page 59

Alder buckthorn
Frangula alnus

Round berries, green at first, then red, then violet-black; $\frac{1}{4}$–$\frac{3}{8}$ in. (6–10 mm). Two to three seeds. Page 61

Black berries

Sweet bay

Laurus nobilis

Oval fruit, dark green for some time; $\frac{3}{4}$ in. (2 cm). One seed. Page 98

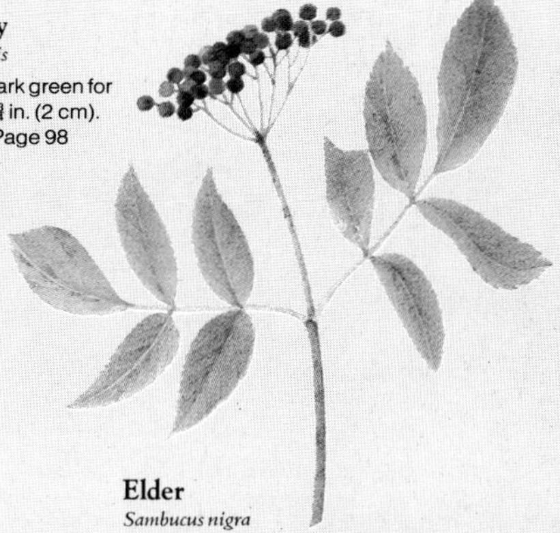

Elder

Sambucus nigra

Round, red-stalked berries hang in dense clusters, green for some time; used to make wine. $\frac{1}{4}$–$\frac{5}{16}$ in. (6–8 mm). Usually three seeds. Page 176

Phillyrea

Phillyrea latifolia

Oval fruits borne in clusters, reddish, then blue-black; $\frac{1}{4}$ in. (6 mm). Usually one seed. Page 120

Oval-leaved privet

Ligustrum ovalifolium

Round, glossy fruits in clustered heads; $\frac{1}{4}$–$\frac{5}{16}$ in. (6–8 mm). One to four seeds. Page 52

Common juniper

Juniperus communis

Single, fleshy, berry-like fruits ripen in two to three years; $\frac{1}{4}$ in. (6 mm). One to six seeds. Page 264

Spurge laurel

Daphne laureola

Round, clustered berries; $\frac{1}{2}$ in. (1·3 cm). One seed. Page 123

Damson

Prunus domestica

Oval fruit, green, then turns purple; $1\frac{1}{2}$ in. (4 cm). One pitted stone. Page 85

Dogwood

Cornus sanguinea

Round fruits in clusters, glossy when ripe; $\frac{1}{4}$–$\frac{5}{16}$ in. (6–8 mm). One stone. Page 62

Blackthorn

Prunus spinosa

Globular fruits, $\frac{2}{5}$–$\frac{3}{5}$ in. (1–1·5 cm). One slightly pitted stone in greenish flesh. Page 57

Purging buckthorn

Rhamnus catharticus

Round berries in small clusters, green for some time, then black; once used for dyeing and as purgative. $\frac{1}{5}$ in. (5 mm). Two to four seeds. Page 60

The pulvinus, or leaf base, stops short of the side buds.

Needles are light green and soft, falling in winter. On long shoots they grow singly; on short shoots they are clustered in rosettes. The twig is straw coloured.

Cones occur all round twig. They are egg-shaped, with tight scales, and stay on the tree for several years after the seed has fallen.

The golden colour of the larch before it sheds its leaves distinguishes it from most other conifers, which are evergreen.

Female flowers

Male flowers

Male flowers are yellow and globe-shaped, female flowers loganberry-red with green stripes, in spring.

Bark is light brown, in fine regular plates.

On a mature tree, the lower stem is clear of branches; the branches higher up are sparse, thick and horizontal. The larch loses its foliage in winter. Grows to 125 ft (38 m).

European larch *Larix decidua*

Between 1740 and 1830 three successive Dukes of Atholl planted more than 14 million larches on their estates in Perthshire. Until then the larch – which was brought to Britain from central Europe about 1620 – had been grown purely as an ornamental tree. The larches are now part of the natural scenery of the area, forming extensive forests near Dunkeld and Blair Atholl. The tree's high-quality timber with its rust-coloured heartwood is used to make staircases, light furniture, wall panelling and many other products.

On the Continent the larch is a mountain species, adapted to long winters and short growing seasons; in Britain it has a longer growing season, and grows quickly in dry areas. It is vulnerable to spring frost and to numerous diseases, especially larch canker. It needs plenty of light and space in which to flourish; to provide the ideal conditions, larch plantations should be thinned.

As the larch does not cast a heavy shadow and is deciduous, grass and brambles grow beneath it, providing food for sheep in upland areas. The tree is often used in forestry to shelter hardwoods. The fast-growing, short-lived larch is felled and sold, allowing the slow-maturing hardwoods to grow on.

The pulvinus, or leaf base, extends up the side of the bud.

Female flowers

Male flower

Male flowers are yellow and globe-shaped; female flowers greenish, occasionally pinkish. The twig is orange.

Cones occur all round twig; they are squat and rounded, with scales turned outwards at the tip, like the petals of a rose.

This deciduous conifer, an oriental cousin of the European larch, grows rapidly and is a major timber tree.

Needles are blue-green, falling in winter. On long shoots they grow singly; on short shoots they are clustered in rosettes.

Japanese larch *Larix kaempferi*

In its native Japan, this ornamental larch was known as the 'money pine'. It was used in bonsai work – the art of developing living dwarf trees by pruning the roots and branches and wiring the branches of normal trees. Some specimens were extremely valuable, or even priceless – hence the Japanese name. The specially dwarfed trees are held to symbolise mortality and the changes wrought by the seasons.

The Japanese larch was introduced to Britain in 1861 and has proved particularly suited to the wetter western side of the country, where its orange twigs colour the hillsides in winter after the needles have fallen. The tree grows quickly and is not susceptible to canker like the European larch. As a result, it is often planted in preference to the European larch, and today forms an important part of Britain's timber resources. As its vigorous growth shades out vegetation, and its wood smoulders rather than burns, it is sometimes planted as a fire-break between more inflammable conifers.

The wood of Japanese larch resembles that of the European larch and is similarly used for fencing and structural work. It has to be sawn carefully to stop the planks from twisting.

Bark is similar to European larch, but more orange.

Branches are horizontal, longer and thicker than those of European larch. The stems of young trees often 'corkscrew'. The tree reaches 115 ft (35 m) in height.

Male flowers are yellow; female flowers vary from loganberry-red to green. Twig is pinkish, sometimes glaucous, or grey-blue.

Female flowers

Male flowers

Cones are egg-shaped or squat, and the scales are sometimes turned outwards.

Needles vary from light green to blue-green, growing singly on long shoots and in rosettes on short shoots.

The vigorous growth of this new hybrid has made it an important timber tree in commercial plantations in Britain.

Hybrid larch *Larix × eurolepis*

The hybrid or Dunkeld larch, a natural cross between the European larch and the Japanese larch, has in recent years become a tree of major commercial importance in this country. Yet the occurrence of the hybrid came about through nothing more than a fortunate accident.

In 1885, about 20 years after Japanese larch was introduced to Britain, the Duke of Atholl planted 11 specimens of the tree at Dunkeld in Perthshire, to produce seed for planting in his forest nurseries. On the hillside above was some European larch, planted more than 100 years before. It is thought that pollen from these trees drifted down and fertilised flowers on the Japanese larch below, so that when the seed was collected, many of the resultant seedlings were hybrids. These seedlings impressed foresters by their vigorous growth.

The hybrid grows more quickly than either parent. It is now produced deliberately in seed orchards, where selected strains of European and Japanese larch are grafted on to young rootstock. This method encourages the trees to seed early, and also produces small bushy trees from which seed can be more easily collected in large quantities.

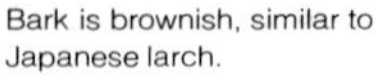

Bark is brownish, similar to Japanese larch.

The pulvinus, or leaf base, just reaches the base of the bud or short shoot.

This cross between European larch and Japanese larch combines features of both parents. Specimens have so far reached 105 ft (32 m).

Male flowers

Flowers are less frequent than on other cedars. Male flowers are erect, releasing yellow pollen in autumn. Female flowers are green.

Female flowers

Single needles grow on the current year's shoot; older needles in rosettes.

Large, barrel-shaped erect cones ripen in two years, then break up to leave a central spike.

The deodar differs from other cedars in its paler green foliage, with longer, softer needles, and triangular shape.

Deodar *Cedrus deodara*

This native of the snow slopes of the Himalayas has religious associations in its native land, where it is also known as the 'tree of God' or the 'sacred Indian fir'. Like other cedars, it is regarded in India as a symbol of fruitfulness and durability, and the timber is traditionally used for building temples and palaces. Its fragrant scent makes it an attractive timber for construction work, though it is also used more prosaically to make railway sleepers and bridges.

This shapely conifer was introduced to Britain in 1831 and soon found favour as an ornamental tree; many specimens may be seen in gardens, parks, churchyards and graveyards. The Commissioners for Crown Lands, forerunners of the Forestry Commission, experimented with the deodar as a forest tree as early as 1860. This was one of many attempts to add a new coniferous timber species to the few conifers then available for commercial purposes in Britain.

The experiment showed, however, that the deodar was not suitable for commercial forestry in Britain, as it comes from a very different climate. Trees from these plantings survive in a few Crown forests, such as the New Forest.

The bark is blackish, with narrow fissures.

Drooping branches distinguish the 'descending' deodar from other cedars. It grows to 110 ft (33 m).

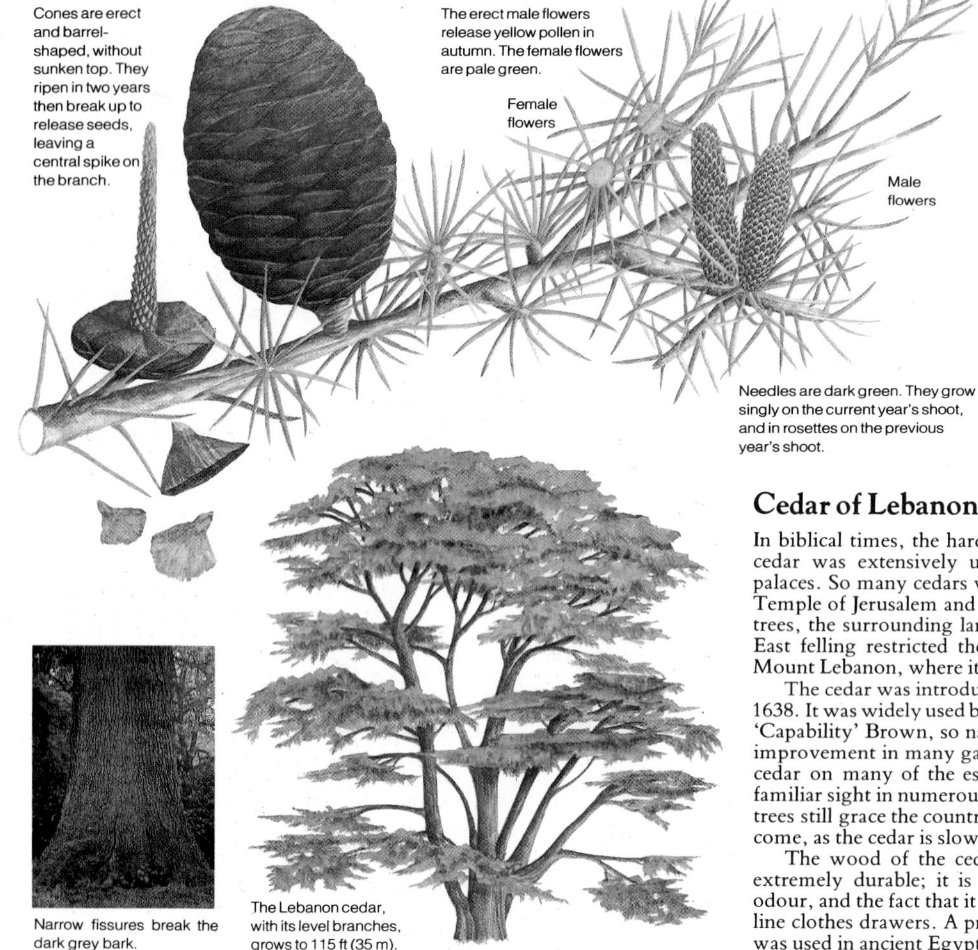

Narrow fissures break the dark grey bark.

The Lebanon cedar, with its level branches, grows to 115 ft (35 m).

Many magnificent trees survive today from extensive planting during the 18th and 19th centuries.

Cedar of Lebanon *Cedrus libani*

In biblical times, the hard and enduring wood of the Lebanon cedar was extensively used in the building of temples and palaces. So many cedars were felled for the construction of the Temple of Jerusalem and Solomon's Palace that, stripped of its trees, the surrounding landscape became a desert. In the Near East felling restricted the cedar to a relatively small area, on Mount Lebanon, where it is now preserved.

The cedar was introduced to Britain as an ornamental tree in 1638. It was widely used by the 18th-century landscape gardener 'Capability' Brown, so named because he saw a 'capability' for improvement in many gardens. Brown planted the flat-topped cedar on many of the estates he redesigned, and it became a familiar sight in numerous parks and large gardens. Many of his trees still grace the countryside, and will do so for some time to come, as the cedar is slow-growing and long-lived.

The wood of the cedar of Lebanon is dense, strong and extremely durable; it is also sweetly scented. Because of its odour, and the fact that it is resistant to insects, it is often used to line clothes drawers. A preservative oil distilled from the wood was used in ancient Egypt to embalm the dead.

Needles, like those of cedar of Lebanon, are blue-green or dark green, growing singly on the current year's shoot and in rosettes on the previous year's shoot.

Female flowers

Pinkish male flowers and green female flowers appear in autumn.

Male flowers

Cone is shaped like a wasp's nest, with a sunken top. It ripens in two years then breaks up, leaving a central spike.

In its native North Africa the Atlas cedar is usually green, but in Britain its blue-green form graces many large gardens.

Bark is dark grey with narrow fissures.

The tree can best be distinguished from other cedars by its rising branches, making it easy to remember as 'Atlas: ascending'. It grows to 120 ft (36 m).

Atlas cedar *Cedrus atlantica*

Most gardeners think of Atlas cedar as the 'blue cedar' because of the attractive blue-green foliage of some specimens. The 'blue' form occurs sporadically in the wild, but there the colour is not as vivid as in the ornamental species cultivated in British gardens. In its native North Africa, the cedar is confined to the Atlas mountains of Algeria and Morocco. It is regarded by some botanists as a western form of the cedar of Lebanon, which it closely resembles.

The Atlas cedar was introduced here in 1841 and grows on sandy soils, loam and limestone. It prefers hotter, drier conditions than most conifers. Fewer large Atlas cedars than cedars of Lebanon exist in Britain, for the Atlas cedar has been grown in this country for less than 150 years, while the first cedars of Lebanon were planted in Britain more than two centuries ago. Because the Atlas cedar reaches a height of around 120 ft (36 m) it needs plenty of space, and specimens planted in small gardens have to be felled before they are fully grown.

Unlike other conifers, the Atlas cedar flowers in autumn. Slug-shaped male catkins then fall in considerable numbers, and often puzzle people as to their origin.

TREES WITH FLAT NEEDLES

Flat needles are characteristic of the largest group of conifers, including all the firs and hemlocks. Flat needles can be subdivided by their length, the way they are arranged, and the contrast in colour between upper and lower surfaces.

Dark green needles

Coast redwood

Sequoia sempervirens

Needles $\frac{1}{2}$–$\frac{3}{4}$ in. (1·3–2 cm) in length, hard and sharp-tipped. Page 222

Common yew

Taxus baccata

Needles $\frac{3}{4}$–$1\frac{1}{2}$ in. (2–4 cm) in length, yellow-green on underside. Page 230

Plum-fruited yew

Podocarpus andinus

Needles $\frac{1}{2}$–$\frac{3}{4}$ in. (1·3–2 cm) in length, with two pale bands on underside. Page 231

Soft, bright green needles

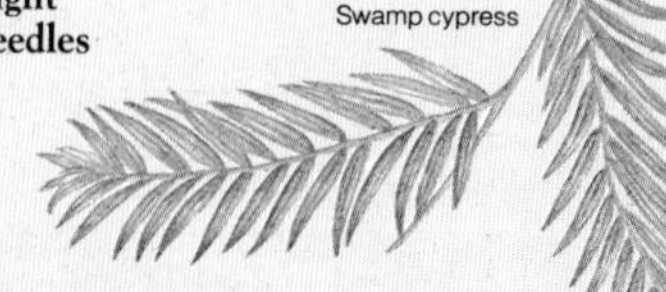

Swamp cypress

Taxodium distichum

Needles $\frac{1}{4}$–$\frac{1}{2}$ in. (0·6–1·3 cm) long, branchlets alternate. Page 225

Dawn redwood

Metasequoia glyptostroboides

Needles $\frac{1}{2}$ in. (1·3 cm) long, branchlets opposite. Page 224

Scattered needles, of varying lengths

Western hemlock

Tsuga heterophylla

Needles $\frac{1}{4}$–$\frac{1}{2}$ in. (0·6–1·3 cm) long, not tapering to tip. Page 220

Eastern hemlock

Tsuga canadensis

Needles $\frac{1}{4}$–$\frac{1}{2}$ in. (0·6–1·3 cm) long, tapering to tip. Page 221

Mountain hemlock

Tsuga mertensiana

Needles $\frac{1}{2}$–$\frac{3}{4}$ in. (1·3–2 cm) long, blue, clustered. Page 219

Large, sharp-pointed needles

Cow's tail pine

Cephalotaxus harringtonia var. *drupacea*

Needles $\frac{1}{2}$–2 in. (1·3–5 cm) long, rows of needles form a V. Page 227

Chinese fir

Cunninghamia lanceolata

Needles $1\frac{1}{2}$–2 in. (4–5 cm) long, with long, slender points. Page 228

California nutmeg

Torreya californica

Needles $1\frac{1}{2}$–2 in. (4–5 cm) long, two marked lines underneath. Page 226

Very broad needles

Monkey puzzle

Araucaria araucana

Needles $\frac{1}{2}$–$1\frac{1}{2}$ in. (1·3–4 cm) long, very broad. Page 229

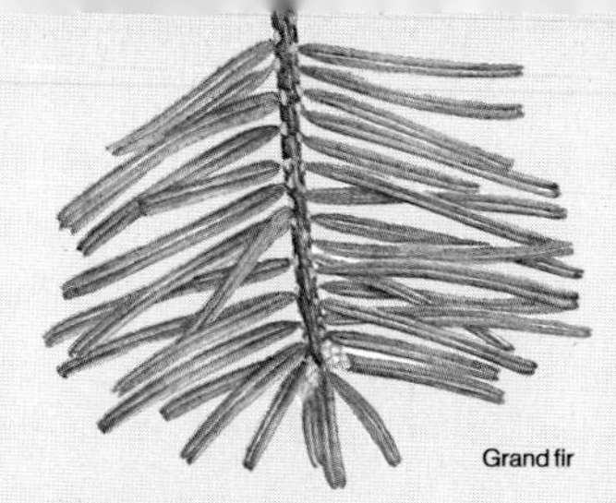

Needles in flat spray

Grand fir
Abies grandis

Needles $\frac{1}{2}$–1 in. (1·3–2·5 cm) long, sparse, not covering shoot. Page 210

Beautiful fir
Abies amabilis

Needles $\frac{1}{2}$–1 in. (1·3–2·5 cm) long, covering shoot. Page 208

Colorado white fir

Blue needles

Colorado white fir
Abies concolor

Needles $\frac{3}{4}$–$2\frac{1}{4}$ in. (2–5·5 cm) long, pointed forwards. Page 211

Noble fir
Abies procera

Needles $\frac{1}{2}$–1 in. (1·3–2·5 cm) long, curving out at right-angles to twig. Page 217

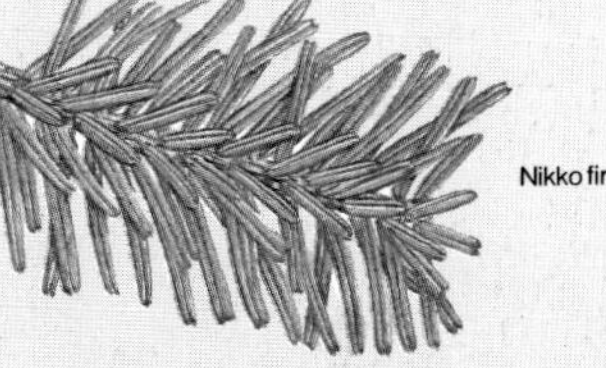

Needles cover upper side of shoot

Nikko fir
Abies homolepis

Needles $\frac{1}{2}$–$\frac{3}{4}$ in. (1·3–2 cm) long, blunt-tipped. Page 215

Caucasian fir
Abies nordmanniana

Needles $\frac{1}{2}$–1 in. (1·3–2·5 cm) long, pointed forwards, notched at tip. Page 207

Needles parted to show shoot

Common silver fir

Common silver fir
Abies alba

Needles $\frac{3}{4}$–$1\frac{1}{2}$ in. (2–4 cm) long, tips notched. Page 206

Douglas fir
Pseudotsuga menziesii

Needles $\frac{3}{4}$–$1\frac{1}{4}$ in. (2–3 cm) long, very soft, pointed. Page 218

Needles with very sharp points

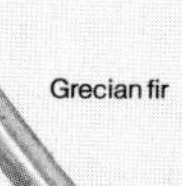

Grecian fir

Grecian fir
Abies cephalonica

Needles $\frac{1}{2}$–1 in. (1·3–2·5 cm) long. Page 213

Spanish fir
Abies pinsapo

Needles $\frac{1}{2}$ in. (1·3 cm) long. Page 212

Needles very white below

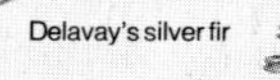

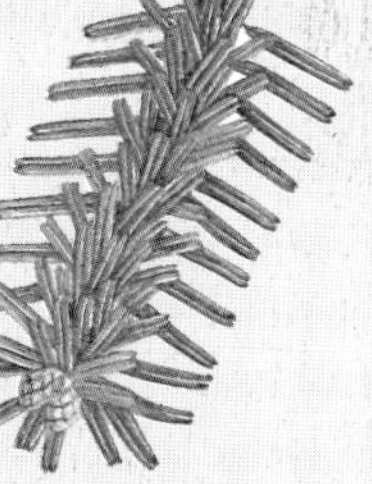

Delavay's silver fir
Abies delavayi

Needles $\frac{1}{2}$–$\frac{3}{4}$ in. (1·3–2 cm) long, margins turned in. Page 216

Veitch's silver fir
Abies veitchii

Needles $\frac{1}{2}$–$\frac{3}{4}$ in. (1·3–2 cm) long, curved forwards. Page 209

Himalayan fir
Abies spectabilis

Needles 1–$2\frac{1}{2}$ in. (2·5–6 cm) long. Page 214

A narrow conical tree that grows slowly at first and can reach 150 ft (46 m).

Yellowish male flowers are grouped on undersides of twigs; green female flowers on upper sides, near top of tree.

Female flower

Male flowers

Needles, shiny green on top and silvery beneath, are parted to either side of twig; upper set shorter and upturned. Tips usually notched.

In central Europe, silver fir is an important timber tree, but in Britain it is prone to damage by aphids.

Young bark grey with resin blisters; cracks with age.

Needles are often attacked by *Adelges* (aphids), which can severely damage or kill the tree.

Cones are borne erect and have protruding bracts.

Common silver fir *Abies alba*

This native fir of central European highlands was widely planted in Britain in the 19th century, both as an ornamental tree and for the sake of its timber. Many large trees still survive, their gaunt 'crow's nests' tops rising high above surrounding trees and making them unmistakable. However, the tree is susceptible to attack by the aphid *Adelges nuslinii*. This aphid sucks sap from the leaves, causing them to become yellow and flabby and eventually to fall; badly attacked trees die. As a result the common silver fir has been largely replaced in Britain by the fast-growing grand fir, *Abies grandis*, from the west coast of North America.

Common silver fir still grows vigorously on the Continent, in such areas as the Black Forest of Germany. This species is the original Christmas tree, although it is the Norway spruce that today provides the Christmas tree of British households.

The timber of common silver fir is white or yellowish-white, with distinct annual rings. It is light in weight, soft and not very strong, but splits easily and can be worked well. Because it is odourless it can be used for food storage without tainting the contents. Resin that has oozed into blisters on the bark of common silver fir is the main constituent of turpentine.

Yellowish-green female flowers appear on young shoots near the top of the tree.

Bracts are prominent on the upright cone.

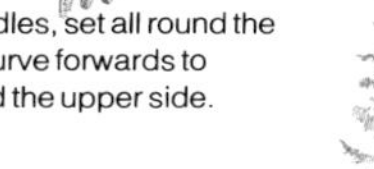

The needles, set all round the shoot, curve forwards to surround the upper side.

Clusters of red male flowers grow on the undersides of shoots, lower down on the tree than females.

This stately and ornamental conifer grows well in Britain, though it is seldom seen outside tree collections and parks.

The smooth, grey bark develops fissures.

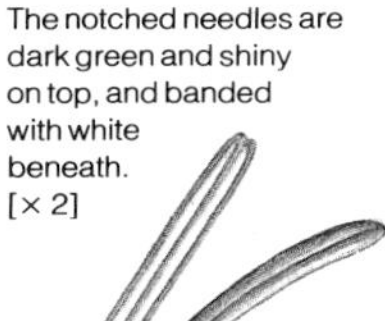

The notched needles are dark green and shiny on top, and banded with white beneath. [× 2]

Denser and darker than most firs, the Caucasian fir has a distinct conical shape and grows up to 150 ft (46 m).

Caucasian fir *Abies nordmanniana*

When a Finnish botanist called Nordmann, working in southern Russia, discovered what was in fact a new species of silver fir in 1836, he was not immediately given the credit he deserved, for the Caucasian fir he had identified was not at first recognised as a distinct species. Two years later, however, its separate identity was recognised, and Nordmann's name was perpetuated in the tree's botanical name.

The initial doubt about Caucasian fir being a separate species is understandable. It has the regular outline characteristic of other silver firs, while its cones stand upright on the shoots and break up to release the seeds when they are ripe – both features that are peculiar to silver firs and to cedars. However, there are distinct points of difference between the Caucasian fir and other silver firs. Its needles are denser, and the bracts on the cones are long, protruding over the cone scales, whereas in some other species of silver fir they are short or completely hidden.

The Caucasian fir grows best in the British Isles in the cool and moist conditions of the west coast. In old age it retains its lower branches down to ground level, instead of losing them like some other firs, and its foliage remains thick.

Needles are flat, dark green and shiny above, silver-white beneath. Shorter central needles point forwards, the longer side needles outwards.

The beautiful fir earns its name by its regular conical shape, and grows to 150 ft (46 m).

Red male flowers are grouped on underside of twig.

The beautiful fir from North America thrives in northern and western Britain in arboreta and large gardens.

Bark is greyish-white, with resin blisters.

Purple female flowers grow on top of the twig.

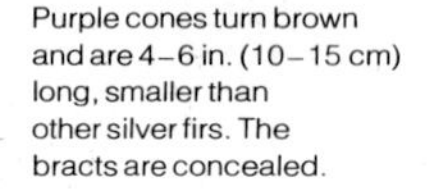

Purple cones turn brown and are 4–6 in. (10–15 cm) long, smaller than other silver firs. The bracts are concealed.

Beautiful fir *Abies amabilis*

On the west coast of North America, where the beautiful fir is a native tree from Oregon to northern British Columbia, it is known by a variety of names, many of which it shares with other silver firs. They include alpine fir, white fir and balsam fir, from its sweet-smelling resin. However, the true balsam fir is a separate species, *Abies balsamea*, valued for its resin which is the source of Canada balsam, a gum used to stick specimens to slides for microscopic study.

Beautiful fir grows further north and at higher altitudes than the grand fir, thriving on mountain-sides at up to 6,000 ft (1,830 m), where the soil is light. In Britain the tree grows well, if slowly at first, but it has not been planted extensively. It is grown as an ornamental species in parks and gardens for its symmetrical shape and attractive needles, which are silvery-white underneath.

The light, moderately hard wood has an even grain and is pale brown in colour, with a darker heart. The beautiful fir produces better-quality timber than most silver firs and is used in North America for buildings, boxes and crates and as a pulpwood. It could become a useful timber tree in Britain.

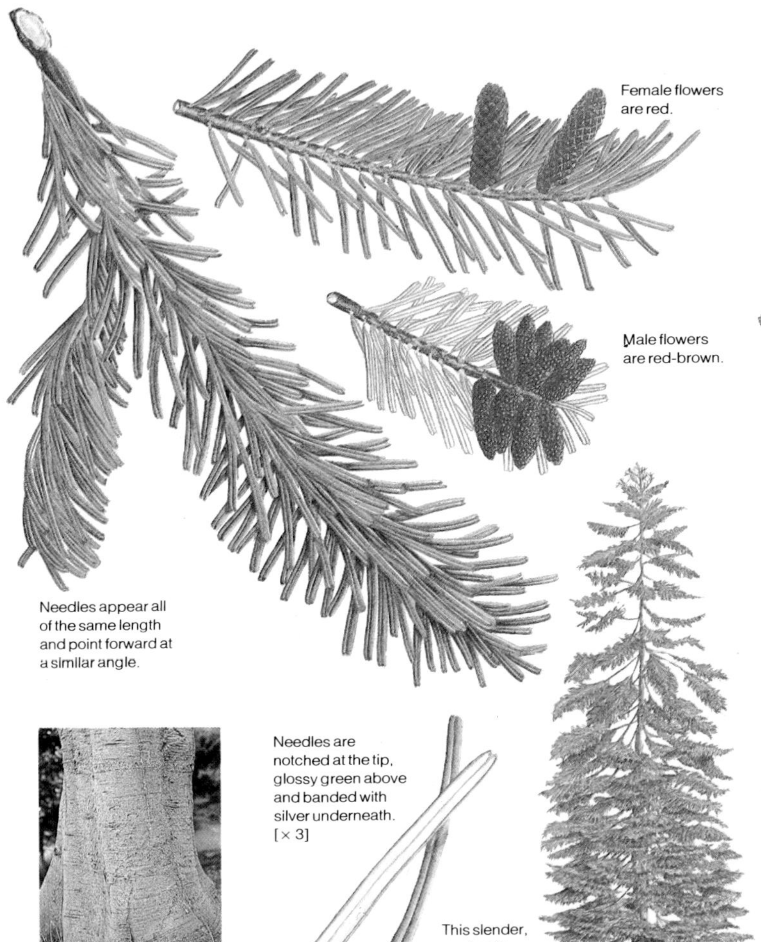

Female flowers are red.

Male flowers are red-brown.

Needles appear all of the same length and point forward at a similar angle.

Needles are notched at the tip, glossy green above and banded with silver underneath. [× 3]

This slender, conical fir grows to 75 ft (23 m). The lower branches are often upswept.

Bark smooth; depressions below branches.

Female flowers become attractive blue cones which turn brown when ripe. Bracts protrude slightly.

This fir is planted as an ornamental tree in gardens and parks. It grows best in western and northern Britain.

Veitch's silver fir *Abies veitchii*

In the late 19th century the Exeter firm of Veitch were the foremost nurserymen in Britain, and internationally famous. They were responsible for the introduction of many exotic species of trees and flowers now cultivated in gardens and parks. In 1860 John Gould Veitch visited Japan, a country which until that time had been inaccessible to foreigners. On that trip he collected many plants that subsequently became popular in Britain, among them the silver fir named after him, which he found growing on the slopes of Mt Fujiyama.

Veitch's silver fir is the smallest of the Japanese firs. It is short-lived, but is one of the easiest Japanese firs to cultivate, being tolerant of pollution and resistant to spring frosts. It is fast-growing, especially in its early years, and soon produces cones and fertile seeds.

Although in Japan the wood is used for paper making, this fir has not yet been grown as a commercial timber tree in Britain – probably because other firs imported from the west coast of America have proved so successful for commercial forests. However, the leaves of Veitch's silver fir have striking silvery undersides that make this conifer a popular ornamental tree.

Male flowers

This majestic tree forms a narrow and symmetrically conical crown; it grows to a height of 180 ft (55 m).

Male and female flowers grow on the same tree; the males are small and purplish, the females green.

Female flowers

In plantations with high rainfall and good soil, the grand fir will produce timber very quickly, reaching full height in 20 years.

The sparse needles vary in length and are strongly flattened on either side of the shoot. They are dark green and shiny on top, and silver beneath.

Bark smooth and grey-green, with resin blisters.

The cone ripens from green to brown, exuding resin; the bracts do not show.

Grand fir *Abies grandis*

Many decorative foreign conifers owe their presence in Britain's parks and gardens to the wave of enthusiasm for landscape gardening in the middle of the 19th century. Among the most successful introductions was the so-called grand fir, discovered by the Scottish tree-collector David Douglas and brought to Britain in 1852 from the banks of the Fraser River in British Columbia. When planted on Scottish estates and in parks as an ornamental tree, it grew so fast that canny estate managers were soon planting it for its timber.

The grand fir has now replaced the European silver fir in plantations as it grows so quickly, and is not prone to disease. The light, soft wood is rather weak and unsuitable for construction work, but it is used to make fruit boxes and crates. This fir grows best in wet districts. In dry areas it may suffer from drought crack when young, with cracks running up the trunk.

The needles are of two types, those growing in shade being much flatter, to present the maximum surface to the sunlight. The litter breaks down readily and is high in mineral content, improving the soil beneath the trees. Fertile seed is produced in Britain and seedlings are found under older trees.

Male flowers

Male and female flowers grow on the same tree. Both are yellow, but the male flowers have a pink tinge and are rounder in shape.

Long fleshy needles are blue-green on both surfaces, and stand away from the twig, curving upwards.

Female flowers

Green cone ripens brown. Its bract scales do not show.

Colorado white fir, a native of the western United States, is found in some British collections of conifers.

Colorado white fir *Abies concolor*

Like all living things, the white fir must adapt itself to its environment or perish. It is a native of western America, where it grows in two forms, both of which have also been planted in Britain. The Colorado white fir, which is the southern form in its homeland, has upward-curving needles with numerous breathing pores on both their surfaces: this is an adaptation to sunny, dry conditions on the part of a very drought-resistant tree. The pores, being filled with air, account for the needles' blue-green colour.

Since the climate is unsuitable, the Colorado white fir is rare in Britain. But Low's fir does better, being adapted to the cooler, wetter conditions of more northerly latitudes. Its needles have few, if any, breathing pores on their upper surfaces, which as a result are greener than those of the Colorado fir's needles.

Low's fir is planted as an ornamental tree in the north, thriving in Northumberland and Argyll, though unusual elsewhere. It can stand a lot of shade throughout its life, and retains branches all the way to ground level, increasing its value as a decorative tree. A dwarf form, with silver-grey leaves, has been developed for rock gardens.

Bark smooth with resin blisters, but may roughen.

Low's fir
Abies concolor var. *lowiana*

The leaves of this decorative northern variety of white fir are green on their upper surfaces.

Branches grow in regular whorls. The tree reaches 130 ft (40 m) in Britain.

Cone is purplish-brown, and more pointed than those of other firs. The bract scales are concealed.

Female flowers

Male flowers

Male and female flowers grow on the same tree. The male flowers are large and cherry-red, the females pale green.

Native to the Sierra Nevada mountains of Spain, this fir thrives on the chalky soils of southern England.

Smooth, dark grey bark becomes roughened with age.

The small, sharp needles on the shoot leave round scars when removed.

The young tree has dense, dull green foliage and a regular, conical shape. In Britain it grows to more than 100 ft (30 m).

Spanish fir *Abies pinsapo*

The quickest and easiest way to identify a Spanish fir is also the most painful. Short, prickly needles spread all around the shoots like the bristles on a bottle-brush, and when they are grasped by the unwary, they show how the tree earned its other name of 'hedgehog fir'.

The Spanish fir is not a native of Britain, but grows wild only in three small areas in the Sierra Nevada mountains of Spain. It is an example of a conifer that was almost wiped out in the Ice Age. When the Ice Age finally retreated, vegetation moved slowly north to re-colonise the areas laid bare by the ice. The spread of the Spanish fir, however, was blocked by the east-west valley of the River Guadalquivir, and it was confined to the region in which the remnants of the native tree grow today, until men began to introduce it as an ornamental tree in gardens elsewhere. It was introduced into Britain in 1839.

The Spanish fir is one of the few silver firs that will flourish on chalky soils, though it does well on other soils if they are not too acid. In Britain it grows best in the warmer south and east where it is planted in parks, gardens and churchyards. It is not a very common tree, however, and grows slowly.

Male flowers

Female flowers

Needles are a dark, shiny green on top and whitish beneath, with sharp points, and are slightly parted below the shoot. Male and female flowers grow on the same tree.

A native of the Greek mountains, the Grecian fir is planted in some large British gardens, particularly in East Anglia.

Cone grows upright on the twig to about 6 in. (15 cm) long. Bract scales protrude and bend downwards.

Light brown surface of bark is broken by dark fissures.

This fir is broad and heavily branched. It is roughly conical, but often has a flattened top. It grows to 115 ft (35 m).

Grecian fir *Abies cephalonica*

Being one of the first silver firs to produce new leaves in spring, the Grecian fir is vulnerable to damage by frost. Once established, however, it grows quickly, and it is valued as an ornamental tree for gardens where there is space for its wide branches to spread. The Grecian fir was introduced to Britain in 1824 from the mountainous country of southern Greece. In its homeland the tree is today less widespread than it used to be, because of devastation by fire and grazing by animals.

The Grecian fir resembles the Spanish fir in having prickly leaves, though they are not quite so stiff. Both trees grow best on chalky soils, and will cross-pollinate naturally when growing close together. The original cross between the two trees, × *vilmorinii*, was brought about in 1868 by pollinating the flowers of the Spanish fir with pollen from the Grecian fir. The tree produced was intermediate in character, and grafts from this are sometimes found growing in collections.

The wood of Grecian fir is similar to that of other firs in being rather soft and not very strong or durable. Grecian fir has the additional drawback that its coarse branching produces many knots, which make weak points in the timber.

The needle is brilliant white below and dark green on top, 1–3 in. (2·5–7·5 cm) long and notched at the tip. [Actual size]

The tree has an irregular crown, with a few heavy, horizontal branches. It has reached 100 ft (30 m).

Needles are parted into two rows either side of the twig, and form a 'V' exposing the shoot.

This fir from Asia's mountain regions is vulnerable to spring frosts in Britain, but grows into a fine tree in mild areas.

Here, lichen covers the greyish-brown bark.

The cone can be as much as 7 in. (18 cm) tall. Pale grey in colour at first, it turns dark purple as it ripens through the winter.

Himalayan fir *Abies spectabilis*

Many of the tea-chests which were once a familiar sight in grocers' shops were made of Himalayan fir – ideal for the purpose because it has no odour to taint the contents. The easily worked wood is white with a straight grain, and it is used for building and general woodwork in India, Pakistan and Afghanistan.

The long cones and the long needles with their silvery-white undersides make the Himalayan fir easy to recognise. The tree is not very hardy in Britain and it is grown mainly in the west, where the Gulf Stream keeps the climate wetter and reasonably warm. In other regions the young buds are often nipped by Britain's late spring frosts.

Himalayan fir produces a small number of heavy branches and is unusual among conifers in growing epicormic branches on the trunk; an epicormic branch grows from a dormant bud, usually when it is suddenly exposed to the light, and this type of growth is more typical of hardwoods. The form of Himalayan fir usually grown in Britain comes from the western part of the tree's native habitat, and has slightly shorter needles than the commonest form of the tree found in its native homeland.

The short needles of the Nikko fir stand upright, almost at right-angles to the twig. They are green on top and whitish beneath.

Being resistant to pollution, Nikko fir, a 19th-century introduction, is well equipped for survival in British city parks.

This native of the Japanese mountains has a symmetrical, triangular shape and grows to 90 ft (27 m) high.

Smooth, light grey bark becomes scaly with age.

Needles are narrow at the base and have rounded tips. [Actual size]

Cones are purple when young, exuding white resin, and ripen brown. The bract scales are concealed.

Nikko fir *Abies homolepis*

A Bavarian-born eye doctor called Philipp Franz von Siebold became in 1854 the first European to collect and record the Nikko fir. Von Siebold was employed by the Dutch East India Company in Japan at a time when that country was developing cautious links with Europe. Because of his skill in curing cataract and other eye diseases, Von Siebold was allowed to visit areas still closed to other Europeans, and he used the opportunity to collect and record many Japanese flowers and trees.

Von Siebold sent specimens of Nikko fir back to the plant nursery he had established at Leiden in Holland. They flourished, and the Nikko fir is now widely planted in parks and gardens in Britain. It is resistant to atmospheric pollution and it survives where other species of silver fir may die.

Nikko fir's appearance is sometimes marred by whiskery shoots growing from its trunk. They arise from dormant buds below the bark which may develop when the amount of light reaching the tree is suddenly increased, as for example by the removal of nearby trees. Wood from Nikko fir is not used commercially, even in Japan, where it usually grows in inaccessible forest areas.

Turned-in edges of needles make them curve away from twig. Undersides of needles are brilliant white. Male flowers are reddish, females blue.

Female flower

Male flowers

The ornamental Delaray's silver fir adapts well to the British climate, but may be damaged by late frosts.

Whorls of branches separated by lengths of stem give the tree a regular pyramid shape. One whorl and one stem length is a year's growth. The tree grows to 65 ft (20 m).

Delavay's silver fir *Abies delavayi*

More than one European plant collector risked death from disease, natural disaster or hostile inhabitants in western China in the 19th century, and the Frenchman Jean Marie Delavay (1834–95) was among the unluckiest. This Jesuit missionary was an avid hunter of new plants. His right arm became paralysed and he caught bubonic plague, from which he never fully recovered. But he never gave up his quest and he continued collecting until his death, still in China.

Delavay sent thousands of carefully dried plant specimens, seeds and young living plants, back to botanists in France but even then his bad luck continued. Many of the dried specimens were ruined after their arrival because they were not looked after properly, and most of the living plants were killed because they were treated as hot-house plants.

Delavay's silver fir grows in the mountains of China at altitudes of between 10,000 and 11,000 ft (3,050–3,400 m). Its attractive blue cones and the white undersides of the needles have made it a garden favourite. The variety most commonly grown in Britain, *forrestii*, was named after one of Delavay's successors – the Scotsman George Forrest (1873–1932).

The bark is smooth and dark grey in colour.

Forrest's fir

Abies delavayi var. *forrestii*

In this variety of Delavay's fir, the tips of the bracts protrude between the cone scales. The needles are less noticeably curved.

Inky blue, barrel-shaped cones appear early in the tree's life. The bracts do not protrude between the cone scales.

Layers of horizontal branches form the regular outline of the noble fir. It grows to 150 ft (45 m).

Female flowers

Male flowers are deep red and cluster under twigs. Females are yellow, upright and shaped like a pastry brush.

Male flowers

Needles in shade are smaller and adhere to the twig.

Needles are blue-green on both sides. On the lower branches they lie close to the twig; in full light on the upper branches they are long and turn upwards.

This imposing American native, occasionally planted for timber in Europe, is widely grown in British gardens.

Upwards curving needle from twig of upper branch.

The smooth, silver-grey bark has resin blisters.

Cones are very big and upright, with protruding, down-turned bracts. The cones break up to leave a thin, central spike.

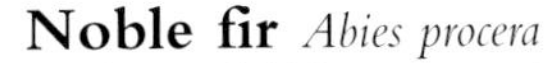

Noble fir *Abies procera*

In the mid-19th century the Scottish tree collector David Douglas introduced this aristocrat of the North American mountains to a new home in the 'policies' or woodlands surrounding Scottish mansions. It is now an established part of the Scottish landscape, standing firm against the wind and snow on exposed northern sites even where the soil is poor. In the less rugged south, the noble fir often sickens and sometimes dies, attacked by a woolly aphis (*Adelges*) which destroys the terminal bud. It also fares badly in shade or on very chalky soils.

A striking feature of the noble fir is the huge, green cone, growing up to 10 in. (25 cm) long and nearly half as broad, with prominent, down-turned bracts. Some of the tree's alternative names refer to the bracts – the 'bracted fir' and the 'feather-cone fir'.

Because it withstands exposure, is resistant to snow damage and tolerates poor soil conditions, the noble fir has been planted as a timber tree, but not in sufficient quantities in Britain to make it commercially significant. However, the wood is light and fairly strong, with a hard, close grain, and in North America it is used for interior building work.

Male flowers

This very tall, conical tree grows to 180 ft (55 m) in Britain and 325 ft (100 m) in its native North American west coast.

Male flowers are yellow; females are red and shaped like a tassel.

Female flowers

Needles grow all round the shoot, but are parted on the upper and undersides, leaving the shoot exposed.

The underside of the leaf has two white bands.

The Douglas fir has been much planted in Britain for its valuable wood, known as Oregon pine when it is imported.

Dark grey or purple with age; fissured and corky.

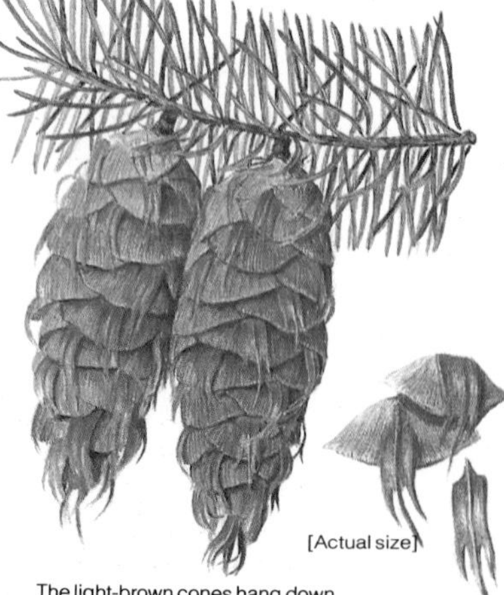

[Actual size]

The light-brown cones hang down and have long, protruding bracts, each with three prongs.

Douglas fir *Pseudotsuga menziesii*

After the coast redwoods, the Douglas fir is the tallest tree growing on the North American west coast. This magnificent conifer is named after David Douglas, the plant collector who introduced its seeds to Britain in 1827. The newcomer was widely planted at first as a decorative tree, particularly in the policies, or private woodlands, around Scottish mansions. It then began to be grown for commercial purposes, and is now an important timber tree in Britain, and also one of the tallest.

The seed sent by Douglas came from an area with conditions similar to those in Britain. Given good soils, the tree grows well and produces some of Britain's finest timber. On shallow soil it is more prone to disease and may be blown down easily. Douglas firs like plenty of light: too much shade encourages a leaf-sucking aphid, which was unwittingly imported with the tree before the dangers were realised.

Many of Britain's Douglas firs are not yet old enough to produce the first-class timber of North America, where it is called Oregon pine. This is heavy and durable, taking paint and polish well. It is excellent for building work, doors, floors, veneers, and high-quality plywood.

Short branches produce a narrow, pointed tree, reaching 65 ft (20 m) in height in Britain.

Bark is reddish-brown, becoming corrugated.

Cones are long and cigar-shaped, with rounded scales. Purple at first, they ripen to brown.

The needles are bluish-green on top and below; they grow all round the stem on long shoots, or in clusters on short shoots, giving a cedar-like appearance.

Male flowers

Female flowers

Male flowers are small and purple; female flowers purple or green and slightly larger. Both appear on the same tree

Its decorative shape and blue-green foliage make this American tree an attractive rarity in British collections.

Mountain hemlock *Tsuga mertensiana*

This stately conifer grows on the very edge of the mountain snows of North America's western coast, taking root at heights of up to 11,000 ft (3,400 m). The rarefied air, gales and fierce sunlight it has to endure at such altitudes cause a tree to lose water rapidly. To combat this, the needles of the mountain hemlock grow in bunches, like those of cedars; this reduces water loss by trapping moisture vapour.

At extreme heights in its native home the mountain hemlock becomes stunted, but lower down the mountain-sides it grows into a tall tree with an elegantly narrow profile. Like other trees native to alpine areas, the mountain hemlock grows only slowly in Britain and does not reach a great height. Although this slow growth makes the tree more suitable than some of the forest giants for ornamental planting, it is still not widely grown.

The mountain hemlock will tolerate a lot of shade, particularly in its younger days. When grown in the open its shapely, dense branches with their bunched, grey-blue needles and purplish young cones offer a handsome spectacle. A hybrid between mountain hemlock and western hemlock known as *Tsuga × jeffreyi* is closer in appearance to its mountain hemlock parent.

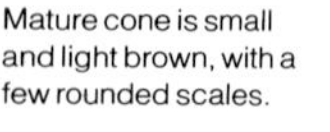

Mature cone is small and light brown, with a few rounded scales.

Needles part to either side of shoot and vary in length, giving a scattered appearance. They are green on top and white beneath. The shoot is hairy.

The western hemlock, which comes from the Pacific seaboard of North America, is grown for ornament and for its wood.

Western hemlock *Tsuga heterophylla*

The Indians of North America made a kind of bread from the inner bark of the western hemlock, but this magnificent conifer was brought to Britain in the last century for its decorative, not its culinary, value. Discovered by the great horticulturalist David Douglas, who gave his name to the Douglas fir, the western hemlock was planted in gardens and woodlands round large houses on Scottish estates.

A graceful, ornamental tree, the western hemlock can be grown on a wide variety of soils, except those containing chalk. It grows rapidly and regenerates easily, producing many seedlings. It reaches a large size and an age of between 200 and 500 years in its native habitat.

When grown commercially, the amount of timber the tree produces per acre is high, especially in western Britain where moisture is plentiful. The wood has the ability to hold nails well, so is much used for making boxes. As with other hemlocks, the seedlings and young trees require shady, moist conditions, and it is therefore useful for planting under other tree crops. The drooping branch tips prevent the young shoots from being damaged by the branches of the trees under which it is growing.

Needles taper to a blunt tip. [× 3]

The purplish-brown bark is fissured, sometimes flaky.

Down-turned branch tips and shoots, giving the whole tree a drooping appearance, make the western hemlock one of the most attractive conifers. In Britain it grows to 115 ft (35 m).

Though not used as a timber tree, eastern hemlock is popular in gardens and parks, particularly in eastern England.

Bark is brownish, deeply furrowed and scaly.

The needles taper from their base to a blunt end. [× 2]

This bushy tree's many-forked stem and its broad, dense, conical crown are distinctive. It grows to a height of 105 ft (32 m).

Eastern hemlock *Tsuga canadensis*

In 1736 Peter Collinson, an amateur collector with a garden in London, introduced to Britain the eastern hemlock from the east coast of North America. Although it is hardier and will grow at higher altitudes than the western hemlock, a later introduction, it does not grow so well in Britain as its relative. Moreover, it forks profusely as it grows, so that it is unsuitable as a timber tree. In North America this forking is not typical of the tree, so that its timber can be used there for construction work as well as for making paper pulp.

In Britain, the eastern hemlock's habit of forking is turned to advantage, for this makes it an effective ornamental tree. Many bushy dwarf forms have been developed for decorative use, especially for rockeries and trough gardens. The tree has the advantage, too, that it will grow on soils over chalk, so long as there is adequate moisture.

The leaves of the hemlocks are very like those of the yew in shape, leading to their being given the generic name *Tsuga*, a Japanese word meaning 'yew-like'. European botanists so named the genus because the first member of it to be discovered was the Japanese hemlock.

Green female flowers are about ¼ in. (6 mm) long.

Needles are bright green above, paler below. They are flattened to either side and end in a sharp point. They often turn brown in winter, but do not fall. The twig is green.

Yellow male flowers grow on tips of small shoots.

Long-lived coast redwoods from California have been planted in many British parks and large gardens.

Cones are rounded and resemble those of cypress. They grow at the tips of larger shoots.

Soft, fibrous, ruddy bark is resistant to fire.

The narrow, column-shaped coast redwood is the tallest tree in the world. One in the Tall Tree Grove, Redwood Creek, California, measures almost 368 ft (112 m).

Coast redwood *Sequoia sempervirens*

At the beginning of the 19th century, as white settlers moved westwards across the United States, a Cherokee Indian called Sequo-yah decided that his people could not hope to retain their independence unless they developed a written alphabet to express their language. Sequo-yah borrowed from English, Greek and Hebrew to create a Cherokee alphabet that is still in use today. His achievement is commemorated in the scientific name of the magnificent coast redwood and in the name of the Sequoia National Park in California.

Fossil remains of coast redwoods have been found from the south-western United States to the Arctic and occur in Britain, but the living tree is now native only to parts of the North American Pacific coast. It was first recorded in 1769, but was not described botanically until 1823, and was introduced to Britain 20 years later. It is grown in Britain mainly for its decorative value, rather than for its light, reddish-brown timber.

Some Californian coast redwoods are more than 2,500 years old, though most are less than half that age. In their native land they grow to heights of 360 ft (110 m) and more, but in Britain they are generally much smaller.

LIFE AMONG REDWOODS

In Britain the coast redwood is an impressive tree that has already reached a height of 140 ft (43 m). In its home on northern California's Pacific coast, it has become the tallest living thing on earth, reaching more than 360 ft (110 m). It is remarkably long-lived: it throws out new shoots after it has fallen, and specimens in America have lived for more than 2,500 years. The oldest and largest stand of redwoods in Britain is the Charles Ackers Redwood Grove near Welshpool, in Powys.

Upswept branches and a conical shape distinguish the dawn redwood from the taller coast redwood. Woodland and shade-loving plants such as red campion, ivy and herb-robert, and plants of grassy places such as common vetch and bird's-foot-trefoil all thrive among redwoods.

When the branches of a coast redwood in the Redwood Grove near Welshpool were driven into the ground as the tree fell, the branches on the upper side of the fallen trunk developed into young trees. After a tree has been felled, coppice shoots spring vigorously from the cut stump, and some will grow into new trees. Treecreepers hollow out roosting places in the redwood's soft bark.

Sparse branches sweep upwards, producing a narrow, conical tree, up to 65 ft (20 m) tall. It sheds its branchlets and needles in autumn.

Needles are broader than those of the swamp cypress. [Actual size]

Branchlets appear opposite each other in pairs. The twig is greenish and the cones are green, globe-shaped or cylindrical, on long stalks.

Thousands of years ago dawn redwoods covered much of the earth; now this 'living fossil' is being planted again.

Dawn redwood *Metasequoia glyptostroboides*

Until 1941 the dawn redwood, or water fir, was known to scientists only from its fossilised remains, and was believed to have been extinct since the Pliocene era, which ended about 2 million years ago. Then botanists in China found more than 100 large specimens growing in Hupeh province, where they had escaped the attention of the European plant-hunters of the 19th century. Later, many more dawn redwoods were discovered in the same region.

Through the efforts of the Arnold Arboretum in the United States, seeds were collected from Hupeh and distributed to tree collections in North America and Europe. It was discovered that the dawn redwood can be reproduced easily from cuttings and it is now widely planted in Britain, except for Scotland where the climate is too cool for it to grow well.

Because the tree is a recent introduction, little is known about the properties of its timber and few specimens are yet old enough to bear flowers and cones. It is one of the few cone-bearing trees that sheds its needles in the autumn. The buds of the dawn redwood are unique, appearing below the branches instead of in the axils above.

Needles turn russet-brown from the tips before falling in the autumn.

Bole is fluted, with shaggy, reddish bark.

Branchlets are alternate, and fall in autumn with the needles. The twig is reddish, and the needles, which do not appear until June, are smaller and finer than those of the dawn redwood.

Female flowers

Female flowers are small and green; male flowers lengthen to form yellow catkins in April.

Male flowers

Green at first, the globe-shaped cone turns purple in autumn before its scales open to release their seeds.

The damp-loving swamp cypress needs warm summers to flourish, so it is seldom seen in northern Britain.

Swamp cypress *Taxodium distichum*

Addicts of old Hollywood films would recognise the swamp cypress on its home ground – the brackish or freshwater swamps of the south-east United States – its fallen trunks festooned with Spanish moss and its weird 'air-roots' sprouting from the mud. Two million years ago the tree grew in Britain, for traces have been found in rocks near Bournemouth. It was introduced in 1640 by John Tradescant, and its spectacular autumn colouring made it a favourite for planting beside lakes.

In the sluggish waters of its native habitat, oxygen is limited. The swamp cypress thrives there because, like the mangrove, it increases the oxygen supply by pushing up air-roots, or pneumatophores, from its root system. These are hollow structures that grow up to 10 ft (3 m) above the ground in the wild. The most usual height is 3 ft (1 m), though where adequate oxygen is available in the soil, the air-roots do not appear at all.

The tree has another habit uncommon in conifers: it sheds its needles in winter, hence its alternative name of 'bald cypress'.

The wood resists damp and insects, and does not shrink; it is also soft and easily worked. These qualities make it popular for window frames and for garden buildings.

Stringy, light brown bark peels off near base.

The triangular outline is distinctive. Air-roots, or pneumatophores, often rise from the surrounding soil: these help breathing in waterlogged conditions when the soil lacks oxygen. The tree grows to 65 ft (20 m).

Male flowers are rounded and yellow. Green female flowers grow on separate trees.

Fruit, green at first and turning purple, contains seeds with nutmeg-like kernels that give the tree its name.

The underside of the needle has two distinct white bands.

The yew-like needles have long; sharp points. They are flattened to either side of the twig and are shiny green on top.

This close relative of the yew, a native of California, grows in spacious gardens mainly in the south and west of Britain.

The slightly ridged bark is greyish-brown in colour.

The tree has a pointed, conical profile; its branches, nearly horizontal, form a whorl around the trunk. The California nutmeg can reach a height of 70 ft (22 m).

California nutmeg *Torreya californica*

In 1849 William Lobb, a Cornish plant collector, went to California on behalf of an Exeter firm of nurserymen, James Veitch and Son. His mission was to send back to England the seeds of interesting and unusual plants and trees. Among these was the rare California nutmeg, which he introduced to England in 1851. It is called nutmeg because the seed kernel resembles the edible nutmeg used to flavour food. The kernel is contained in a fleshy, purple fruit. A less pleasing name for this ornamental tree is stinking yew – a reference to the unpleasant smell of the leaves and bark when they are bruised.

The California nutmeg can exist on chalky soil, but it likes plenty of moisture. Like the related common yew, it flourishes in shade and forms dense thickets; the seedlings need shady conditions in order to survive. The spiky foliage of the mature tree casts a dense shade in which very little will grow.

The tree – which is only found in a few large parks and gardens – grows slowly and it is believed that it will prove to be long-lived. Its light, hard-grained wood is lemon yellow in colour; although it is durable, the trees from which it comes are too few for it to be of any great commercial use.

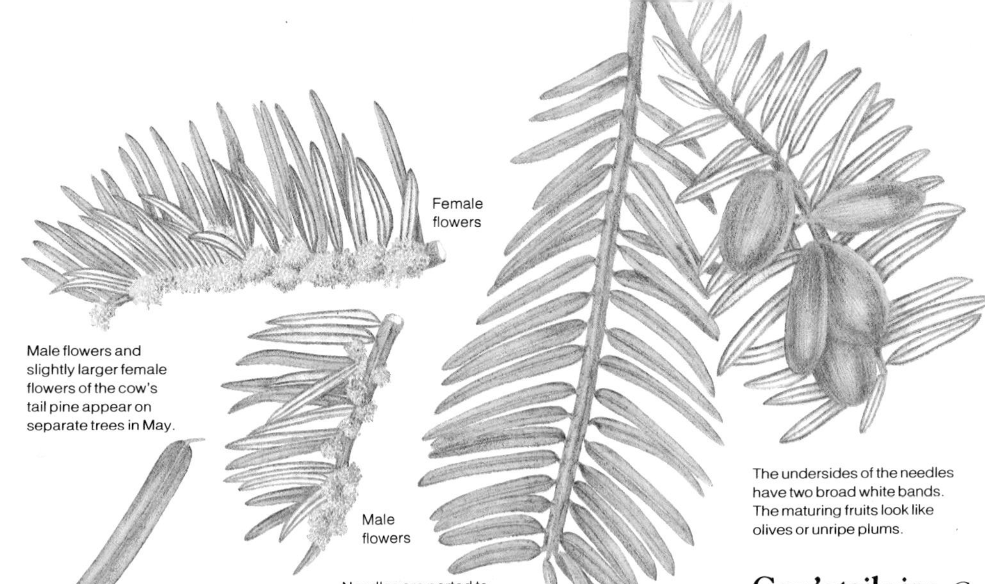

Male flowers and slightly larger female flowers of the cow's tail pine appear on separate trees in May.

Yellow-green needles are less sharply tipped than those of Californian nutmeg, with prominent central rib. [Actual size]

Needles are parted to either side of the twig, and curve upwards to form a V-shaped trough.

The undersides of the needles have two broad white bands. The maturing fruits look like olives or unripe plums.

The bushy shape of the cow's tail pine, a native of China and Japan, is sometimes seen in British parks and gardens.

Dense branches form a low, spreading tree which rarely reaches its maximum height of 40 ft (12 m) in Britain.

The greyish bark is divided into narrow strips.

Cow's tail pine *Cephalotaxus harringtonia* var. *drupacea*

Introduced to Britain from the Far East in the 19th century, cow's tail pine is planted mainly as a screening shrub. It does not mind a shaded position, can be pruned heavily without damage and, except for chalk, grows well on most types of soil.

The origin of the tree's most common name is not clear, for there is nothing about it that resembles a cow's tail. It is more accurately described by its two alternative names of Japanese plum-fruited yew and plum-fruited cephalotaxus, for it has fleshy, plum-like fruits that are borne in heads: *cephalos* is Greek for 'head'.

In its native lands of China and Japan, cow's tail pine grows at altitudes up to 3,000 ft (900 m). In cultivation in Britain it remains low and shrubby, rarely reaching its maximum height. In fact, in Britain it seldom grows to more than 10 ft (3 m). Of the various garden forms that are available, one – 'Fastigiata' – has dense upright branches and resembles the Irish yew. The leaves of the 'Fastigiata' cultivar are very dark, almost black, and are arranged right round the shoots. The wood of cow's tail pine is yellow and moderately hard, but it is not available in any appreciable quantity.

The immature cone is a shiny, vivid green.

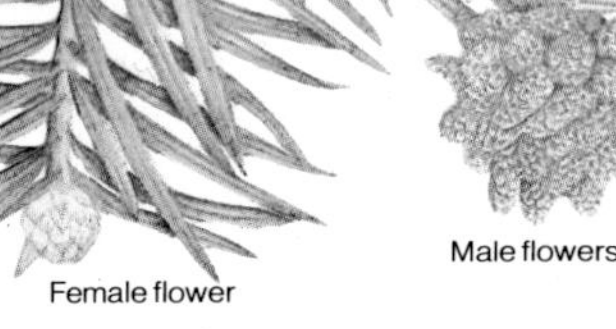

Female flower

Male flowers

Needles are long, narrow and triangular, and shiny green on top. Female flowers are yellow, orange or pale green in colour.

Underside of needles has two pronounced greenish-white lines. The small male flowers appear in a bunch at the end of the shoot.

The Chinese fir grows fast when young. It is uncommon, and is seen mainly in botanical gardens in southern England.

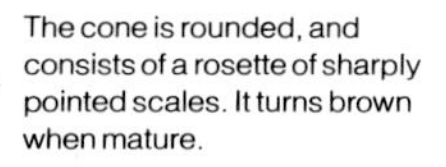

The cone is rounded, and consists of a rosette of sharply pointed scales. It turns brown when mature.

The stringy bark is a rich brown colour.

The Chinese fir is a column-shaped or conical tree with sparse branches; in healthy trees the lack of branches is concealed by their foliage. The tree can reach a height of 100 ft (30 m).

Chinese fir *Cunninghamia lanceolata*

In China, which is its native home, this tree is known as Sam-Shu or common evergreen, for it is extremely abundant. Its yellow wood is soft, easily worked and notably durable, and is especially prized for making coffins. Timber of old trees which have fallen and been buried and have become dark in colour is particularly highly valued. Chemicals contained in the bark make it weather-resistant, and it is widely used in China for making roof shingles.

The Chinese fir was seen in 1702 by James Cunningham, a surgeon with the East India Company who made several voyages to China before the country became inaccessible to foreigners. An avid botanist, Cunningham travelled extensively and was the first Englishman to collect plants in China. The tree was not, however, introduced to Britain until 1804, when a collector named William Kerr brought back specimens for Kew Gardens.

Sunny situations on light, well-drained soils suit this tree best. Once they are more than 3–4 ft (1 m) high, young trees grow very quickly. Chinese fir is liable to frost damage, particularly in the autumn, but unlike other conifers the tree sheds its frost-damaged tip and new shoots arise from the healed wound.

The monkey puzzle has a domed crown, and often the lower branches fall, leaving a clean stem. The tree reaches a height of 80 ft (24 m).

The branchlets are completely clothed in overlapping dark green leaves. These are broad and triangular, and have sharp spines.

Female flower

Male and female flowers grow on separate trees. The female flowers appear singly, the male flowers in groups.

Male flowers

The monkey puzzle became popular in Victorian times and is still a feature of many parks and suburban gardens.

Bark is thick and grey, with horizontal rings.

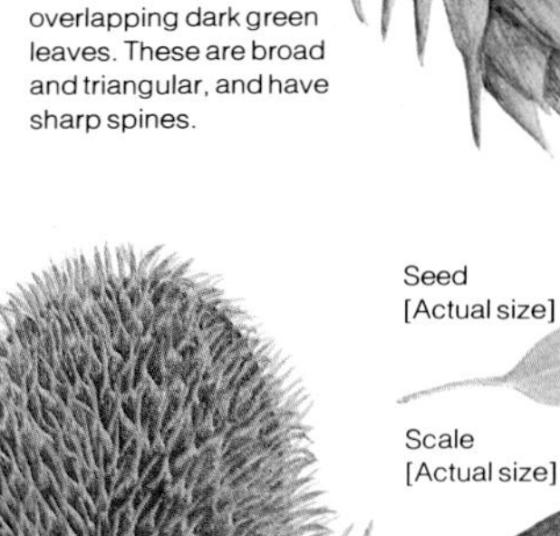

Seed [Actual size]

Scale [Actual size]

The cone takes two to three years to ripen, by which time it has become brown and up to 6 in. (15 cm) in diameter. It breaks up to release seeds and scales.

Monkey puzzle *Araucaria araucana*

The monkey puzzle, or Chile pine, became known to Europeans in the 17th century because the Spaniards needed timber to build and repair their ships while they were exploiting the treasures of South America. Its discoverer was an explorer named Don Francisco Dendariarena, whom the Spanish government sent to South America specifically charged with the mission of finding a source of strong but easily worked timber.

The tree's scientific name is derived from the Araucanian Indians, who inhabited the area of southern Argentina and Chile in which it was found. The traditional explanation of the common name is that the task of climbing the tree, with its sharp, close-set leaves, would puzzle even a monkey.

The seeds of the monkey puzzle were eaten, fresh or boiled, by the Araucanian Indians. The tree was introduced to Britain in 1795 by Archibald Menzies, who saved the edible seeds served to him as a dessert and planted them on board the ship *Discovery* on which he was travelling as a botanist. The trees seldom live longer than 100 years, so no specimens of the original plantings survive today. The timber of trees grown in Britain is too knotty to be of commercial use.

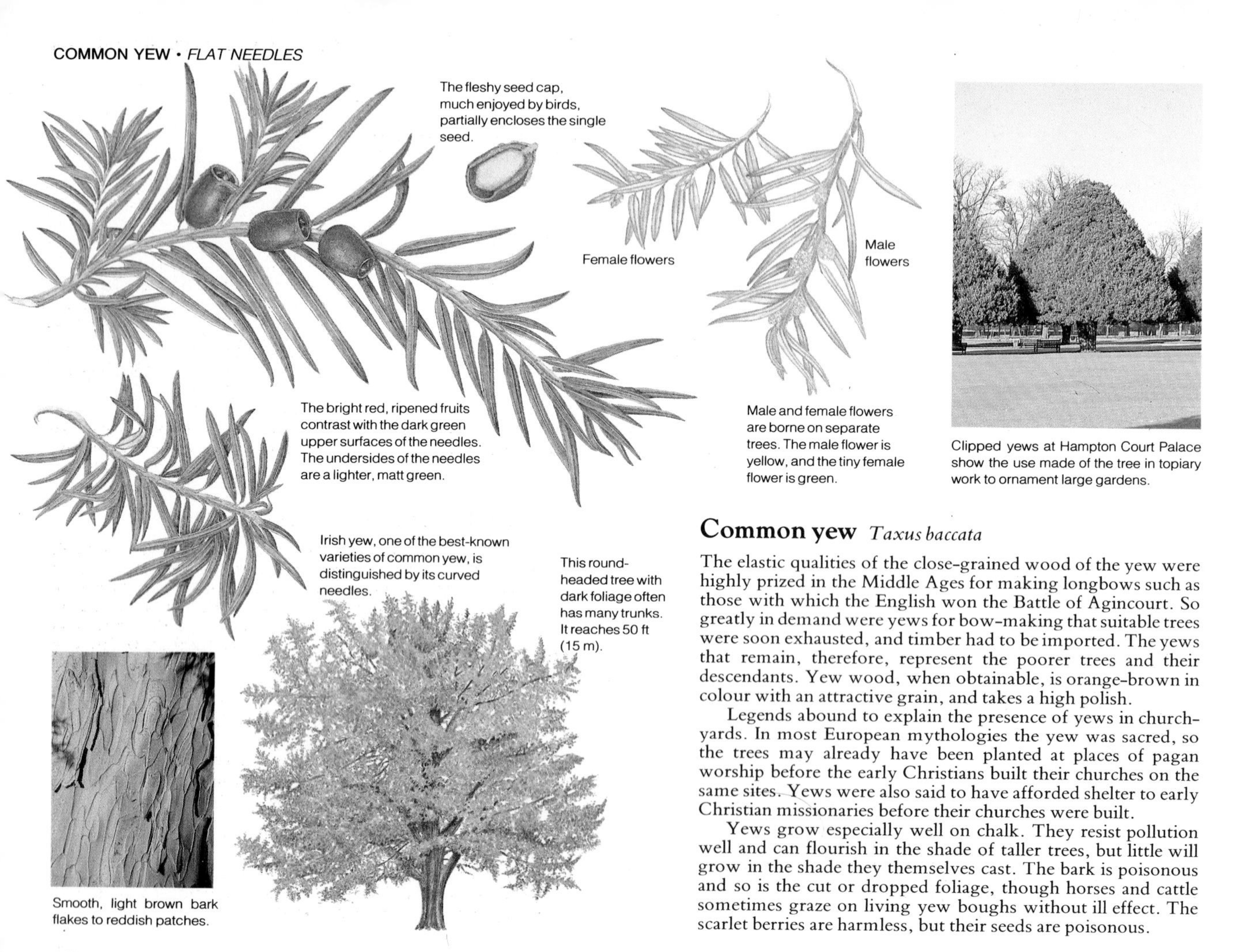

The fleshy seed cap, much enjoyed by birds, partially encloses the single seed.

The bright red, ripened fruits contrast with the dark green upper surfaces of the needles. The undersides of the needles are a lighter, matt green.

Male and female flowers are borne on separate trees. The male flower is yellow, and the tiny female flower is green.

Clipped yews at Hampton Court Palace show the use made of the tree in topiary work to ornament large gardens.

Irish yew, one of the best-known varieties of common yew, is distinguished by its curved needles.

This round-headed tree with dark foliage often has many trunks. It reaches 50 ft (15 m).

Smooth, light brown bark flakes to reddish patches.

Common yew *Taxus baccata*

The elastic qualities of the close-grained wood of the yew were highly prized in the Middle Ages for making longbows such as those with which the English won the Battle of Agincourt. So greatly in demand were yews for bow-making that suitable trees were soon exhausted, and timber had to be imported. The yews that remain, therefore, represent the poorer trees and their descendants. Yew wood, when obtainable, is orange-brown in colour with an attractive grain, and takes a high polish.

Legends abound to explain the presence of yews in churchyards. In most European mythologies the yew was sacred, so the trees may already have been planted at places of pagan worship before the early Christians built their churches on the same sites. Yews were also said to have afforded shelter to early Christian missionaries before their churches were built.

Yews grow especially well on chalk. They resist pollution well and can flourish in the shade of taller trees, but little will grow in the shade they themselves cast. The bark is poisonous and so is the cut or dropped foliage, though horses and cattle sometimes graze on living yew boughs without ill effect. The scarlet berries are harmless, but their seeds are poisonous.

Male flowers are yellow and grow in clusters on separate trees from the female flowers. They open in June.

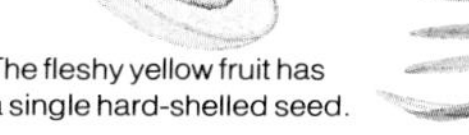

The fleshy yellow fruit has a single hard-shelled seed.

Female flowers are slender and green.

Plum-fruited yew, first imported from Chile in the 19th century, grows mainly in mild areas of Britain, in botanical gardens.

Fruits grow in clusters of two to six. They are apple-green with white flecks, turning to yellow when ripe.

Smooth, dark brown bark becomes grey when old.

Needles are blunt-tipped, bright green on top and pale green beneath.

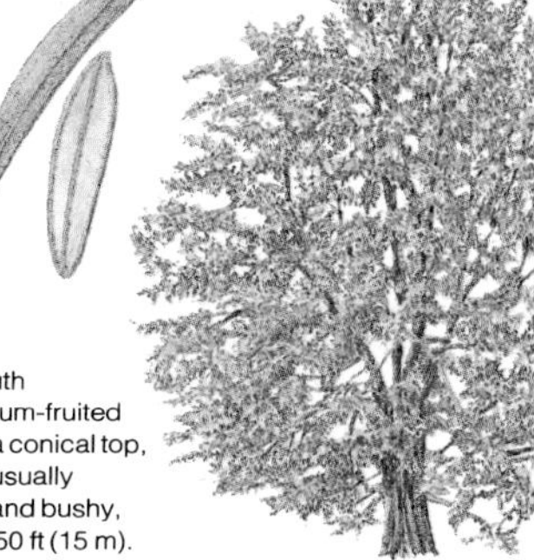

In its native South America, the plum-fruited yew develops a conical top, but in Britain it usually remains small and bushy, no higher than 50 ft (15 m).

Plum-fruited yew *Podocarpus andinus*

In their native region, the Andes mountains of southern Chile and Argentina, plum-fruited yews grow at altitudes of up to 6,000 ft (1,830 m). As the name suggests, the fruit, which turns yellow when ripe, looks like a small plum and is sweet-tasting. South American Indians also eat the kernel of the stone, after removing its hard shell. In its native lands, the plum-fruited yew is prized for its wood, used as a decorative feature in cabinet-making. It is hard and yellow, giving the family of trees to which it belongs the alternative name of 'yellow woods'.

The plum-fruited yew is the only yellow wood that can be grown out of doors in the British Isles. Because of its mountain origin, it starts growth early and is vulnerable to late spring frosts; it therefore does best in the south and west, in places that are sheltered from cold winds. Like yew, it can be grown as a hedge.

The tree is difficult to propagate from seed, as the hard shell of the stone must be broken down before germination will take place. The stone has to be 'stratified' – put in sand and kept moist for several months – or else prepared by scraping it thinner with a knife or treating it with chemicals.

The tree forms a regular conical shape, with the higher branches ascending and lower branches either level or drooping. It can reach 130 ft (40 m).

All children know this spruce as the familiar Christmas tree.

The light green needles are short and prickly, protruding on all sides of the shoot. The cones are long and cigar-shaped with rounded scales, and they hang down.

A native of continental Europe, the Norway spruce is widely grown for its timber, or is cut young for Christmas trees.

Bark is light brown and smooth, cracking with age.

Flowers open in May. Yellow male flowers cluster at the ends of shoots; erect female flowers are pink; cones ripen in autumn.

Norway spruce *Picea abies*

The Christmas tree so familiar to many a British household is Norway spruce. It is not considered a native tree, but it grew here during warm episodes in the last glaciation. Driven south by the last Ice Age, it was slow in recolonising northern Europe. Changing climate and human activities have led to its spread in the last 5,000 years. But by this time, Britain was cut off from the Continent by sea. Although reintroduced by about 1500, its use at Christmas dates only from Victorian times, when Prince Albert brought a Norway spruce to Windsor Castle from Coburg.

The tree serves as much more than a Christmas decoration. It produces a high yield of good-quality timber for building work, pit-props, packing cases and boxes. It is also very suitable for paper pulp, as the wood is composed of long fibres that bind together well.

The timber of Norway spruce is sometimes known as 'violin wood' because of its use for the sounding board, or front, of the violin, and the sound post between front and back. Its function is to transmit vibrations from the strings to the hard maple wood of the sides and back. Pitch and turpentine used to be made from the resin, and a spruce beer from the twigs.

LIFE IN A MAN-MADE FOREST

Some of the wildlife that had become very scarce by the end of the 19th century, due to persecution by man and the reduction of its forest shelter, is now recovering in the spreading woodland of commercial plantations. In young forest, small mammals breed prolifically, providing food for birds of prey. Here, too, small birds shelter. As the conifers grow and become dense, larger animals such as deer and foxes move in. The trees let in more light as they grow taller, encouraging ground vegetation and harbouring tits, siskins and wrens in their branches.

Young spruce trees.

Mature Norway spruce plantation.

Red squirrels and other small animals breed and feed in man-made forests, where they may raid birds' nests for eggs. Small birds such as crossbills, treecreepers and coal tits nest in coniferous trees. Sparrowhawks and other birds of prey nest at the forest edges.

Bramble, bracken, foxglove and rosebay willowherb spring up among the younger spruces. The rides and other open spaces provide feeding grounds for deer in the early morning and evening, and the dense plantations provide refuges in which they hide during the day. Hen harriers favour this habitat for nesting.

Regular horizontal branches give the blue spruce an attractive narrow, triangular shape. Up to 80 ft (24 m).

Sharp, stiff needles grow all round the top of the shoot and point forwards. They are blue-grey, sometimes powder blue. Flowers open in May.

Scales are brown and papery. [× 2]

Light brown cones hang downwards and are similar to those of the Sitka spruce, though longer.

Bark is dark brown in colour and scaly.

Blue spruce grows well throughout Britain, and is widely planted as an ornamental tree in parks and gardens.

Blue spruce *Picea pungens* 'Glauca'

High in the Rocky Mountains of North America, the Colorado spruce grows on soil drier than that tolerated by other spruces. To reduce water loss, the needles have air-filled breathing pores and a waxy coating; these features also give the needles their bluish-grey, or 'glaucous', colouring. By selecting the bluest of the seedlings of Colorado spruce and propagating them by grafting, tree growers have produced the distinctive deep colour of the blue spruce, an ornamental feature of many British gardens and parks.

Most of the blue forms of Colorado spruce are grouped together under the name 'Glauca', from the Latin word for a blue-grey-green shade. The cultivar most commonly planted in small gardens is 'Koster'. Another cultivar, 'Prostrata', is produced from side branches of the parent tree rather than from the stem, and so hugs the ground.

The Colorado spruce and its cultivated forms have stiff, sharp-pointed needles, giving them their Latin name of *pungens*, meaning 'stabbing' or 'pricking'. The Colorado spruce itself is rarely planted as an ornamental tree, as its foliage is regarded as less attractive than that of the blue cultivars.

Needles are sickle-shaped and too sharp to be grasped. Chestnut-brown bud scales persist and are seen as lumps on underside of shoot.

Male flowers

Male flowers are yellow, female flowers green.

Female flower

Prickly foliage makes the tiger tail spruce unsuitable for all but the largest gardens and tree collections.

The narrow tiger tail spruce has the conical shape typical of most spruces. It reaches 60 ft (18 m) in Britain.

Rough, grey-brown or purplish bark has large scales.

Cones hang down from twig. Rounded, broad scales have light-coloured edges.

Forward-curved, rigid needles are the sharpest of any spruce. [Actual size]

Tiger tail spruce *Picea polita*

Either the long, dangling branches on older trees or the sharp-pointed needles, which are painful to grasp even lightly, may have earned this spruce its name of tiger tail – *torano-wo-nomi* in Japanese. It comes from the cool, temperate regions of Japan, and grows wild only in inaccessible valleys, where it sometimes occurs in mixed clumps with hardwoods. Its timber is soft and white, giving it the alternative name of white fir which it shares with various other species. The wood is sometimes used for building or for pulp, but is generally of little commercial importance, because of the remoteness of its growing areas.

Tiger tail spruces are widely planted as ornamental trees in Japan, often to provide shade for Shinto and Buddhist temples. In Britain, where they were introduced in the 19th century, they lend an exotic eastern appearance to many tree collections. Mirroring the Japanese custom of siting them in holy places, a few have been planted in English churchyards.

In Japan, the tiger tail spruce grows to about 130 ft (40 m), but in Britain few have attained half that height. Like all spruces, its root system is shallow and it is easily blown down if exposed to strong winds.

Needles are long, thin and sharp, dark green above and blue-green below. Twigs are yellowish.

Attacks by spruce aphid often defoliate the tree in summer, but seldom kill it.

Female flowers

Male flowers

Male flowers are pale yellow; female flowers, often clustered at the top of the tree, are greenish-red.

Growing exceptionally fast on poor exposed and wet sites, the Sitka spruce is ideal for commercial forestry in Britain.

Cones are light brown, with crinkled, papery scales and blunt tips.

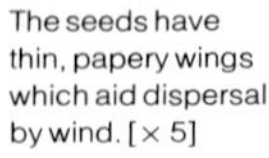

The seeds have thin, papery wings which aid dispersal by wind. [× 5]

The smooth grey bark peels off in thin plates.

This tall, vigorous tree is conical in shape with long, heavy lower branches. It commonly reaches a height of 150 ft (46 m).

Sitka spruce *Picea sitchensis*

Since it was introduced to Britain in 1831, Sitka spruce has become the most widely planted commercial forest tree in the country. It grows quickly on many different types of soil, and yields large quantities of excellent timber. So far it has proved resistant to disease, though in exceptionally dry conditions it may lose its needles to the attacks of the spruce aphid. Deer and voles, which attack other conifers, cause little damage to the Sitka spruce, deterred perhaps by its sharp foliage.

Sitka spruce requires plenty of moisture, and thrives in the wetter areas of western Britain, where conditions resemble those of its native home on the west coast of America. The name Sitka comes from Sitka Sound in Alaska. Because the roots are shallow, trees growing in exposed situations may be uprooted by high winds. The tree is also vulnerable to damage by spring frosts, and in frost hollows the hardier Norway spruce is usually planted.

The white or pale brown wood is light but strong – qualities which made it a suitable material for the construction of Mosquito aircraft during the Second World War. It has long fibres, ideal for paper-making, and it is also used to make boxes.

The tree is conical and narrow. Top branches are level, lower ones droop. Up to 100 ft (30 m).

Needles are white-streaked on underside and parted, exposing yellowish twig.

Female flowers

Male flowers

Needles look darker from above, overlapping like fish scales and covering the twig. Female flowers, larger than male, grow near top of tree.

In Britain, this Japanese variety of an Asian species is mainly confined to large gardens and formal collections.

Hondo spruce *Picea jezoensis* var. *hondoensis*

Hondo in Japanese is an alternative name for the island of Honshu, where this variety of spruce originated. Although *Picea jezoensis* is widespread in Korea, Manchuria and Japan, the few specimens in this country are slow-growing and stunted. Only the Hondo variety is planted with success in Britain.

The hardy Hondo spruce grows evenly and steadily to form a slim, towering pyramid. With its graceful outline and needles of contrasting colours, it makes an attractive ornamental tree in parks and larger gardens.

In Japan, Hondo spruce is a major source of building timber, and of woodpulp for paper production. The timber is light-weight, soft in texture and creamy coloured. Like all spruces it is long fibred, so that it holds nails well and is most useful for joinery and box making. Used outdoors, spruce timber is not particularly durable, but it readily absorbs preservatives that make it resistant to fungi and insects. For indoor use, spruce wood has to be seasoned by drying soon after felling, or else its natural moisture will make it warp and rot. Timber left to dry in the sun is vulnerable to fungus infection and insect attacks, so commercial mills use artificial drying methods.

Bark brown; may be white-flecked. Greys with age.

Mature cone is 2–3 in. (5–7·5 cm) long, with rounded tip and toothed, papery scales.

Female flowers

Male flowers

Male and female flowers are crimson when unripe, but turn yellow when they ripen, before shedding pollen.

Needles have blunt tips and are greenish on top and whitish beneath. They point outwards at the side of the shoot and forwards at the end. The twig is reddish.

The Serbian spruce is a popular choice of ornamental tree for parks and gardens. It is sometimes found in small plantations.

Bluish foliage, reaching to the ground, and a very narrow crown distinguish the Serbian spruce; it grows to about 85 ft (26 m).

The reddish-brown bark scales off in plates.

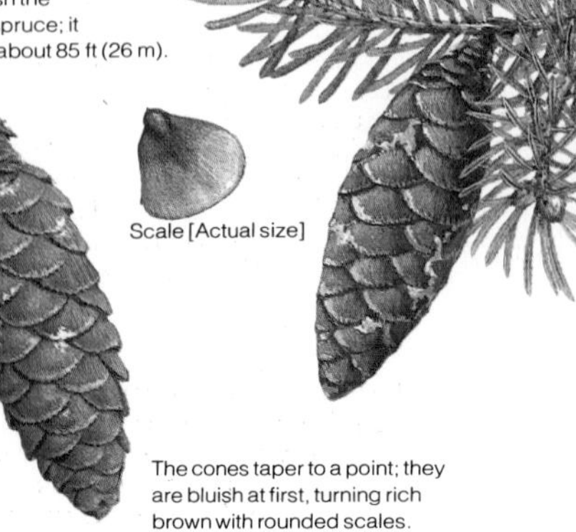

Scale [Actual size]

The cones taper to a point; they are bluish at first, turning rich brown with rounded scales.

Serbian spruce *Picea omorika*

The only place where the Serbian spruce survived the advance and ravages of the sheets of ice during the Ice Age was a valley in Yugoslavia. There it clung tenaciously to the limestone mountains, as it does to this day. Competition from other species is small, and the cool, moist conditions favour its growth. In 1889 the tree was introduced to Britain.

Since the tree is so hardy, it had been hoped that the Serbian spruce could be grown as a forest tree, but it grew too slowly. Instead, with its crown like a spire, it is often grown as a striking ornamental conifer. It grows well on chalky soils, but is very adaptable and will grow equally well on a wide range of soils.

The Serbian spruce is less damaged by frost than either the Norway or Sitka spruces, because it comes into leaf later in the year when the risk of frost is reduced. It grows slowly but surely, stands firm against strong winds, tolerates pollution and is not affected by insect pests. There are a number of garden cultivars and there exists a hybrid with the fast-growing Sitka spruce. Hopes that this would combine hardiness with fast growth have been disappointed; it still grows too slowly to provide a good source of commercial timber.

The glossy, dark green needles, which have rounded ends, are shorter than those of any other spruce. Immature cones are pale green.

Male flowers

This narrow, conical tree has dense branches and foliage. It grows to about 130 ft (40 m). A dwarf form is often grown in rockeries.

Dwarf form

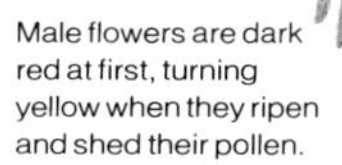

Male flowers are dark red at first, turning yellow when they ripen and shed their pollen.

The oriental spruce, from the Caucasus mountains of Turkey, is common throughout Britain in large gardens.

Cones are narrow and slightly curved, tapering at both ends.

Light brown bark curls into flakes on older trees.

Oriental spruce *Picea orientalis*

In its homelands in the Caucasus and Eastern Europe the oriental spruce grows at altitudes of up to 7,000 ft (2,130 m). In Britain, where it has been grown since 1839, the tree is found most frequently in parks and gardens, where it is grown in a number of forms. Its cultivars include the particularly attractive 'Pendula', with weeping branches, and 'Aurea' which, as a dwarf tree, is spectacular in the spring.

Very small needles, which lie close to the stem and have blunt, rather than pointed tips, distinguish oriental spruce from the similar and more widely grown Norway spruce. The tree grows slowly at first but, once established, grows rapidly in height and girth. When grown in forest plantations in Britain it has produced high yields of timber similar to that of the Norway spruce.

Because sites where the oriental spruce would grow well are already occupied by the Norway spruce, the tree has not been planted extensively for timber. But it is hardy, adaptable, grows in a wide range of conditions and is believed to be less susceptible to attack by insects than the Norway spruce. So it may one day find a place in Britain's countryside as well as in gardens.

Male flowers

Female cone

Long, pointed needles, shiny green on both sides, curve forwards. Buds are large and red-brown. Flowers open in May.

The morinda is a spruce native to the Himalayas, from Afghanistan to Nepal. It is also called West Himalayan spruce.

Hanging foliage gives the same weeping appearance as Brewer's spruce, but the curtain effect is less marked. Trees usually grow to about 120 ft (36 m).

The cone ripens to a shiny brown.

The young cone is light green with a long, pointed outline. Its scales are smoothly rounded.

Bark is dull grey, breaking into thin plates.

Morinda *Picea smithiana*

The drops of resin found on the young cones of this tall, handsome conifer gave rise to its native name of morinda, a Himalayan word meaning 'the honey of flowers'. Among its alternative names is weeping fir, descriptive of its characteristic drooping branches. Their shape is helpful in allowing the morinda to shed the great weight of snow that it has to bear, for it grows in the Himalayas up to a height of 12,000 ft (3,700 m). The wood is soft and white, rather like Norway spruce.

The morinda was introduced to Britain in 1818, the Smith referred to in its botanical name being the gardener of Hopetoun House, Lothian, who first grew it in Scotland. It makes a distinguished tree in big parks and gardens, where it has ample space to grow; and although the young tree is prone to damage by spring frosts, it is hardy once established and grows rapidly. It can withstand moderate shade and grows best in moist soils.

The only other spruce with which the morinda might be confused is Brewer's spruce, a native of the Oregon and California mountains with long, drooping branches. The morinda, however, has round and not flat needles like those of Brewer's spruce, and its shoots are hairless.

Dark foliage hangs like curtains from the upswept branches, and takes on a shimmering silver appearance after rain. Trees reach 50 ft (15 m) in Britain.

Long, slightly curved cones ripen to brown in the autumn.

The foliage enables this spruce to shed snow easily in its mountainous homeland, so reducing branch damage.

Pinkish-grey bark, like that of larch, breaks into scales.

Female flowers

Male flowers

Stiff, fleshy needles thrust out almost at right-angles to the shoot. The upright female flowers are greenish; male flowers are orange.

Brewer's weeping spruce *Picea brewerana*

This tree has been described as the most beautiful of all conifers – an understandable superlative. Dense masses of foliage hang from drooping branches in curtains, giving the tree the 'weeping' appearance referred to in its name. When the sky clears after rain the effect is most striking of all, as the wet foliage glistens in the sunlight. As the tree grows slowly and does not reach a large size, it is very suitable for smaller gardens. Unless it is a grafted specimen, however, it does not show 'weeping' foliage until late in life. The tree can be grown in sun or shade, and does best on moist soil.

Brewer's weeping spruce is an uncommon tree in its native land – the inaccessible mountain ranges of the Oregon-California boundary in the north-western United States. It was found and described by Professor W. H. Brewer, a 19th-century Californian botanist, after whom it is named.

The tree was introduced to Britain in 1897, when a single specimen was planted at Kew Gardens; it was widely planted from the early 1900s, and it is now one of the most popular of all ornamental conifers. Older trees are found in large gardens and arboreta, and young ones in parks and smaller gardens.

PINE NEEDLES AND BUDS

Trees with needles grouped in twos, threes or fives are easily identified as pines. The needles differ in size, and buds also aid recognition: these may be small and pointed, large and fat, bullet-shaped or cylindrical.

Bhutan pine
Pinus wallichiana

Bud cylindrical, with long, pointed scales. Five needles, $7\frac{1}{2}$ in. (19 cm) long, stiff. Page 257

Maritime pine
Pinus pinaster

Bud stout, with fringed scales. Two needles, $6\frac{3}{4}$ in. (17 cm) long, grey-green. Page 250

Western yellow pine
Pinus ponderosa

Bud long, resinous. Three needles, 7 in. (18 cm) long, stiff. Page 252

Monterey pine
Pinus radiata

Bud parallel-sided. Three needles, $4\frac{1}{2}$ in. (12 cm) long, soft. Page 253

Mexican white pine
Pinus ayacahuite

Bud conical. Five needles, $5\frac{1}{2}$ in. (14 cm) long, drooping. Page 254

Austrian pine
Pinus nigra

Bud large, fat, onion-shaped. Two needles, $3\frac{1}{2}$ in. (9 cm) long, coarse. Page 246

Corsican pine
Pinus nigra ssp. laricio

Bud medium-sized, onion-shaped. Two needles, $4\frac{1}{2}$ in. (12 cm) long. Page 247

Stone pine
Pinus pinea

Bud long, with turned-back white scales. Two needles, $4\frac{1}{4}$ in. (11 cm) long, dark green. Page 251

Weymouth pine
Pinus strobus

Bud small, pointed. Five needles, $3\frac{1}{2}$ in. (9 cm) long, slender, soft. Page 256

Arolla pine
Pinus cembra

Bud long, pointed. Five needles, $3\frac{1}{4}$ in. (8 cm) long, bluish. Page 258

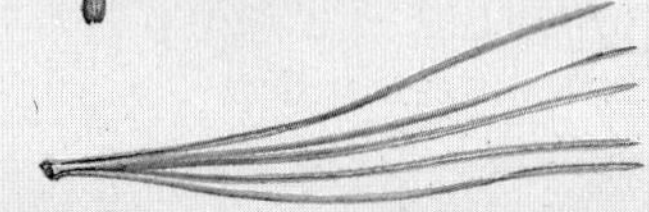

Macedonian pine
Pinus peuce

Bud oval, with sharp points. Needles $3\frac{1}{4}$–$4\frac{1}{2}$ in. (8–12 cm) long, thin. Page 259

Scots pine
Pinus sylvestris

Bud small, pointed, red-brown. Two needles, $2\frac{1}{2}$ in. (6 cm) long, blue-green. Page 243

Shore pine
Pinus contorta

Bud bullet-shaped. Two needles, 2 in. (5 cm) long, twisted, yellow-green. Page 248

Mountain pine
Pinus mugo

Bud cylindrical, blunt, resinous. Two needles, 2 in. (5 cm) long, with long sheath. Page 249

Japanese white pine
Pinus parviflora

Bud small, rich brown. Five needles, $2\frac{1}{2}$ in. (6 cm) long. Page 255

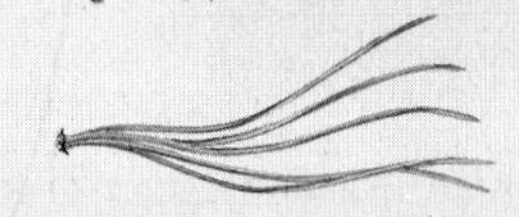

Crimson female flowers are carried in pairs at the end of the current year's shoot.

Male flowers grow at the base of the shoot.

A new bud tips each branchlet in winter. Cones nearest the tip were fertilised in the previous spring. Cones below are two years old, maturing; the lowest cones are three years old and ripe.

Paired needles are usually twisted, and, at 2–3 in. (5–7·5 cm), shorter than those of most pines.

A native of the once-extensive Caledonian pine forests, the Scots pine still graces Highland lochs and mountains.

Upper bark is warm red; lower bark deeply fissured.

Winged seeds are released when cone scales open. [Actual size]

The fully branched, narrow outline alters as a maturing tree loses its lower branches and forms a flatter, spreading crown, rising to 120 ft (36 m).

Scots pine *Pinus sylvestris*

As the glaciers retreated from northern Britain at the end of the Ice Age, one, and only one, large conifer was able to struggle back to the ravaged land left by the ice before the English Channel opened. Even today the Scots pine retains its ancestral pioneering habits, clinging to the poor soils of the Highland slopes and to infertile lowland sands.

Only a few remnants survive of the native pine forests of the Highlands, for they provided top-quality timber. Water provided an easy means of transport for the heavy logs, which could be floated across lochs and down rivers to be sawn into planks for building purposes, and made into ships' masts. Moreover, the Scots pine was a major source of turpentine, resin and tar; its wood was used for charcoal, and for making flaming torches.

Scots pine wood is strong, yet soft and easily worked, making it suitable for furniture, chipboard, boxes, fencing, telegraph poles and many other wood products. Imported Scots pine is known as red or yellow deal. The attractive red colouring of the upper stems of mature trees, contrasting with their dark green foliage, has made them a popular addition to landscapes on both sides of the border.

LIFE IN A NATURAL PINE FOREST

Fragments of Britain's primeval wilderness live on in Scotland, where they harbour a wealth of rare wildlife. Britain's only large native conifer, the Scots pine, was once much exploited for its valuable timber, but now most forest tracts containing this survivor from prehistoric times are protected in nature reserves. They can be seen in such places as Glen Affric, west of Inverness, on Deeside and Speyside, and in the Black Wood of Rannoch. The pine forest protects, in turn, the elusive pine marten and the wild cat. It shelters the capercaillie, once extinct in the British Isles, and also the crested tit, which is known nowhere else in Britain. Rare and lovely wild plants flourish, and these forests have always been the natural habitat of the magnificent red deer.

Young pines spring up in the open woodland unless the heather and moss become very dense, when the pine seeds cannot reach the soil. Another native conifer, the juniper, occurs in the pine woods.

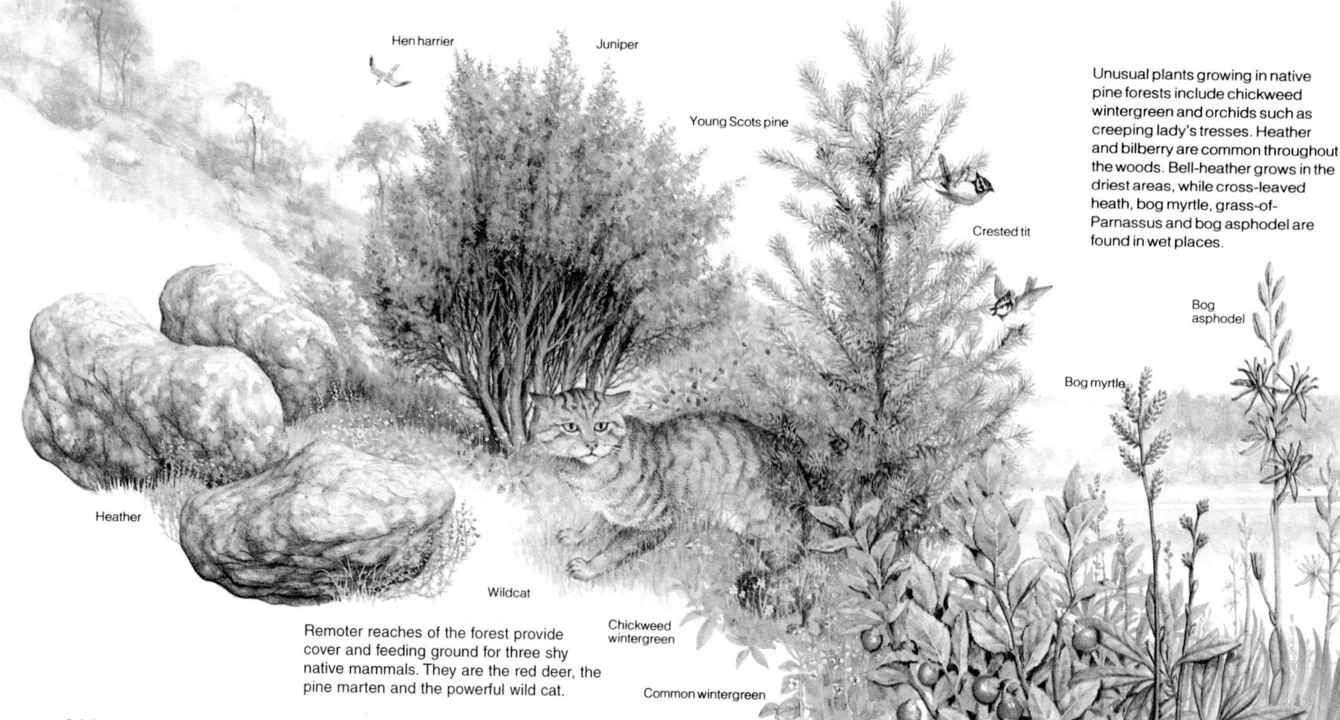

Unusual plants growing in native pine forests include chickweed wintergreen and orchids such as creeping lady's tresses. Heather and bilberry are common throughout the woods. Bell-heather grows in the driest areas, while cross-leaved heath, bog myrtle, grass-of-Parnassus and bog asphodel are found in wet places.

Remoter reaches of the forest provide cover and feeding ground for three shy native mammals. They are the red deer, the pine marten and the powerful wild cat.

The remnants of the once-extensive Caledonian pine forests today form attractive, open woodlands which regenerate themselves freely and contain trees of various ages. The older trees have flattish tops and bare stems; younger trees are narrow-crowned, with branches to the ground.

Birds of prey such as the hen harrier flourish in the forest; the osprey or fish eagle is re-establishing itself on the forest lochs, and the golden eagle is widespread.

This dark, rough-looking, heavy-branched tree attains a height of around 100 ft (30 m).

Bark is dark grey or almost black, with ridges.

Ripening cones are green and elongated. When mature, the cones are large, brown and rounded. They take two and a half years to ripen.

The long, paired needles are sharp, stiff and coarser in texture than those of other pines. They are grouped in distinct whorls on the branchlets.

Female flowers

Male flowers

Red female flowers grow in pairs; yellow male flowers are clustered.

Its dense and dark foliage makes the Austrian pine stand out from other trees. It is useful as a windbreak.

Austrian pine *Pinus nigra* ssp. *nigra*

Charles Lawson (1794–1873), the Scottish nurseryman after whom the widely planted Lawson cypress is named, introduced the Austrian pine to Britain in 1835. He suggested that it should be grown not only for ornament, but also as a plantation tree for its wood. However, it was not a success as a timber tree because it is coarse, and its heavy branches form large knots which weaken planks made from it, reducing their value. Where the branches are not at right-angles to the trunk, the knots extend at an oblique angle into the tree, weakening the wood. The Austrian pine is not now grown for timber and has been replaced in plantations by the finer-branched Corsican pine.

As an ornamental tree, Lawson's import has proved more successful. It can withstand exposure to salt-laden winds and to industrial pollution, so it is often planted as a windbreak or screen, and it flourishes on most dry soils, particularly those overlying chalk.

Two cultivars of the Austrian pine are sometimes grown in British gardens. One, *Pinus nigra* 'Hornibrookiana', was developed by grafting from a 'witch's broom' – a dense, bushy outgrowth on a tree caused by insects.

Female flowers

Male flowers

The male flowers are yellow, and cluster around the base of the shoot. The red female flowers appear in pairs at the tip of the shoot as the needles emerge.

This fast-growing tree, a native of the Mediterranean, grows in forests, parks and gardens throughout Britain.

Needles are long, arranged in pairs on the twig, and sometimes twisted. The mature cone is rounded, and takes two years to ripen. The bud is large and fat, with turned-back scales.

Bark is dark grey, fissuring and flaking off with age.

The Corsican pine is a conical tree, slender in outline when young. Its branches are more horizontal than those of other pines. It grows to about 115 ft (35 m).

Corsican pine *Pinus nigra* ssp. *laricio*

This tree is a subspecies of Austrian pine, and has much greater value as a timber tree because of its thinner branches and straight, cylindrical trunk. It was introduced to Britain from Corsica in 1799, and proved suitable for planting in the drier areas of the country. Commercial forests of this pine now grow well on the light, sandy soils of the East Anglian Breckland, where they also provide a suitable habitat for deer and birds.

Corsican pine is successful, too, on sand dunes, such as those at Culbin, to the east of Inverness, provided that the sand is prevented from moving by 'thatching' it with cut branches. Pines, unlike spruces, grow a thick tap root and few side-shoots, and so hold firm against the wind once the seedlings are established. Corsican pines need plenty of light, and plantations are kept carefully thinned out to encourage the remaining trees to grow quickly.

The timber of the Corsican pine is made into pit props and is used in general building work. Some goes into plywood: for this purpose, thin strips of wood are shaved from the log in a spiral, then glued together in layers, the grain running at opposite angles in successive layers for strength.

Male flowers grow at base of current year's shoot, female flowers at the tip, under the bud. Buds are bullet-shaped and resinous.

Male flowers

Female flowers

This tall pine grows erect to 80 ft (24 m), even in wet peats and impoverished soils.

The needles are in pairs, short, yellowish-green and twisted. Cones are clustered, and stay long on tree, ripening brown.

Caterpillars of the pine beauty moth strip plantations.

Because it grows on poor soils, the lodgepole variety of shore pine is used for upland planting in Britain.

Brown cracks divide bark into corky squares.

The lodgepole pine (var. *latifolia*) has longer, less-dense foliage of a brighter green.

Shore pine (Lodgepole pine) *Pinus contorta*

The particular shore that gives this pine its name is that of the north-western seaboard of North America. Its ability to flourish in a harsh coastal climate also makes it suitable for survival on poor, high moorland in Scotland and north-east England, where shore pine prepares the ground for other species by suppressing the heather that competes for nutrients in the soil.

A variety of shore pine which is more commonly grown in British forestry plantations is the lodgepole pine *Pinus contorta* var. *latifolia*, from further inland on North America's western mountains. It was used by North American Indians as the central pole supporting their *tepees*, or tent-like 'lodges'. The cones of the lodgepole pine are notable for one of nature's most remarkable survival mechanisms: they stay closed for many years, until the heat of a forest fire opens the scales, releasing the seeds and sending forth new growth to re-colonise burned land.

Lodgepole pine has a narrower crown and lighter branches than shore pine, making it more useful for commercial forestry. But both varieties are vulnerable to pine beauty moth caterpillars, which eat the needles. The trees are protected by regular aerial spraying with chemicals.

This shrub-like conifer usually grows close to the ground and rarely attains its maximum height of about 33 ft (10 m).

The cones are small, with prickles on the scales.

The scaly bark is usually grey-brown in colour.

Female flowers

The paired needles are in long sheaths and grouped in whorls on the branches.

Various dwarf forms of mountain pine make ideal rockery plants.

Male flowers

Numerous yellow-orange male flowers cluster at the base of each small new shoot of the mountain pine. They ripen in mid-June.

Different forms of mountain pine can adorn a garden – or shelter valuable timber crops on exposed slopes.

Mountain pine *Pinus mugo*

The hardy mountain pine comes from the slopes of the Alps and occurs in two different forms. The dwarf variety, var. *pumilio*, was introduced to Britain in the 18th century and is often featured in garden rockeries. The commonest form, a later introduction, is larger and shrub-like. Its leading bud does not suppress the side buds, so the pine grows as a bush with no distinct leading shoot. A similar and closely related species is *Pinus uncinata*. It is altogether more tree-like with a sturdy, conical shape, and forests of it are found high up on the mountains of western Europe, including the Pyrenees.

Mountain pine makes a decorative garden tree in any of its forms, and its hardiness and bushiness make it useful for land conservation projects in mountain areas. It is often planted on the edges of shelter belts to prevent the wind from sweeping in under the lower branches of taller trees, and on mountain slopes it helps to break up avalanches by dividing the sliding snow.

Foresters use mountain pine to protect young plants of more valuable trees such as Scots pine and Sitka spruce. Planted among them, the mountain pines give shelter and impede the growth of heather that could smother the young trees.

Female flowers

Male flowers

Male flowers are yellow at the base of new shoots; red female flowers cluster around the terminal bud.

This pine likes sandy soil and grows on Britain's southern coast, where it is shaped by the prevailing winds.

In older trees, a long, bare pole ascends to the widely spaced branches of an open crown up to 110 ft (33 m) high.

The dark purplish bark is deeply fissured into plates.

The stout, grey-green needles are grouped in twos, and longer than those of any other two-needled pine. The long, stalkless cones are clustered and persist for many years on the branches.

Maritime pine *Pinus pinaster*

As early as 1789, vast areas of sand-dunes in the south of France were being reclaimed by the use of maritime pine. The seed was sown mixed with broom seeds to fix nitrogen in the soil, and covered with branches to stop the sand from blowing away. The forests that resulted have since furnished an important supply of resin and turpentine. Similar techniques have been used in Britain for afforesting sand-dunes, but maritime pine is not generally used for this purpose in this country, as the climate is not warm enough in most districts. However, the tree does grow well in the south of England, where it is sometimes known as Bournemouth pine.

Maritime pines grow quickly, and in young plantations the crowns of the trees soon form a wind-resistant barrier. In exposed situations, especially near the sea, the prevailing wind bends the tree at the base of its trunk, compressing the wood on one side; branches are bent over in the same way.

Prehistoric man used such 'compression wood' from pines to make skis; a prehistoric rock-carving in Norway shows that the art of skiing is at least 4,000 years old. Maritime pine has a reddish-brown heartwood and white or yellow sapwood.

Female flower

Needles grow in pairs, dark green, long and sparse. Golden male flowers open in June.

Cones are large, heavy and globe-shaped and take three years to ripen.

This curiously shaped pine, typical of Mediterranean scenes, occasionally grows in southern England.

Stone pine *Pinus pinea*

To Roman soldiers garrisoned in the cold northern provinces of the empire, the nuts – actually seeds – of the stone pine were a delicacy. Their husks have been found on military camp sites in Britain, but the seeds from which they came must have been imported. For the stone pine is a Mediterranean tree that was not introduced to Britain until long after Roman times, and its seeds do not ripen in Britain except in warm summers.

In its Mediterranean homeland the tree is planted largely for its seeds, which are eaten raw or roasted, or mixed into cakes. They are kept stored in their cones until they are ready to be eaten, for once removed they become rancid. In Britain the stone pine is grown as an ornamental tree only, and flourishes in the warmer parts of southern England, especially near the coast. Its seeds provide a feast for squirrels, dormice and crossbills.

Like other pines, the stone pine gives off volatile oil from its leaves, producing the characteristic smell of pine woods. The vapour is thought to deter grazers. The wood contains resin – a waste product of the tree. Insects have been found in lumps of fossil pine resin (amber) after being trapped in its sticky embrace thousands of years ago.

The light brown bark fissures into long, flat plates.

The unusually broad, flat crown above a tall, bare trunk, and the branches radiating upwards like umbrella ribs, give this tree its second name of 'umbrella pine'. It grows to 100 ft (30 m).

Seeds [Actual size]

The mature cone sheds fat seeds, containing an edible kernel.

Upper branches are ascending, but lower branches droop downwards. The tree reaches 105 ft (32 m) in height.

Mature cones have a sharp prickle or spine, curving slightly downward, on their scales. The cones are egg-shaped and up to 4 in. (10 cm) long.

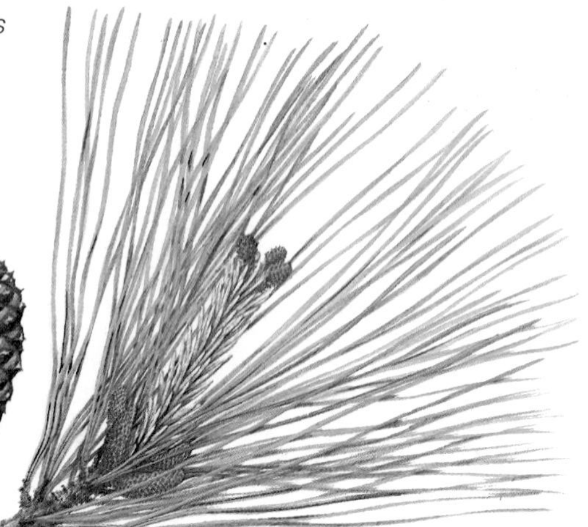

Long, dark green or grey needles are slender, sharp-tipped and bunched together in groups of three. Male flowers are purple. Dull red female flowers appear at the tips of the shoots.

Lofty western yellow pines, widespread in western North America, have been planted as ornamental trees in Britain.

Yellow-brown bark breaks up into thick plates.

Jeffrey's pine
Pinus jeffreyi

Jeffrey's pine, also from western North America, is similar in appearance to the western yellow pine, but its needles are shorter and stiffer and its cones are much larger.

Western yellow pine *Pinus ponderosa*

It was with this pine that the technique of dendrochronology, or tree-ring dating, was first developed in the western United States in 1901. Every year, trees in temperate regions add to their girth by laying down a light-coloured band of spring wood and one of darker summer wood. Their width depends on whether the year is wet, producing a broad band, or dry, when the band is narrow. If the annual ring patterns are compared with those from tree remains on archaeological sites, climatic variations over time can be deduced and the wood can be dated.

The wood of the tree is yellow, as its name suggests. The alternative names of big pine and bull pine indicate the size to which the tree can grow. A fourth name, heavy pine, is a further reference to the wood, which is hard compared with that of the white or soft pines. It is close-grained and easy to work, but is not used commercially in Britain.

Western yellow pine is planted in Britain as an ornamental tree, but because it reaches such a large size, it can only be planted in big gardens. Like all pines it likes plenty of light, though it will stand shade better than some species. A very similar tree, *Pinus jeffreyi*, has shorter, darker, and stiffer needles.

Long, slender needles are a characteristic grass-green. Male flowers crowded at the base of new shoots are yellow in spring. Female flowers are set in clusters of three to five.

Male flowers

Female flowers

Although the Monterey pine is found wild only in a small area of its native California, it grows well in southern England.

Mature trees have a dense, high dome with many branches; younger trees have a more conical shape. The tree grows to 100 ft (30 m).

The squat, lop-sided cones of the Monterey pine may remain on the tree for many years before falling.

Needles are straight and set closely together in groups of three.

Thick, dark brown bark has deep fissures.

On the coast of California, the Monterey pine is low-growing. It grows taller and straighter in Britain. In New Zealand, it has reached 185 ft (56 m).

Monterey pine *Pinus radiata*

The cold that spread out from the Arctic in the Ice Age pushed the conifers of North America southwards. With the retreat of the ice, the trees moved north again, but one species remained restricted to the Monterey peninsula of California. There – and nowhere else in America – they still survive precariously. The Monterey pine has, however, been successfully introduced to other countries, including Britain, to which it was brought in 1833 by the tree collector David Douglas.

In Britain the tree grows very quickly, and in the south-west continues to grow throughout most of the year. Some trees put on two whorls of branches in a year instead of the single whorl which normally represents a season's growth. The Monterey pine's rapid growth, dense needles and ability to withstand exposure at low altitudes, especially near the sea, make it ideal for planting in rows to form a windbreak. East winds cause excessive water-loss and browning of the needles.

Another name for the tree is 'remarkable cone pine'; a reference to its habit of retaining its cones on the tree for 20-30 years. The wood is light, soft and rather brittle, with light brown heartwood and yellowish sapwood.

Needles are spread out, with dull blue-green or yellow-green outer and blue-white inner surfaces. Male flowers are yellow; females are red and upright on short stalks.

Male flowers

Female flowers

The Mexican white pine, an attractive introduction from Central America, is usually found in Britain only in tree collections.

Tapering cones hang downwards and are about 12 in. (30 cm) long. Immature cones are green; ripe cones have pale orange-brown scales, turning back near base.

Long, slender needles, sometimes bent near their base, are in groups of five.

Thin bark has wide, shallow pinkish fissures.

This conical pine has long, sinuous, level lower branches and more densely set, upward-pointing branches towards the top. When young, the tree has a broader crown. It reaches 80 ft (24 m).

Mexican white pine *Pinus ayacahuite*

In 1836 Karl Theodor Hartweg, a clerk at the Horticultural Society of London, was promoted and sent to Central America in search of exotic flowers and trees. Hartweg, a German, spent almost seven years in the wilds of Mexico, Guatemala and the Andes. Among the many specimens he sent back was the tender Mexican white pine. The tree is one of Hartweg's few introductions which has flourished outside its native habitat, and it grows well in Britain except in Scotland and on the east coast of England.

Mexican white pine has crossed with the very similar Bhutan pine at Westonbirt Arboretum in the Cotswolds, where the two species grow together. Pollen from the Bhutan pine fertilised the cones of a Mexican white pine. Seed was collected and grown about 1904, but the resulting seedlings were not recognised as hybrids until they produced cones in 1933. The vigorous hybrid is called Holford's pine after the then owner of Westonbirt.

The banana-shaped cones of the Mexican white pine are the longest of all the five-needled pines. The cones differ from those of the Bhutan pine in that the scales at their bases curl back towards the stalk.

Small, upright cones have thick scales. Green when young, they ripen orange-brown and then dark purple.

Unripe cone

Male flowers

Short needles, blue-green above, whitish below, are bunched in groups of five. Pink or purple female flowers appear at the end of shoots. Male flowers are yellow or brown, and clustered round the shoot.

Female flowers

This Japanese tree can be found occasionally in large gardens, but it occurs more often in a dwarf form.

The Japanese white pine is familiar from willow-pattern plates. The pine is also widely used in *bonsai* – the Japanese art of growing miniature trees.

Here, lichen covers the purple-grey bark.

Layered foliage is borne on level or slightly drooping branches, forming a wide, usually low, crown. The tree grows to 65 ft (20 m), but is usually no more than 33 ft (10 m) tall.

Japanese white pine *Pinus parviflora*

When the 19th-century tree collector John Gould Veitch was attached to the staff of the British Ambassador in Japan, Sir Rutherford Alcock, he travelled the country in search of picturesque species. He was fascinated by the popular and ornamental Japanese white pine, which was trained and moulded by native gardeners. In 1861, Veitch introduced the slow-growing, semi-dwarf form of the tree to England.

Unlike other pines, the Japanese white pine does not often shed its distinctive needles, which are short, blunt and twisted. It retains them for as long as four years and so always has very dense, layered foliage. But it resembles other pines in having large terminal buds, which contain the following year's growth in an unexpanded form. The buds break in the spring and the shoots extend rapidly, with growth ceasing early in the summer. The rest of the growing season is spent laying down the shoots for the next year in the new buds. At this stage, water is not as important as sunshine, and pines grow better than other conifers in places with hot, dry summers.

Like many pines with needles in fives, this Japanese tree has whiter timber, with a finer texture, than that of other pines.

Long cone scales are thickened at the end, like a duck's bill, and open to release seed. [Actual size]

Seed [Actual size]

Pointed, banana-shaped cones are 4–6 in. (10–15 cm) long, on short stalks. They often bear white resin.

Male flowers

Female flowers

Blue-green needles grow in fives and are short, soft and slender. Male flowers are yellowish; female flowers at ends of shoots are pinkish.

Weymouth pines, natives of eastern North America, are subject to disease and are therefore rarely planted now.

Young bark is smooth and grey, becoming furrowed.

Mature trees have an irregular conical shape, with upswept or horizontal branches. Shoots on the upper branches are spiky. Trees grow to 115 ft (35 m).

Blister-rust is caused by a fungus which passes through most of its life-cycle on the leaves of blackcurrants.

Weymouth pine *Pinus strobus*

The Duchess of Beaufort introduced this North American pine to England in 1705. It grew well on her estate at Badminton, Gloucestershire; however, the tree was not named after her. That honour went to Lord Weymouth who, a short while later, planted the pine extensively on his domains at Longleat, Wiltshire. It was valued for its excellent timber, which was used for building and for making boxes.

Unfortunately, the tree is subject to a fungal disease called blister-rust, which attacks the upper stem. Ultimately this kills the pine, so it is no longer planted on a commercial scale. The disease crossed from Europe to America in 1892, where it spread rapidly and caused extensive damage. The fungus lives for part of its life on fruit bushes such as blackcurrants, and the Weymouth pine is at risk wherever these bushes grow. Trees whose bark has been damaged by the rust are often attacked by voles, which find the damaged bark palatable.

The pine grows rapidly and is resistant to frost. It thrives on light, moist soils and can live to between 100 and 200 years old. Today, most Weymouth pines in Britain are old trees in parks and churchyards, as few young ones have been planted.

This pine, with its open, conical crown, has wide-spreading, heavy, drooping branches. It reaches 115 ft (35 m).

Mature cones are brown, flecked with white resin. The scales are not bent backwards. They are 8–12 in. (20–30 cm) long.

Bluish-green needles are grouped in fives. The long curved cones, green when immature, hang down.

Bhutan pine, from the mountains of the Himalayas, has been planted in many British parks for its attractive foliage.

Thin, resinous bark is fissured on older trees.

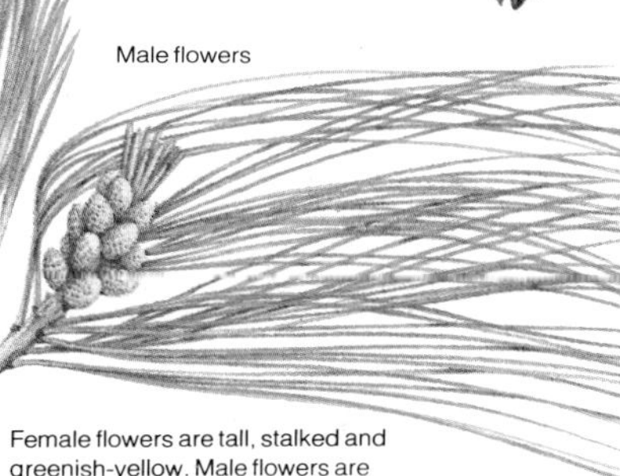

Female flowers are tall, stalked and greenish-yellow. Male flowers are grouped, and appear yellow in June.

Bhutan pine *Pinus wallichiana*

Although this pine may not be long-lived – it has not been cultivated in Britain long enough for horticulturists to be sure – it is extensively planted in parks and gardens for its attractive, bluish-green foliage and orange or pink bark. It grows on a wide variety of soils, and tolerates a certain amount of lime; but too much lime reduces the intake of potassium and iron and turns its foliage yellow. Introducing fertiliser into the soil helps to mitigate this effect.

Bhutan pine – also known as blue pine, Himalaya pine or lofty pine – was introduced to Britain from Nepal in 1823. To the people of the Himalayas it is one of the most important conifers, for its hard, durable wood is used for building work and for making tea-chests. In Britain the timber is only available from solitary trees, so it is not commercially significant.

The heartwood is red and the sapwood creamy-white. An oil extracted from its roots was used as an insect repellent in rice fields, until modern chemicals superseded it. Like the Mexican white pine – with which it has accidentally crossed – the Bhutan pine has long, banana-shaped cones, but is distinguished from Mexican white pine by its smooth, hairless shoots.

The knotty trunk has short, level branches that often grow almost down to the ground. The tree can reach a height of 70 ft (22 m).

The dense, stiff needles grow in groups of five. They are shiny green on top and whitish beneath, with hairy shoots.

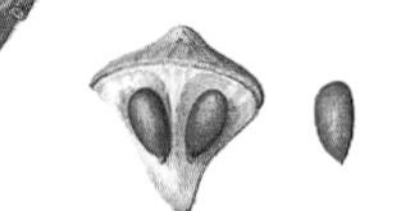

The large seeds are extracted from the scales of the cones by birds and animals.

The small, erect cones are egg-shaped; they are deep blue in summer, ripening to red-brown.

Alpine in origin, the Arolla pine adds its decorative, bushy profile to parks, large gardens and tree collections.

Young bark has resin blisters; later becomes scaly.

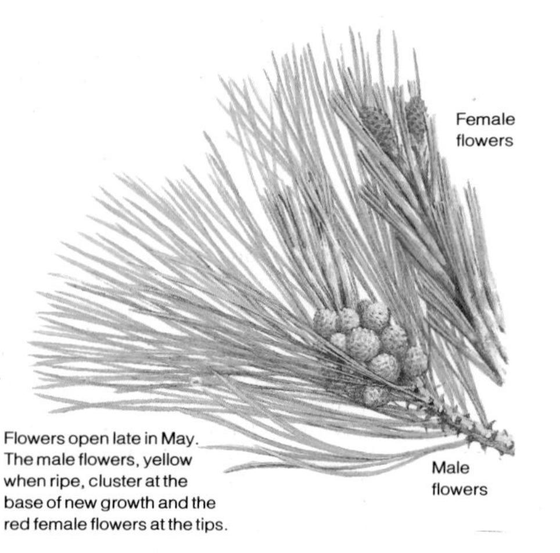

Flowers open late in May. The male flowers, yellow when ripe, cluster at the base of new growth and the red female flowers at the tips.

Arolla pine *Pinus cembra*

This small, densely branched tree, introduced to Britain in 1746 by the Duke of Argyll, grows at higher altitudes than any other European pine, and is found at 5,000–8,000 ft (1,500–2,400 m) in its native Alps and Carpathians. It grows slowly, an advantage in smaller gardens. It keeps its lower branches right down to the ground as it grows older, and its hairy young shoots are orange-brown in colour, distinguishing it from other pines with five needles, such as the Macedonian pine. These features, together with the attractive purple cones – produced when the tree is about 25 years old – make it a decorative ornamental tree for light, well-drained soils.

Unlike other pine cones the cones of Arolla pine never open naturally. The seeds are dispersed only when the cone rots on the ground or is opened by squirrels and birds seeking the seeds. As the tree does not use the wind to spread its seeds, they have no 'wings' like those of other pine seeds.

When free of knots, the soft wood of Arolla pine is easily worked and valued in its mountain homeland for decorative panelling. In the Austrian Tyrol it is used for carving small figures and animals.

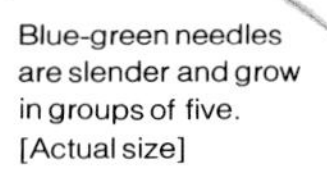

Blue-green needles are slender and grow in groups of five. [Actual size]

Needles are bunched towards the ends of the twigs. The fairly large, cylindrical immature cones are bright green and hang down.

This pine, native to the south-western Balkans, is planted in tree collections and in a few large gardens.

This pine can grow to 70 ft (22 m). Its dense crown is similar to that of the Arolla pine. The lower branches are often heavy but keep a symmetrical shape.

Cone is long, resinous and curved. It ripens to red-brown.

Thin, brown bark remains smooth, with few fissures.

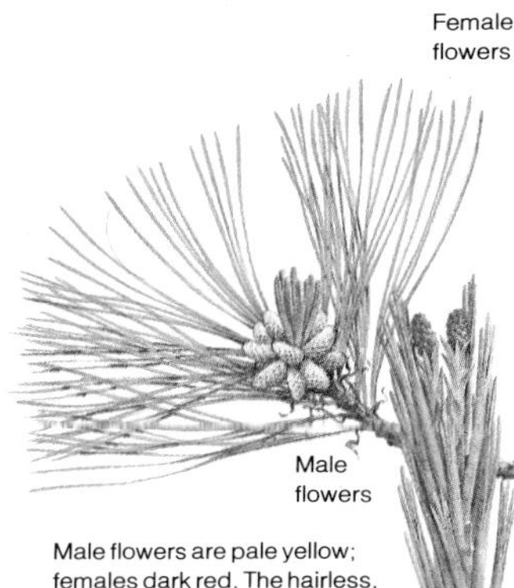

Female flowers

Male flowers

Male flowers are pale yellow; females dark red. The hairless, light green shoot distinguishes this tree from the Arolla pine.

Macedonian pine *Pinus peuce*

A native of three small areas in the Balkans, the Macedonian pine was introduced to Britain in 1864. It grows slowly and steadily, forming a very regular outline, which should make it attractive to landscape designers; but it has not been grown to any great extent outside arboreta. A few experimental forestry plantations have been established on exposed high ground in northern Britain, where the tree has shown itself able to withstand severe cold and wind.

The Macedonian pine is useful as a windbreak tree because it retains its branches right down to the ground as it grows older, the deep blue-green branches of needles forming dense foliage and an efficient barrier. The persistent branches means that the timber is knotty and of poor quality, so that the future of the tree in Britain seems to be limited to ornamental uses as an addition to parks and tree collections.

The apple-green colour of its shoots distinguishes the Macedonian pine from all other pines commonly grown in Britain. The cones are long and similar to those of the Bhutan pine, to which the tree is closely related; but they are smaller. Much resin oozes out if the bark of the tree is damaged.

TREES WITH SCALE-LIKE LEAVES

In some conifers, particularly cypresses, the adult leaves are reduced to scales closely pressed against the twig. This helps to reduce water loss. The juvenile leaves, which are produced first, are sharp and awl-like.

Single large leaves

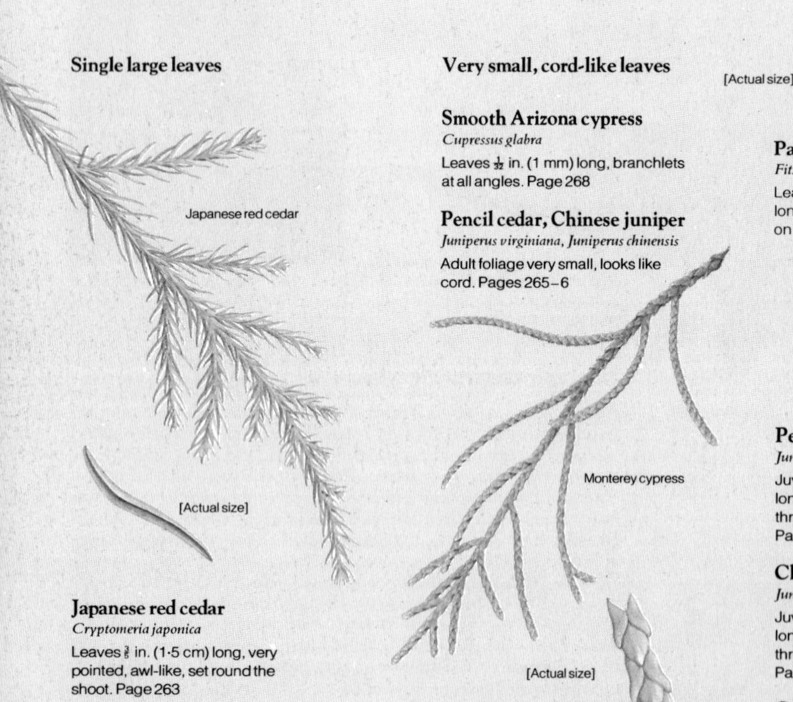

Japanese red cedar

Cryptomeria japonica

Leaves $\frac{5}{8}$ in. (1·5 cm) long, very pointed, awl-like, set round the shoot. Page 263

Wellingtonia

Sequoiadendron giganteum

Leaves $\frac{1}{6}$ – $\frac{5}{16}$ in. (4–8 mm) long, sickle-shaped, curvng away from twig. Page 262

Very small, cord-like leaves

Smooth Arizona cypress

Cupressus glabra

Leaves $\frac{1}{32}$ in. (1 mm) long, branchlets at all angles. Page 268

Pencil cedar, Chinese juniper

Juniperus virginiana, Juniperus chinensis

Adult foliage very small, looks like cord. Pages 265–6

Monterey cypress

Cupressus macrocarpa

Leaves $\frac{1}{32}$ in. (1 mm) long; branchlets point forwards. Page 269

Leaves in threes

Patagonian cypress

[Actual size]

Patagonian cypress

Fitzroya cupressoides

Leaves $\frac{1}{16}$ – $\frac{1}{6}$ in. (2–4 mm) long, broad, two white bands on each surface. Page 267

Pencil cedar

Juniperus virginiana

Juvenile leaves $\frac{1}{4}$ in. (6 mm) long, growing in groups of three at tips of shoots. Page 265

Chinese juniper

Juniperus chinensis

Juvenile leaves $\frac{3}{8}$ in. (1 cm) long, growing in twos and threes at base of shoots. Page 266

Common juniper

Juniperus communis

Leaves $\frac{1}{2}$ in. (1·3 cm) long, growing in threes; spiky and blue-green, with broad white band on upper side. Page 264

Common juniper

[Actual size]

Flat branchlets with white on undersides

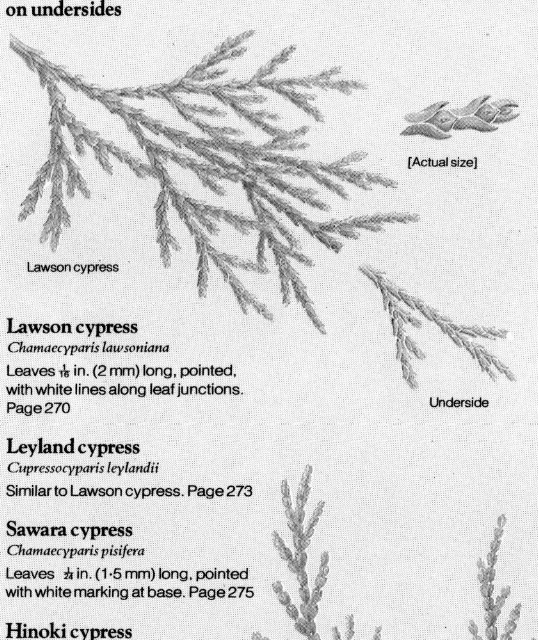

Lawson cypress
Chamaecyparis lawsoniana

Leaves $\frac{1}{16}$ in. (2 mm) long, pointed, with white lines along leaf junctions. Page 270

Leyland cypress
Cupressocyparis leylandii

Similar to Lawson cypress. Page 273

Sawara cypress
Chamaecyparis pisifera

Leaves $\frac{1}{24}$ in. (1·5 mm) long, pointed with white marking at base. Page 275

Hinoki cypress
Chamaecyparis obtusa

Leaves $\frac{1}{24}$ in. (1·5 mm) long, with blunt tips and white bases. Page 274

Western red cedar
Thuja plicata

Leaves $\frac{1}{16}$ in. (2 mm) long, with blunt tips and small white patches. Page 277

Hiba
Thujopsis dolabrata

Leaves $\frac{1}{16}$–$\frac{1}{5}$ in. (2–5 mm) long, with large white patches and a plastic appearance. Page 279

Flat branchlets with yellowish-green undersides

Nootka cypress
Chamaecyparis nootkatensis

Leaves $\frac{1}{16}$ in. (2 mm) long, with sharp points. Page 272

Underside

White cedar

[Actual size]

White cedar
Thuja occidentalis

Leaves $\frac{1}{16}$ in. (2 mm) long, with blunt tips. Page 276

Flat branchlets with green undersides

Chinese thuja
Thuja orientalis

Leaves $\frac{1}{24}$ in. (1·5 mm) long, blunt. Page 276

Underside

[Actual size]

Incense cedar

Incense cedar
Calocedrus decurrens

Leaves $\frac{1}{8}$–$\frac{1}{5}$ in. (3–5 mm) long, very flattened, with sharp points standing away from the stem. Page 278

This narrow, conical tree, with a pointed crown, has branches that sweep down, then up at their ends. It reaches 150 ft (46 m) in Britain.

The small leaves curve away from the twig. Cones, large and corky when ripe, have scales with a characteristic groove.

The cones, green when immature, take two years to ripen.

The Wellingtonia's crown is often seen rising above the tops of trees in avenues and parks in lowland Britain.

Bark is thick and fibrous, with soft ridges.

Female

Male

Male flowers are pale yellow in spring. Female flowers are green. Both grow at the ends of the shoots.

Wellingtonia *Sequoiadendron giganteum*

Avenues of Wellingtonia were planted on many large estates in Britain soon after the tree was discovered in America in 1852. Among the most famous of these avenues is one on the Duke of Wellington's estate at Stratfield Saye in Hampshire, where this conifer was first planted in 1857. In Britain the tree was named after the 'Iron Duke', who died in the year of its discovery; but in America it is called by a variety of names reflecting its great size – among them big tree, mammoth tree and giant sequoia.

The Wellingtonia has lived up to 3,400 years in its native California. Until recently, it was thought to be the oldest-known living tree, but the bristle cone pine was found to be even longer-lived, by some 1,600 years. The Wellingtonia grows well in Britain on a wide range of soils, though its remarkably tall crown is often struck by lightning and dies at the top.

The purplish or red-brown wood is very light and brittle, so that when large trees are felled they often break up and are of little use. The thick, spongy bark is fire-resistant, as it does not contain resin. It is rich in tannins and other chemicals, and even when a fallen tree has lain on the forest floor for many years it decays hardly at all.

Male flowers

Female flowers

Long, awl-like needles are arranged round the shoot. Male flowers are globular, brownish-yellow; females are small green rosettes.

This Japanese ornamental tree is common in larger gardens in rural areas, growing best in cool, damp parts.

The common garden cultivar 'Elegans' retains its juvenile juniper-like foliage throughout its life. The soft grey-green needles turn a rich bronze in autumn.

The soft, thick, fibrous bark peels off in long strips.

A bright green, narrowly conical crown and pale brownish-red bark distinguish the Japanese red cedar, which attains a height of 115 ft (35 m).

Round cones, with curved hooks on scales, ripen dark brown. Part of the shoot may stick out of the top.

Japanese red cedar *Cryptomeria japonica*

In its native Japan, the ornamental red cedar is often planted in gardens and along avenues near temples. It is known there by such picturesque names as 'peacock pine' and 'goddess of mercy fir'. The tree is a close relative of the Wellingtonia, which it resembles in shape and form, though it is smaller in size. It also occurs naturally in China, but it is the Japanese form – with shorter leaves – that was introduced to Britain in 1861.

Japanese red cedar grows quickly in Britain and is found in many gardens, as are its numerous cultivars, some of which retain their long, feathery, juvenile foliage for life. The tree can be coppiced, or cut down near the ground to produce new shoots, which is unusual among conifers. It withstands a lot of shade and flourishes if grown under other trees. Its dense foliage keeps out a great deal of sunlight, and so prevents the growth of weeds. The lower branches are shed early in life and produce fragrant, knot-free timber without pruning.

The timber has red heartwood and yellowish sapwood, and is strong, durable and easy to work. In Japan, it is used for building and general purposes; but in Britain it has only occasionally been planted as a forest tree.

The common juniper may be a small, conical tree up to 20 ft (6 m) tall, or a low, twisted shrub with spreading branches.

Male and female flowers grow on separate trees; males are yellow and females green.

Cultivars popular in gardens include Irish juniper, 'Hibernica', with its attractive narrow upright shape, and the prostrate golden 'Depressa Aurea', ideal as a ground-cover plant.

Rich, reddish-brown bark shreds and curls in strips.

Berries ripen dark purple in the second year.

The spiky, blue-green needles, ½ in. (1·3 cm) long, are in groups of three. Each has a white band on upper side. Berries are green in first year.

Juniper is often seen growing on moorland in the Lake District and Scotland, and on chalk uplands in the south.

Common juniper *Juniperus communis*

The ancient Egyptians used cedar oil made from the aromatic leaves of the juniper – together with other oils and sweet-smelling substances – in the preservation of the bodies of their dead by mummification. In medieval Europe, the leaves and branches were burned to keep away evil; and, together with beechwood, to smoke and preserve hams. The berries provided a brown dye and, used medicinally, were said to resist the plague, cure the bites of savage beasts, and generally act as an antidote to poison. The berries are still used for flavouring gin and its Dutch equivalent, geneva.

The juniper is one of Britain's native conifers, and grows naturally in a variety of situations. In the south it grows on chalk downs, but has become increasingly scarce because of fungal disease; further north it grows on limestone moorland, while in Scotland it flourishes on the acid soils of pine forests.

Since this shrub – or small tree – varies greatly in form, it has been cultivated by gardeners in numerous ways on a wide range of soils. Variant forms include the Irish juniper, 'Hibernica', which is a narrow, pointed column. Dwarf forms are often used to decorate rock gardens.

The pencil cedar has a narrow profile and straight stem; it grows to a height of 45 ft (14 m).

The reddish-brown bark peels off in long strips.

The needle-like juvenile leaves appear in threes at the tips of shoots, above the mature scale leaves. The oval fruits ripen in one year.

The cultivar 'Burkii', with its conical, upswept crown and blue-green foliage, is one of the most popular garden forms.

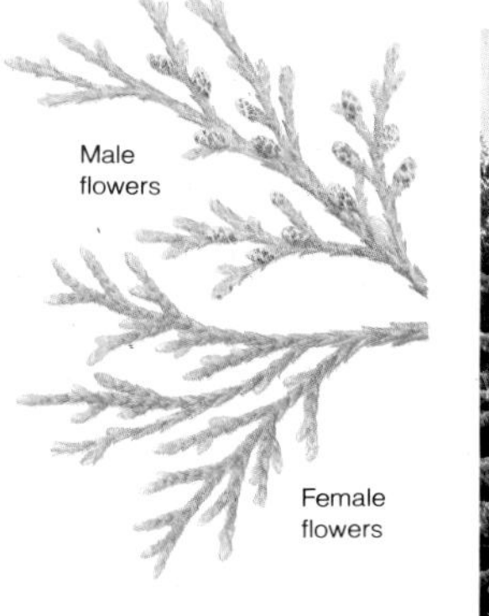

The male flowers are round and yellow; female flowers are smaller and green. Both open in March, on separate shoots.

This slender, elegant tree takes varied forms, and is sometimes seen in large gardens as a dense pillar of foliage.

Pencil cedar *Juniperus virginiana*

As its name suggests, the wood of this cedar used to be much in demand for making pencils, as it is easily sharpened and does not splinter. Today, however, the tree is no longer so abundant, and its wood is used only in the manufacture of the finest quality pencils. The wood is light, soft and aromatic, and has a fine texture, with rose-red heartwood and white sapwood. It is durable and resists attacks by insects, and has been used to make moth-proof linings for chests and wardrobes; wood shavings from the tree used to be put in drawers to keep moths away. Cedar oil is an ingredient of some soaps and perfumes.

The pencil cedar, tallest of the junipers, was introduced from eastern North America to England as an ornamental tree in 1664. It is hardy and very adaptable, growing in a wide variety of situations; it does particularly well on drier soils. Like the common juniper, it is very slow-growing, and appears in dwarf form in rockeries.

The aromatic leaves are needle-like when young. Older trees develop cypress-like leaves, but juvenile leaves are often retained at the branch tips; some cultivated varieties never develop adult foliage.

The golden foliage of the slender cultivar 'Aurea' makes it a popular ornamental tree.

A very narrow, conical, many-branched profile and an open crown characterise this juniper. It reaches a height of 60 ft (18 m).

Mature foliage consists of very small, scale-like leaves and branchlets with a spotted appearance. Juvenile leaves, ⅜ in. (1 cm) long, are awl-shaped and grow in twos and threes.

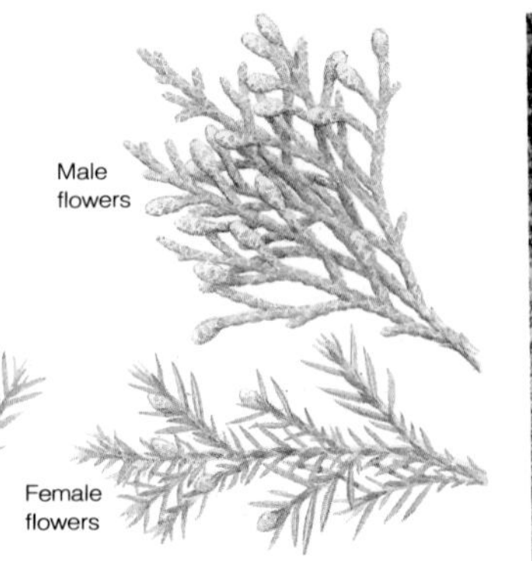

Male flowers are numerous and bright yellow; green female flowers are inconspicuous, in leaf axils.

Chinese juniper is the most commonly planted juniper in British gardens; it is also found in parks and churchyards.

The reddish-brown bark peels off in long strips.

The numerous fruits, blue-green when immature, take two years to ripen to dark purple.

Chinese juniper *Juniperus chinensis*

The bluish berries of the Chinese juniper are an attractive addition to any park or garden. In order to produce the berries – which take two years to mature – the trees are best planted in groups, as the male and female flowers are on separate trees. Numerous cultivars of the Chinese juniper can be grown; some of them are different forms of the same species, while others are crosses with other species of juniper.

One of the most popular garden forms is 'Pfitzerana', a hybrid between the Chinese juniper and the savin (*Juniperus sabina*) – a European juniper grown in Britain since 1548. The spreading 'Pfitzerana' cultivar is very suitable for low ground cover. A number of blue and grey-blue forms are also available, and many retain their awl-shaped juvenile leaves for life. Another greatly admired cultivar is 'Aurea', a golden tree.

Chinese juniper and the pencil cedar are the only junipers that assume tree form; the other junipers are really shrubs. The tree and its cultivars are slow-growing and short-lived, and thrive on a wide range of soils and situations. This ornamental tree came to Britain from the Far East in 1804, and in Japan it is grown in gardens and near temples.

The foliage of the Patagonian cypress hangs in drooping sprays. In Britain, the tree has so far grown to about 60 ft (18 m).

The leaves are in threes, as on junipers, but they are blunt and much shorter, with two white bands on each surface. The scales of the small brown cone are few, and open very widely when it is ripe.

Female flowers

The female flowers are abundant but seldom produce ripe seed, as the male tree is not common in Britain.

Bark is dark and furrowed; it peels in long strips.

This South American tree is grown in gardens and arboreta in the west and south for its attractive drooping foliage.

Patagonian cypress *Fitzroya cupressoides*

Captain Robert Fitzroy was the commander of HMS *Beagle*, the ship on which the naturalist Charles Darwin made the five-year voyage around the world which resulted in the writing of his epoch-making book *On the Origin of Species*. In 1849, 13 years after the *Beagle* returned to England, the Patagonian cypress was introduced to Britain and its generic name is a tribute to Captain Fitzroy. The tree was discovered on marshy ground in Patagonia, at the southern tip of South America – one of the regions visited earlier by the *Beagle*.

Most trees of this species cultivated in Britain appear to be female. As a consequence the cones have only sterile seed, but this cypress can be propagated by cuttings. Male and female flowers are usually produced on separate trees, although some bear flowers of both sexes. As with all conifers the seed is not enclosed in an ovary, but lies on the upper surface of the cone scale.

Once established, the Patagonian cypress is hardy. It is a graceful, very slow-growing tree, whose reddish-brown wood has a straight grain and is easily worked. Its timber is used in Chile to make, amongst other things, masts for ships.

This cypress is notable for its even, conical outline, dense foliage and upswept branches. It grows to 65 ft (20 m).

Very small, scale-like leaves give the dull green foliage a stringy appearance. Some leaves have white spots. Rounded branchlets spread in all directions. The many yellow male flowers are present throughout winter.

This well-shaped ornamental conifer is a very common garden tree, sometimes planted to form a hedge.

The large round cones may remain on the tree for many years after shedding their seeds.

Purple bark blisters and flakes in patches.

The silvery-blue foliage of the cultivar 'Pyramidalis' and its conical shape have made it one of Britain's most popular garden trees.

Smooth Arizona cypress *Cupressus glabra*

Although this graceful tree formed large forests in its native central Arizona, it is normally planted in Britain as an individual tree, or as a hedge. It was introduced in 1907 and has become a favourite in small gardens, with its attractive purple-coloured bark and its grey-blue and grey-green leaves. The oil produced by the leaves is thought to be an adaptation to reduce water loss in the tree's dry homeland. As a result, the cypress grows well on dry soils, and is not badly affected by drought.

For more than 70 years the smooth Arizona cypress was mistakenly known as *Cupressus arizonica*, and is still so called in some garden catalogues. The true *Cupressus arizonica*, or rough-barked Arizona cypress, is a very similar tree, but one that is rarely found in Britain. It is distinguished from the smooth Arizona cypress by its stringy, furrowed bark and much greener leaves. Also, its leaves are frequently without the white spots seen on those of the smooth cypress.

A number of cultivars are grown, some of them selected for their blue foliage. They include the beautiful 'Pyramidalis', with its brilliant, silver-blue leaves, nearly all of which have a prominent, central white spot.

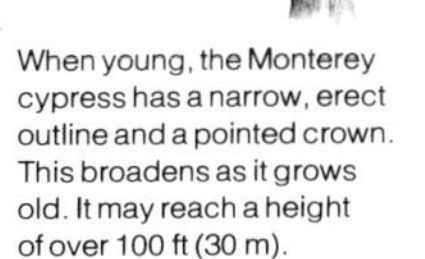

When young, the Monterey cypress has a narrow, erect outline and a pointed crown. This broadens as it grows old. It may reach a height of over 100 ft (30 m).

Bark is yellowish-brown, with long ridges.

The dull gold colour of the cultivar 'Lutea' provides a contrast with darker greens when planted in gardens.

Cones are large, with lumpy, leathery scales; leaves are very small. Branchlets all point forwards.

The small, yellow, egg-shaped male flowers appear in late spring.

Because it resists salt winds, this tree has probably been used more than any other for seaside planting in Britain.

Monterey cypress *Cupressus macrocarpa*

When it was introduced to Britain from west California in 1838, the Monterey cypress was mainly used as a windbreak or hedge. It thrives in the south and west of Britain, where it grows on a wide range of soils. Although it is damaged and sometimes killed by frost, it is resistant to salt winds. But today its role as a hedge plant has been taken over by the faster growing Leyland cypress, a cross between this species and the Nootka cypress.

On the Monterey peninsula in California, the tree is characteristic of a narrow zone lying between the beach and the area occupied by the Monterey pine. Some of the older trees are shaped into picturesque silhouettes by the wind. Like the Monterey pine, the Monterey cypress grows well in Africa and Australasia, where it is an important timber tree. The fragrant, yellowish wood is of good quality, but it is only obtainable in small quantities in Britain.

The cypress needs to be planted out young as – like pines – it later develops a strong tap root which is easily damaged during transplanting. Container-grown plants solve this problem. The young tree has to be supported by a stake if it has much foliage, otherwise the wind may catch it and work the tree loose.

A slender tree with a tall crown and a drooping leading shoot. Branches are small, with pendulous foliage; stems are numerous and forked. The tree can reach a height of more than 120 ft (36 m).

Male flowers

Female flowers grow on the ends of small branchlets. Male flowers grow on the ends of branches and have black scales edged with white, becoming red when ripe.

Female flowers

Lawson cypresses are planted for ornamental purposes and for hedging; a few are grown for timber.

Lawson cypress *Chamaecyparis lawsoniana*

Britain's most popular garden conifer, the Lawson cypress, indirectly owes its presence in this country to the mysterious disappearance of the Scottish botanist, John Jeffrey. He vanished without trace while on a collecting expedition in northern California at the beginning of 1854, and one of those who went in search of him was a fellow botanist, William Murray. During his search – which proved fruitless – Murray came across this cypress in the valley of the Sacramento River. He sent the first consignment of seed to an Edinburgh seed firm, Messrs Lawson, from which the tree took its name.

The tree was soon planted in many gardens, and before long cultivars were selected. The process continues today, when around 165 different types can be obtained, ranging from dwarf and prostrate forms to tall trees, some with drooping foliage. They occur in a variety of golds, yellows, greens and blues, and some of the cultivars retain their long juvenile leaves, giving the foliage a feathery appearance.

The long-lived Lawson cypress grows on a wide variety of soils, providing there is sufficient moisture. The yellowish timber is hard and durable, and used for fencing.

Smooth, rich brown bark becomes finely fissured.

Foliage is soft and light green, with a purplish tinge on the shoot. Leaves are dark green on top and a lighter green below, with whitish lines between the scales. The scales of open cones resemble tacks.

'Allumii'

Compact shape is suited to small gardens. Foliage flattened, dull grey-green. Grows to 6 ft (1·8 m) in ten years, then to 50 ft (15 m).

'Ellwoodii'

Close green foliage; variants tinged gold, silver or white. Grows to 6 ft (1·8 m) in ten years and finally to 20 ft (6 m).

'Green pillar'

This tree resembles 'Erecta', but is a brighter green and less liable to damage by snow. It reaches a height of 6 ft (1·8 m) in ten years, and after that grows to about 40 ft (12 m).

'Pygmaea argentea'

Bluish foliage has silvery-white tips, often browned by frost or sun. Reaches 10 in. (25 cm) in ten years, on to 3 ft (1 m).

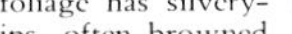

'Westermannii'

With its large sprays of pendulous, yellowish foliage, this unusual tree reaches 33 ft (10 m); it grows to 10 ft (3 m) in ten years.

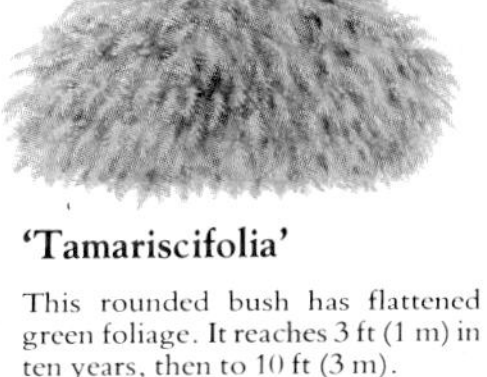

'Tamariscifolia'

This rounded bush has flattened green foliage. It reaches 3 ft (1 m) in ten years, then to 10 ft (3 m).

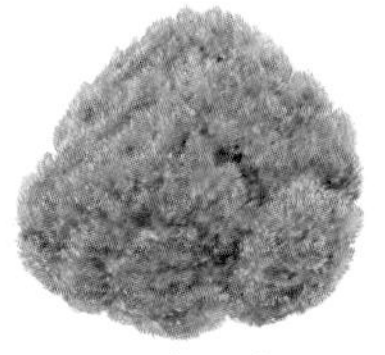

'Minima glauca'

Dwarf tree, green foliage. Reaches 1 ft (30 cm) in ten years, then to 5 ft (1·5 m).

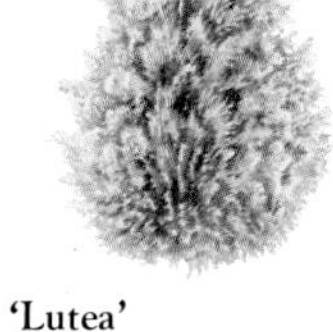

'Lutea'

Yellow foliage. 6 ft (1·8 m) in ten years, then 40 ft (12 m).

'Pottenii'

Slender; grows to 8 ft (2·5 m) in ten years, then to 50 ft (15 m).

'Spek'

Spectacular, ice-blue foliage gives this tree its alternative name of 'Glauca Spek'. It reaches 6 ft (1·8 m) in ten years, and grows to 30 ft (9 m).

'Wisselii'

Darkish, blue-green foliage; tiny, dark-red spring flowers; twisted sprays. Fast-growing, reaching 10 ft (3 m) in ten years and growing to 40 ft (12 m).

'Lanei'

The handsome golden foliage keeps its colour all year in a south-facing situation. It grows to a height of 50 ft (15 m), reaches 6 ft (1·8 m) in the first ten years.

'Erecta'

Erect branches provide name. Flame-shape is often spoiled by heavy snow. Growth rate is 6 ft (1·8 m) in ten years and ultimately reaches 50 ft (15 m).

Cypresses for park and garden

Lawson cypress only grows naturally in two small locations on the borders of Oregon and California: one on the coast around Port Orford and the other in the Siskiyou mountains. The tree is known in the United States as Port Orford cedar. The lumber is exported in large quantities to Japan, where it is prized for its light, durable and easily worked timber.

In Europe, however, the chief use of Lawson cypress is as a garden ornamental tree, producing a wide range of cultivars of various shapes and colours. Some 165 different types are available, and new ones are named regularly, making Lawson cypress probably the most common evergreen garden tree in Britain.

The bright green leaves are pointed and form flattened branchlets. The tiny rounded cones, are ½ in. (1·3 cm) in diameter, and have prominent spikes.

The conical crown is very regular; the foliage droops. Upper branches are small and slightly ascending. The tree grows to 80–115 ft (24–35 m).

Thin, red-brown bark cracks into small scales.

Seeds are released when the cones ripen in the spring.

The dark, yellowish-green foliage of the cultivar 'Pendula' hangs in long, curtain-like masses. In summer the cones turn shiny blue.

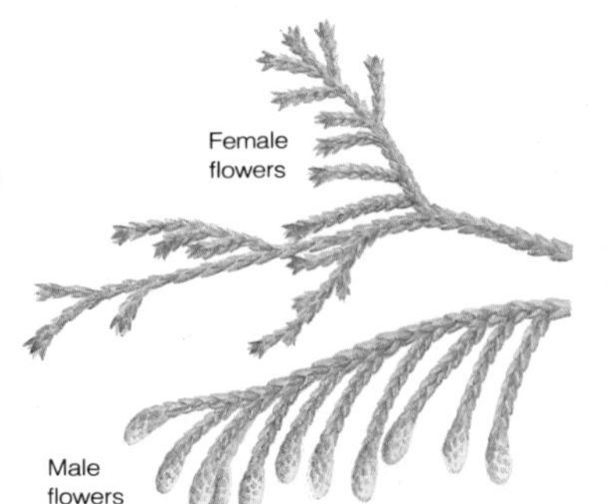

Green female flowers hang on the shorter branchlets; their cones mature in second year. Yellow male flowers open on the tips of hanging branchlets.

This very hardy cypress is planted in parks, large gardens and churchyards, sometimes in a yellow-leaved form.

Nootka cypress *Chamaecyparis nootkatensis*

Popular for its own sake as an ornamental tree in large parks and gardens, the Nootka cypress is also one of the parents of the hybrid Leyland cypress. Its outstanding quality is its extreme hardiness, which has been passed on to the hybrid. The Nootka cypress was introduced from north-west America in 1853, where ages of 300 and 400 years have been recorded, and takes its name from the Nootka Indians who live on Vancouver Island.

The Nootka cypress prefers moist soils, but will grow well on drier soils if they are of good quality. It can tolerate shade, and the young trees actually grow better in such conditions. The dark green, fern-like foliage hangs down on either side of the branches and has a thick, oily aroma when crushed. The pendulous sprays are harsh and rough if rubbed the wrong way. A few cultivars are grown in Britain, mainly with yellow foliage.

The fine-grained wood is a distinctive sulphur-yellow in colour and it cleaves and works easily. Because of this, the timber is valuable in North America; in Canada it is known as canoe cedar and is used for boat-building. In Britain, most trees are relatively young and the species has not been exploited commercially for its timber.

The small, densely packed, leaves are bright green and very like those of Lawson cypress. The inconspicuous green female flowers and yellow male flowers appear infrequently.

Female flowers

Male flowers

The Leyland cypress has a narrow, column-like crown. Its numerous branches extend from crown to base. It has reached a height of 100 ft (30 m) in Britain.

The bark is reddish-brown and fissured.

[×2]

The round, brown cones occur only occasionally, at the tips of branches. Small winged seeds have so far been only rarely produced.

This hardy, fast-growing natural hybrid is found on a variety of soils and sites, and is very popular for hedges.

Leyland cypress × *Cupressocyparis leylandii*

Although hybrids occur quite frequently between closely related trees, it is not often that a cross occurs naturally between trees of different genera. This happened when the cones of Nootka cypress (a 'false' cypress of the *Chamaecyparis* genus), were fertilised by pollen from Monterey cypress (a true cypress of the *Cupressus* genus). The cross took place in 1888 on the Leighton Estate, Welshpool, and the hybrid was given the name of C. J. Leyland, brother-in-law of the owner of the estate, who took some of the seedlings and planted them on his own estate at Haggerston Castle in Northumberland.

Twenty-three years later, a further cross occurred at Leighton Estate. This time the cones of the Monterey cypress were fertilised by pollen from the Nootka cypress. The result of this cross was a second hybrid, given the name of 'Leighton Green'.

The first cross is known as 'Haggerston Grey', as its scale-like leaves are often grey at the base. It is now the most commonly grown of the two crosses. In either form, Leyland cypress combines the hardiness of Nootka cypress with the fast growth of Monterey cypress; in fact, it is the fastest-growing conifer in Britain, growing as much as 4 ft (1·25 m) a year.

This ornamental tree has a broadly conical crown, with very dense foliage. It reaches a height of 120 ft (36 m).

The bright green, glossy leaves are blunt-tipped, flattened and scale-like. The pea-sized cones ripen to brown in a year.

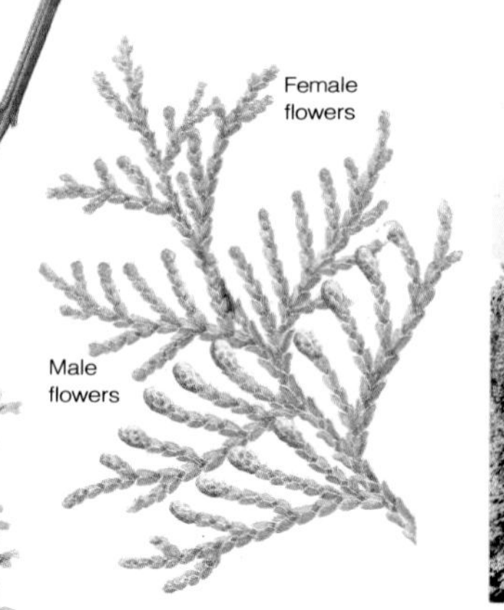

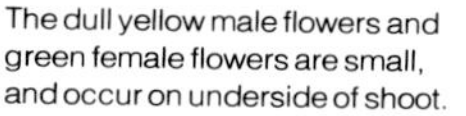
The dull yellow male flowers and green female flowers are small, and occur on underside of shoot.

The tree grows best in western parts of Britain, where it is frequently found in large gardens. It is rare in the east.

Hinoki cypress *Chamaecyparis obtusa*

In the middle of the 17th century, when the population of Japan grew and wood was much in demand for building, laws to conserve forests were introduced and five trees were reserved for use by the Emperor and for religious purposes. The Hinoki cypress was one of these; the other four were the Sawara cypress, the Japanese umbrella pine, the hiba, and the Japanese arbor-vitae.

The Hinoki cypress was dedicated as the 'Tree of the Sun'. It was often planted near temples, and many dwarf forms were cultivated in gardens. It was introduced to Britain in 1861 by the collector J. G. Veitch, and is frequently seen in large gardens. It does well on moist soils, including those which are slightly acid. Numerous cultivars have been propagated, many of them slow-growing dwarf forms which are planted in rockeries. In eastern areas it is more often seen as the cultivar 'Crippsii', grown in small gardens and parks.

The bark resists decay and, in Japan, is used for roof shingles. The wood is white, fragrant, easily worked and durable. It has a beautiful grain and is much used in furniture-making in its native land.

The red-brown bark shreds into coarse, parallel strips.

Undersides of leaves have pronounced white markings.

The golden cultivar 'Crippsii' grows slowly and suits rockeries. It tolerates shade.

This hardy tree has a pyramidal, frequently broad crown. The branches are usually level, but sometimes bend down and form layers at the tree base. The tree can grow to 65 ft (20 m).

The small, sharp-pointed leaves form compact sprays. The small brown cones have few scales.

Female flowers

Male flowers

Minute male and female flowers occur on the underside of the shoots. The pale brown male flowers shed pollen in April.

Cultivars of the Sawara cypress, with feathery, light green foliage, are widely planted in gardens and arboreta.

Rich brown bark is finely fissured in long ridges.

The cultivar 'Squarrosa' is one of the many garden forms of this tree which have retained their juniper-like foliage and do not produce flat, adult, scale-like leaves.

Leaves have white markings on the undersides. [× 2]

Sawara cypress *Chamaecyparis pisifera*

Like the Hinoki cypress, the Sawara cypress was one of the five sacred trees of old Japan. Varieties cultivated there were introduced to Britain by the collector Robert Fortune in 1861, and cultivars are now widespread in this country; but the tree in its original form is not so often seen. Many of the cultivars retain their juvenile, juniper-like leaves, which at first led botanists to place them in a separate group called *Retinospora*, meaning 'net-like foliage'. Not until later was it realised that the imported cultivars were in fact a juvenile form of the Sawara cypress, and they are still often referred to by their 'wrong' name.

The cultivars are frequently found in parks, town gardens and churchyards. They include 'Plumosa aurea', whose bright gold form pales with age and sometimes reverts to green; the broad, many-stemmed 'Filifera'; a bright gold beehive-shaped bush, 'Filifera aurea'; and 'Squarrosa', with its fluffy, bluish-green foliage.

The Sawara cypress is slow-growing, but succeeds in most good soils. It prefers those where there is plenty of moisture, and it does not like lime. When crushed, the foliage has a resinous, acrid aroma.

Chinese thuja

Thuja orientalis

This ornamental tree differs from white cedar in having leaves that are dark green on both sides, in dense flattened sprays. The blue-green cones, hooked at the top, turn brown when ripe.

Brownish-orange bark is vertically fissured.

Leaves are dark on top and yellowish-green below. Cones are yellow at first, ripening to brown.

The young tree's profile is narrowly conical, with open crown and steeply rising branches. It grows to a height of 65 ft (20 m).

Male flowers are small and red-brown, growing at the tips of the shoots. The female flowers are green or purple.

This native of North American swamps is best known in its various garden forms. Its shape broadens with age.

White cedar *Thuja occidentalis*

In the century following the discoveries of Christopher Columbus, European explorers investigating the eastern seaboard of North America found many trees and plants hitherto unknown to them. One was the white cedar, the first conifer introduced to Britain from America. It arrived in the second half of the 16th century, and was planted by the herbalist John Gerard in his garden. In Britain the white cedar grows slowly; it will adapt itself to a wide variety of soils, but being native to swamplands it likes plenty of moisture.

Although white cedar is sometimes grown as a hedge, it is usually seen in the form of one of its many cultivars. As with so many cypress-like trees, some cultivars retain their juniper-like juvenile foliage, which the tree in its original form normally loses when two or three years old. One of the cultivars most often grown is the rich golden 'Rheingold'.

The light brown timber is fragrant, like that of all thujas, which is why they are popularly called cedars; the word 'thuja' is derived from a Greek word meaning a resinous tree. The timber is light and soft, and was much used in Canada for building lightweight boats before being largely replaced by glass fibre.

The single upright leading shoot at the top of this tree distinguishes it from the cypresses that it otherwise resembles. It grows rapidly in damp, cool areas, reaching a height of about 83 ft (25 m) in 30 years.

The leaves are broader than those of cypresses, bright green on top with white patches below. The leafy cones mature in one year.

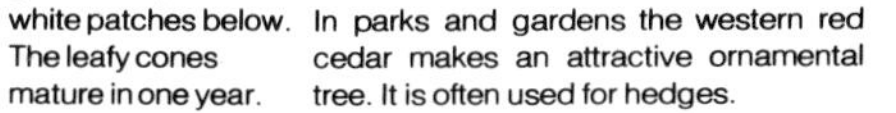

In parks and gardens the western red cedar makes an attractive ornamental tree. It is often used for hedges.

Western red cedar *Thuja plicata*

North American Indians used the timber of western red cedar for their canoes and totem poles. Today it is familiar in Britain as the reddish-brown wood used for the roofing shingles and wall cladding of modern bungalows, and for garden sheds. The American Indians discovered many centuries ago that the fibrous timber cleaves readily; the fibres are therefore not cut, so that water runs off easily and the wood does not decay.

The tree was introduced to Britain in 1853, when it was sent from the west coast of North America to the nurseries of John Veitch in Exeter. It quickly became popular as an ornamental tree, being particularly suitable for formal avenues and hedges, and in 1876 it was first planted as a forest tree at Benmore in Argyllshire. It is planted under other trees because it does not mind shade, and its narrow shape makes it ideal as a 'nurse' crop to shelter young oaks, because its branches do not spread and damage the surrounding trees.

In its native land the western red cedar grows from Alaska to California. It is not a true cedar, but was given its name by early settlers who believed it to be related to the cedars of Lebanon mentioned in the Bible.

Reddish bark peels off in strips; bole is often fluted.

Male and female flowers are borne at the end of short branches. The male flowers are reddish, the female flowers yellowish-green, opening in March.

The tightly packed foliage of the incense cedar forms a dense and narrow column when the tree is grown in British parks and gardens. It reaches 115 ft (35 m).

The bright green leaves are closely pressed to the stem, but with points turned outwards. The cones, about 1 in. (2·5 cm) long, are vase-shaped with the tips of the scales turned out.

The incense cedar was first planted in Britain by 19th-century landowners for its very slim and elegant shape.

Female flowers

Bright cinnamon-coloured bark breaks into ridges.

Male flowers

Male and female flowers grow on the same tree. Male flowers are golden-yellow; green female flowers develop into rich brown cones.

Incense cedar *Calocedrus decurrens*

The cedar-like aroma of its wood and the sweet smell produced when its resin is burned have given this tree its common name of incense cedar, though it is not in fact a cedar but a member of the cypress family. It is a handsome tree, tall and very slim with a spire-like crown and bright green foliage.

In its native North America, where it grows from mid-Oregon to southern California, incense cedar timber is used for buildings, pencils, fences and rails; in the wild it is not usually as slim as trees propagated for ornament. In Britain the tree has been grown as an ornamental tree since its introduction in 1853. It was imported by the Oregon Association, a group of Scottish landowners who arranged to have the seeds of exotic trees collected and planted in woodlands around their large houses.

The foliage of incense cedar is also strongly fragrant, and the large winged seeds are carried considerable distances by the winds. The timber is yellowish-brown, with a fine grain, and is very durable. The tree grows well on most soils and in a wide range of conditions, tolerating shade but needing more light as it gets older. Related species occur in China and Taiwan, and fossil remains have been found in Europe and Greenland.

The cones, oval when closed, have few scales, each with a protuberance near its tip. They open widely to release seed. The cones are about ⅝ in. (1·6 cm) in length.

The shiny leaves have the artificial look of plastic. They have conspicuous broad white patches with a narrow green border on the undersides.

The decorative hiba is often found in large parks and gardens, especially down the western side of Britain.

The cylindrical, regularly shaped hiba is densely clothed with foliage. The tree grows 50–65 ft (15–20 m).

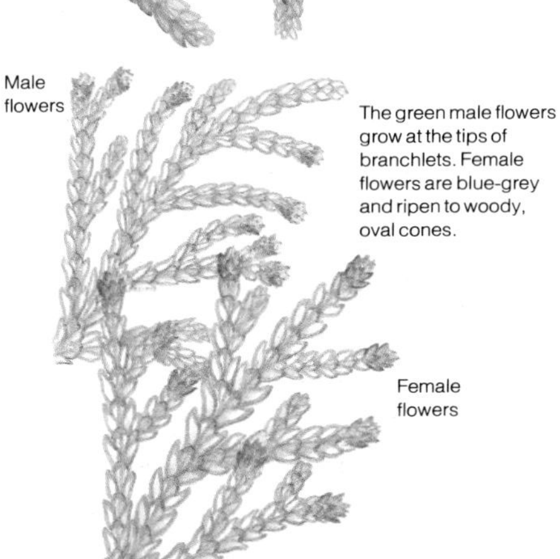

The green male flowers grow at the tips of branchlets. Female flowers are blue-grey and ripen to woody, oval cones.

Hiba *Thujopsis dolabrata*

The hiba's species name of *dolabrata* – from the Latin *dolabra*, 'hatchet' – refers to the shape of its scale-like leaves, which are thought to resemble an axe-head. They are a shiny bright green, with undersides boldly marked in white, and so perfect that they seem almost artificial. Because of the continuous luxuriance of its foliage, the hiba is one of a group of trees sometimes known as *Arbor vitae*, 'tree of life'; the others are the closely related thujas.

The timber is used for building in Japan, as it is light but strong, easy to work and durable. The hiba was one of the five sacred trees of old Japan, preserved for use by the royal family and in religious practice. It was introduced to Britain in 1853, in its southern and somewhat shrubby form. The first plant to be introduced died, but others arrived in 1859 and 1861.

In Britain, the hiba is seen purely as an ornamental tree, which thrives on soils that are not lime-rich. When trees are grown in open surroundings, the branches often touch the ground and will sometimes take root. The cone scales each bear three to five seeds, unlike the thujas which have only two seeds to each scale.

IDENTIFYING CONES

All cones have a similar seed-bearing function and are similar in structure; but they and their component parts may vary widely in appearance. For instance, the cone scales are tack-shaped in cypresses, thin and papery in spruces, and thick in silver firs; while in pines they bear a lump called an umbo.

In addition to cone scales, cones also bear much thinner bract scales, which bear the seed. In trees such as the noble and Douglas fir, the bract scales show between the cone scales of the mature cone. In trees such as the grand fir they are concealed.

All cones are green when they first form, and most turn various shades of brown as they ripen; but others go yellow, purple or blue. All cones stand upright until they are ripe and ready to shed their seeds. Then most turn over to hang downwards, allowing the seeds to fall out. But the cones of cedars and silver firs stay upright, and the scales fall to release the seed.

Barrel-shaped, erect cones

While all cedar cones look very much alike, the cones of silver firs vary widely in shape, size and colour; their bract scales may be concealed or protruding. The monkey puzzle cone is unique in appearance and has fat, edible seeds.

Forrest's fir

Abies delavayi var. *forrestii*

Bracts showing; cone ripens to blue, 3½ in. (9 cm). Page 216

Forrest's fir

Grand fir

Abies grandis

Bracts concealed; turns brown, to 3 in. (7·5 cm). Page 210. Bracts concealed also on Colorado white fir, p. 211; Nikko fir, p. 215; Spanish fir, p. 212; Veitch's silver fir, p. 209; beautiful fir, p. 208; and Himalayan fir, p. 214.

Grand fir

Noble fir

Abies procera

Large, ripens to brown, conspicuous down-turned green bracts. 8–10 in. (20–25 cm). Page 217. Similar cones, with conspicuous bracts, are borne by Caucasian fir, page 207, common silver fir, page 206, and Grecian fir, page 213. All ripen to brown; up to 6 in. (15 cm) long.

Noble fir

Atlas cedar

Atlas cedar

Cedrus atlantica

Depression in top, ripens to pale purplish-brown. 3¼ in. (8 cm). Page 203. Cedar of Lebanon, page 202, turns purple-brown; deodar, page 201, larger, turns light grey-brown.

Monkey puzzle

Monkey puzzle

Araucaria araucana

Pineapple-shaped, ripens to green with golden spines. Seeds large, with awl-like points. 4–7 in. (10–18 cm). Page 229

Long, hanging cones

These cones hang throughout the winter, shed their seeds with the first warm days of spring, then fall. Some have woody cone scales, are often blotched with white resin, and take two years to ripen. Others have soft, thin, often papery cone scales, and ripen in one year. Of these, only the Douglas fir cone shows its bract scales.

Morinda

Morinda
Picea smithiana

Scales soft and thin; ripens to brown, 4¾–6 in. (12–15 cm). Page 240

Bhutan pine

Bhutan pine
Pinus wallichiana

Woody cone scales; turns dark brown; may show resin. To 12 in. (30 cm). Page 257. Mexican white pine, page 254, similar.

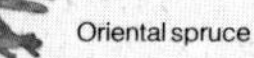

Oriental spruce
Picea orientalis

Ripens to ashy-brown, 2¾ in. (7 cm). Page 239. Brewer's weeping spruce, page 241, is similar.

Norway spruce

Norway spruce
Picea abies

Scales soft and thin; ripens to brown, 4¾–6 in. (12–15 cm). Page 232

Sitka spruce

Sitka spruce
Picea sitchensis

Scales very thin and papery, turns light brown; to 3 in. (7·5 cm). Page 236. Similar cone on blue spruce, page 234, and Hondo spruce, page 237.

Weymouth pine

Weymouth pine
Pinus strobus

Woody cone scales, curved and ripening to brown. 4–6 in. (10–15 cm). Page 256. Macedonian pine, page 259, has similar cone.

Douglas fir

Douglas fir
Pseudotsuga menziesii

Prominent three-pronged bracts protrude between cone scales, ripens to brown. 2–3 in. (5–7·5 cm). Page 218

Serbian spruce

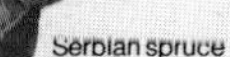

Serbian spruce
Picea omorika

Ripens to red-brown, 2½ in. (6 cm). Page 238. Mountain hemlock, page 219 and tiger tail spruce, page 235, are similar.

Round, hanging cones

Some of these cones have diamond-shaped, stalked cone scales. The remainder – all pine cones – have scales that are woody, thickened at the edges and often armed with prickles. They take two years to ripen, and some do not fall until long after the seed has been shed.

Corsican pine

Pinus nigra ssp. *laricio*

Woody scales; ripens to grey-brown, $2\frac{1}{2}$–$2\frac{3}{4}$ in. (6–7 cm). Page 247. Austrian pine, page 246, has similar cones.

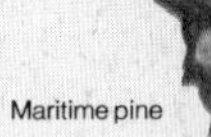

Maritime pine

Pinus pinaster

Woody scales; cone asymmetrical, with sharp prickle, ripens to shiny brown; persists on tree. 4 in. (10 cm). Page 250. Similar but larger cones on Monterey pine, page 253, and Western yellow pine, page 252.

Coast redwood

Coast redwood

Sequoia sempervirens

Scales diamond-shaped. Stalked, ripens to brown in one year. $\frac{3}{4}$ in. (2 cm). Page 222

Shore pine

Shore pine

Pinus contorta

Woody scales; cones in whorls. 2 in. (5 cm). Page 248. Stone pine, p. 251, larger, with lined scales. Arolla pine, p. 258, and Japanese white pine, p. 255, also have small round cones.

Swamp cypress

Taxodium distichum

Few, diamond-shaped scales, tiny spines; turns purple. 1 in. (2·5 cm). Page 225. Dawn redwood, page 224, is similar.

Swamp cypress

Wellingtonia

Wellingtonia

Sequoiadendron giganteum

Scales diamond-shaped. Stalked, ripens to grey-brown in two years. Scales corky, depressed at centre. 3 in. (7·5 cm). Page 262

Scots pine

Scots pine

Pinus sylvestris

Woody scales; ripens to grey-brown, 2–$2\frac{1}{2}$ in. (5–6 cm). Page 243. Mountain pine, page 249, has similar cones.

Cones with few scales

This group consists of small, rather inconspicuous cones which are varied in shape and have few scales. In most cases the cones remain on the tree after they have shed their seeds.

Western red cedar

Thuja plicata

Leaf-like scales. Ripens to brown. $\frac{3}{8}$ in. (1 cm). Page 277

Similar cones on white cedar and Chinese thuja, p. 276, incense cedar, p. 278 and hiba, p. 279, all turning yellow.

Nootka cypress

Chamaecyparis nootkatensis

Round, with tack-shaped scales. Ripens in two years. $\frac{3}{8}$ in. (1 cm). Page 272. Hinoki, page 274, and sawara cypress, page 275, resemble Nootka but open in one year.

Western hemlock

Tsuga heterophylla

Small, egg-shaped scales. Ripens to pale brown in one year. $\frac{3}{4}$–1 in. (2–2·5 cm). Page 220. The ripe cone of eastern hemlock, page 221, is smaller and darker.

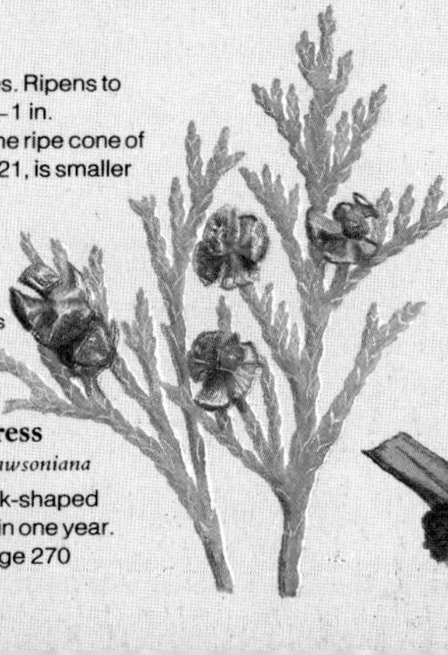

Lawson cypress

Chamaecyparis lawsoniana

Round, with tack-shaped scales. Ripens in one year. $\frac{1}{5}$ in. (5 mm). Page 270

Round cones scattered on twig

These rounded or egg-shaped cones do not turn right over as they ripen in order to shake out their seeds. After shedding their seed they often remain on the tree. They ripen in one year.

Japanese red cedar

Cryptomeria japonica

Few, tight scales with two or three curved spines on each scale. $\frac{3}{4}$ in. (2 cm). Page 263

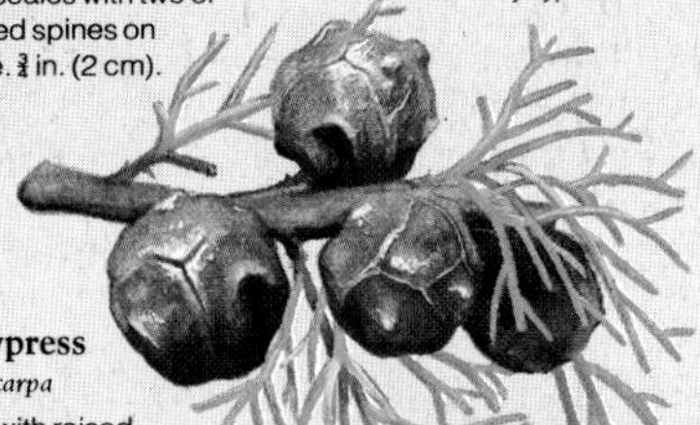

Monterey cypress

Cupressus macrocarpa

Few flat scales with raised centres, 1–1$\frac{1}{2}$ in. (2·5–4 cm). Page 269. Similar cones on Leyland cypress, page 273; Patagonian cypress (very small triangular scales), page 267; and smooth Arizona cypress (central spine on scales), page 268.

Japanese larch

Larix kaempferi

Many round scales, tips turned back. 1 in. (2·5 cm). Page 199. Hybrid larch, page 200, resembles both European and Japanese larch.

European larch

Larix decidua

Many round scales, tips not turned back. $\frac{3}{4}$–1$\frac{1}{2}$ in. (2–4 cm). Page 198

TREES PAST AND PRESENT

Britain's changing landscape

The vegetation cover provided by trees, shrubs and other plants in what is now the British Isles has varied dramatically over the millions of years of geological time.

Some 310 to 290 million years ago, the climate was equatorial, and luxuriant rain forest covered much of the land. The remains of this forest, with its gigantic club mosses up to 130 ft (40 m) tall and great tree ferns and horsetail plants, eventually formed the coal seams that are mined today.

Scorching deserts

By about 290 million years ago, Sahara-like conditions prevailed. Most vegetation had disappeared and there were vast areas of sand-dunes, which today form the sandstones of areas such as south-east Devon.

Sub-tropical forest flourished some 140 to 120 million years ago. Conifers, ferns and horsetails, along with palm-like cycads, were the main plants, for true flowering plants did not appear until about 130 million years ago.

A land bridge joined Britain to the rest of Europe for much of geological time, and across this bridge, tree and plant species spread. By about 50 million years ago, Britain's rich and varied cover included magnolias, giant redwoods and palms. All this was to change in the coming Ice Age.

The northern ice sheets began to edge southwards about 2 million years ago. They were to advance and retreat many times, and as they advanced, tree and plant species moved southwards, returning northwards as the sheets retreated. At the time of their maximum extent, about 400,000 years ago, the ice sheets covered virtually all of Britain north of the Thames and the Severn estuary, and only tundra vegetation managed to survive in the region to the south of this cold frontier line.

Retreat of the ice

The ice began its last withdrawal about 10,000 years ago, and the temperate climate of today developed. Trees and plant species re-invaded northern Europe and spread into Britain, and our native trees, shrubs and plants date from this time. Willow, dwarf birches and juniper were the vanguard of the advancing forest. Birches and pines followed. Later, as the climate began to resemble that of today, broad-leaved forests, including oak, elm, hazel and alder became established.

However, the sea level was rising as the ice melted, and about 7,500 years ago Britain was severed from the Continent as the sea broke through to make the Strait of Dover. Many European tree species, including the Norway spruce (the 'Christmas tree'), European larch and European silver fir, did not have time to reach Britain before the land bridge disappeared. As a result, our range of native trees is very limited compared with what it was in the past, totalling only 35 tree species and a few shrubs.

A land of vast forests

Successive waves of migrant peoples from the Continent crossed to Britain. The earliest were the Stone Age hunters and gatherers who, even with their primitive stone tools, made the first inroads on Britain's forests. About 3500 BC, people with a more settled way of life, based on farming, arrived. Their methods of cultivation rapidly intensified the clearance of the woodland, and this clearance was to continue at an increasing rate for the next 4,000 years.

The early farmers found almost all of Britain covered by trees. There was dense forest, largely of oak, elm, alder, lime and hazel extending over much of lowland Britain, with more open forest of oak, alder and hazel on the uplands of Wales. Scots pine, sessile oak and juniper clothed the uplands of Scotland.

Sharp-edged tools of flint enabled the farmers of the 'New Stone Age' to fell trees for fuel, to provide building material for their primitive houses, and to make clearings in which to graze their livestock and grow their crops, including barley and oats. These clearings were most easily made and maintained in the open woodlands on the dry chalk and limestone soils of the south-east and on the sandstone ridges. It is in these regions that the tree cover has been removed for the longest time.

Many of the raw materials available to prehistoric people came from trees and shrubs, and they very early learned how to produce staple items from wood. For instance, the coppicing of hazel and other species, developed about 5,000 years ago, produced long straight rods for the fences needed to protect livestock.

Axes of bronze, sharper and more durable than those of flint, were common in Britain by about 1000 BC and contributed considerably to the destruction of woodlands, especially in the uplands. More efficient iron tools helped the Celts, who began arriving in Britain about 500 BC, to carve out even more farmland from virgin forests.

By the time the Romans arrived, much of upland Britain had been stripped of its forest cover. The Romans removed broad swathes of vegetation along their roads to prevent their enemies using them as cover.

Land-hungry Saxon farmers

The Saxons laid down a pattern of farming communities that survived into recent times. When the Domesday Book was compiled for William the Conqueror in 1086, on a basis of a nationwide survey of resources, it disclosed that only 20 per cent of England was still covered by forests. This was the first written estimate of the extent of Britain's tree cover.

The Normans, with their love of the chase, found it necessary to designate certain areas as 'Royal Forests'. Several of these royal hunting preserves, including the New Forest and Forest of Dean, survive today as areas that were probably always wooded.

Dwindling forest resources

During the following centuries, many factors conspired to deplete Britain's forests even more, and to prevent the land cleared of trees from reverting to woodland. By Tudor times exports of wool were vital to the economy of an energetic and ambitious England. Large parts of the country, particularly the Cotswolds, were used for grazing sheep, and young tree seedlings and saplings stood little chance against the voracious animals. Scotland, too, was a mainly pastoral nation, and by 1500 most of the great Caledonian pine forest had been destroyed.

South-east Britain also suffered. Extensive ship-building in the reigns of Henry VIII and Elizabeth I led to the destruction of much of the oak forest of the Kent and Sussex Weald. The production of charcoal for the area's flourishing iron industries was largely supplied by renewable methods of wood production, such as coppicing, but the building of Wealden timbered houses played its part in forest losses.

Even before its heyday in Tudor and Elizabethan times, the wool trade led to the enclosure of great tracts of Saxon open fields to provide pastures. At first, wattle fences were used, but the planting of hedgerows followed as a means of demarcating boundaries. These were often of hawthorn, and furnished an ideal environment in which other trees could grow. In this way Britain's vast mileage of hedgerows with trees – such a dominant feature of many landscapes today – came into being.

However, there was little incentive for people to try to re-establish Britain's forests as they had existed in earlier centuries. Even in the 18th and 19th centuries, when the Industrial Revolution greatly increased the demand for timber, the country was wealthy enough to buy from abroad.

The successful industrial families of the time often spent much of their wealth in the countryside, establishing landed estates, but they were not interested in replacing woodland, for which there was scant need. Instead, they employed landscape architects such as 'Capability' Brown to supervise extensive ornamental tree planting, which added to the variety of trees to be seen in the landscape.

Hope for the future

It was not until the First World War that home-grown timber was needed again in any quantity. The German blockade prevented imports; large-scale tree felling on private estates ensued, and by 1918 only some 4 per cent of Britain was still covered by woodland.

This state of affairs led to the setting up of the Forestry Commission to undertake a national forestry programme and to encourage private owners in commercial timber production. Today, despite extensive felling in the Second World War, about 11 per cent of the island carries productive, commercial woodland and forest.

Trees and man

If a farmer from pre-Roman times were to return to Britain today, he would be amazed at the variety of trees and shrubs growing in the countryside. He would recognise only about one in five of the species, for the rest have been introduced since his day, from other parts of the world.

It was the Romans who began the diversification of Britain's treescape. The ever-practical conquerors brought in the walnut and the sweet chestnut for the sake of their edible seeds. The other trees which they may have introduced include the sycamore and the holm oak.

In the Middle Ages, as contact between Britain and the Continent increased, more and more trees were shipped to a 'second home' in Britain. Monks were constantly in touch with their European counterparts and probably introduced fruit and timber trees for their economic value, though no record of particular species exists.

About 100 years before the birth of Elizabeth I, the Norway spruce – the now familiar Christmas tree – was introduced. Other introductions took place in the Elizabethan age, including the medlar from southern Europe and the black mulberry from Asia, both of which were wanted for their fruit. The common silver fir arrived in 1603, and in 1616 the horse chestnut was brought from Greece or Albania. It was followed by the European larch, which was thought to have been brought back from Russia by John Tradescant around 1618 – 11 years before he became gardener to Charles I. Tradescant also persuaded ships' captains bound for North America to bring back tree seeds. His son, John Tradescant junior, later sailed across the Atlantic and between them they introduced many American trees, including the locust tree in about 1636, swamp cypress around 1640, and the tulip tree some ten years later.

Conifers from North America

Throughout the 17th and 18th centuries, gardeners and botanists were commissioned by wealthy patrons to collect the seeds of ornamental trees and shrubs. One such patron was Peter Collinson, a successful London draper, who planted many North American trees in his garden near Hendon, North London. The land now forms part of the grounds of Mill Hill School, and some of the trees – including a swamp cypress, a cedar of Lebanon, an oriental plane and a Caucasian wing nut – are still standing. Also from North America came conifers such as the Douglas fir and the Sitka spruce.

Similar collections were made by the Botanic Gardens of Oxford and Edinburgh, and by the Oregon Association, formed by Scotsmen in the mid-19th century to exploit the natural products of North America. The Horticultural Society of London, founded in 1804, sent David Douglas to the west coast conifer forests of North America. In the late 1820s he was the first person to collect the seeds of the Douglas fir, which was named after him, the noble and grand firs, and numerous other trees. More than 20 years later the Oregon Association sent John Jeffrey – who, like Douglas, was a native of Perthshire – to California, from where he sent back several species, including Jeffrey's pine and western hemlock.

Although China and Japan were not open to European travellers until the end of the 19th century, the tree of heaven was discovered in China by a French monk named Pierre d'Incarville, who had been allowed into the country as a missionary, and was introduced to Britain in 1751. Seven years later it was followed by the maidenhair tree, or ginkgo, which came from China via Japan. The Japanese larch arrived in 1861, when it joined other oriental trees such as the Chinese juniper, the Chinese fir and the graceful deodar cedar, the last of which arrived from Kashmir in 1829.

Ornamentals from the Orient

Another collector who introduced ornamental trees long cultivated in the Far East was the Cornishman, William Lobb, who worked for the enterprising nursery firm of James Veitch. Lobb was rivalled by Robert Fortune of the Horticultural Society, and between them they were responsible for the introduction of many trees, including the Japanese red cedar in 1842. Delavay's silver fir was introduced from China by Father Jean Marie Delavay at the beginning of the 20th century.

One of the most valuable acquisitions was made in 1904 by Henry 'Chinese' Wilson, who brought the handkerchief or dove tree to England. China also provided Britain's most recent introduction, the dawn redwood (1946). It was previously known as a fossil and was not found living in China until 1941. Today its bronze autumn foliage enriches many gardens and tree collections.

Trees for pleasure and profit

Many of the treescapes planned by the great landscape gardeners of the 18th century can still be seen today; and it was also in the 18th century that private landowners first started the extensive planting of conifers typical of modern commercial timber forests.

The 'natural look', in which gardens were an extension of the countryside, was pioneered early in the 18th century by the Yorkshireman, William Kent – the acknowledged father of English gardening. He was succeeded by his pupil Lancelot 'Capability' Brown, a Northumbrian who gained his nickname from his habit of riding round a site that he was about to redesign and listing its 'capabilities' for improvement. He rejected formal features such as straight avenues in favour of clumps of trees and winding lakes.

Brown remodelled or laid out the grounds of the Nuneham Courtenay House, near Oxford, as well as those at Kew and Blenheim Palace, Oxfordshire, the home of the Duke of Marlborough – all of which are wholly or partly open to the public today.

On Capability Brown's death in 1783 his mantle was donned by Humphry Repton, a failed general merchant and unsuccessful investor. He developed his own technique, in which he sketched the faults of an estate and then provided an overlay drawing which showed his potential clients the 'before and after' effect. His first major creation was at Cobham Hall, Kent, around 1790. Today the 150 acres of grounds of what is now a school are open to the public during the holidays, and the specimen trees growing there include some giant cedars. Repton was employed by many of the leading noblemen of his day.

Tree planting in the 18th century was not all for ornament. Some had a practical purpose, and trees originally introduced from abroad for their botanical interest were eventually used for their timber as well. Early in the 18th century Lord Weymouth extensively planted at Longleat in Wiltshire the eastern American white pine that was to be named after him in Britain. At about the same time the 3rd Duke of Atholl – the owner of large Perthshire estates – began the widespread planting of European larches, earning himself the nickname of 'the planting duke'. He and his successors planted some 27 million trees. The most successful introductions of all were the many conifers brought over from the west coast of North America, which are now Britain's most highly valued timber trees.

For a long time private landowners were alone in exploiting the potential of such introduced trees, and they did it only to a limited extent. However, following the acute timber shortage of the First World War, the Forestry Commission was set up in 1919 to establish supplies of home-grown timber. It achieved this by planting on marginal uplands, and by helping private owners to regenerate their woods and to establish new ones.

Timber and recreation

In the last 60 years British foresters have pioneered nursery practices, from seed-sowing to soil management, and have introduced special afforestation techniques to establish the seedlings on what would once have been regarded as unsuitable ground.

The intensive development of forestry, particularly in our uplands, where ploughing and deep draining for conifer plantation has been extensive, has led to concern for the conservation of some habitats. The needs of timber production must be balanced with the protection of our distinctive blanket bogs and moorland.

The introduction of trees has benefited Britain in many ways, not least of which is that plantations provide the public with places for recreation. Walking, horse-riding, birdwatching and path-finding are all the more enjoyable in a forest setting – provided that visitors respect the surroundings and appreciate that the area's main purpose is the production of timber.

The age of trees

The oldest living things in the world are trees: short, twisted bristle-cone pines in the White Mountains of California, North America, which have been standing for nearly 5,000 years. They were already more than 1,000 years old when the Ancient Greek civilisation first stirred into life about 1200 BC. Nearly as long-lived are the massive Wellingtonias of California, which are known to have survived for 3,400 years.

Britain's longest-lived tree is the yew, which can reach an age of more than 1,000 years, although few standing today are as old as this. Many yew trees have several younger stems growing round a long-dead central stem, leaving a hollow centre. The Fortingall Yew near Aberfeldy in Tayside, Scotland, has just such a hollow shell. Reputedly Britain's oldest tree, it is believed to be at least 1,500 years old, and may have been a sapling in Roman times.

Trees of 100–200 years old are not uncommon, and there are still some healthy oaks and sweet chestnuts in British parks and gardens that have been standing for four or five centuries. Strollers beneath their young branches discussing the news of the day could have been talking of events such as the defeat of the Spanish Armada.

How rings are formed

When a tree growing in a temperate climate such as that of Britain is cut down, a series of rings can be seen on the stump of the tree and on the end of the severed trunk. Each ring marks one year's growth.

Trees grow only in the warmer part of the year – generally from March to October – and the growth of the woody parts in spring differs from growth in summer. In spring, thin-walled cells with large central spaces are formed to conduct water and minerals (sap) from the roots to the rapidly growing parts of the tree. In summer, cells with thicker walls are formed to give strength to the new growth.

The thin-walled spring wood is lighter in colour than the thick-walled summer wood, and although the two merge during a year's growth, the dark summer wood formed at the end of the growing season shows up distinctly against the light spring wood of the following season, so forming a ring.

Telling the age of a living tree

Annual rings are not necessarily all evenly spaced. They reveal not only the tree's age but also its history – showing, for example, a year of drought when growth was limited and the ring narrow. They also show setbacks to growth such as frost, fire damage or damage by grazing animals.

It is possible to count the annual growth rings in a living tree. This is done with an instrument called an increment borer, which is driven into the trunk straight towards the centre. It cuts out a core of wood about as thick as a pencil, and when this is pulled out the number of rings can be counted.

Another way of finding the age of a larger tree is by measuring the girth of its trunk at a height of about 5 ft (1.5 m) above the ground. Even though an old tree will cease to grow in height, it must continue to form annual rings in order to feed itself, so its girth expands throughout its life.

Alan Mitchell, who worked for the forestry commission, measured and recorded many large trees and found that, on average, a tree with a full crown expands by about 1 in (2.5 cm) in girth each year, if growing in uncrowded conditions. Trees growing in a wood, in competition with others, take about two years to expand by the same amount, and those partially confined in, say, an avenue, take about one and a half years.

Although young trees usually grow faster and old trees slower than 1 in (2.5 cm) a year, this is the average expansion. So a tree with a girth of about 8 ft (2.5 m) growing in the open, is probably about 100 years old.

Coniferous trees

The age of a coniferous tree can also be assessed by its branch pattern, a method that is accurate while it is still fairly young. The branches occur in whorls – several growing out almost horizontally round the stem at the same height. Such whorls can be seen on all conifers up to 40 or 50 years of age, except cypresses, but are most noticeable on silver firs and pines.

The whorls are formed from side buds grouped round the base of the leading bud, and each spring all the buds develop into branches. Each whorl of branches is therefore separated by a length of stem developed from the leading bud, and the whorl and the stem above it are one year's growth. Although other side buds do develop from a leading shoot, they do not occur in whorls and are never as large as those in the whorl.

A tree's age can be found by counting the whorls, but it is always safest to allow a few extra years for lower branches that may have been lost in early life. Branches that have been cut off usually leave a scar that can be seen for many years. A whorl of scars indicates the beginning of a year's growth.

On occasions, however, a tree will develop two whorls in one year. This may occur in a season with a long summer and mild autumn, when buds that have developed during summer for the following season's growth are stimulated by the good weather to open in late August. This extra growth is known as Lammas growth, named after Lammas Day on August 1. It is commonest on the Douglas fir.

The record of the rings

By counting the annual rings of a tree it is possible to tell how old it is. The rings also record years of drought when the tree grew less than usual, moist summers when it grew fast, and incidents that occurred during its lifetime.

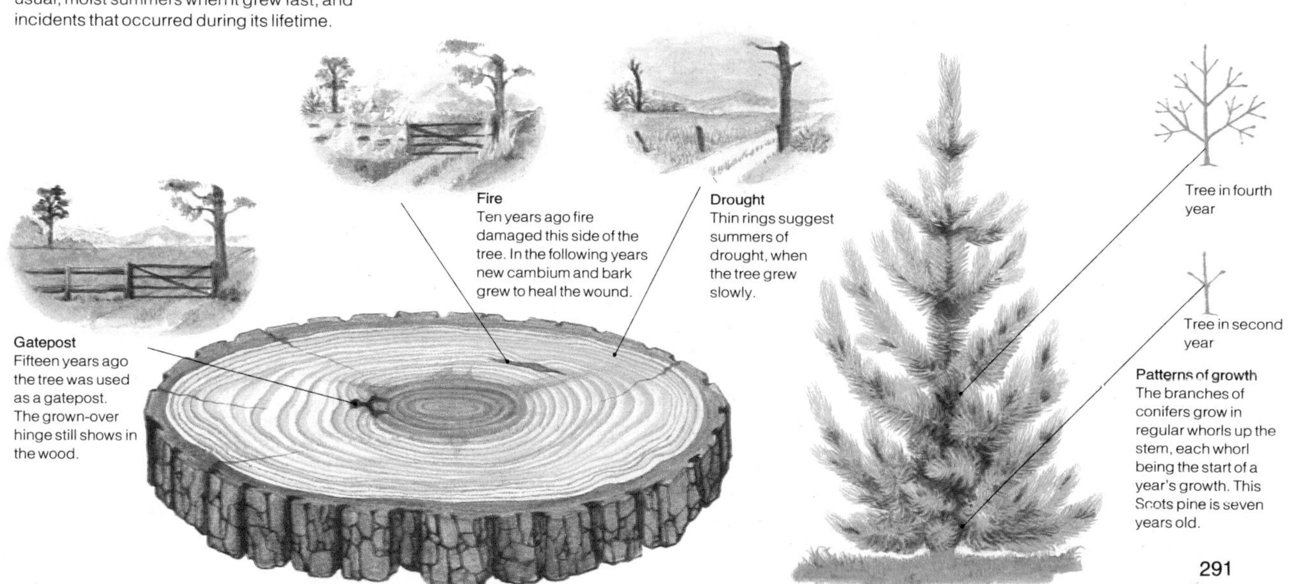

Fire
Ten years ago fire damaged this side of the tree. In the following years new cambium and bark grew to heal the wound.

Drought
Thin rings suggest summers of drought, when the tree grew slowly.

Gatepost
Fifteen years ago the tree was used as a gatepost. The grown-over hinge still shows in the wood.

Patterns of growth
The branches of conifers grow in regular whorls up the stem, each whorl being the start of a year's growth. This Scots pine is seven years old.

Where to see trees

Botanic gardens, forest parks and the grounds of many great estates in all parts of Britain provide numerous opportunities to study and enjoy the wide range of trees that grow in this country.

Some of the oldest collections of trees were originally physic gardens, where plants and some trees were grown for medicinal purposes. The botanic gardens at Oxford and Cambridge are examples. A garden laid out in 1759 in the grounds of a royal palace became the basis of the famous Royal Botanic Gardens at Kew.

One outcome of the Industrial Revolution was the accumulation of wealth by successful businessmen, whose families often invested their money in landed estates and employed gardeners such as Capability Brown to landscape their grounds. Many landowners travelled abroad and brought back choice specimens for their gardens, vying with each other in the splendour and variety of their collections. A number of these estates now belong to the National Trust and are open to the public.

In more recent times, arboreta and forest gardens have been established where species can be tested and studied. Although the aims of such collections are mainly scientific, they are of equal interest to the amateur tree-lover. In addition to these specialised collections, the Forestry Commission – whose primary role is timber production – has established forest parks and developed forest walks, nature trails and other opportunities for the study of trees and wildlife – all of which are managed by its agency, Forest Enterprise.

All the tree collections listed in the gazetteer which follows are open to the public, some throughout the year and some for more restricted periods, as indicated in the text. The positions of all the sites listed are shown on the map, page 294. Properties which are administered by the Forest Enterprise (FE) and the National Trust (NT) are indicated by initials.

Argyll Forest Park Argyll. FE
The park covers 55,000 acres (22,000 ha) of the Cowal peninsula. The first and, arguably, the finest of the Forestry Commission's parks, it offers a rich landscape of rugged mountains, coniferous forests, broadleaved woodland and a loch. Forest Enterprises provides about 38 miles (60 km) of waymarked walks through a variety of different types of forest. The network of 93 miles (150 km) of forest road is open to pedestrians and cyclists.

Batsford Arboretum Moreton-in-Marsh, Gloucestershire.
The arboretum contains a notable and varied collection of rare trees, shrubs and bamboos. Originally created as a wild garden by Lord Redesdale, British attaché in Tokyo in the 1860s, it was developed into an arboretum in the 1950s by the second Lord Dulverton. It is now administered by the Batsford Foundation. Oriental influence is seen in Lord Redesdale's grouping of trees to reflect his observations of landscape composition. To this Lord Dulverton has added collections of oaks, pines, firs, magnolias, birch, maples, mountain ash, Japanese walnuts and other rare trees.

Bicton Park Gardens East Budleigh, Devon.
The gardens and a pinetum are largely set in a shallow valley, backing onto a tree-fringed lake. The three main gardens – the American, the Italian and the Hermitage – altogether contain more than 500 different species of trees and shrubs. They range from the tallest tree in the gardens, the 133 ft (41 m) high western red cedar, to pines, cypresses, maples, spruce, planes, hornbeams and oaks.

Blair Castle Blair Atholl, Perthshire.
Almost 130 trees grow in the 2 acres (1 ha) of the estate known as Diana's Grove. Of these, 13 are over 160 ft (48 m) tall and include the tallest Japanese larch and the tallest red fir in Britain. The Grove was originally laid out in 1737, but the lime avenue and most of the large conifers were not planted until the 1870s. Further plantings have since followed, including some Wellingtonias, Japanese larch and a variety of cypresses, hemlocks and cedars.

Bodnant Garden Tal-y-cafn, Conwy. NT
The garden lies on sloping ground above the River Conwy and is divided into two parts. The

Terrace Gardens – with their cedar of Lebanon and Atlas cedar – are built around the house. Lower down is the Dell, which contains a wild garden and pinetum. Among the outstanding trees are cypresses, firs, Japanese maple and dawn redwood. There are some uncommon shrubs, such as Hemsley's styrax from China.

Brecon Beacons National Park Powys. www.breconbeacons.org
A forest reserve and five national nature reserves fall within the 520 square miles (1,347 km²) of the park. They contain oak, birch, alder, beech, larch and horse chestnut. In the forest reserve, in the Taf Valley, small-leaved lime and a unique sub-species of whitebeam occur. The 50 acre (20 ha) nature reserve at Cwm Clydach has one of Wales's few surviving native beech woods.

Cambridge University Botanic Garden Cambridge. www.plantsci.cam.ac.uk
Although the eastern half of this garden was not developed until 1951 – more than a century after the western half was planted – it has numerous trees on show including pines, alders, cedars, cypresses, hazels and larches. The western section features, among others, limes, maples, mulberries, yews, walnuts, willows and horse chestnuts. The garden is too dry to suit some conifers, but it has some unusual broad-leaved trees – including Warburg oak, Caucasian wing-nut and a fine collection of limes.

Cannock Forest Staffordshire.
This area of forest and heath is rich in birch and alder, and the planted woodlands contain oak, poplar, beech and sweet and horse chestnut. The present large conifer plantations were created by the Forestry Commission between 1920 and 1950 with annual plantings of Scots and Corsican pine, and European and Japanese larch.

Charles Ackers Redwood Grove and Naylor Pinetum near Welshpool, Powys.
The 33 coastal redwoods in the main grove were brought from California in pots in 1858. They stand where they were first planted, and their average girth is 12 ft (3.6 m). The tallest of the trees is about 127 ft (38.5 m); on average, they grow to around 115 ft (35 m). The grove and the surrounding woodland were presented to the Royal Forestry Society of England, Wales and Northern Ireland in 1958 by the late Mr Charles Ackers, an imaginative and forward-looking forester. The Naylor Pinetum contains more than 120 specimens of spruce, cypress, firs, cedars and pines.

Crarae Forest Garden near Inveraray, Argyll and Bute.
Although it covers only 38 acres (15 ha), the garden contains around 100 plots of conifers and a collection of rhododendrons. The principal trees are firs, spruces and hemlocks; among the more unusual specimen trees are eucalyptus and South American beech. The coniferous and broad-leaved trees have been planted since 1933.

Dalby Forest North Yorkshire. FE
There was no forest at Dalby until the 20th century, because the rabbits and sheep of the scrub woodland and steep-sided valleys ate all the seedlings. In 1921 the Forestry Commission began to plant more than 6,000 acres (2,500 ha) of pine, spruce, larch, Douglas fir and beech. Now, broad-leaved trees are being planted, too.

Delamere Forest Park Delamere, Northwich, Cheshire. FE
This mature conifer plantation stands on part of the ancient hunting grounds of the Earls of Chester. Today it contains numerous Scots pines and Corsican pines, some of them more than 80 ft (24 m) high. Hemlock, larch and broad-leaved trees are also present. The forest's annual timber yield is about 5,000 tons, and each year thousands of people go there to buy Christmas trees.

Dyffryn Gardens St Nicholas, near Cardiff, Vale of Glamorgan
A large collection of Japanese maples and paper-bark maples from West China are among the highlights of the 55 acre (22 ha) gardens. There is an outstanding magnolia collection, which includes such species as Veitch's hybrid magnolia, cucumber tree, large-leaved cucumber tree and yellow cucumber tree. Among other notable specimens are a tulip tree, Monterey cypress, Brewer's weeping spruce and male and female maidenhair trees. Confirmed champion trees include paper bark maple, Lebanese oak, Chinese elm and Chinese wing-nut.

Exbury Gardens near Beaulieu, Hampshire
A comprehensive collection of rhododendrons and azaleas is the main attraction of the woodland gardens, which were laid out in 1918 by the zoologist Lionel de Rothschild, of the banking family. The Exbury strain of hybrid azaleas, developed in the 1930s, is renowned – as are the many award-winning hybrid rhododendrons bred here over the past 70 years. The gardens cover some 200 acres (80 ha), and are also noted for their colourful spread of spring bulbs, and their camellias and

magnolias. The gardens are open from March to November.

Exeter University Grounds and Gardens
The 300 acre (120 ha) estate sweeps across hills that contain a wide range of trees and plants from various parts of the world. It was laid out in the 1860s, but was almost derelict when it was acquired by the University in 1922. Many of the original plantings were still standing, and today the specimens include cypresses, junipers, maples, firs, chestnuts, birches, pines, beeches, ashes, oaks and willows.

Forest of Dean Gloucestershire, Monmouthshire and Herefordshire. FE
The 27,000 acres (11,000 ha) of woods are noted for their numerous timber trees, including oaks, beeches, spruce and larch. The area has been a royal hunting ground since the time of the Saxon kings. Some of Britain's finest small-leaved lime trees grow in the lime-rich soil of the Forest Nature Reserve at Wyndcliff, near Chepstow.

Galloway Forest Park
Dumfries and Galloway. FE
The tallest mountain in the south of Scotland – Merrick, more than 2,760 ft (841 m) high – dominates the fells, crags, rivers and loch that make up the park. The peaty grassland is ideal for the principal trees planted there – Norway and Sitka spruces. Other trees that grow well are Scots pine, lodgepole pine and Douglas fir.

Glen More Forest Park Highland. FE
Wind-bent Scots pines hug the sandy beaches of Loch Morlich, which lies in the heart of the

park. The trees are remnants of the ancient Caledonian pine forest which once stretched across the 3,500 acres (1,400 ha) of woodland. Among them are thickets of juniper and birch. Within the area of the park, exotic trees are gradually being removed and the Caledonian pine forest is being restored. There is a visitors' centre and a network of walks and cycle paths.

Greenwich Park Greenwich, London.
The stump of an oak – under which Queen Elizabeth I is said to have played as a child – can be seen, mounted on a plinth in the park. The queen was born in Greenwich Palace 100 years after the ground was enclosed under licence from Henry VI, so making it the first of London's royal parks. Today the avenues are lined with sweet and horse chestnuts; English oaks, holm oaks, cedars and some beeches can be seen in the flower gardens.

Grizedale Forest Park Cumbria. FE
Until the end of the 19th century the area around Grizedale Forest was a centre for forest industries. The broad-leaved trees were used to produce charcoal for iron smelting, and a restored bobbin mill is working 8 miles (13 km) away. The Forestry Commission has planted thousands of acres of Sitka spruce, Japanese larch, Scots pine, Norway spruce and European larch. In wet areas, hardwoods are being restocked – hazel, rowan, alder and willow. There are forest trails and a visitors' centre.

Hampton Court and Bushy Park Richmond-upon-Thames, London.
Two monarchs, Charles II and William III, were responsible for planting limes whose successors still stand; and ancient yews line the avenues. The notable trees at Hampton Court include a stone pine planted in the early 18th century, a silver lime, an unusual hardy rubber tree, and a common chestnut (also called Hampton Court Gold, because it was first discovered there). William III, advised by Sir Christopher Wren, created the imposing Chestnut Avenue in nearby Bushy Park. Also in Bushy Park are two of the country's largest swamp cypresses and a lime avenue. Among other trees growing in the two royal parks are oaks, hawthorns, willows, planes, birches, spruces, cedars, sycamores, alders and pines.

Harlow Carr Botanical Gardens Harrogate, North Yorkshire.
Wind-breaks of spruce and larch provide shelter for the young trees – beech, chestnuts, willows, rowans, red oaks and a wide range of conifers – that are an outstanding attraction of the arboretum. The Broad Walk is flanked by ornamental trees – among them crab and flowering cherries – and colourful flowering shrubs. Among the more recent plantings is the bristle-cone pine from the Rocky Mountains. The acid soil is suited to rhododendrons, of which there are more than 300 species and hybrids. The gardens are run by the Northern Horticultural Society.

The Sir Harold Hillier Gardens and Arboretum Ampfield, near Romsey, Hants.
This arboretum covers 180 acres (73 ha) and has one of the largest collections of trees and shrubs in the temperate world. The arboretum was started in 1953 by Sir Harold Hillier who planted numerous shrubs and trees, including witch hazel, oaks and dwarf conifers. Gradually hollies and rhododendrons were introduced, and today there are more than 11,000 different taxa.

Inverewe Gardens Poolewe, Highland.
The gardens are on the same latitude as Moscow to the east and Labrador to the west, but they benefit from the relatively warm waters of the North Atlantic drift. As a result there is a profusion of trees including copper beech, oaks, ashes, cedars, Douglas firs, Scots pines and 24 varieties of eucalyptus. Altogether there are 86 different types of tree in the gardens. Three large Wellingtonias are more than 100 years old. The most unusual tree is a variegated Turkey oak, given to the gardens by Marie Sawyer in 1952. Until recently, no one was able to name the tree or propagate it, but this has since been successfully achieved.

Jodrell Bank Science Centre, Planetarium and Arboretum Cheshire.
More than 2,000 different species, varieties and cultivars of young trees and shrubs grow in the 35 acre (14 ha) arboretum, which was founded in 1971. The main and, so far, more flourishing specimens include maples, crab apples, rowans, whitebeams, alders, birch, cypresses, junipers, limes and barberries. The arboretum – which is administered by the University of Manchester – is open daily from Easter to the end of October and also on winter weekends.

Kielder Forest Park FE
The 148,000 acre (60,000 ha) forest lies mainly in Northumberland and Cumbria and the two main species are Norway spruce and Sitka spruce; there are also Japanese larch, lodgepole pine and some broad-leaved trees. Much of the

timber is used in construction, and some is pulped. It has a multi-purpose nature, combining a working forest with facilities for recreation and conservation.

Kilmun Forest Park near Dunoon, Argyll. FE
Because of the area's mild oceanic climate, the arboretum was established in 1930 to contain trees from all parts of the world. Three recommended walks take visitors through collections of Australian eucalyptus, South American southern beeches, western North American silver firs, Japanese larch, Norway maple, limber pine, mountain hemlocks and Delavay's fir among many other coniferous and deciduous trees. There is also a southern beech from Tierra del Fuego. Unusually, the trees are planted in groups rather than as individual specimens. Visitors should note that the terrain is steep.

London Parks
Among the splendours of London are its five central parks, a source of delight to tourists, office workers and city dwellers. Although Regent's Park is best known for its zoo, there are many splendid trees growing there including paulownia, Turkey oak, evodia, honey locust, Caucasian elms and Kentucky coffee trees. In Hyde Park there are ginkgo, pendent silver limes and Caucasian wing-nut, among other species. Kensington Gardens are noted for a rare date plum, an equally rare evodia and a Montpelier maple. Visitors to Green Park can enjoy the planes, balsam poplars, hawthorns and Indian bean-trees. In St James's Park, in addition to the cherries, planes, swamp cypresses, willows and chestnuts, there are Dawyck beeches, evodias, Golden Rain trees and Tree of Heaven. Usually, only deciduous trees are planted in the parks – originally because they were less affected by London's smoke, but now because they are considered more traditional than conifers.

Muncaster Castle Ravenglass, Cumbria.
A nature trail containing almost 100 different species is one of the main attractions of this 13th-century estate. Among the outstanding trees are Southern beech – including one of the biggest in the country – English oak, coast redwood, wild cherry, Chilean yew, eucryphya cordofolia and Himalayan tree rhododendrons. The castle has extensive woodland gardens with fine magnolias, rhododendrons and azaleas.

National Pinetum Bedgebury, Kent. FE
A lake, two streams and almost 300 acres (121 ha) of undulating ground make up this pinetum, parts of which are nearly 300 ft (91 m) above sea-level. The first modern plantings were made in 1925, when increasing pollution at the Royal Botanic Gardens, Kew, affected the growth of conifers and a new site was sought for them. Among the many trees which flourish at Bedgebury are Colorado blue spruce, silver fir, white fir and red fir; Japanese black pine and Bosnian pine, Polish and Sudeten forms of the European larch, coastal redwoods and Serbian spruce more than 60 ft (18 m) high. They also have national collections of junipers, Lawson cypress cultivars and yews.

New Forest Hampshire. FE
The Tall Trees Walk contains some of the tallest specimen trees in Britain. Bolderwood Drive contains numerous trees such as spruce, native Scots pine and Douglas fir. The 145 square mile (375 km^2) forest, was established by William the Conqueror in 1079 and is the largest pasture woodland in Europe. In many places old woodlands of oak, birch, beech, yew and holly survive.

Oxford Botanic Garden Oxford.
The University of Oxford Botanic Garden has stood on the same site for more than 375 years. One English yew was planted during the Civil War, soon after the garden was founded in 1621. The 135 trees that can be seen today have been planted since 1750. The Austrian black pine, planted in 1800, is the largest and oldest specimen in the UK, as are a pair of service trees, both the apple and pear-fruited forms. From China there are magnolias, acers and the exquisite dove tree. Seven glasshouses contain trees from every continent. The gardens also run the Harcourt Arboretum at Nuneham Courtenay, 6 miles (10 km) south of Oxford, with many trees from North America, planted in the 1930s.

Queen Elizabeth Forest Park Aberfoyle, Stirling. FE
The park consists of four forests – Achray, Loch Ard, Buchanan and Strathyre – and commemorates the coronation of Queen Elizabeth II in 1953. By far the most common trees are Sitka and Norway spruces. These are followed by Scots and lodgepole pine, European and Japanese larch, Douglas fir, silver fir and western hemlock; and broad-leaved oaks and beeches; a total of more than 23 species. The visitor centre, just north of Aberfoyle (tel. 01877 382 258), offers a wide range of information and advice.

Queenswood Country Park Dinmore Hill, Leominster, Herefordshire.

On either side of the hill (which contains Sites of Special Scientific Interest) 103 acres (32 ha) of natural wood support oak, birch and ash. From the 67 acre (26 ha) of arboretum at the top of the hill it is possible to see Hereford, the Black Mountains and the Malverns. A numbered collection of more than 600 species includes alders, ashes, beeches, cedars, cherries, chestnuts, cypresses, firs, hemlocks, larches, limes, pines, poplars, spruces and yews. The arboretum was bought by public subscription in 1935 to commemorate the Silver Jubilee of King George V.

Richmond Park Richmond-upon-Thames, London.
The green sward, plantations, dells, hills and sweeps of bracken are decorated with a highly varied collection of trees. The three main species are oak, beech and hornbeam; there are also numerous limes, poplars, horse chestnuts, rowan and various thorn trees, as well as a large collection of unusual specimen trees. The park was created in 1637 by Charles I who, like his son Charles II, used it as a hunting ground. Since the reign of William and Mary, the park has been open to the public. It is the largest of the royal parks, covering some 2,400 acres (970 ha), and two herds of the Queen's deer – 400 fallow deer and 300 red deer – roam free. The Isabella plantation contains rhododendrons, magnolias, azaleas, camellias and heathers.

Royal Botanic Garden Edinburgh, Lothian.
A large collection of trees from all parts of the world, including pines, maples and birches, grows in the garden. Despite the harsh climate many trees – such as foxglove trees from China, Chilean firebush and Nymans hybrid eucryphia – flower outdoors. There are also satellite gardens at Benmore, in Argyll, which is noted for its mature conifer trees, including spruces and silver firs; Logan, near Stranraer, with its cabbage palms, chusan palms and tree ferns; and Dawyck Botanic Garden, near Peebles, with mature plantings of Douglas firs, Brewer's weeping spruce and Dawyck beech.

Royal Botanic Gardens Kew, Richmond-upon-Thames, London. www.kew.org
The 18th-century botanist and wealthy patron Sir Joseph Banks sent young men to various parts of the world to bring back trees and shrubs for Kew. Today many of these prizes are on show; they include collections of poplar, willow, birch, ash, alder, oak, mulberry, cedar, maple, sweet chestnut and juniper. In 1841 the gardens were given to the state and opened to the public, and since then they have been increased in size to just over 300 acres (120 ha), containing more than 38,000 different species of trees and plants.

Scone Palace Tayside. www.scone_palace.co.uk
In 1823 the botanist David Douglas, who had worked as a boy in the palace gardens at Scone, was sent by the Royal Horticultural Society to America to collect tree specimens. He brought back the first Douglas fir, which he planted at Scone and which is still growing. The pinetum was planted 25 years later and includes many species of American conifer of which Douglas collected the first seed. The most notable specimens include noble fir, grand silver fir, red fir, coast redwood and Brewer's weeping spruce.

Sheffield Park Gardens near Uckfield, East Sussex. NT
The original landscape was designed by Capability Brown around 1775. But the gardens, set around four lakes, were extended by successive owners in the late 19th century. They contain more than 300 varieties of conifer, including Montezuma pines, Monterey pines, Brewer's weeping spruce from Oregon, and a 125 ft (38 m) high Wellingtonia. Other trees include tupelo or black gum from eastern North America, oriental spruce, yellow Lawson's cypress, swamp cypress from the southern USA, many Japanese maples, American big-cone pine and two 100 ft (30 m) maritime pines.

Snowdonia National Park North Wales. FE
Snowdonia contains two forest parks, at Coed Y Brenin in the south and Gwydyr in the north, planted with spruce, pine, larch and other conifers, as well as some broad-leaved varieties. Coed Y Brenin has a visitors' centre at Maesgwm (tel. 01341 440666).

Stourhead Garden Stourton, near Mere, Wiltshire. NT
In the mid-18th century the owner of Stourhead estate, Henry Hoare, planted the hillsides to the east and west of the lake with a mixture of conifers and deciduous trees. When Stourhead passed to his descendants, numerous exotic trees and shrubs were planted. Many of these were the first of their type and still survive. They are rarely seen outside these gardens and because of the favourable conditions, some have become champions. Visitors today can admire cedars, magnolias, spruces, birches, chestnuts, crab apples, cypresses, poplars, willows, yews, maples and redwoods.

Studley Royal Deer Park Fountains, Ripon, North Yorkshire. NT www.fountainsabbey.org.uk
For more than 400 years herds of deer have lived in the park, feeding off the fruits of the many oaks, beeches and sweet chestnuts; in the summer the larch and beech copses provide cover for the fawns and calves. The park is perhaps best seen in the autumn, when the deciduous and evergreen trees provide a palette of colours ranging from deep green to lime, and from the palest yellow through gold russet, copper and brown. Among the outstanding trees are a wild cherry, an English oak 120 ft (36 m) tall, and a mile-long (1.6 km) avenue of limes.

Syon Park and Gardens Hounslow, London.
In the late 18th century, the 1st Duke of Northumberland paid Capability Brown the then handsome sum of £1,956 to redesign the parks and gardens, and to plant foreign and native trees. Later owners have added to the collection, which is particularly strong in North American trees, especially oaks, and the swamp cypresses are some of the finest in the country. Other rare specimens include Turkish hazels, tulip trees and Liquidambars, as well as fine examples of Caucasian wing-nut and Indian bean-tree. A programme of replanting has been initiated by the present owners.

Thetford Forest Suffolk and Norfolk. FE
In an area that was once bleak, infertile heathland, 52,000 acres (21,000 ha) of forest now flourish. In 1922 the Forestry Commission began planting Thetford Forest, mainly with Scots and Corsican pines. Today Thetford is the largest lowland forest in England. It is the most mature of the forests established by the Forestry Commission, and contributes more than 8 per cent of the commission's total timber output.

Tresco Abbey Gardens Tresco, Isles of Scilly.
Despite being set on a small Atlantic island and exposed to extremely strong and salty winds, these gardens contain one of the finest outdoor collections of Southern Hemisphere trees to be seen in the Northern Hemisphere. These include the banksia from Australasia, phoenix palms from the Canaries, Cape silver trees from South Africa, the orange-barked myrtle from Chile, the lily-of-the-valley tree from Madeira and the Norfolk Island pine from New Zealand. The most noted individual specimen is the 120-year-old 'Christmas Tree', also from New Zealand. Many trees have had to be cut back after suffering from storms.

Westonbirt Arboretum near Tetbury, Gloucestershire. FC
Many of the 18,000 trees in the 600 acre (240 ha) arboretum are grouped according to the seasons in which they are seen at their best. Willows flower in the late winter, followed by spring-flowering trees such as Campbell's magnolia, alder and handkerchief trees. In summer, the snowbell tree, the Indian horse chestnut, the fairly rare Pyrenean oak, the white-flowered Stuartia and others are on display. Autumn colours come from scarlet oak and Japanese maples. The national collection of Japanese maples and willows is here.

Wilton House near Salisbury, Wiltshire.
Pride of place in the 20 acres (8 ha) of lawn goes to the giant cedars of Lebanon, the oldest of which was planted in 1630. Other trees of historical interest include an oak planted in 1817 by the Grand Duke Nicholas, who became Nicholas I, Emperor of Russia. Wilton House is the Earl of Pembroke's home, and the grounds are open every day from Easter to October. The most common trees are holm oaks, Turkey oaks, tulip trees and planes. A fine golden oak stands by the 18th-century Palladian Bridge.

Wisley Gardens near Woking, Surrey.
The principal garden of the Royal Horticultural Society, the garden is open throughout the year except for Christmas Day. (Members only on Sundays.) The gardens contain many fine specimens, including 11 champions (tallest of their type in the British Isles). A 200-year-old English oak guards the entrance. The 32 acre (13 ha) Jubilee Arboretum, opened in 1978, has 1,400 different trees planted in various themed groups, for seasonal interest, habitat and botanical purposes. The 15 acre (6 ha) pinetum, planted in 1910, contains fine specimens of Brewer's spruce, Holford's pine and more than 50 other different conifers.

Woodland Park Brokerswood, near Westbury, Wiltshire.
In the 80 acres (32 ha) of woodland open to the public are 28 paths, all clearly marked and lined by trees, most of them self-generated, either by root suckers or by seeds; some conifers and hardwoods have been planted. Among the trees are horse chestnut, yew, laurel, cricket-bat willow, oak, sycamore, Norway spruce, bird cherry, silver birch, dogwood and hazel. Although the trees are comparatively young, the area has been woodland since primeval forests covered much of the area. There is a woodland heritage centre.

Tree organisations

Voluntary organisations

ROYAL SCOTTISH FORESTRY SOCIETY *The Stables, Dalkeith Country Park, Dalkeith, Midlothian* DH22 2NA. Believed to be the oldest forestry society in the English-speaking world, it was founded in 1854. It arranges meetings on forestry topics and publishes *Scottish Forestry*.

ROYAL FORESTRY SOCIETY OF ENGLAND, WALES AND NORTHERN IRELAND, *102 High Street, Tring, Hertfordshire* HP23 4AF *www.rfs.org.uk* The largest of the UK's tree societies, founded in 1882. It arranges field meetings at home and study tours overseas, and offers professional examinations in arboriculture.

INTERNATIONAL TREE FOUNDATION, *Sandy Lane, Crawley Down, Crawley, West Sussex* RH10 4HS. An international society which aims to foster an appreciation of the necessity and beauty of trees, and to encourage planting and protection on a world scale.

ARBORICULTURAL ASSOCIATION, *Ampfield House, Romsey, Hampshire* SO51 9PA *www.trees.org.uk* Ensures a high standard of professionalism among arboriculturalists.

WOODLAND TRUST, *Autumn Park, Dysart Road, Grantham, Lincolnshire* NG31 6LL *www.woodland-trust.org.uk* The trust was formed in 1972 to conserve old broad-leaved woodlands and to establish new ones. It acquires areas of woodland and manages them with the minimum of interference.

TREE COUNCIL, *51 Catherine Place, London* SW1E 6DY *www.treecouncil.org.uk* A forum for all organisations with an interest in the place of trees in the landscape. It publicises the need for trees in industrial and urban communities and raises money for tree planting and maintenance by grants and other means.

Official bodies

FORESTRY COMMISSION, *231 Corstorphine Road, Edinburgh* EH12 7AT. *www.forestry.gov.uk* (Regional offices throughout the country.) A government department, consisting of the Forestry Authority (the regulatory body) and two agencies, Forest Research and Forest Enterprise (which manages the national forests and forest parks). The commission's aim is to protect and expand Britain's forest and woodland, and to increase their value to society and the environment.

COUNTRYSIDE AGENCY, *John Dower House, Crescent Place, Cheltenham, Gloucestershire* GL50 3RA. *www.countryside.gov.uk* The commission reviews landscape conservation and enhancement and provides facilities for enjoyment of the countryside. It designates national parks and areas of outstanding natural beauty, recommends country parks and long-distance footpaths and publishes guides.

COUNTRYSIDE COUNCIL FOR WALES, *Plas Penrhos, Ffordd Penrhos, Bangor, Gwynedd* LL57 2LQ *www.ccw.gov.uk* The executive authority for the conservation of habitats and wildlife in Wales. Through partners such as local authorities, voluntary organisations and interested individuals, the commission promotes the protection of landscape, opportunities for enjoyment and the support of those who live and work in the countryside.

SCOTTISH NATURAL HERITAGE, *12 Hope Terrace, Edinburgh* EH9 2AS *www.snh.org.uk* Scottish Natural Heritage is responsible for providing facilities for the enjoyment of the countryside in Scotland, and for enhancing and maintaining the natural beauty of the landscape.

Glossary

Abscission layer Cork layer forming at base of leaf-stalk of DECIDUOUS tree in autumn, causing leaf to fall.
Alternate Term used of leaves or buds of broad-leaved trees that arise first on one side of a twig, then on the other.
Annual ring Ring of wood laid down in stem and branches of tree or shrub during one growing season.
Aril Fleshy cup formed from fused CONE SCALES surrounding seed.

Bark Protective layer on the outside of stems and branches, consisting of living cork cells on the inside and dead cells on the outside.
Bract scale Thin, papery, seed-bearing structure rising from CONE AXIS above CONE SCALES.
Branchlet Small branch, between branch and twig in size.
Bud scale Scale that covers and protects a developing leaf.

Cambium Layer of living cells just under bark and at growing tips of shoots and roots, from which new growth develops.
Catkin Male or female flowers hanging in chains; they lack coloured petals because they are wind-pollinated.
Clone Identical plant arising from a single parent by VEGETATIVE PROPAGATION.
Compound Term describing leaf that consists of several LEAFLETS.
Cone axis Central core of cone.
Cone scale Woody structure rising from CONE AXIS, enclosing developing seeds.
Coniferous Term describing tree that bears cones.
Coppicing Cutting of woody stem at ground level to encourage growth of several stems from one root system.
Cotyledon SIMPLE leaf formed in the seed; the first to emerge on GERMINATION. Also called seed leaf.
Cross-fertilisation FERTILISATION of the OVULE of one individual plant by the pollen from another.
Crown Branches and upper part of trunk of tree.
Cultivar Variation of a SPECIES arising in cultivation, and propagated for some unusual characteristic such as leaf colour or shape.
Cuticle Waxy surface of a leaf, reducing water loss and protecting against damage.
Cutting Non-reproductive part of a plant, stimulated artificially to form an identical new individual.

Deciduous Term describing tree or shrub that retains its leaves for one growing season only, dropping them before the following winter.

Entire Term describing leaf without lobes, teeth or other indentations in margin.
Evergreen Tree or shrub that retains its leaves all year.

Family Large group of similar

plants, made up of several genera (see GENUS).

Fastigiate Term describing a tree with nearly vertical branches.

Fertilisation Union of a male pollen grain with a female OVULE to form the embryo of a new individual.

Genus Group of closely related species distinct enough not to interbreed. Plural: genera.

Germination Development of seedling from fertilised seed.

Glaucous Term describing waxy film on the surface of a leaf or stem, giving it a bluish appearance and serving to reduce water loss.

Grafting Artificial union of the aerial parts of one plant with the vigorous ROOTSTOCK of another.

Hardy Tolerant of adverse conditions of climate and soil.

Heartwood Dead wood consisting of several ANNUAL RINGS at centre of tree trunk or branch, no longer water-conducting tissue but providing structural support.

Hybrid Offspring of different species.

Lateral roots Shallow roots running out sideways from stem.

Layering Term describing the development of a new individual plant from a branch or stem that has rooted into the ground.

Leading shoot Main shoot that develops from the terminal bud at the top of a tree each year.

Leaflet Leaf-shaped subdivision of a COMPOUND leaf.

Lenticel Small pore in bark aiding gaseous exchange with atmosphere.

Lobe Round indentation on leaf margin.

Native A species that is thought to have reached Britain since the Ice Age without the aid of humans.

Nutlet Small nut, usually one of several in the same fruit.

Opposite Term used of buds or leaves of broad-leaved trees that are arranged in pairs on the twig.

Ovule Unfertilised potential seed of a flowering plant.

Perfect Term describing flower with both male and female parts.

Persistent Term describing part of a plant that does not fall, wither or disappear, as is usual with the same parts of other plants.

Petals Parts of a flower that surround the reproductive organs. They are often coloured to attract insects.

Photosynthesis Chemical process carried out by green plants in the presence of light, which combines carbon dioxide from the atmosphere with hydrogen from water to form sugars as food for the growing plant.

Pinnate Term used of leaf completely subdivided into several LEAFLETS ranged along either side of the midrib.

Pollarding Lopping off the branches of a tree at about 5 ft (1.5 m) to encourage shoots to arise all at the same level.

Pollen Male reproductive cell that is transferred to the female reproductive structure (pollination), germinates and fertilises the female OVULE.

Pore Opening between cells in the surface of a leaf or in bark that permits exchange of oxygen and carbon dioxide between the tree and the atmosphere. See STOMATA

Pulvinus Base of a leaf stalk: the swollen part of a shoot from which the leaf arises.

Respiration Absorption of oxygen and release of carbon dioxide formed in a plant when energy is liberated from stored foods: the reverse of PHOTOSYNTHESIS.

Root hairs Fine structures at tips of young roots, through which water and mineral salts are absorbed from soil.

Rootstock Root of common plant onto which a less common plant is joined by GRAFTING.

Sapwood Living wood consisting of outer ANNUAL RINGS in a tree trunk, through which water from the soil is conducted up a tree.

Scale See BRACT SCALE, BUD SCALE, CONE SCALE.

Seed Small body that develops from the fertilisation of the OVULE, and from which a new plant develops after GERMINATION.

Seed leaf See COTYLEDON.

Sepal An organ that is often green and leaf-like and covers and protects the developing flower.

Short shoot Shoot which extends only a little each year.

Simple Term describing a leaf that is not divided into LEAFLETS.

Species Group of plants similar in all respects and able to interbreed.

Springwood Inner part of ANNUAL RING, formed early in the growing season, consisting of thin-walled vessels for conducting water.

Stipule Leaf-like growth on stem at base of leaf stalk, often in pairs.

Stomata Breathing PORES in leaves, often concentrated on the underside.

Sucker Shoot arising directly from a root, or at the base of a stem.

Summerwood Outer part of ANNUAL RING, formed during middle and later part of growing season, consisting of thick-walled vessels conducting water up the stem.

Tap root Main, downward-growing root of seedling.

Tooth One of a series of small, regular points on a leaf margin.

Variety Variation of a SPECIES, usually differing only in one characteristic, such as colour or leaf shape.

Vegetative propagation Reproduction by CUTTINGS, LAYERING and GRAFTING; not involving FERTILISATION.

Whorl Structures such as buds, leaves and branches arising three or more at a time around a stem at the same point.

Index

Page numbers in **bold type** denote full-page illustrated entries. Page numbers in roman type denote additional references to a species in leaf keys and charts, or shorter profiles of less common species.

Acknowledgments

Artwork in *Trees and Shrubs of Britain* was supplied by the following artists:

3 Richard Bonson · 8–19 Delyth Jones · 20–23 Charles Raymond · 24–25 Jim Russell · 26–29 Richard Bonson · 30–33 Brian Delf · 34–37 Shirley Felts · 38–47 Brian Delf · 48–49 Derek Rodgers · 50–55 Nicolas Hall · 56–63 Ann Savage · 64–75 Brian Delf · 76–87 Ian Garrard · 88–91 Ann Savage · 92–99 Nicolas Hall · 100–3 Ann Savage · 104–5 Bruce Whatley · 106–13 Ian Garrard · 114–25 Ann Savage · 126–36 Shirley Felts · 137–45 Derek Rodgers · 146–75 Brian Delf · 176–93 Ann Savage · 194–7 Charles Raymond · 198–222 David Salariya · 223 Richard Bonson · 224–31 David Salariya · 232–79 Richard Bonson · 280–3 Bruce Whatley · 284–5 Jim Russell · 291 Bruce Whatley

Photographs in *Trees and Shrubs of Britain* were supplied by the following photographers and agencies. Names of photographers are in roman type and those of agencies in capital letters. The following abbreviations are used:
NHPA – Natural History Photographic Agency.
NSP – Natural Science Photographs.
OSF – Oxford Scientific Films.
Commissioned photographs are credited in *italics*. Where only one name is listed for a page containing two photographs, the photographer named was responsible for both.

28 OSF/G. A. Maclean; John Vigurs · 29 Gerald Wilkinson; NSP/G. A. Matthews · 30 Gerald Wilkinson · 31 A–Z COLLECTION/M. Nimmo; Heather Angel · 32 Gerald Wilkinson; Michael Warren · 33 A–Z COLLECTION/M. Nimmo · 34 Gerald Wilkinson; NSP/G. A. Matthews · 35 Gerald Wilkinson; A–Z COLLECTION/M. Nimmo · 36 Brian Hawkes; Heather Angel · 37 Gerald Wilkinson; NHPA/S. Dalton · 39 RIDA/Gerald Wilkinson · 40 *Gerald Wilkinson*; Heather Angel · 42 *Gerald Wilkinson* · 43 *Gerald Wilkinson*; A–Z COLLECTION/M. Nimmo · 44 A–Z COLLECTION/M. Nimmo; BRUCE COLEMAN/Eric Crichton · 45 *Gerald Wilkinson* · 46 A–Z COLLECTION/M. Nimmo; *Gerald Wilkinson* · 47 *Gerald Wilkinson* · 50 HARRY SMITH COLLECTION · 51 A–Z COLLECTION · 52 A–Z COLLECTION/G. W. Miller · 53 A–Z COLLECTION · 54 HARRY SMITH COLLECTION; A–Z COLLECTION/M. Nimmo · 55 Heather Angel · 56 Gerald Wilkinson · 57 A–Z COLLECTION/M. Nimmo; BRUCE COLEMAN/S. C. Porter · 58 Gerald Wilkinson; Heather Angel · 59 Heather Angel; Gerald Wilkinson · 60 *Gerald Wilkinson* · 61 Heather Angel · 62 *Gerald Wilkinson*; Tony Evans · 63 A–Z COLLECTION/M. Nimmo; Michael Warren · 64 NHPA/E. A. Janes; Gerald Wilkinson · 65 A–Z COLLECTION/G. A. Matthews; A–Z COLLECTION/M. Nimmo · 66 *Gerald Wilkinson*; Brian Hawkes · 67 A–Z COLLECTION/M. Nimmo · 68 A–Z COLLECTION/M. Nimmo; Heather Angel · 69 *Gerald Wilkinson* · 70 HARRY SMITH COLLECTION · 71 OSF/G. A. Maclean; Heather Angel · 72 ARDEA/P. M. Morris; A–Z COLLECTION/M. Nimmo · 74 RIDA; Michael Warren · 75 A–Z COLLECTION/M. Nimmo; *Gerald Wilkinson* · 76 BRUCE COLEMAN/John Sims; Heather Angel · 77 *Gerald Wilkinson*; ARDEA · 78 A–Z COLLECTION/M. B. Jones; Gerald Wilkinson · 79 P. Lawson; *Gerald Wilkinson* · 80 RIDA; Alan Beaumont · 81 Heather Angel; BRUCE COLEMAN/John Sims · 82 A–Z COLLECTION/M. Nimmo; Heather Angel · 83 P. Lawson; A–Z COLLECTION/M. Nimmo · 84 *Gerald Wilkinson*; Gerald Wilkinson · 85 A–Z COLLECTION/M. Nimmo; *Gerald Wilkinson* · 86 *Gerald Wilkinson*; Robin Fletcher · 87 NSP/G. A. Matthews · 88 Gerald Wilkinson; Robin Fletcher · 89 Heather Angel; HARRY SMITH COLLECTION · 90 NHPA/M. Savonius · 91 A–Z COLLECTION/Elsa Megson · 94 Gerald Wilkinson; HARRY SMITH COLLECTION · 95 Heather Angel · 96 NHPA/M. Savonius · 97 A–Z COLLECTION/M. Nimmo · 98 BRUCE COLEMAN/E. Crichton · 99 *Gerald Wilkinson* · 100 Oleg Polunin; Gerald Wilkinson · 101 *Gerald Wilkinson*; Gerald Wilkinson · 102 Heather Angel; Eric Crichton · 103 David Sutton; Gerald Wilkinson · 106 A–Z COLLECTION; *Gerald Wilkinson* · 107 *Gerald Wilkinson* · 108 Heather Angel; NSP/M. Chinery · 109 Gerald Wilkinson; Maurice Nimmo · 110 HARRY SMITH COLLECTION; ARDEA/A. Paterson · 111 *Gerald Wilkinson* · 112 *Gerald Wilkinson* · 113 Heather Angel · 114 OSF/G. A. Maclean · 115 *Gerald Wilkinson* · 116 Brian Hawkes; Gerald Wilkinson · 117 Heather Angel; BRUCE COLEMAN/Eric Crichton · 118 NHPA/G. E. Hyde; OSF · 119 NHPA/N. R. Coulton · 120 Gerald Wilkinson; Michael Warren · 121 *Gerald Wilkinson* · 122 A–Z COLLECTION/Elsa Megson · 123 Heather Angel · 124 A–Z COLLECTION/M. Nimmo; *Gerald Wilkinson* · 125 Heather Angel; A–Z COLLECTION/M. Nimmo · 128 Ron & Christine Foord; Heather Angel · 129 Heather Angel; Gerald Wilkinson · 130 JACANA/C. Nardin; Gerald Wilkinson · 131 FORESTRY COMMISSION; A–Z COLLECTION/M. Nimmo · 132 Heather Angel · 133 Heather Angel; Gerald Wilkinson · 134 Ron & Christine Foord · 135 A–Z COLLECTION; A–Z COLLECTION/M. Nimmo · 137 John Sims; A–Z COLLECTION/M. Nimmo · 138 Gerald Wilkinson; NSP/G. A. Matthews · 139 Gerald Wilkinson; A–Z COLLECTION/M. Nimmo · 140 Gerald Wilkinson; BRUCE COLEMAN/Eric Crichton · 141 Gerald Wilkinson; BRUCE COLEMAN/Eric Crichton · 142 Gerald Wilkinson · 143 Eric Hosking · 144 A–Z COLLECTION; Gerald Wilkinson · 145 Gerald Wilkinson · 147 Gerald Wilkinson · 148 Eric Crichton; Heather Angel · 149 Heather Angel · 152 FORESTRY COMMISSION; Michael Warren · 153 Ron & Christine Foord · 154 Heather Angel; Michael Warren · 155 Heather Angel; Oleg Polunin · 156 Heather Angel · 157 Heather Angel; Robin Fletcher · 158 RIDA/D. Bayliss; A–Z COLLECTION/M. Nimmo · 159 A–Z COLLECTION/M. Nimmo; A–Z COLLECTION · 160 Gerald Wilkinson; Robin Fletcher · 161 A–Z COLLECTION/M. Nimmo; NHPA/M. Savonius · 164 A–Z COLLECTION/M. Nimmo · 165 Heather Angel; John Sims · 166 Eric Hosking; Gerald Wilkinson · 167 Heather Angel; A–Z COLLECTION/M. Nimmo · 168 Heather Angel; Michael Warren · 169 David Sutton · 170 Gerald Wilkinson · 171 John Sims; A–Z COLLECTION/M. Nimmo · 172 *Gerald Wilkinson*; Robin Fletcher · 173 Gerald Wilkinson; Robin Fletcher · 174 John Sims · 175 A–Z COLLECTION/M. Nimmo; Heather Angel · 176 Heather Angel; OSF · 177 Heather Angel; A–Z COLLECTION/M. Nimmo · 178 A–Z COLLECTION/M. Nimmo; A–Z COLLECTION/Elsa Megson · 179 John Sims; Roy Lancaster · 180 Brian Hawkes · 181 Heather Angel · 182 Gerald Wilkinson · 183 Robin Fletcher · 198 Heather Angel; Robin Fletcher · 199 A–Z COLLECTION/M. Nimmo · 200 A–Z COLLECTION/M. Nimmo; *Gerald Wilkinson* · 201 A–Z COLLECTION/M. Nimmo; Robin Fletcher · 202 A–Z COLLECTION/M. Nimmo; BRUCE COLEMAN/Eric Crichton · 203 A–Z COLLECTION/M. Nimmo; Michael Warren · 206 A–Z COLLECTION/M. Nimmo · 207 A–Z COLLECTION/M. Nimmo; FORESTRY COMMISSION · 208 *Gerald Wilkinson* · 209 *Gerald Wilkinson* · 210 A–Z COLLECTION/M. Nimmo · 211 Robin Fletcher; HARRY SMITH COLLECTION · 212 *Gerald Wilkinson*; FORESTRY COMMISSION · 213 A–Z COLLECTION/M. Nimmo; Ron & Christine Foord · 214 *Gerald Wilkinson*; Alan Mitchell · 215 A–Z COLLECTION/M. Nimmo; Gerald Wilkinson · 216 *Gerald Wilkinson*; FORESTRY COMMISSION · 217 BRUCE COLEMAN/Eric Crichton; FORESTRY COMMISSION · 218 Robin Fletcher · 219 *Gerald Wilkinson* · 220 Heather Angel; A–Z COLLECTION · 221 A–Z COLLECTION/M. Nimmo · 222 David Sutton; Heather Angel · 224 Heather Angel; HARRY SMITH COLLECTION · 225 HARRY SMITH COLLECTION; Heather Angel · 226 Gerald Wilkinson · 227 *Gerald Wilkinson*; Michael Warren · 228 John Sims; Heather Angel · 229 Gerald Wilkinson; A–Z COLLECTION/G. W. Miller · 230 BRUCE COLEMAN/Jane Burton; RIDA/D. Bayliss · 231 *Gerald Wilkinson* · 232 VISION INTERNATIONAL/Robin Fletcher; Heather Angel · 234 *Gerald Wilkinson*; Eric Crichton · 235 A–Z COLLECTION/M. Nimmo · 236 Heather Angel; Robin Fletcher · 237 *Gerald Wilkinson* · 238 Gerald Wilkinson; Robin Fletcher · 239 Gerald Wilkinson; FORESTRY COMMISSION · 240 Alan Mitchell; Heather Angel · 241 John Sims; Gerald Wilkinson · 243 NSP/G. A. Matthews; Heather Angel · 246 Heather Angel; John Sims · 247 *Gerald Wilkinson* · 248 A–Z COLLECTION/M. Nimmo · 249 John Sims; Michael Warren · 250 John Sims; NHPA/M. Savonius · 251 Eric Crichton; NSP/M. Chinery · 252 A–Z COLLECTION/M. Nimmo; ARDEA/K. W. Fink · 253 A–Z COLLECTION/M. Nimmo; Oleg Polunin · 254 Heather Angel · 255 Heather Angel; Gerald Wilkinson · 256 A–Z COLLECTION/M. Nimmo · 257 David Sutton; Eric Crichton · 258 A–Z COLLECTION/M. Nimmo; Heather Angel · 259 John Sims; Heather Angel · 262 NSP/G. A. Matthews; Gerald Wilkinson · 263 Heather Angel · 264 A–Z COLLECTION/M. Nimmo; NSP/M. Chinery · 265 Heather Angel; Ron & Christine Foord · 266 Ron & Christine Foord; Michael Warren · 267 Heather Angel; Ron & Christine Foord · 268 Heather Angel; John Sims · 269 A–Z COLLECTION/M. Nimmo; Scott Leathart · 270 Michael Warren; Heather Angel · 272 John Sims; Heather Angel · 273 Heather Angel; Eric Crichton · 274 FORESTRY COMMISSION; A–Z COLLECTION/M. Nimmo · 275 Gerald Wilkinson; Michael Warren · 276 Heather Angel; HARRY SMITH COLLECTION · 277 *Gerald Wilkinson* · 278 Heather Angel; Robin Fletcher · 279 Michael Warren

The publishers acknowledge their indebtedness to the following books which were consulted for reference.

British Trees by Miles Hadfield (Dent) · *British Trees and Shrubs* by R. D. Meikle (Eyre and Spottiswoode) · *Conifers for your Garden* by Adrian Bloom (Floraprint) · *Conifers in Britain* by B. Alwyn Jay (Adam & Charles Black) · *Conifers in the British Isles* by A. F. Mitchell (HMSO, Forestry Commission Booklet) · *Evergreen Garden Trees and Shrubs* edited by Anthony Huxley (Blandford Press) · *A Field Guide to the Trees of Britain and Northern Europe* by Alan Mitchell (Collins) · *Flora of the British Isles* by A. R. Clapham, T. G. Tutin and E. F. Warburg (Cambridge University Press) · *Forest Trees of the Pacific Slope* by George B. Sudworth (US Dept of Agriculture, Forest Services) · *The Glory of the Tree* by Dr B. K. Boom and H. Kleijn (Harrap) · *Handbook of Coniferae* by W. Dallimore and A. B. Jackson (Edward Arnold) · *Hilliers' Manual of Trees and Shrubs* (David and Charles) · *The Illustrated Encyclopedia of Trees Timbers and Forests of the World* by Herbert Edlin and Maurice Nimmo (Salamander) · *The International Book of Trees* by Hugh Johnson (Mitchell Beazley) · *Japanese Maples* by J. D. Vertrees (Timber Press) · *Know Your Broadleaves* by Herbert L. Edlin (HMSO, Forestry Commission Booklet) · *Know Your Conifers* by Herbert L. Edlin (HMSO, Forestry Commission Booklet) · *Living Trees of the World* by Thomas H. Everett (Thames and Hudson) · *The Nature Trail Book of Trees and Leaves* by Ingrid Selberg (Usborne) · *The Observer's Book of Trees* edited by W. J. Stokoe (Warne) · *The Oxford Book of Trees* by B. E. Nicholson and A. R. Clapham (Oxford University Press) · *Spotters Guide to Trees* by Esmond Harris (Usborne) · *The Tree Key* by Herbert L. Edlin (Warne) · *Trees and Bushes* by H. Vedel and J. Lange (Methuen) · *Trees and Bushes of Europe* by Oleg Polunin (Oxford University Press) · *Trees and Shrubs Hardy in the British Isles* by W. J. Bean (J. Murray) · *The Trees and Shrubs of Britain* by J. C. Loudon (Longman, Brown, Green and Longmans) · *Trees for your Garden* by Roy Lancaster (Floraprint) · *Trees in Britain, Europe and North America* by Roger Phillips (Pan) · *Trees in the Wild* by Gerald Wilkinson (Stephen Hope) · *Trees of the World* by Scott Leathart (Hamlyn)

Typesetting: VANTAGE PHOTOSETTING CO. LTD, EASTLEIGH
Separations: MULLIS MORGAN LTD, LONDON
Printer/Binder: MILANOSTAMPA, ITALY

400-081-02